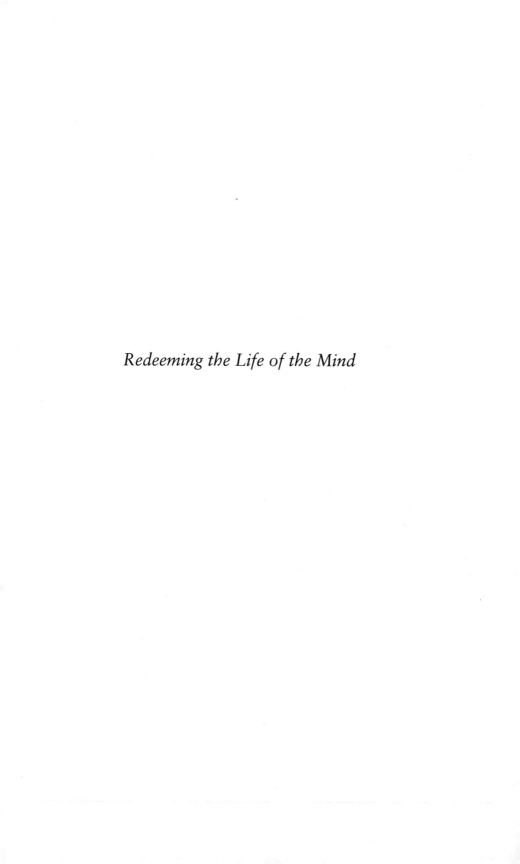

Redeeming the Life of the Mind

Redeeming the Life of the Mind

Essays in Honor of Vern Poythress

Edited by
John M. Frame, Wayne Grudem,
and John J. Hughes

FOREWORD BY J. I. PACKER

WHEATON, ILLINOIS

Redeeming the Life of the Mind: Essays in Honor of Vern Poythress

Copyright © 2017 by John M. Frame, Wayne Grudem, and John J. Hughes

Published by Crossway
        1300 Crescent Street
        Wheaton, Illinois 60187

Cover design: Jordan Singer

First printing 2017

Printed in the United States of America

Unless otherwise indicated, Scripture quotations are from the ESV® Bible (The Holy Bible, English Standard Version®), copyright © 2001 by Crossway, a publishing ministry of Good News Publishers. Used by permission. All rights reserved.

For other Scripture versions cited, please see the appendix.

All emphases in Scripture quotations have been added by the authors.

Hardcover ISBN: 978-1-4335-5303-5
ePub ISBN: 978-1-4335-5306-6
PDF ISBN: 978-1-4335-5304-2
Mobipocket ISBN: 978-1-4335-5305-9

Library of Congress Cataloging-in-Publication Data

Names: Poythress, Vern S., honouree. | Frame, John M., 1939– editor.
Title: Redeeming the life of the mind: essays in honor of Vern Poythress / edited by John M. Frame, Wayne Grudem, and John J. Hughes; foreword by J. I. Packer.
Description: Wheaton: Crossway, 2017. | Includes bibliographical references and index.
Identifiers: LCCN 2016055814 (print) | LCCN 2017034986 (ebook) | ISBN 9781433553042 (pdf) | ISBN 9781433553059 (mobi) | ISBN 9781433553066 (epub) | ISBN 9781433553035 (hc)
Subjects: LCSH: Theology. | Christian philosophy.
Classification: LCC BR118 (ebook) | LCC BR118 .R434 2017 (print) | DDC 230—dc23
LC record available at https://lccn.loc.gov/2016055814

Crossway is a publishing ministry of Good News Publishers.

SH		27	26	25	24	23	22	21	20	19	18	17
15	14	13	12	11	10	9	8	7	6	5	4	3	2	1

To the glory of our Trinitarian God:
Father, Son, and Holy Spirit

Contents

Foreword

Among today's senior Reformed theologians, Dr. Vern Poythress may well be identified as the dark horse.

I recall President Edmund Clowney of Westminster Theological Seminary enthusing to me about Vern's arrival on the seminary faculty, dwelling on the gain that Vern's combination of skills in mathematics, linguistics, and biblical disciplines brought to the seminary, despite his hesitant manner as a teacher and his gentle personal style. Dr. Clowney urged me to get to know Poythress, and he was right to do so. Vern is modest and unassuming, but he is a polymath of outstanding quality and has contributed much of importance to evangelical thought at a foundational level. The present Festschrift clearly shows this, and it is a privilege to be introducing it.

A polymath—what is that? Answer: a scholar who is on top of several academic disciplines and for whom questions of correlating and integrating them with each other have perennial interest. In a series of writings on Holy Scripture, Poythress shows himself both true to type as a polymath and true to God as a Christian, and it should not cause surprise when book after book that he writes gets hailed as the best in its class.

Some who shared in the inerrancy debates of the past half century stopped short by offering negations, sometimes facile, of the assertions of others, but what Poythress did time after time was to work the discussions round to some aspect of the quest for God-centered coherence and truth that, according to such a polymath as Abraham Kuyper in his marvelous *Encyclopedia of Sacred Theology*, we all should be seeking all the time. With Poythress, theocentric rationality and enhanced doxology break surface all the time.

Two linked themes on which Poythress has dug most deeply are the theological and cultural frame of biblical inerrancy and God's use of language to communicate with mankind. What he has written on these matters stirs a strong desire for more.

So, on behalf of all who have had anything to do with this book, I wish him many more years of focusing for us the true biblical faith.

J. I. Packer
Board of Governors' Professor of Theology
Regent College

Preface

Westminster Theological Seminary has played a major role in the history of orthodox Reformed theology in America. Upon its founding in 1929, its original faculty affirmed that the seminary would continue the historic position of "old Princeton Seminary." Princeton had for many decades represented the theology of Calvin and the Westminster Confession of Faith, as opposed to the liberal theology taught after 1929 by many professors at "new Princeton." But Westminster was not merely a clone of the older school. Although committed to the Reformed doctrinal standards, it quickly displayed a pattern of creative thought within the bounds of Reformed orthodoxy.

Westminster professors produced many books and articles defending orthodoxy against threats that were distinctive to the modern period. The chief founder of Westminster, J. Gresham Machen, brought his great expertise in modern European theology and biblical criticism to the new faculty, as can be seen in his books *The Virgin Birth of Christ*,[1] *The Origin of Paul's Religion*,[2] and *Christianity and Liberalism*.[3] Cornelius Van Til, professor of apologetics, also attacked liberal theology, but from a new biblical epistemology that became known as *presuppositionalism*. Many Westminster professors also advocated the "biblical theology" of Geerhardus Vos, a Princeton professor who was too much neglected during his years at Princeton. John Murray in systematics focused like a laser on the basis of Reformed doctrines in the biblical texts themselves. So at

---

1. New York: Harper, 1930.
2. New York: Macmillan, 1921.
3. New York: Macmillan, 1923.

Westminster, there was a strong defense of the old doctrines by some strikingly new methods.

The 1960s marked significant changes at Westminster. The "boys" that Machen brought with him from Princeton began to retire and go to glory. I studied, largely with this old faculty, from 1961 to 1964, earning my BD degree, which is now called the MDiv. My time at Westminster was a great blessing as I grew in my understanding of the Word of God. But it was also an intellectual treat, and when I went on for graduate work at Yale, I felt well prepared, for Westminster taught me not only to embrace Reformed orthodoxy but also to think carefully and creatively about theology and Scripture. When I returned to Westminster in a teaching capacity in 1968, I was determined to continue for my students both the oldness and the newness that had characterized Westminster's heritage. In time, that led me to examine American language-analysis philosophy, just as Van Til and Robert Knudsen had studied European philosophy and theology. And it led me to develop a theological method called *triperspectivalism*, about which there will be more references in this book.

In the late 1960s and early 1970s, there was an atmosphere of transition, as new faculty were added and new thoughts entered our corporate discussion: Jay Adams's "nouthetic counseling," Jack Miller's views of how to outgrow the ingrown church, and D. Clair Davis's Jesus-centered understanding of church history. Discussions in my classes often felt like "passing the torch," as I taught and learned from many students who turned out to be notable thinkers in their own right, bringing forth in the Westminster tradition ideas old and new. Among those students were Wayne Grudem, later author of a wonderful systematic theology and coeditor of this volume; Greg Bahnsen, who defended theonomy and Van Til's apologetics with rigor; Dennis Johnson, now a professor at Westminster Seminary California; John Hughes, who taught theology at Westmont College and is coeditor of this volume; Bill Edgar, who now teaches at Westminster; Jim Hurley, who founded the Marriage and Family Therapy program at Reformed Theological Seminary in Jackson, Mississippi; Dick Keyes, who for many years has directed the L'Abri program in Southborough, Massachusetts; and Tiina Allik, who doctored at Yale and taught for some years at Loyola University in New Orleans.

Others, too, who attended Westminster at that time later entered the theological profession. Willem VanGemeren taught Old Testament for many years at Reformed and Trinity Seminaries. Moisés Silva was a professor of biblical studies at Westmont College and Gordon-Conwell Seminary. Andrew Lincoln served as Portland Professor of New Testament at the University of Gloucestershire from 1999 to 2013. And Susan Foh later wrote *Women and the Word of God*.[4] There was also a group of academically sharp students who followed and sought to apply the teachings of Herman Dooyeweerd. When I think of having many of these students in the same classroom, I wonder how I managed to survive those years. Yet I remember them as a group that loved Jesus and who sought to dig deeply into the Word of God, following its teaching wherever it led.

Vern S. Poythress fit right in with this group. I remember well the faculty meeting in which President Edmund P. Clowney told us that we needed to have something new, an "experimental honors program." Clowney had often spoken to students at Harvard, and he had met Vern there, concluding that the present Westminster program would not be sufficiently challenging for Vern. Vern had a PhD in mathematics from Harvard. He had also studied theology extensively and wanted to earn a theology degree. So our faculty voted to establish a program in which especially gifted students would not have to attend regularly scheduled classes (though they could attend any lectures they desired), but would take comprehensive exams and write papers in major areas of theology.

As it turned out, many of the lectures that Vern chose to attend were in my courses, so he joined the group to which the torch was being passed. In fear and trembling, I presented my triperspectival method in these classes with Vern and the others listening carefully; and, somewhat to my surprise, Vern found this approach fascinating and consonant with his own thinking. He had studied linguistics with Kenneth Pike, the inventor of "tagmemics," the theory of linguistics that governed the Bible translation work of Wycliffe Bible Translators. Vern found that my triperspectival triad of normative, situational, and existential perspectives was congruent with Pike's distinction between

---

4. Phillipsburg, NJ: Presbyterian and Reformed, 1978.

particle, field, and wave, as well as the other concepts of Pike's linguistic theory. Then in 1976 Vern wrote a book called *Philosophy, Science, and the Sovereignty of God,*[5] in which he correlated these triads and many others, developing doctrines of ontology, methodology, and axiology. Throughout the 1970s, he worked with Wycliffe Bible Translators and earned a DTh degree in biblical studies at the University of Stellenbosch in South Africa. From 1976 to the present, he has been a professor of New Testament at Westminster.

Throughout his career, Vern's work has illumined many fields of study, as the bibliography in this volume will attest—from biblical theology and mathematics, to sociology, philosophy, logic, theory of chance and determinism, hermeneutics, and biblical authority. Many of us will testify that his character is equally inspiring. Vern believes that the work of the scholar must be done not only from God's Word and in God's name but also in the *presence* of God.[6] Vern is God-centered in the workplace and in his family. Many of us have been moved by the way he has taught his two sons, Ransom and Justin. Both boys attended public school, but Vern and his wife, Diane, understood that a secular education was not enough. Students from Christian families needed to be untaught a great many things to make sure their own thinking would reflect biblical presuppositions. So Vern and Diane taught Ransom and Justin intensively in biblical content and theology. They prepared both boys for what they called Bar Yeshua ceremonies. These were similar to the Bar Mitzvah ceremonies of the Jewish people, but full of gospel content. You will learn some of the results of this from the Poythress sons themselves in the first section of this book, "Sons of Yeshua." And in those essays you can find some beautiful testimonies of Vern's godly character.

In this volume we also seek to honor Vern by presenting to him essays from his fellow scholars on topics of concern to him through the years of his ministry. Following "Sons of Yeshua," part 1 of our book, we present groups of essays on biblical exegesis, the doctrine of the Trinity, worldview, history, and ethics.

---

5. Nutley, NJ: Presbyterian and Reformed, 1976.
6. See especially his *Reading the Word of God in the Presence of God: A Handbook of Biblical Interpretation* (Wheaton, IL: Crossway, 2016).

In part 2, on biblical exegesis, Greg Beale, Vern's Westminster colleague, presents in chapter 3 "The New Testament Background of ἐκκλησία Revisited Yet Again," a study of the term in Scripture. Beale argues that the main background of this term is to be found in the Septuagint translation of the Old Testament, not in secular Roman usage. He concludes that the church of the Old Testament and the church of the New Testament are the same church.

In chapter 4, In Whan Kim, president and vice chancellor of Swaziland Christian University in Mbabane, Swaziland, contributes his essay "The Divine Choice between the Offerings of Cain and Abel," arguing that what differentiates the offerings of the two brothers is not something in the offerings themselves but whether the brothers were moved to act from hearts of faith: Abel sought above all to please God, and Cain did not.

Brandon Crowe, another of Vern's colleagues, in his essay "Reading the Lord's Prayer Christologically" (chap. 5), teaches us how to do what the title of his essay communicates. Like his colleagues, Vern has always taught that Christ is the center of the Scriptures, both the Old and the New Testaments. Crowe shows how a Christological focus sheds light on all the petitions of the Lord's Prayer.

Then Robert J. Cara, vice president in charge of academic affairs at Reformed Theological Seminary, who has studied with Vern, continues the Christological theme, considering in chapter 6 "Psalms Applied to Both Christ and Christians" in the New Testament. As in Vern's teaching, Christological exegesis not only gives us facts about Christ but also applies Scripture to our own lives in the most helpful way.

Next, Iain Duguid, who teaches Old Testament at Westminster, in his contribution "What Kind of Prophecy Continues? Defining the Differences between Continuationism and Cessationism" (chap. 7), takes up "cessationism," the question of whether and in what form the charismatic gifts of the New Testament (tongues, prophecy, healing) continue today. He follows Vern's own treatments of this controversial and difficult issue with a careful, nuanced discussion. Duguid believes that we should give more consideration to the variations in the biblical concepts. This carefulness will lead to the conclusion that the cessationist Richard Gaffin and the continuationist Wayne Grudem (who both have essays in this volume) are not as far apart (or as far from Vern) as they might initially appear.

Lane Tipton, who teaches New Testament at Westminster, addresses in "Christocentrism *and* Christotelism: The Spirit, Redemptive History, and the Gospel" (our chap. 8) a recent controversy within the seminary faculty. He helpfully employs Vos's distinction between symbol and type, yielding two ways in which Christ is the theme of the Old Testament: the symbols point to Christ as the substance of Israel's present life, and the types point to him as the future consummation of Israel's hope. Neither of these requires an explanation in terms of "Second Temple hermeneutics."

Richard B. Gaffin is a longtime (and recently retired) colleague of Vern's at Westminster. His essay "What 'Symphony of Sighs'? Reflections on the Eschatological Future of the Creation" is our chapter 9. Gaffin draws on his recent work of translating the *Reformed Dogmatics* of Geerhardus Vos, and develops cogent reasons for seeing the new heavens and new earth as a purification of the old, rather than an annihilation of the old and replacement with something totally different.

Part 3 of our book is dedicated to the doctrine of the Trinity, one of the major areas of theological discussion in evangelicalism today. Vern has taken a great interest in this doctrine. In the context of his triperspectivalism, he sees the Trinity as the root of all the unity and diversity of the creation. Camden Bucey begins this discussion in chapter 10 with his contribution "The Trinity and Monotheism: Christianity and Islam in the Theology of Cornelius Van Til."

Combining in chapter 11 Vern's concern with the Trinity and his interests in language and linguistics, Pierce Taylor Hibbs writes "Language and the Trinity: A Meeting Place for the Global Church."

In chapter 12, Jeffrey C. Waddington contributes his "Jonathan Edwards and God's Involvement in Creation: An Examination of 'Miscellanies,' no. 1263." There has long been controversy over Edwards's "occasionalism." Some have suspected Edwards of pantheism or panentheism, since for him everything in nature immediately depends on God, making Edwards an advocate of "continuous creation." At the end of his essay, Waddington makes comparisons between Edwards's views and Vern's essay "Why Scientists *Must* Believe in God," the remarkable apologetic that begins his book *Redeeming Science*.

Part 4 of our collection deals with worldview, a central concern of Vern's writings, inherited from Van Til. In chapter 13, Peter A. Lillback, president of Westminster, presents "Redeeming the Seminary by Redeeming Its Worldview." My essay in chapter 14, "Presuppositionalism and Perspectivalism," discusses two matters of central concern to Vern and me. I try there to show how presuppositionalism, an apologetic focused on worldview (developed by Van Til), is quite compatible with triperspectivalism and indeed inseparable from it. Chapter 15 is the deeply stimulating essay "The Death of Tragedy: Reflections upon a Tragic Aspect of This Present Age," by the Westminster church historian Carl Trueman. In chapter 16, Brian Courtney Wood brings part 4 to an inspiring conclusion in his "Beholding the Glory of Jesus: How a Christ-Centered Perspective Restores in Us the Splendor of God's Image." Here the emphasis on Christian worldview combines with the emphasis on Christ-centered exegesis, reminding us that Christ-centered exegesis of Scripture *is* the Christian worldview.

Part 5 deals with history, a somewhat neglected area of Christian philosophy. The essay by Luke Lu in chapter 17 is "Christian Missions in China: A Reformed Perspective." Vern's wife, Diane, has long had a special concern with China. She speaks fluent Mandarin, and she and Vern have had a special ministry to Chinese students on the Westminster campus, as well as to other international students. Diane herself brings her missions interests to bear on the philosophy of history in chapter 18, "Historiography: Redeeming History." Diane is herself a working historian, and in this essay she supplements her husband's "Redeeming" books, adding another important realm to the discussion of Christ's lordship over all realms of life. She shows that in the Christian worldview, God is in control of time as well as space. So there can be no religious neutrality in the way we interpret history.

Part 6 concludes our volume with a question Francis Schaeffer asked: "How should we then live?" Two of the book's coeditors (and good friends of Vern's) here contribute essays on biblical ethics. In chapter 19, Wayne Grudem presents "Christians Never Have to Choose the 'Lesser Sin.'" And in chapter 20, John Hughes presents a triperspectival analysis of some ethical terms in Paul's letter to the Romans: "Perspectives on the Kingdom of God in Romans 14:17."

We trust God that this collection will honor Vern and, above all, as Vern certainly would wish, honor the Lord Jesus Christ. May it promote Vern's vision among God's people, a vision to glorify Christ's lordship over all areas of human life, redeeming all realms of human thought.

John M. Frame

Acknowledgments

It has been our pleasure to work with Vern's family—Diane, Ransom, and Justin—and with so many of his friends to produce this Festschrift in his honor.

Special thanks go to Diane for the many ways she helped us from start to finish.

To this volume's many contributors, we express our thanks for their labors and contributions in Vern's honor.

We also would like to thank Justin Taylor at Crossway for supporting this project, for encouraging us, and for his flexibility with the deadline.

Finally, we would like to thank Crossway's Thom Notaro for the professional copyediting skills he has brought to our project.

May our Trinitarian God be glorified by this book.

John M. Frame
Wayne Grudem
John J. Hughes

Abbreviations

AB	Anchor Bible
ANF	*The Ante-Nicene Fathers*. Edited by Alexander Roberts and James Donaldson. 1885–1887. 10 vols. Repr., Peabody, MA: Hendrickson, 1994
BDAG	Bauer, Walter, Frederick William Danker, William F. Arndt, and F. Wilbur Gingrich. *A Greek-English Lexicon of the New Testament and Other Early Christian Literature*. 3rd ed. Chicago: University of Chicago Press, 2000
BECNT	Baker Exegetical Commentary on the New Testament
EBC	Expositor's Bible Commentary
ESV	English Standard Version
GKC	*Gesenius' Hebrew Grammar*. Edited by E. Kautzsch. Translated by A. E. Cowley. 2nd ed. Oxford: Clarendon, 1910
GTJ	*Grace Theological Journal*
HCSB	Holman Christian Standard Bible
ICC	International Critical Commentary
IJST	*International Journal of Systematic Theology*
Institutes	Calvin, John. *Institutes of the Christian Religion*. Edited by John T. McNeill. Translated by Ford Lewis Battles. 2 vols. The Library of Christian Classics 20–21. Louisville: Westminster John Knox, 1960
JASA	*Journal of the American Scientific Affiliation*
JBMW	*Journal for Biblical Manhood and Womanhood*
JETS	*Journal of the Evangelical Theological Society*
JSNT	*Journal for the Study of the New Testament*
KJV	King James Version
LXX	Septuagint
NA^{28}	*Novum Testamentum Graece* (Nestle-Aland). 28th ed. Edited by Barbara Aland, Kurt Aland, Johannes Karavidopoulos, Carlos M. Martini, and Bruce M. Metzger. Stuttgart: Deutsche Bibelgesellschaft, 2012

NASB   New American Standard Bible

NEB   New English Bible

NET   NET Bible

NICNT   New International Commentary on the New Testament

NIGTC   New International Greek Testament Commentary

NIV   New International Version

NIVAC   NIV Application Commentary

NJB   New Jerusalem Bible

NKJV   New King James Version

NLT   New Living Translation

NPNF¹   *The Nicene and Post-Nicene Fathers*, Series 1. Edited by Philip Schaff. 1886–1889. 14 vols. Repr., Peabody, MA: Hendrickson, 1994

NRSV   New Revised Standard Version

NTS   *New Testament Studies*

PNTC   Pillar New Testament Commentary

PTR   *Princeton Theological Review*

RSV   Revised Standard Version

SBT   Studies in Biblical Theology

SJT   *Scottish Journal of Theology*

SNTSMS   Society for New Testament Studies Monograph Series

TNIV   Today's New International Version

TNTC   Tyndale New Testament Commentaries

TOTC   Tyndale Old Testament Commentaries

UBS⁵   *The Greek New Testament* (United Bible Societies). 5th ed. Edited by Barbara Aland, Kurt Aland, Johannes Karavidopoulos, Carlos M. Martini, and Bruce M. Metzger. Stuttgart: Deutsche Bibelgesellschaft, 2014

WBC   Word Biblical Commentary

WCF   Westminster Confession of Faith

WJE   Edwards, Jonathan. *The Works of Jonathan Edwards*. Edited by Paul Ramsay et al. Vols. 1, 3, 6, 17, 21, 23, 26. New Haven, CT: Yale University Press, 1957, 1970, 1980, 1999, 2003, 2004, 2008

WLC   Westminster Larger Catechism

WTJ   *Westminster Theological Journal*

Part 1

SONS OF YESHUA

1

Redeeming Science

A Father-Son Tale

RANSOM POYTHRESS

Many people have a love-hate relationship with the sciences. They see them either as the bedrock for life and the proper understanding of the universe or as some enigmatic intellectual pursuit they escaped from after that one required college course. People can talk with polarizing, emotionally charged language about their feelings on the sciences, the way they might speak about politics, the Yankees, or dark chocolate.

Some think only a certain type of person has what it takes to thrive in the sciences. This person must have a certain type of brain, a particular personality, and a special genetic predisposition to really enjoy the sciences. They believe the sciences are not for everyone.

This mistaken view can be used to ill effect by people on either side of the divide. Those who have embraced the sciences can sometimes see themselves as elite and superior. They are above and beyond the huddled, ignorant masses. They wield intellectualism as a weapon to intimidate others by using scientific language, like a password to a

secret society, to exclude and diminish their peers. "You don't understand what I'm saying when I spout a long list of complicated scientific
terms? You poor soul. Just trust that I know what I'm talking about
and believe that I'm smarter than you and know truth better than you."
They set themselves up as arbiters of truth in order to achieve power
and position. This is science at its worst, used to confuse instead of
clarify, to subjugate instead of serve.

On the flip side, those not drawn to the sciences will sometimes try
to separate themselves through a different kind of derision. They por-
tray scientists as awkward, geeky, and introverted. To them, scientists
are people who sit in dark, windowless labs poring over data because
they're too antisocial to form functional human relationships. These
individuals laugh at the pocket protectors and the frequently parodied
inability of scientists to perform in the "real" world. To them, scientists
are like that out-of-place kid brother they condescendingly tolerated
and begrudgingly assisted when he was out of his depth. Alternatively,
some feel like they are the kid brother, and science is the scary, inac-
cessible older brother. So, they distance themselves to avoid potential
embarrassment and rejection.

At times, these differing stances can set up invisible battle lines,
trying to disparage one another in order to elevate themselves. I regard these two prevailing positions as fatally flawed because the battle
line creates a false dichotomy. The tension rests on the presupposition
that some gifts are better than others. Although some may have more
aptitude in the sciences, that doesn't make them inherently better (or
worse) than anyone else. Job description doesn't make you superior.
The CEO in a penthouse office isn't better than the janitor who cleans
his office. Putting value on ability isn't biblical—it's cultural. Although
there may be real, ordained differences in authority, there is no inherent difference in the value of the work. All work done to the glory of
God is glorious.

God created work for his glory and for love of neighbor, not for
societal standing, monetary advantage, or selfish gain. As a result, I
believe everyone can appreciate the fundamentals of any job or task,
from changing diapers to leading a country. This includes the sciences
as well. If we can't explain our work in a way that is accessible to every-

one, it's a failure on our part rather than a reflection of the inadequacy of the hearer. Owing to our human nature as image bearers, not only are the sciences understandable to everyone—they are also potentially enjoyable by everyone. Even if some individuals may not gravitate toward the sciences, they can praise God as they discover what science reveals about "his eternal power and divine nature" (Rom. 1:20).

I have my father, Vern Sheridan Poythress, largely to thank for my perspective on science and, more generally, all facets of creation. It was he who taught me from an early age to search out how God is revealed in all aspects of life. Whether through Old Testament law pointing forward to Christ, redemptive themes abounding in film, or bare winter branches demonstrating God's artistry, my father pointed out God's revelation and how we, in relationship, respond to him. This vision of the world became most apparent to me as I journeyed through the sciences. My understanding matured with time as my father helped open my eyes to a more expansive vista of creation.

I don't recall exactly when or how my interest in the sciences originated, though my parents tell me it was from a young age. I do remember that my father actively nurtured those early feelings. I recall my excitement upon receiving what was, at the time, a fairly expensive oil immersion compound light microscope. With my primitive tools and technique, I eagerly dissected small insects or birds that had perished in our backyard, and mounted samples on microscope slides. I pored over books on animal behavior and watched National Geographic documentaries on repeat. Those early years of uninhibited exploration provided much of the groundwork for my future interest in the sciences.

However, the rigor and routine of school and the pressure of grades soon infiltrated my carefree revelry. During those teen years, my father stoked the fire as he patiently and painstakingly held my hand through science fair projects. His contagious excitement reignited in me those wonder-filled moments that made the sciences so appealing. I'll probably never truly know exactly how many hours he dedicated as he explained, re-explained, and further explained endless sheets of mathematical equations. Yet through it all, there was no concealing the pleasure he got from being involved.

The flat, disinterested style of the public schools seemed to almost intentionally disfigure the sciences into a set of lifeless obstacles to be surmounted on the way to some nebulous idea of comfort and success. My schoolteachers reduced science to pragmatic tools, meaningless rules, and rote memorization. But at home, I watched my father come alive expounding on the beauty of consensus and cooperativity in creation. The sciences took on new life for me under his tutelage. He delightedly tried to explain a new system of annotating, describing, and manipulating very large numbers; he got carried away teaching me how to use exponential regression to compare evolutionary models with typological-cladistic arrangements of animal phyla, and I found myself caught up in the fervor with him.

Eventually, I went off to college, and although I persevered, much of the zeal dried up. Science lost its sheen, its spark fading beneath mounds of droning professors, stuffy classrooms, and inane paperwork with only the occasional flash of what I knew must be hidden somewhere below the surface. Where was that thrill of discovery? Or being gleefully astonished by two disparate ideas joining together in harmony? I knew something was missing, and I graduated confused and disheartened. Science, real science, was entombed somewhere beneath my feet. I could feel that it was there. I could see the headstone, yet it felt beyond my power to unearth the captive realm.

My time of study at Westminster Theological Seminary finally exhumed the precious jewel of science. Through my work there and hours of conversations with my father, I started to see the wellspring of my zeal for the sciences. He helped me see not just that I love science but also where that love came from, something I had not been able to grasp until then. He wasn't just encouraging a love of science, but explaining and showing *why* I love science in the first place—because I love God. In showing me why I love science, by extension, he showed me why I had lost science. When anything displaces God as the focal point, you no longer see it through the light of the Son, and its gleam is lost. It's like trying to use the moon for light after you've removed the sun from the sky.

When you love God, by extension you love everything about him, everything that proclaims him, everything that is brought forth by him, everything that reminds you of him. If you enjoy anything in life, it's because first and foremost you see God in it (although non-Christians would deny it—Romans 1). Pleasure of any kind is a shadow of the fulfillment we find in relationship with God. It's all meant to point and drive us toward him. So I am excited by science because my heart sees God there and delights in God's revelation of himself. The experiments I do with my hands and the results I see with my eyes reveal God's beauty, organization, sovereignty, care, power, tenderness, inscrutability, and a host of other attributes. Those flashes of majesty I glimpsed throughout my life in science fully reveal themselves when they're connected to the majesty and worship of the one true Creator God.

Furthermore, humans are the only creatures capable of this connection. As image bearers, we are able to enter into a personal relationship with God in a way that nothing else in creation can. A human soul is more significant than all the marvels of science because of this alikeness. Therefore, as our understanding of science grows in scope and grandeur, by association our worship of God for the special place of humankind in creation expands proportionally.

These truths struck me with irrepressible clarity on one particularly memorable occasion. In my early years of graduate school, my father came to Boston University to give an open lecture on science and faith. There were about a hundred people in the audience ranging from freshman music majors to the senior president of the atheist club on campus. Many people were drawn by my father's reputation for superior academics and a sharp theological mind. I remember sitting in the front row nervously preparing my introductory comments and watching him off to the side. His physical presence isn't particularly commanding—tall and lanky, always lecturing in a full suit, seemingly unaware of the definition of "relax." A brief summary of his résumé intimidates. You quickly realize the magnitude of his genius accompanied by wisdom, maturity, and a degree of solemnity that comes from years of world experience. Yet, there is none of the pride or abrasive confidence that often accompanies such knowledge. He possesses a quiet, gentle, and inspiring humility. I sometimes notice the slightly awkward way he stands, a little too stiff, a little too uncomfortable, with his hands clasped strangely, looking off into a corner, his mind traveling at light speed. It's endearing, and—without disrespect—I'd almost describe it as adorable, like a sweet, absent-minded professor.

Once I survived the nerve-wracking ordeal of introducing the greatest man I know, I settled down to listen to his talk. I had heard several versions of it in bits and pieces through the years—at the dinner table and scattered throughout chapters of his books. Although the content itself wasn't new, it was the presentation that gripped my attention. Being personable and sociable isn't one of my father's strongest traits, but he knows it's a way of demonstrating love for others, so he works hard at it. This adds to his adorable quirkiness, but it also means his lectures can be didactic and dry, relying more on audience interest in material than on charisma and panache. However, as his talk wore on, the entire audience pulsed in rapt attention. For a large group of college-age students, this was no small feat. Every day hundreds of professors across the country fail to keep students awake, let alone attentive. How was this possible? It became all the more remarkable as the subject material increased in complexity to the point where I was sure no one in the audience had the faintest clue what he was talking about. There is no way a freshman business major could have the slightest idea how drawings of boxes connect to four-dimensional symmetries and Maxwell's equations of light, yet everyone was transfixed.

Then I saw it. My father was overjoyed with what he was saying. He didn't just think intellectually that God was revealed in all creation; he felt it. In his talk, he actively worshiped God for the beautiful harmonies revealed in creation. He glorified God for the way he revealed himself. Here was a man with two PhDs enamored and animated, rocking back and forth, hardly able to contain his giddy enthusiasm! He was full of child-like amazement, and it was infectious. We all wanted that. We all wanted to be so captivated and entranced by our studies, our work, our lives, that we couldn't contain our joy. I finally felt like I understood what Jesus meant in Matthew 18:2–3: "And calling to him a child, he put him in the midst of them and said, 'Truly, I say to you, unless you turn and become like children, you will never enter the kingdom of heaven.'" Here was a man who didn't use tips from the latest book on presentation style, or techniques from pop psychology on how to keep people engaged. He used no flashy PowerPoint tricks or catchy animations to elicit a cheap laugh. There was no mask, no artificially constructed barrier between him and what he articulated; he lived his love of God. It was uncontainable and utterly desirable. I can imagine him and King David dancing together, their hearts singing,

> The heavens declare the glory of God,
>   and the sky above proclaims his handiwork. (Ps. 19:1)

I finally realized I had an example to help me embody my joy and interest in the sciences. But this was not limited to how my love of science provides a clear avenue for glorifying God personally. When you are filled to overflowing with awe and exuberance, you can't help but want to share that. Now I want to communicate my joy to others so they might experience the same delight, as in the parable of the woman who lost her coin. She gave all her time and energy to find it and, when she found it, called others to celebrate with her (Luke 15:8–9). I "found" God in the sciences and want everyone else to see the splendor of the Creator with the same clarity. The way my father and I get excited about science, the way a child gets excited about a new toy, or a college graduate celebrates his first job, or parents cherish their first child, all of this points us to God and his care, sovereignty, love, and grace. Yet, as praiseworthy as these things are, they are but small shadows, pale reflections of the enthusiasm we should feel for the gospel of Jesus Christ. We should all be so moved by the gospel that our exuberance is uncontainable (Matt. 5:14–16).

This joyful response isn't just limited to the sciences. By extension, this same gospel connection applies to every area of work, study, or play. Art, sports, politics, insurance, Wall Street, custodial services, parenting—they can all be done in connection to, pointing toward, and to the glory of the one true God. God, by his Spirit, has revealed the truth of himself and his once-for-all salvific work through the sacrifice of his Son, Jesus Christ, as an atonement for sin. This is an astonishing truth. Seeing God's glory revealed in Scripture and in creation should elicit such responses as joy, fear, awe, and worship. Like the disciples during the transfiguration, when we see God displayed specifically in our daily lives, we should fall on our faces before his majesty (Matt. 17:6). Then we reflect the image of his glory as we ourselves are transformed. "And we all, with unveiled face, beholding the glory of the Lord, are being transformed into the same image from one degree of glory to another" (2 Cor. 3:18a). Glimpses of glory in work done in accordance with God's will reveal what a magnificent, astounding God we serve. John Piper says this beautifully in his book *Think: The Life of the Mind and the Love of God*:

> All branches of learning exist ultimately for the purposes of knowing God, loving God, and loving man through Jesus. And since loving man means ultimately helping him see and savor God in Christ forever, it is profoundly right to say all thinking, all learning, all education, and all research is for the sake of knowing God, loving God, and showing God.[1]

In June 2014, I had the amazing honor of standing beside my father as we gave presentations on science and faith and answered questions on a panel. For more than twenty years I had witnessed and experienced the wondrousness of God through my father, and now, for the first time, I shared it with others in a large public setting. For me, this felt like a momentous induction and commissioning. My father trained me in word and deed. He passed on his excitement rooted in the truth, and the time has come to share what I've learned. I'll never be my father, but I hope by God's grace that, like him, I can embody the truth of creation as revealed by God. I pray that I can manifest a genuine exhilaration that comes from the full realization of the overflowing mercy and grandeur of God. I aspire to pass on to future generations what I have learned by the Holy Spirit through my father. Abraham Kuyper once said, "There is not a square inch in the whole domain of our human existence over which Christ, who is Sovereign over *all*, does not cry: Mine!"[2] Vern Poythress, my father, has helped me realize that not only is this true, but it's a truth worth celebrating and proclaiming with all my heart.

---

1. John Piper, *Think: The Life of the Mind and the Love of God* (Wheaton, IL: Crossway, 2010), 175.

2. Abraham Kuyper, inaugural address at the opening of the Free University of Amsterdam, October 20, 1880, quoted in Abraham Kuyper, "Sphere Sovereignty," in *Abraham Kuyper: A Centennial Reader*, ed. James D. Bratt (Grand Rapids, MI: Eerdmans, 1998), 488, emphasis original.

2

The Grace and Gift
of Differentness

JUSTIN POYTHRESS

"So how much will it be, total?" my dad asked.

"Well," the man shifted, looking up and stroking his chin. "I think I said three thousand. But when we go to get the paperwork done at the DMV, we can just write it down as a gift, and that way you don't have to pay any taxes."

I was lost. It was the first time I'd ever been involved in a vehicle transaction, and because of the last-second nature of getting this teaching job in Tennessee, we had found, sought out, and were now buying a 1997 Crown Victoria in the space of twenty-four hours.

"No," my dad said softly, and with a gentleness that betrayed his distaste for any sort of confrontation. "I don't think that's the right way."

"No, no, it's fine!" the man assured us. "I'm happy to do it. I do it all the time for people I sell to, and it just saves you the taxes, is all." He was a little irritated that we would be refusing his warm generosity, more than that, refusing his willingness to put himself on the line for our benefit.

"I understand," my father said doggedly, his voice now rising in its steadiness and firmness. "But see, we are followers of Jesus Christ, so we want to obey the law; we'll pay the full taxes on it."

"Ah, oh yes, of course, I get that," the man shuffled and sputtered. "Wanting to help you all out was all, but I understand."

The seller was not the only one out of sorts.

"Followers of Jesus Christ"? The phrase was echoing in my own head. Who says that? "We don't want to break the law"? You don't phrase it like that to someone who is trying to do you a favor. If you must, you let him down gently. And why bring Christ into it? A person can just be honest without having to say it's because of Jesus. Good grief. And to top it all off, I was going to have to pay back my dad for the vehicle. So, yeah, maybe the whole no taxes thing wouldn't have been so bad. After all, both my dad and I were on the same page against big government, so why did we have to make such a fuss about giving them more money?

This was my father, though, and this story exemplifies one of the many ways in which he is—there's no other word for it—*different*. That word can come with a lot of baggage, but I intend to show primarily, as in the above case, how it describes him with the best possible nuances of that word. We as Christians are called to be different. We are sojourners and exiles in this world. And no matter what I might have thought about how my father chose to phrase that particular refusal of tax evasion, I could not help but feel, even in that moment, the thawing warmth of gospel reverence so manifest in my dad's character. There was something so solid, so unshakeable, so unflinching in his unashamed embrace of the shame of Christ.

It will not come as a surprise to anyone reading this collection that Vern Poythress is a godly man. One simply cannot live the sort of life he has, with the career path he has chosen, and the works he has contributed, without an accompanying measure of authentic faith. Yet this is perhaps the area where I can best provide illumination, seeing as my father has not been one to maintain an extensive social circle. It is within a man's private life, in the refuge of recreation, in those "unseen hours," where his character is most laid bare. And so it is there that I wish to speak on behalf of his "differentness."

One of the first areas where I encountered this different godliness was in his Bible knowledge. Every seminary professor or man in ministry knows his Bible, or at least would like to appear to know his Bible; so such a statement can seem a truism. Yet my exposure to this reality was more organic and thus made a stronger impression. We did morning and evening devotions as a family, and I knew my father read his Bible in the morning. But I also remember other occasions, such as Saturday afternoons, or evenings, or during vacation times, hearing—of all things—a sanctified hissing noise.

The noise would come from his bedroom, the door slightly ajar, and I discerned the cause of the hissing to be my father's voice as he read the Bible to himself at a volume just above a whisper. The result, audible to someone outside the room, was a series of *s* sounds echoing faintly in the hallway. When I peeked in, he would sometimes raise his eyes and offer the faintest smile before returning to the Scripture. He was always willing to be disturbed, but if left alone, he would proceed for long durations, reading large chunks in a sitting.

Slowly, as I grew in my own Bible education, I became aware that Daddy could serve as a biblical encyclopedia. And not just to answer questions about any and every theological term, or church structures, or clarifying how to interpret a tricky passage. He knew where every story or doctrine was in the Bible. I still remember being stunned at about age ten when my mother revealed to me that you could quote or read any selection from the Bible and my dad would be able to tell exactly what chapter and verse it came from. Naturally, I had to test this a few times and soon discovered that my dad had indeed mastered this neat little party trick, though I saw little more value to it at the time.

When I got into college and seminary, that's when I started hearing the stories. A seminary employee recounted the following to me: Upon seeing Vern Poythress eating his lunch in the Machen dining hall by himself, the man observed that my father was whispering over a Bible.

"What are you doing?"

"Memorizing the book of Habakkuk," Dad replied.

"Why Habakkuk?"

"Because it's the next one."

There's not much one can say after a response like that. Eventually,

I was able to goad out of Dad more precisely how much of the Bible he had memorized: the entire New Testament, the Psalter, the second half of Isaiah, Ecclesiastes and the Song of Solomon, all the Minor Prophets, Ruth, and other select portions of Old Testament narrative. That adds up to about half the Bible, at least as far as direct memorization is concerned. I then discovered that in order to keep it from fading, he tries to make a daily practice (who knows where he finds this time) to review six chapters of memorized material, in addition to his daily review of Hebrew vocabulary flashcards.

So when Dr. Poythress gives his plug each year in his hermeneutics class for really "knowing your Bible" and, during sermon preparation, memorizing the passage, it's not empty counsel, though he'd never willingly give his credentials.

That's another part of what has made my father different: his humility. I don't know if I've ever encountered a more thoroughly gospel-humble man. If you ever want to see Vern Poythress become uncomfortable, I can offer you a tried and tested way to do so: Without warning, launch into how much you appreciate his work, or how God has used him in your life, or how remarkable you've found a book or teaching of his. Immediately, he will begin squirming, shuffling, and grimacing, as if you were jabbing at him with a red-hot poker. So fearful is he of pride, and of allowing a foothold for conceit, that if ever the conversation turns around to congratulating him on his achievements or character, it produces an immediate shutdown. He revealed on multiple occasions, much to my disbelief, that his greatest fear and greatest weakness was his pride. So he would never engage in talk that openly lent itself to building his acclaim.

The same could be said about gossip. I've heard my father engage in gossip approximately the same number of times I've seen him get angry, which is to say, never. This doesn't mean that he would never have strong opinions or feel the weight of folly or injustice, which would stir him up to agitation; but if he ever sensed that a conversation was descending to mudslinging, he clammed up. And being sinfully inclined toward gossip and dirt myself, I remember trying to lob him softballs. People who stood against him, who attacked him, or whose foolishness paraded itself and worked to his detriment—I would try goading him to attack them, yet without success. I never witnessed such perseverance in guarded understatement. I never perceived in my father, by deed or word, any ill will toward another human being. He forgave anyone in our family so effortlessly that I always found it nearly impossible to harbor resentment toward him, even if I chafed at some decision he made.

I think his ability to forgive and reconcile relations is an outworking of his genius of multiperspectivalism. That lens of perception is not merely an abstract theological theory used to peel apart multiple layers of symphonic biblical truth, but it applies to how he deals with people in the real world. My father has an uncanny ability, which frequently served him in his efforts as peacekeeper within our house, to see, understand, and sympathize with every person's perspective in turn, while not necessarily agreeing with it. He can slip from one man's shoes into another's with such remarkable alacrity that you must often wait a long time hoping to hear his own personal opinion.

Such deference and desire to see the best in others reflects my father's "differentness" in godliness worked out in humility. That humility is so deeply rooted within his character that it routinely overflows in a simplicity that structures and pervades his entire life.

It is in relation to the subject of simplicity that we find a sharp irony that surfaces when exploring the contours of my father's worldview. On the one hand, he is a marrow-deep academic. If one ever wished to paint a caricature of the consummate scholar—the professor squirreled away in his office, hunched over massive tomes in the solitude of his ivory tower, poring over the obscure thought of specialized internal academic debates, perfectly content to sail for days through the mental waters of writing, thought, and logic, with nary a human interaction— Vern Poythress could serve well as your model.

Yet, on the other hand, I don't believe I've ever encountered someone who so derides, disparages, and deconstructs the very academic world he orbits. He is only too eager to thrust aside the scholarly blinders. He observes with disgust how so many of his colleagues clutch these blinders, believing they guide them into a more distinguished, loftier focus. In doing so, however, my father, in Kuyperian fashion, sees them rejecting the fullness of the manifestation of God's glory as it appears in things like children's cartoons and McDonald's, just as much as it appears in symphonies and foreign delicacies. Instead of bequeathing a subscription to the snobbery of academia, he steadfastly cultivated in us a deep reverence for the ordinary, for the unassuming, for the simple. He would regularly direct us to observe how, more often than not, it was the lowly and meek and simple to whom God granted his Spirit of understanding and faith. Oh the joy that he takes in simplicity! He continues eschewing every form of extravagance, finding peace in not being haughty, but always associating with the lowly (cf. Rom. 12:16).

Two examples serve as illustrations. The first occurred while we awaited the opening curtain of a high school musical we attended to support the child of a family friend. I was complaining about the definitive lack of quality we were about to witness. My father chided me about such an attitude. He warned that our ease of access to the cream of the crop in all branches of entertainment had numbed our ability to appreciate the amateur arts. Yet these stand, in God's sight, as equally pleasing artistic expressions of his glory and thus should be enjoyed as such. My father has helped me seek, incrementally, to become a person who, like him, does not despise the day of small things (cf. Zech. 4:10).

Another example would be football. It is not so "different" in modern America to enjoy football (often to excess). But it is different for someone like my father. For a man who himself has only ever been tangentially athletic to be introduced (through his wife) to football, and to then develop a passion for the grind of the gridiron, is quite unusual. On New Year's Day, he can contentedly join with, and even lead, the family in watching a full day's worth of unbroken bowl games. He is different in the way he watches football. He steadfastly demurs to root for any team as his favorite, being willing to side with those closest to him, but preferring most to watch the game for the game itself. He watches for the artistry, and the drama, and the chess match of coaching.

It was on account of his Kuyperian "every inch is Christ's" mentality that I was inundated, willingly or not, with explanations of how everything I did or enjoyed pointed to Christ. Playing Pokemon was patterned after a healthy exercise of dominion over the created order. Batman and Superman, as defenders of the oppressed, upholders of justice, and deliverers of redemption were types of Christ. We practiced good table manners because God is a God of order, and structure, and respect. I loved football because it displayed the exercise of Christ-given talents in analogical patterns to the Christian life of competing, strategizing, and striving until the end. There was no escape. However, God used those truths to break in when I least expected it. The transforming of one's mind is a lifelong process. I still remember how revolutionary it was when my father explained that God made the sun as the sustaining force of all life on Earth, and created the very phenomenon of light so that we could understand better who God is. Not only are these objects helpful resources that God permits us to use in making imperfect analogies, but God actually created everything, including the sun, primarily for the purpose of better knowing who he is. That is a Copernican notion to our human understanding.

This Christ-centeredness went far beyond merely sucking the fun out of comic book heroes and video games. It has characterized all of my father's life, and it came through in the holistic way my parents thought about and structured home life. We always had morning and evening devotions. Church, Sunday school, and youth group were non-negotiables. Our conversations with friends or public school lectures were dissected and then reconstructed and guided by a biblical framework. Both my brother and I went through a Christian rite of passage to manhood, which they termed a Bar Yeshua. This was totally different, and completely new cultural territory, but in matters of Christian living, navigating new and different waters was never something my parents shied from. One of the things I recall and respect dearly about my mom and dad, as I reflect back on their Christ-centered parenting, is how intentional and diligent they were in discharging this duty. They did not stray or waver from their plans, no matter how different, strange, and unfruitful their efforts at fulfilling Deuteronomy 6:6–9 might appear at a given time.

The stark, bold differentness my father maintains has been protected and reinforced by his different personality as it pertains to relationships. It's not that he does not love and appreciate the warmth and intimacy of family and friends. He does. However, because of his intellect and disposition, God has enabled him to hold these things more loosely. So once you extend outside his immediate circles of family and friends, it is not the slightest overstatement when he tells me that he doesn't care what others think of his work. This has freed him to pursue the topics, thought, and writings he feels God is leading him toward, without concern about reception.

Yet he balances that with a level of appropriate concern for how his efforts will land. He warns against the vanity of seeking to be different for the sake of being different. He has always striven to work in ways that will make an eternal impact. For him, this has meant honest reckoning with his own gifts in his place and time in the world. He rarely travels. He does not seek speaking engagements. He doesn't blog. His writings are almost never reactionary, but instead he embraces the power of the positive. The apologetic work of deconstruction must be done ten times over for any one error, and then will have to be repeated and modified to fight a slightly different strain of the same virus one generation later. However, if he contributes something positive, if he sets himself to the vastly more challenging task of blazing a new trail, if he builds something the right way, not out of hay or straw, but out of gold, that particular construction may never have to be laid again, but only added on to.

As I reflect personally on the most lasting impact of my father's legacy in my life thus far and into the future, it has been his character. Through all his brilliance, his thoughts, his biblical understanding, and his orchestrating of family life, what has been most enduring to me is the differentness of his godly character as a father. As any Van Tilian knows, there is a pretty wide Creator-creature distinction. God is different—fundamentally, innately different and peculiar. God is different down to the level of substance, of *ousia*. And so, when I give thanks for my earthly father's differentness, the most significant and lasting mode in which this has appeared to me has been in the way he has reflected and displayed God as Father.

Perhaps one of the most glorious, personal, and uplifting revelations of the New Testament is its new and different focus on relating to God as our Father through Jesus Christ. This is one of the most meaningful paradigms through which God intends for us to view him. And the longer I have known my own father, the more I have come to appreciate my own spiritual blessing in this regard, especially when compared with others who may have to work their entire lives to push past the damaged, broken, or absent images that represent all they have ever known of fatherhood. God created fatherhood, like he created the sun, not because of any creational necessity, but in order that we could better understand his character. Our dependency on human fathers; our reverence and fear of them; their love, compassion, wisdom, strength, justice, and mercy—all these things give us an abundance of tangible displays through which God wants us to grasp our way toward comprehending the one relationship that will shape our lives for eternity.

My father, Vern Poythress, will not be with me forever, but he has left me something far more significant than any legacy, inheritance, book, or even life lesson. He has laid before me, as a human model, a grid or a matrix through which I can continue to move forward in seeing and loving my heavenly Father, who is very different.

God promises to transform our entire character in Jesus through his Spirit—which makes it impossible, when I reflect on my father's legacy as a living portrayal of *the* Father, to identify clear boundary lines of where that begins and ends. So also, in the Christian life, the dynamic of fatherhood, or relating to God as Father, does not fall within neat boundaries. It pertains to all aspects of our life, and though it will change in expression, our Father-son relation with the Lord will have no end throughout eternity.

Part 2

EXEGESIS

3

The New Testament
Background of ἐκκλησία
Revisited Yet Again

G. K. BEALE

I am happy to write an essay in honor of my colleague Vern Poythress. He has been gracious and helpful to me since I came to Westminster Theological Seminary. Vern's interests and skills are wide-ranging. He is as comfortable with systematic theology, philosophy, linguistics, logic, and math as he is with exegesis and biblical theology. I have enjoyed our many conversations about exegesis and biblical theology. Vern is truly a man without guile.

• • •

In 2015 the *Journal for the Study of the New Testament* published my article titled "The Background of ἐκκλησία Revisited."[1] The purpose of the article was to enter into the recent debate about whether the

---

1. *JSNT* 38 (2015): 1–18.

background for Paul's use of ἐκκλησία was primarily Greco-Roman or from the Greek Old Testament. The article attempted to provide further evidence that, while there may be some influence from the use of ἐκκλησία as a civil assembly in the Greco-Roman world, the Septuagint was the main background for Paul's use of the word, especially for his multiple uses of "church [assembly] of God" (ἐκκλησία τοῦ θεοῦ).[2] Nehemiah 13:1 is the only place in all of the Septuagint where the phrase ἐκκλησία + θεοῦ occurs. In this case, not only is there a unique combination of words in the very same order, but there is almost the exact verbal expression: "They read in the book of Moses in the ears of the people; and it was found written in it [Deut. 23:3–5] that the Ammonites and Moabites should never enter *the assembly of God* forever."[3]

In addition to the clear verbal correspondence, the thematic similarity of Nehemiah 13:1 to the New Testament occurrences is evident, since it is the only passage in the Old Testament where the word is directly related to "reading in the book of Moses." Here "the people" are to be identified with the "assembly" (ἐκκλησία), so that the "assembly" is the place not only where unclean people are to be kept out, but also where the Scripture is read as part of worship. (Note also Neh. 8:1–2, where "the law of Moses" was read and explained in the area of the Water Gate to the "assembly" [ἐκκλησία].) Likewise, an aspect of worship by the church in Acts, in Paul's letters, and in Revelation included teaching, which involved instruction founded not only on apostolic tradition but also on the Old Testament, which was clearly part of the apostolic doctrine (e.g., 1 Cor. 15:1–3) and was read in early church worship.[4] This likeness between Nehemiah and the Pauline churches in their reading and teaching of Scripture could have been part of what sparked Paul to allude to "the assembly of God" from Nehemiah 13:1.

---

2. Except for translations from the Septuagint, Scripture quotations in this chapter are from the New American Standard Bible, copyright © 1960, 1962, 1963, 1968, 1971, 1972, 1973, 1975, 1977, 1995 by The Lockman Foundation. Used by permission.

3. In the LXX of Nehemiah, only the article τοῦ is missing before θεοῦ, though it is included before the divine name in some LXX manuscripts of Neh. 13:1 (A ℵc.a). The Hebrew text of Neh. 13:1 indeed includes the definite article before "God" (בִּקְהַל הָאֱלֹהִים), although it is not to be translated into English. Paul may well be alluding to the Hebrew text, since he includes the article τοῦ before θεοῦ, but he may be alluding to some of the significant LXX manuscript traditions of Neh. 13:1 that include the article, or he may have merely inserted the article, since it is implied in the LXX because "God" is certainly "definite" with or without an article.

4. On which see Beale, "Background of ἐκκλησία Revisited," 4.

The conclusion of my earlier article was that the early Christian "assembly" (usually translated "church") was the continuation of the true Israelite "assembly of God" in the new covenant age[5] and *implicitly* stood in contrast to the pagan civic "assemblies of the world."

In the 2015 article, except for Acts 19–20, I did not address uses of ἐκκλησία outside Paul in the New Testament and how some of them might relate to the Old Testament. As far as I am aware, such a study has not been done. It is this to which we now turn. The purpose of this study is to see whether or not other kinds of allusions to a Greco-Roman background or to other Old Testament allusions are linked with the uses of ἐκκλησία. If other allusions to a pagan background are detected, then this would point to a greater probability of a civic background for New Testament uses of ἐκκλησία. On the other hand, if other Old Testament allusions are found directly linked to New Testament uses of ἐκκλησία, then the Old Testament background of ἐκκλησία would be seen as predominant in those uses.

The remainder of this essay does not address all the other uses of ἐκκλησία outside of Paul in the New Testament, but only those in Ephesians, Colossians, 1 Timothy,[6] Hebrews, and Revelation (excluding, e.g., Matthew, Acts [outside of chaps. 19–20], James, and 3 John). The reason for this limitation is that the only allusions we have found directly linked to ἐκκλησία are Old Testament allusions in these five New Testament books. Beyond these references, I have not observed other uses of ἐκκλησία in this extra-Pauline corpus to be linked with any allusions to a Greco-Roman background or to the Old Testament. We proceed to examine these other relevant New Testament uses.

Uses of ἐκκλησία in the Later Pauline Epistles

Of course, there are many who would not hold to Pauline authorship of Ephesians, Colossians, and 1 Timothy. I accept these epistles as

---

5. For this conclusion, see, among others, not only P. Trebilco, "Why Did the Early Christians Call Themselves ἡ ἐκκλησία?," *NTS* 57, no. 3 (2011): 440–60, but also earlier works by I. Howard Marshall, "The Biblical Use of the Word 'ἐκκλησία,'" *Expository Times* 84, no. 12 (1973): 359–64, and Peter T. O'Brien, *Colossians, Philemon*, WBC 44 (Nashville: Thomas Nelson, 1982), 57–61, all of whom also argue for a predominate LXX influence.

6. Though I did address 1 Timothy briefly in the 2015 article.

authored by Paul. There is not space here to argue for this, but that has been done well by others.[7] Nevertheless, even if these three epistles were not written by Paul, they would still give evidence of a developed Pauline tradition later in the first century. We will see that the use of ἐκκλησία in direct linkage with the Old Testament in these epistles coheres with the same kind of usage elsewhere in Paul, especially in 1 Corinthians and 1 Thessalonians (discussed in the earlier article). This observation will point further to the genuine Pauline nature of Ephesians, Colossians, and 1 Timothy. Because of the direct connection of ἐκκλησία to Old Testament allusions and quotations in the following references, that term should be seen to have some link itself to the Old Testament rather than to a Greco-Roman concept of the civic assembly. Furthermore, if the following Old Testament citations and allusions about Israel or her king are fulfilled in the Christian covenant community (whether as direct or typological prophecies), is it not natural that ἐκκλησία would be applied to that community, since that was one of the main words for the Old Testament covenant community?

1. Ephesians 1:22 begins with an acknowledged quotation of Psalm 8:6, "He put all things in subjection under His feet," which is applied to Christ's ruling position at God's right hand (Eph. 1:20–21). In the psalm David sees that Israel's hope is in an ideal Adam, who will rule over all the earth (Ps. 8:6–8). This hope has begun fulfillment in Christ, which is immediately related to and explained as Christ being the "head over all things to the church" (Eph. 1:22). Christ rules over the entire earth in fulfillment of the psalm, and this rule is for the advantage of the "church" (ἐκκλησία), the continuation of authentic Israel, whose hopes have begun to be realized in Christ's inaugurated rule.

2. In Ephesians 3:9–10, Paul says that grace was given to him so that "the manifold wisdom of God," which "has been hidden" in a "mystery," "might now be made known through the church [ἐκκλησία] to the rulers and the authorities in the heavenly places." This

---

7. E.g., see D. A. Carson and Douglas J. Moo, *Introduction to the New Testament* (Grand Rapids, MI: Zondervan, 2005), 479–97 (on Ephesians), 516–31 (on Colossians), and 571–77 (on 1 Timothy).

continues the discussion of the revealed "mystery" from verses 3–8. The revelation of the "mystery" is not that the concept of the church (Jew and Gentile in Christ) is now revealed for the first time, nor that Gentiles can be saved, nor that Gentiles form part of true Israel with believing Jews in Christ, but *how Gentiles (together with believing Jews) become part of* the true Israel: by submission only to and identification only with Jesus the Israelite King, not submission to and identification only with the ethnic identification marks of the Mosaic law (circumcision, dietary laws, Sabbath laws, etc.), though there is not space here to argue this.[8]

An allusion in Ephesians 3 to the book of Daniel affirms this thought. Through ten significant parallels, Caragounis ties the revealed mystery in Ephesians 3 with the mystery in Daniel 2.[9] The expression "by revelation there was made known to me the mystery" (κατὰ ἀπο-κάλυψιν ἐγνωρίσθη μοι τὸ μυστήριον) in Ephesians 3:3 is a literary allusion to Daniel 2:28 (Theodotion), which reads, "There is a God in heaven who reveals mysteries, and He has made known to King Nebuchadnezzar . . ." (ἔστιν θεὸς ἐν οὐρανῷ ἀποκαλύπτων μυστήρια καὶ ἐγνώρισεν τῷ βασιλεῖ Ναβουχοδονοσορ).

What added significance could the Daniel background contribute to what we have concluded thus far about the unveiled mystery, especially as this bears upon the use of "church" in Ephesians 3:10? As in Daniel, the Ephesian mystery concerns the Messiah establishing Israel's kingdom after he defeats evil rulers in the end time (see Eph. 1:9–10, 20–22; cf. 3:5, 10 ["now"]). In this light, the divulged mystery in Ephesians 3 explains the new entrance requirements for becoming citizens of the Israelite kingdom prophesied in Daniel 2: namely, identifying the kingdom's head, the Messiah, as the only identification tag of being a true Israelite and not identifying with the marks of the old Torah. Recall that the "stone" in Daniel 2 smote the statue (representing evil kingdoms), and the parallel with the "stone" in Daniel 7 is the "Son of Man" (7:13), who rules over evil kingdoms. Furthermore,

---

8. See, further, G. K. Beale and Benjamin L. Gladd, *Hidden but Now Revealed: A Biblical Theology of Mystery* (Downers Grove, IL: InterVarsity Press, 2014), 159–73; see further secondary sources cited therein in support of various aspects of the argument here and below.

9. Chrys Caragounis, *The Ephesian Mysterion: Meaning and Content*, Coniectanea Biblica: New Testament 8 (Lund: Gleerup, 1977), 123–26.

Matthew 21:42–44 identifies the "stone" of Daniel 2 with Christ, who will judge unbelievers. Recall that the "stone" of Daniel 2 "filled the whole earth" (2:35), indicating that the Israelite kingdom led by the Messiah would include some Gentiles who would willingly submit to him. The "church" composed of believing Jews and Gentiles, which is the fulfillment of this Israelite kingdom, is the vehicle through which the content of God's wise mystery about the "church" is proclaimed (Eph. 3:10).

3. Genesis 2:24 is formally quoted in Ephesians 5:31, and then verse 32 refers to the Old Testament quotation as a "mystery," which pertains not directly to husbands and wives but "to Christ and the church" (ἐκκλησία). There is much discussion of the alternative ways to understand the relation of the Genesis 2 quotation to Christ and the church, which is the key to understanding the "mystery." Some see various kinds of analogies between Genesis 2:24 and the human marriage relationship, as well as the Christ-church relationship. Others understand Genesis 2:24 as a typological foreshadowing of the Christ-church relationship (though human marriage is not out of mind), though this also has alternative versions. What is clear is that there is some relationship between the Old Testament quotation in Ephesians 5:31 and Christ and the church in 5:32 so that, again, we have the "church" inextricably linked to an Old Testament reference and thus to be understood in some way in the light of that reference.[10]

4. In line with the above uses, the fact that the reference to "the church" in Colossians 1:18 is in an immediate context (1:15–19) that is saturated with allusions to the Old Testament and to Judaism concerning the coming Messiah, and not a Greco-Roman background, shows the likelihood that "church" here, to one degree or another, reflects an Old Testament background: Christ is "head of the body, the church; and He is the beginning, the firstborn from the dead, so that He Him-

---

10. Note also that several commentators see an allusion to Ezek. 16:9, 13–14 in Eph. 5:26–27: both speak of a bride who is washed by water and thus is made perfect. For example, see NA[28]; Andrew T. Lincoln, *Ephesians*, WBC 42 (Waco, TX: Word, 1990), 376–77; Peter T. O'Brien, *The Letter to the Ephesians*, PNTC (Grand Rapids, MI: Eerdmans, 1999), 422–23; Ernest Best, *Ephesians*, ICC (Edinburgh: T&T Clark, 1998), 543, 546; Frank Thielman, *Ephesians*, BECNT (Grand Rapids, MI: Baker, 2010), 385–86. For instance, compare Eph. 5:26 (ἁγιάσῃ καθαρίσας τῷ λουτρῷ τοῦ ὕδατος ἐν ῥήματι) with Ezek. 16:9 (ἔλουσά σε ἐν ὕδατι καὶ ἀπέπλυνα τὸ αἷμά σου ἀπὸ σοῦ καὶ ἔχρισά σε ἐν ἐλαίῳ). This is a probable allusion and, once again, connects ἐκκλησία in Eph. 5:27 directly with the covenant community of Old Testament Israel.

self will come to have first place in everything." In addition, Christ as the "firstborn" who has the supremacy in everything in Colossians 1:18 is directly linked to Christ as the temple in 1:19.

In this regard, some commentators have observed that the combined wording of "well pleased" and "dwell" in verse 19 is traceable to the LXX of Psalm 67(68):17:[11] Colossians 1:19 can be translated "because in him [ἐν αὐτῷ] all the fullness [*of deity*] was well pleased [εὐδόκεω] to dwell [κατοικέω]" (alternatively, "in him he was well pleased *for* all the fullness [*of deity*] to dwell"); and the Psalm 68 passage reads, "God was well pleased [εὐδόκεω] to dwell [κατοικέω] in it [ἐν αὐτῷ, i.e., Zion] . . . the Lord will dwell [there] forever . . . in *the holy place* [τῷ ἁγίῳ, which renders קֹדֶשׁ[12]]."

The unique wording shared by Psalm 68(67) and Colossians 1 points to the probability of such an allusion: Psalm 67:17a is the only place in the LXX where the words "well pleased" (εὐδόκεω) and "dwell" (κατοικέω) occur together ("dwell" in 67:17a, as well as "dwell" [κατασκηνόω] in 67:17b and 67:19; and 68[67]:17 is a reference to the temple, as most English translations render the last phrase of the Hebrew and the LXX).

It is perhaps no mere coincidence that ἐκκλησία occurs only a few verses later, in Psalm 67:27 of the LXX (ἐν ἐκκλησίαις εὐλογεῖτε τὸν θεόν), which refers to "praising God" in the context of "the sanctuary," and that context is explicitly referred to again in 67:30

---

11. In this respect, see Christopher A. Beetham, *Echoes of Scripture in the Letter of Paul to the Colossians*, Biblical Interpretation Series 96 (Leiden: Brill, 2008), 144–56, as well his list of scholars who also see the allusion to Ps. 68(67):17 (on which see ibid., 143). In addition to that list, see also G. Münderlein, "Die Erwählung durch das Pleroma," *NTS* 8, no. 3 (1962): 266–70, who sees a clear connection between Ps. 68(67):17 (esp. the Targumic version) and Col. 1:19; N. T. Wright, *Colossians and Philemon*, TNTC 12 (Leicester, UK: Inter-Varsity Press, 1986), 78; Margaret Y. MacDonald, *Colossians and Ephesians*, Sacra Pagina (Collegeville, MI: Liturgical, 2000), 63, says the wording "calls to mind the Jewish Scripture . . . LXX Ps. 67:17, for example"; M. Wolter, *Der Brief an die Kolosser: Der Brief an Philemon*, Ökumenischer Taschenbuchkommentar zum Neuen Testament 12 (Gütersloh: Mohn, 1993), 85, argues that the wording comes from the Jewish Old Testament background, especially Ps. 68(67):17 (and, secondarily, from Ps. 132:13–14 [131:13–14 LXX]; 2 Macc. 14:35; 3 Macc. 2:16); T. K. Abbott, A *Critical Commentary on the Epistles to the Ephesians and the Colossians*, ICC (Edinburgh: T&T Clark, 1897), 219, sees an echo of the Psalm text; G. R. Beasley-Murray, "The Second Chapter of Colossian," *Review and Expositor* 70, no. 4 (1973): 177, says that Ps. 67:17 (LXX) is a "parallel that is more than a matter of vocabulary."

12. Most translations render קֹדֶשׁ as "holy place" or "sanctuary" (ESV, HCSB, KJV, NIV, NJB, NLT, NRSV, RSV; so also 3 En. 24:6–7), though a few translate it as "holiness" (e.g., NASB, NEB). What confirms the rendering of "holy place" instead of "holiness" is that the ב preposition is followed by the article "the" (indicated by a short "a" vowel under the ב and a dagesh forte in the ק). On the other hand, "in the holiness" would result in a rather awkward rendering.

("because of your temple in Jerusalem will kings bring presents to you" [= 68:29 in English versions]). The observation that about nineteen of the seventy-three uses of ἐκκλησία (rendering קָהָל) in the LXX are also directly linked to a temple context may show that the link between ἐκκλησία and temple in Colossians 1:18–19 was a natural one to make.

Thus, ἐκκλησία in Colossians 1:18 likely has an Old Testament ring and identifies the Christian church with the covenant assembly of old Israel and her temple.

5. In 1 Timothy 3:15 "the household of God" is further defined as "the church of the living God, the pillar and support of the truth." The phrase οἴκῳ θεοῦ can be rendered "household of God" or "house of God." The phrase is used often (about seventy-five times) in the LXX to refer to the temple, and it never refers to a "household." The phrase "the pillar and support of the truth" also reflects, at least in part, Old Testament temple language. For example, 2 Chronicles 4:11–12 refers to Chiram making for Solomon "in the house of God two *pillars* [στύλους]," referring to the pillars at the entrance of the Holy Place. (See also 1 Kings 7:3: Chiram "cast the two *pillars* [στύλους] for the porch of the house"; so also Josephus, *Jewish Antiquities* 8.77; Ezra 5:16, "the *foundations* of the house of God," though θεμελίους is used and not στύλους; Ezra 2:68 refers to people "establishing" the "house of God . . . on its *prepared* [ἑτοιμασίαν] place.") That "the house of God" is equated with "the church of the living God" in 1 Timothy 3:15 points further to the notion of a temple, since God dwelt in Israel's temple. We have also seen earlier that about nineteen of the approximately seventy-three uses of ἐκκλησία (rendering קָהָל) in the LXX are also directly linked to a temple context. Of particular interest is Nehemiah 13:1–2, where ἐκκλησία τοῦ θεοῦ occurs in association with four repetitions of "house of God" (ὁ οἴκος τοῦ θεοῦ) in the following context (Neh. 13:4, 7, 9, 11), and where the two expressions are closely related (see also, e.g., 2 Chron. 23:3 and Ezra 10:1, where "the assembly" of Israel gathers before the "house of God"). Likewise, 1 Kings 8 refers four times to the ἐκκλησία of Israel, which are in close proximity to reference to the temple.

Some commentators acknowledge a reference to the temple in 1 Timothy 3:15,[13] while others argue against it.[14]

Conclusion to the Uses in the Later Pauline Epistles

Paul's above uses of ἐκκλησία occur in relation to direct or typological prophecies about the Messiah or the Christian community, which favors mainly an Old Testament background for ἐκκλησία rather than a predominant Greco-Roman one. These uses indicate, to one degree or another, that Christians are the continuation of the true people of God, true Israel, with the Messiah as their King, in contrast to Israel according to the flesh or, perhaps, even the ἐκκλησίαι of the pagan Greco-Roman world.

Uses of ἐκκλησία in Revelation

Another important piece of evidence for the New Testament use of ἐκκλησία against an Old Testament background is the range of uses of ἐκκλησία in Revelation, which are also directly linked to Old Testament allusions and not to Greco-Roman civil assembly uses. Out of eighteen uses of ἐκκλησία in the book, at least eleven are directly linked in the same verse to clear Old Testament allusions. These Old Testament allusions are not greatly debated, so here we can merely give the references and a summary of their content.[15]

1. In Revelation 1:20, the "lampstands" of Zechariah 4:2, 11 (on which see Rev. 1:12) are equated with "the seven churches [ἐκκλησίαι]." Even if this verse were not a specific allusion to Zechariah 4:2, 11, it is still an obvious reference to the temple lampstand in the Old

---

13. I. H. Marshall, *A Critical and Exegetical Commentary on the Pastoral Epistles*, ICC (Edinburgh: T&T Clark, 1999), 507–9 (citing others in support), sees "household" as the focus but with the idea of temple included; similarly Luke Timothy Johnson, *The First and Second Letters to Timothy*, AB 35A (New York: Doubleday, 2001), 231; William D. Mounce, *Pastoral Epistles*, WBC 46 (Nashville: Thomas Nelson, 2000), 220; George W. Knight III, *The Pastoral Epistles*, NIGTC (Grand Rapids, MI: Eerdmans, 1992), 179–81. Note Eph. 2:19–22, where both ideas of "household" and "temple" are in mind: those in "the household of God" dwell in his "holy temple."

14. E.g., Philip H. Towner, *The Letters to Timothy and Titus*, NICNT (Grand Rapids, MI: Eerdmans, 2006), 273. Other commentators do not even mention the possibility that the notion of the temple could be in mind.

15. See, e.g., G. K. Beale, *Revelation*, NIGTC (Grand Rapids, MI: Eerdmans, 1999), for discussions of the validity and use of these eleven allusions. Similarly, the NA[28] cites ten of these as allusions (Rev. 1:20 [see 1:12]; 2:7, 12, 17, 18, 23; 3:7, 14; 22:16). Many commentators typically follow suit.

Testament (e.g., see Exodus 25 and 37). Thus, the churches are equated with a feature of Israel's temple.

2. In Revelation 2:1, "to the angel of the *church* [ἐκκλησία] in Ephesus"[16] directly associates the "church" with the "lampstands," which Revelation 1:20 has equated with "the seven churches." Christ is the Lord, who "walks" as the sovereign Priest among these lampstands. The reference to "golden lampstands" more precisely identifies these with the lampstand of the Old Testament temple, as in Revelation 1:12, based again on Zechariah 4:2, 11 (and, more generally, Exodus 25 and 37).

3. In Revelation 2:7, the one among "the *churches*" (dative ταῖς ἐκκλησίαις) "who overcomes" will "eat of the tree of life which is in the Paradise of God," the latter expression based on Genesis 2:8–9 and 3:2–3, 22, 24 (LXX).

4. In Revelation 2:12, "the church [ἐκκλησία] in Pergamum" is directly related to Christ, who is portrayed as having "the sharp two-edged sword." This refers back to Revelation 1:16, which says that "out of His mouth came a sharp two-edged sword." It is a clear allusion to Isaiah 49:2, where God makes the servant's "mouth like a sharp sword." Thus, Christ stands over the church as their kingly Lord, who threatens them with judgment (cf. Rev. 2:16), just as was the case with God's former relationship to the assembly of Israel.

5. In Revelation 2:17, the one "who overcomes" among "the churches [ταῖς ἐκκλησίαις]" will be given "the hidden manna," a partial allusion to the manna given to Israel in the wilderness, which is given eschatological significance. Furthermore, any "who overcomes" will also receive "a new name," an allusion to Isaiah's prophecy that end-time Israel would be given a "new name," indicating a new married status of Israel with her God (Isa. 62:2; 65:15). Thus, "the church" is identified directly with Old Testament allusions about Israel's messianic servant and Israel's end-time rewards, respectively, at the beginning and end of the letter to Pergamum.

---

16. "The angel of the church" addressed here (and in Rev. 2:18; 3:7, 14) could refer to (1) an actual angel who represents the church; (2) a letter carrier to the church, who is to convey the message to the church; (3) a church official (e.g., an elder); or (4) a personification of the church. Options 1 or 2 are most preferable. Whichever among these options is correct, the church in one way or another is being addressed, especially through a representative (and so also in the introduction of the following six prophetic letters).

6. In Revelation 2:18, the "church [ἐκκλησία] in Thyatira" is directly associated with the "Son of God, who has eyes like a flame of fire, and His feet are like burnished bronze." "Son of God" likely comes from the messianic reference to God's Son in Psalm 2, which anticipates the full quotation from Psalm 2:8–9 at the end of the letter to this church (Rev. 2:26–27). The reference to the Son's fiery eyes and feet like bronze comes from Daniel 10:6, which describes an angel. Christ again is portrayed with Old Testament ascriptions of the Messiah and the Danielic angel of God in addressing the church.

7. In Revelation 2:26–27, Christ promises the one "who overcomes" a share in the messianic kingdom prophesied in Psalm 2:8–9, the authority of which he himself has already received: "to him I will give authority over the nations; and he shall rule them with a rod of iron, as the vessels of the potter are broken to pieces." The reference to the "morning star" at the end of Revelation 2:28 is also another Old Testament allusion, this time to Numbers 24:17 (where the future end-time ruler of Israel is called a rising "star"). That believers would be identified with this star enhances further their identification with the messianic kingdom in Revelation [2:26–27]. Then, directly after these Old Testament allusions identifying believers with the messianic kingdom, there follows the exhortation, the one "who has an ear, let him hear what the Spirit says to the churches [ταῖς ἐκκλησίαις]" (Rev. 2:29). This directly identifies those who "overcome" among the churches with the messianic kingdom.

8. In Revelation 3:7, "the church [ἐκκλησία] in Philadelphia" is addressed by Christ, "who has the key of David, who opens and no one will shut, and who shuts and no one opens." This is a quotation from Isaiah 22:22, which is a description of Eliakim, who was in charge of the Israelite king's court. Now Christ is a greater Eliakim in his address to the church.

9. Revelation 3:12 is more saturated with the Old Testament than many other passages in Revelation. There are at least three allusions here: (a) "He who overcomes, I will make him a pillar in the temple of My God, and he will not go out from it anymore" is a clear allusion generally to the Old Testament temple; (b) "and I will write on him . . . the name of the city of My God, the new Jerusalem" is a clear reference

to the Old Testament city of Jerusalem; and (c) "My new name," as we saw in Revelation 2:17, is a specific allusion to Isaiah 62:2; 65:15, Isaiah's prophecy that end-time Israel would be given a "new name" as an indication of a new eschatological relationship with her God. The first two allusions refer to Old Testament realities that are eschatologically escalated to apply to Christians, so that they are identified with these heightened realities. The "new name" from Isaiah is a prophecy first fulfilled by Christ (note "*My* new name") and then identified with Christians, who thus also are part of its fulfillment.

Then immediately in Revelation 3:13 those in "the churches [ταῖς ἐκκλησίαις]" are exhorted to "hear" and identify with the realities described in verse 12, as well as to pay heed to the earlier parts of the letter.

10. Revelation 3:14 says, "To the angel of the church in Laodicea write: The Amen, the faithful and true Witness, the Beginning of the creation of God, says this." There is general consensus that "the Amen" is an allusion to Isaiah 65:16, where Yahweh is twice called "the God of Amen." Now Christ is identified with Yahweh of the Isaiah text.[17] Once again Christ addresses the "church" (ἐκκλησία) as her sovereign Lord, just as Yahweh addressed Israel as her sovereign Lord in Isaiah 65:16.

11. In Revelation 22:16 we read: "I, Jesus, have sent My angel to testify to you these things for the churches. I am the root and the descendant of David, the bright morning star." Jesus "testifies" through his angel to the "churches" (ταῖς ἐκκλησίαις). To state his credentials in doing so, he identifies himself as a "descendant of David" and "the bright morning star," a repeated allusion to the messianic prophecy of Numbers 24:17, which has already been made at Revelation 2:18 (discussed above). Thus in speaking to the "churches," he identifies himself with the fulfillment of the hopes of David and of the prophecy in Numbers.

Conclusion to the Uses in Revelation

In all of the above Revelation texts, two observations can be made: (a) the "church" (or "churches") is directly addressed by Christ, who

---

17. In fact, even the following wording "the faithful and true" is likely an interpretative expansion of "Amen" that reflects the multiple witness of the Septuagintal exegetical tradition of Isa. 65:16.

is identified with Old Testament realities and prophecies, and this indicates that the church now stands as the eschatological Israel who is
addressed by her Messiah, who is sometimes identified with Yahweh;
(b) the "church" (or "churches") is identified with Old Testament realities or is seen as part of the fulfillment of Old Testament prophecies,
further identifying them with the end-time hopes of Israel. To say the
least, the "church" is seen to be inextricably linked with Israel of the
Old Testament. We also observed this above in several texts of Paul
and in the disputed Pauline letters.

Uses of ἐκκλησία in Hebrews

Finally, the book of Hebrews uses ἐκκλησία twice. Hebrews 2:12 is
part of an allusion to Psalm 22:22. The hearers of that epistle would
certainly have identified themselves with the "church" mentioned in
the Psalm quotation. Likewise, Hebrews 12:22–23 equates Christians
who have "come to Mount Zion and to . . . the heavenly Jerusalem"
with "the general assembly and the church [ἐκκλησία] of the firstborn," which includes Old Testament and New Testament saints together. These are obvious Old Testament references that equate with
the "church." Then in Hebrews 12:24, Christians are said to have
come "to Jesus, the mediator of a new covenant," and they have come
"to the sprinkled blood, which speaks better than the blood of Abel"
(cf. Gen. 4:9–10), another clear Old Testament allusion linked to the
Christian "church" in Hebrews 12:23.

Overall Conclusion

The above observed combination of ἐκκλησία with Old Testament
allusions—and not Greco-Roman background references in Paul, the
later Pauline epistles, Revelation, and Hebrews—provides further evidence that ἐκκλησία in the New Testament is more influenced by an
Old Testament background than by the Greco-Roman world. Though
the word ἐκκλησία does not occur often in the LXX context of the
above Old Testament quotations and allusions,[18] it is still clear that

---

18. For significant exceptions, note the LXX of Ps. 88:6 in 1 Cor. 14:33; of Ps. 67:17–18 (cf.
v. 27) in Col. 1:19; and of Ps. 22:22 in Heb. 2:12, to which may also be added Acts 7:38 and Acts
20:28, where ἐκκλησία is substituted for συναγωγὴ of the Old Testament texts.

ἐκκλησία in its New Testament contexts is often directly associated with the Old Testament. In his survey of ἐκκλησία in Paul's writings and Revelation, with the exception of Hebrews, Paul Trebilco does not make the above observations of the direct linkage with Old Testament allusions. Had he done so, I believe his overall position that the Greek Old Testament is the background for the New Testament use of ἐκκλησία would have been strengthened.[19]

Some have proposed that the Greco-Roman background of ἐκκλησία, referring typically to pagan civic assemblies or city councils, is the main backdrop for understanding the meaning of the word in the New Testament (to which reference is clearly made in Acts 19:32, 39, 40–41).[20] According to such a view, the church gatherings would best be understood in light of the political civic gatherings in the Greco-Roman world. If this were the case, then one might be able to conclude that the church is the true assembly in opposition to the pagan assemblies of the unbelieving world. If we had found that ἐκκλησία was *often* associated with various kinds of Greco-Roman allusions, then it would have been plausible to conclude that the Greco-Roman civic assembly is the likely backdrop in these cases. But we have not found this.[21] We have found only other Old Testament allusions in direct connection to uses of ἐκκλησία.

Thus, the biblical-theological upshot of this essay is that the Old Testament "church" ("assembly") and the New Testament "church" ("assembly") are one and the same organically, the former prophetically anticipating fulfillment in the latter. The New Testament "church" is the inaugurated eschatological Israel.

---

19. Paul Trebilco, *Self-Designations and Group Identity in the New Testament* (Cambridge: Cambridge University Press, 2012), 170–80, 183, 201–7.

20. In these verses the city council of Ephesus met because of the disturbance Paul's ministry had caused in the city.

21. See Beale, "Background of ἐκκλησία Revisited," for more in-depth discussion of the debate about whether the Old Testament Greek or the Greco-Roman use is the main background, and for the conclusion that the former is clearly predominant.

4

The Divine Choice between the Offerings of Cain and Abel

In Whan Kim

In Genesis 4:1–15 Moses records a story about two sons of Adam and Eve who offered sacrifices to the Lord. The narrative reveals that the Lord accepted the offering of Abel while he rejected that of Cain. Cain was angry at the choice of the Lord, and he killed his brother, Abel. In this way Cain became not only the first murderer but also the first to commit fratricide in the history of mankind, a symbol of an atrocious human being.

Why did the Lord accept the offering of Abel while rejecting that of Cain? This question highlights the standard by which the Lord accepts one offering and rejects the other in this narrative. Moses only records the historical event itself and does not provide any clear clues to answering this question. Many scholars have attempted to give an answer, but no consensus has been reached to date.

This chapter will propose an answer from a structural and redemptive-historical perspective.

Diverse Proposals of Scholars

It is necessary for us to see how scholars have attempted to answer this
question in order to show why we need to understand the narrative
from a structural and biblical-theological perspective.

Gordon J. Wenham, F. A. Spina, Jack P. Lewis, and Youjin Chung
have summarized the diverse scholarly discussions on the subject.[1]
Their summaries are not substantially different, but Wenham's summary is the most comprehensive. He explains that there are five different views on why God accepted Abel's offering while rejecting that
of Cain:[2]

1. God prefers shepherds to gardeners (Gunkel).
2. Animal sacrifice is more acceptable than vegetable offering
   (Skinner, Jacob).
3. God's motives are inscrutable: his preference for Abel's sacrifice
   reflects the mystery of divine election (von Rad, Vawter, Golka,
   Westermann).
4. The different motives of the two brothers are known only
   to God (Calvin, Dillmann, Driver, König).
5. The brothers differed in their approach to worship and in the
   quality of their gifts.

Wenham maintains that among these views, the fifth has been the
most commonly accepted since ancient times.[3] He supports this position by saying that "the acceptance of Abel's sacrifice in contrast to
the rejection of Cain's is not just an illustration of the election of the
younger brother, but emphasizes that only those who offer the best in
their sacrifices are acceptable to God."[4]

Chung has recently analyzed each of the views and pointed out
weaknesses inherent in each.[5] She especially refutes the third view since

1. Gordon J. Wenham, *Genesis 1–15*, WBC 1 (Waco, TX: Word, 1987), 104; Frank A. Spina, "The 'Ground' for Cain's Rejection (Gen. 4): 'ádámá' in the Context of Gen 1–11," *Zeitschrift für die alttestamentliche Wissenschaft* 104, no. 3 (1992): 320; Jack P. Lewis, "The Offering of Abel (Gen 4:4): A History of Interpretation," *JETS* 37, no. 4 (1994): 481–96; Youjin Chung, "Conflicting Readings in the Narrative of Cain and Abel (Gen. 4:1–26)," *Asian Journal of Pentecostal Studies* 14, no. 2 (2011): 241–54.
2. Wenham, *Genesis 1–15*, 104.
3. Ibid.
4. Ibid., 117.
5. Chung, "Conflicting Readings in the Narrative," 244–47.

God's process of election in this view appears to attribute a capricious character to God. Maintaining that this view makes God the cause of trouble, she proposes that Cain's own dishonest desire was the main reason why God rejected his sacrifice. Her proposal is based on her own understanding of the narrative, as follows:

> First, the narrative itself is neutral. There is no indication in the text that the offering of Abel is better than Cain's, nor vice-versa. Rather, both brothers bring their best in an appropriate way. Second, God Himself is neutral. There is, in other words, no hint that God discriminates or prefers one to the other. Third, God Himself is free. As such His freedom sometimes goes beyond logical comprehensions, so it creates even disruption, tension and a shadowy side of reality. Fourth, Cain himself is volitional. Without a doubt, "God tells Cain that he can do better. Not in using a better technique of sacrifice, but in not taking God for granted." Therefore, it is Cain's own choice to agree or disagree with God's word.[6]

Even if we grant her criticism of the scholarly views on why God rejected Cain's sacrifice, her own proposal falls short because it excludes the role that God played in choosing between them. The fact remains that God was the subject who rejected Cain's sacrifice, and Cain's anger was followed by God's sovereign rejection.

Each view has its own merits. However, because the text itself does not give a clear reason why the Lord rejected Cain's offering and accepted Abel's, the various viewpoints share a common weakness: they are derived from speculative reasoning and inferences made from the theological perspectives of their proponents, as Spina points out.[7] Thus, none of them provides a conclusive answer to the thorny question as to why God rejected Cain and his sacrifice while he accepted Abel and his.

This fact has led Spina to focus on the text itself and to devote attention to the source of Cain's offering, an approach in line with J. Halevy, Benno Jacob, Thomas Mann, and Northrop Frye. Like them, Spina believes that the cursed ground (or "soil," אֲדָמָה) was a key factor in

---

6. Ibid., 247–48, quoting Andre LaCocque, *Onslaught against Innocence: Cain, Abel, and the Yahwist* (Eugene, OR: Cascade, 2008), 25.
7. Spina, "The 'Ground' for Cain's Rejection," 320.

Cain's rejection, since it was the source of Cain's offering.[8] He, therefore, regards the cursed אֲדָמָה as the reason for Yahweh's rejection of
Cain, and he attempts to show how the אֲדָמָה functions in the context
of Genesis 1–11.[9] Spina notes that the cursed state of the אֲדָמָה was
maintained "until God announced an 'uncursing' of the אֲדָמָה (Gen.
8:21)" in the days of Noah after the flood. In this context, he infers, the
production of the cursed אֲדָמָה was also cursed. However, he excludes
all animals except the Serpent from this category because he believes
that God cursed only the Serpent, and "all the other animals presumably remained unscathed."[10] Spina then reasons that "because the אֲדָמָה
was cursed, God refused Cain's offering."[11] In this way, he proposes
that the אֲדָמָה, the cursed soil or ground, is the unique standard by
which God made a choice between the two offerings.

Spina's approach is a fresh alternative to the others mentioned. He
does not, however, do full justice to the context of Genesis 1–4. He
also does not properly understand what the אֲדָמָה pointed to when he
limits the scope of the divine curse on the אֲדָמָה only to the agricultural
productions and excludes animals that lived on the אֲדָמָה. He overlooks
the fact that the curse of God embraced all creatures that God put
under the dominion of man in the covenant relationship. Furthermore,
his position that only the agriculture in the land and the Serpent were
cursed by God is contrary to biblical attestation. The Old and New
Testaments alike consistently attest that all creatures—whether agricultural, oceanic, aerial plant, or animal, which were created and put
under the dominion of man by God—were cursed because of man's
sin and were also waiting for the redemption in the eschatological age
(Rom. 8:19–22). Therefore, Spina's position does not answer the question at hand. We need to see the narrative from a different perspective.

An Analysis of the Offerings of Cain and Abel
COMMONNESS BETWEEN THE OFFERINGS

Offerings as מִנְחָה. Cain as "a worker of the ground" (Gen. 4:2)
"brought to the LORD an offering [מִנְחָה] of the fruit of the ground"

---

8. Ibid., 323–24; see also his notes 13–16.
9. Ibid., 324–32.
10. Ibid., 326.
11. Ibid., 332.

(4:3), and Abel as "a keeper of sheep" (4:2) "brought of the firstborn of the flock and of their fat portions" (4:4). Moses used the word מִנְחָה to designate the offerings of both Cain and Abel. This is an important clue that the standard by which God accepted Cain's and Abel's offerings did not concern whether the offering was an animal or a grain.

Diverse words have been employed to designate the offerings that people brought to God in the Old Testament. Among them, the term מִנְחָה is used in a general sense as well as a cultic sense. In extra-biblical literature, this term is also used broadly. In Akkadian, Ugaritic, Phoenician, and Arabic literature, it designates a thanksgiving present, or payment of obligations, or a tribute offered by a lower-ranking person to a higher-ranking person in religious or political contexts.[12] Such a use of the word in the surrounding culture is maintained in the Old Testament without significant change. Averbeck argues that the fundamental meaning of מִנְחָה is "gift" to God or to people. Based on this, he classifies its meaning or use in the Old Testament in four categories: (1) in the cultic contexts, as a general term for offering, whether from crops or flocks/herds (Gen. 4:3–4; 2 Chron. 32:23; Isa. 1:13; 66:20; Jer. 17:26; Mal.1:13); (2) as a specialized term for grain offering (Lev. 2:8); (3) in non-cultic (or secular) contexts, as a general word for a gift or present between people (Gen. 43:26; 1 Sam. 10:27); and (4) in a specialized sense, for tribute to a superior in political contexts (2 Chron. 17:11).[13]

In Genesis 4:3–4, the term is used without distinguishing crops and flock offerings. Moses, in employing the term מִנְחָה, makes it clear that both offerings of Cain and Abel were thanksgiving gifts to God for giving them fruits.[14] From this perspective, Waltke rightly argues that "in any case, by using מִנְחָה Moses virtually excludes the possibility that God did not look on Cain's offering because it was bloodless."[15] If God accepted Abel's offering because it was a bloody offering, Moses would not have used the same term; he would have used a different word to designate the two offerings, corresponding to the nature of each, in order to distinguish Abel's offering from Cain's and to emphasize the

---

12. Richard E. Averbeck, "מִנְחָה" in *Dictionary of Old Testament Theology and Exegesis*, ed. Willem A. VanGemeren, 5 vols. (Grand Rapids, MI: Zondervan, 1997), 2:978–79.
13. Ibid., 2:979–80.
14. Bruce K. Waltke, "Cain and His Offering," *WTJ* 48, no. 2 (1986): 368.
15. Ibid., 366.

significance of the bloody offering. Since Moses used the same word for both offerings, the two offerings can equally be considered gifts to God, seeking the favor of God.

In this regard, both offerings are acceptable to God in substance.

Offerings according to the vocations. Moses reveals that Cain's and Abel's offerings differed in their content. Cain brought the fruit of the ground, and Abel offered the firstborn of his flock, including their fat portions. Such a difference reflected the difference in their professions. However, what is common is that each brought to God the fruits he produced from his own profession.

How did the brothers know to bring God their offerings? It is not clear where the system of offering originated in the days of Cain and Abel. However, Moses gives us a clue to its origin in the phrase "in the course of time," in verse 3. The phrase implies that when they brought the offerings to God, a good period of time had passed since they were born. A literal translation of the Hebrew text, וַיְהִי מִקֵּץ יָמִים, is "at the end of days" or "after the days." Wenham thinks it refers specifically to a year, in light of the context—that is, "at the end of the agricultural year," rather than to "an indefinite period, short or long."[16] However, he overlooks that when a term refers to a definite period of time, it is accompanied by expressions such as "forty days" or "ten years" (cf. Gen. 8:6; 16:3; 41:1; etc.). Therefore, it is more appropriate to regard וַיְהִי מִקֵּץ יָמִים as an idiomatic expression implying an indefinite period of time, short or long (cf. 2 Sam. 14:26; 1 Kings 17:7; Jer. 13:6). Hence, this phrase, following what Genesis 4:1–2 says, denotes that a period of time passed in which Cain and Abel grew up to be a farmer and a shepherd, respectively, and then Cain and Abel brought God their offerings. If so, they might have had an opportunity to learn from someone about the practice of giving offerings to God.

Kenneth A. Matthews maintains that Adam might have taught them how to bring offerings to God. He further holds that Cain's and Abel's offerings in Genesis 4 were not their first but were within their customary practice.[17] His argumentation is very probable, although

---

16. Wenham, *Genesis 1–15*, 103.
17. Kenneth A. Matthews, *Genesis 1–11:26: An Exegetical and Theological Exposition of Holy Scripture NIV Text* (Nashville: Broadman & Holman, 1996), 267.

we cannot find specific biblical support. God the Creator probably revealed to Adam some kind of offering system right after the fall, and Adam most likely taught it to his children. If not, Cain and Abel would have invented a system of offering, which is unthinkable.

Therefore, the offerings of Cain and Abel were common in the sense that they brought them from their vocations. Their offerings were not accidental but a kind of mandatory cultic activity imposed by God, and hence each of the offerings was legitimate as such.

THE DIFFERENCE BETWEEN THE OFFERINGS

Despite such common factors embedded in Cain's and Abel's offerings, the narrative also reveals some differences between them. The obvious difference lies in their selection of the items offered: Cain, as the worker of the ground, selected the fruit of the ground, while Abel, as the keeper of the sheep, selected the firstborn of his flock and their fat portions. Moses's description of their offerings reveals that Cain did not pay as much attention as Abel did to his selection of an offering: whether or not they were the firstfruits, a symbol of the choicest and of thankfulness. Hence, Cain's offering was, as Matthews points out, "in contrast with the offering of Abel who brought not only some of his firstborn (בְּכֹרוֹת) but the best of the animal, the fatty portions (v. 4)."[18]

However, Skinner does not see any difference between the two offerings. He regards Cain's offering of the fruits from the ground as analogous to the Hebrew ritual offering of the firstfruits from the ground, because the Hebrew ritual offering of the firstfruits from the ground originates in the custom of the Carthaginian fruit offering, which consists of a branch bearing fruit. From this he argues that Cain also selected the best item from what he had for God.[19] Skinner seems to do justice to his critics' presupposition that the Pentateuch was written after the days of Moses to justify a Hebrew ritual tradition that had already been established. However, during the time of Cain and Abel, there was no Jew or Carthaginian. Therefore, his position is not acceptable.

More recently, G. Ch. Aalders and F. F. Bruce have argued that

---

18. Ibid.
19. John Skinner, *Critical and Exegetical Commentary on Genesis*, 2nd ed., ICC (Edinburgh: T&T Clark, 1930), 104.

Cain's offering was also the firstfruits from the ground, simply because the text does not say anything in detail except that Cain offered the product of the ground from his own vocation.[20]

It is true that there is no reason to maintain that Cain's offering was or was not the firstfruits and that he did or did not select the offering at random if the text does not clearly indicate as much. However, the text itself emphasizes Abel's careful selection of the items of his offering. The word גַּם־הוּא ("he also"—Gen. 4:4) in the text explains that Cain offered first and then Abel offered after him. The sacrifice that Abel offered was "the firstborn of his flock and of their fat portions" (מִבְּכֹרוֹת צֹאנוֹ וּמֵחֶלְבֵהֶן)—Gen. 4:4). Here the ו is not simple *waw copulativum* but rather *waw explicativum*, explanatory rather than simply copulative.[21] This, therefore, indicates that Abel's offering consisted not of two kinds of offerings—namely, the firstborn of his flock and their fat portions—but of one kind—namely, the firstborn of his flock and of the fat thereof, the best of its kind. This is a double emphasis with two expressions. Cassuto puts it very aptly:

> On the other hand, it is clear that since in regard to Cain it is stated simply that his offering was *of the fruit of the ground*, and in Abel's case the Bible uses two expressions to emphasize that the oblation was the best of its kind (*of the firstlings. . . . and of* THEIR FAT PORTIONS), this distinction is not made pointlessly. On the other hand, it must be noted that although there is a *distinction*, there is no *contrast*. Apparently the Bible wished to convey that whilst Abel was concerned to choose the finest thing is his possession, Cain was indifferent. In other words: Abel endeavored to perform his religious duty ideally, whereas Cain was content merely to discharge this duty.[22]

Therefore, it is apparent that Cain's attitude was different from Abel's in the selection of their offerings.

---

20. G. Ch. Aalders, *Genesis*, trans. William Heynen, 2 vols., Bible Student's Commentary (Grand Rapids, MI: Zondervan, 1981), 1:120; F. F. Bruce, *The Epistle to the Hebrews*, rev. ed., NICNT (Grand Rapids, MI: Eerdmans, 1990), 283. Aalders thinks that since the text does not rule it out, we cannot exclude the possibility that Cain's offering also "consisted of the first fruits of his harvest."

21. GKC, §154, 1, (b).

22. U. Cassuto, *A Commentary on the Book of Genesis: From Abram to Noah*, pt. 1, trans. Israel Abrahams (repr., Jerusalem: Magness, Hebrew University, 1972), 205.

The Standard of Yahweh

Yahweh responded differently to the brothers' offerings. He did not accept Cain's offering, while he did accept Abel's. What kind of standard did Yahweh employ in his selection? Although the narrative text clearly reveals a distinction between the attitudes of Cain and Abel in their selection of offerings, as discussed above, the narrative does not hint that this difference serves to determine the standard of God. Nor does the text explain exactly what kind of offering each of them made to God. It is, therefore, not easy for us to know the standard of Yahweh's selection from the narrative itself.

Some scholars have paid attention to the words in Genesis 4:7 "If you do well, will you not be accepted?" to find a clue as to the standard of Yahweh. Calvin was one example. He regarded this statement as related to Cain's offering. Accordingly, if Cain had offered his sacrifice in a right way, Yahweh would have accepted it and Cain would not have been angry. Therefore, Cain's anger or hatred toward his brother could not be justified.[23] However, most scholars and commentators since then have not understood the text as simply as Calvin did. God's statement cannot be that simply interpreted; furthermore, a serious grammatical issue impinges on the interpretation of the words. Some interpreters have even emended the text and interpreted it according their own perspectives.[24]

One thing is clear: no one can successfully make the text itself explain the wrongdoings involved in Cain's offering, no matter how he or she interprets the text. Hamilton's comment regarding this is noteworthy: "Perhaps the silence is the message itself. As outside viewers, we are unable to detect any difference between the two brothers and their offerings. Perhaps the fault is an internal one, an attitude that is known only to God."[25]

Where, then, can we find the answer to the question before us? If not in the text itself, then we must turn our eyes to the context in which the text is placed or in other Scripture that deals with this text.

---

23. John Calvin, *Commentaries on the First Book of Moses Called Genesis*, trans. John King (repr., Grand Rapids, MI: Baker, 1979), 200–201.

24. See Cassuto, *Book of Genesis*, 2008–13; Wenham, *Genesis 1–15*, 104–6, and Victor P. Hamilton, *The Book of Genesis, Chapters 1–17*, NICOT (Grand Rapids, MI: Eerdmans, 1990), 224.

25. Hamilton, *Book of Genesis, Chapters 1–17*, 224.

Contextual Consideration

WITHIN THE BOOK OF GENESIS

The book of Genesis can be divided into two main parts: the overall account of God's creation of the heavens and the earth (1:1–2:3) and the account of the human responses to the lordship of the Creator (2:4–50:26). The first part not only explains the origin and the function of the heavens, the earth, and all the creatures in them in light of God's purpose for his creation; it also explains the lordship of God over his creation under the covenant he made with the first man, whom he created in his own image in order to fulfill his purpose for creation. Hence, this account necessitates another record of how the man and his descendants responded to God's lordship in their lives. This record is found in the second part, which consists of ten "generations" (תוֹלְדוֹת). Therefore, the first and the second parts are inseparably connected with each other. Given their structural unity, the second part cannot be properly understood apart from the first.

The first "generation" (2:4–4:26) of the second part is of the heavens and the earth. Seemingly, it is a repetition or an extension of the first part (1:1–2:3). This fact has led many scholars and commentators into confusion and misunderstanding of the creation narrative in the history of interpretation. If we take seriously the unity established between the two parts, we should not understand the first generation of the heavens and the earth as a separate, different, independent creation story from the one in Genesis 1:1–2:3, as the old proponents of the documentary hypothesis and many contemporary critics have done.

Meredith Kline, noting the consistent usage of the word תוֹלְדוֹת in Genesis, aptly argues that "Genesis 2:4 must be understood as the superscription not for an account of the origins of the heaven and the earth, but rather for an account of their subsequent 'family' history."[26] Bruce Waltke maintains, in the same vein, that the word "תוֹלְדוֹת, which was derived from the root ילד, meaning 'to bear children,' here signifies 'what is produced or brought into being by someone' and that 'the account [Gen. 2:4–4:24] pertains to what the cosmos has generated, not

---

26. Meredith G. Kline, *Kingdom Prologue: Genesis Foundations for a Covenantal Worldview* (Eugene, OR: Wipf & Stock, 2006), 9.

the generation of the cosmos.'"[27] Therefore, the first generation is nothing else than an account of the response of the world of humanity to the cosmos, the workmanship of God the Creator—the response generated in 2:4–4:24 to the covenant of the Creator explained in the account of 1:1–2:3. The narrative of the offerings of Cain and Abel should thus be understood within the immediate context of Genesis 2:4–4:24.

In this first-generation narrative, Moses records in Genesis 2 the first stage of the heavens and the earth after God created them, and then he proceeds to record how God made man in his own image, placed him in the garden of Eden, and entered into a covenant relationship with him—what is called the covenant of creation—giving him a covenant mandate with the divine sanction of blessing and curse. Moses then continues to record why God made a woman for man, that is, to be his helpmate. In this way, God created the marriage ordinance for the man and the woman and instituted a family system by which man and wife in a marital relationship could obey God and fulfill the covenant mandate to multiply and rule the earth for him.

In Genesis 3, Moses recorded the first response of the man and the woman to the covenant of creation, explaining not only their disobedience to God and his subsequent judgment and curse upon them, but also God's plan to save them from his curse under the covenant of redemption. In God's redemptive plan he set an enmity between the Serpent and the woman and between their descendants too, and one single male son of the woman would ultimately conquer the Serpent and its descendants. In this redemptive covenant administration, God renewed the first covenant—the covenant of creation—which he made with man before the fall. Hence, the covenant of creation both continued and discontinued in this newer covenant. The fundamental arrangements and purpose of the covenant of creation continued, and hence man had to carry out all the responsibilities of the covenant of creation. However, the creation covenant could be fulfilled no longer by humans, who were totally corrupted, but by the sovereign commitment of God out of his grace and love.

Such a divine commitment must have planted a seed of hope and faith in the hearts of Adam and the woman. Hence, Adam named the

---

27. Bruce K. Waltke, *Genesis: A Commentary* (Grand Rapids, MI: Zondervan, 2001), 83.

woman Eve, believing that she would be the mother of all the living. In Genesis 4, Moses tells the first story of how such a divine plan of redemption began to be fulfilled by the sovereign commitment of God through the life of Adam and Eve and their descendants, Cain and Abel, and then Seth, the substitute after Abel was killed by Cain. And then Moses closes the narrative of the first generation.

Since the stories in the first generation are in unity, Moses employs the same words, motifs, and themes to maintain the stream of thought when he writes the narrative of the offerings of Cain and Abel. This results in close similarities between the narrative of Cain and Abel and its proceeding narrative. Hauser has explored and proved the structural, linguistic, and thematic links between the two narratives[28] and has concluded that "the two stories have been closely and carefully interwoven. . . . Any attempt to interpret the accounts without reference to their unity is likely to obscure and distort what the writer intended to say."[29] Lohr backs him up.[30] Ross, connecting this narrative with Genesis 3, maintains that the design and motif are in parallel with those in Genesis 3, and that the narrative in Genesis 4 is an extension of the narrative in chapter 3.[31]

They all, however, miss a very important purpose of the author, which is to reveal how the covenant made between God and the man after the fall would be fulfilled progressively in the history of redemption. Hence, they overlook the interrelationship between God's divine commitment to fulfill his redemptive plan in Genesis 3:15 ("I will put enmity between you and the woman, / and between your offspring and her offspring; / he shall bruise your head, / and you shall bruise his heel") and the narrative of the offerings of Cain and Abel. An exegetical analysis of the narratives demonstrates that the two texts have a close relationship and proves that the Genesis 4 narrative records the inaugural fulfillment of the divine commitment in the history of redemption.

---

28. Alan J. Hauser, "Linguistic and Thematic Links between Genesis 4:1–16 and Genesis 2–3," *JETS* 23, no. 4 (1980): 297–305.

29. Ibid., 305.

30. Joel N. Lohr, "Righteous Abel, Wicked Cain: Genesis 4:1–16 in the Masoretic Text, the Septuagint, and the New Testament," *Catholic Biblical Quarterly* 71, no. 3 (2009): 485–96.

31. Allen P. Ross, *Creation and Blessing: A Guide to the Study and Exposition of Genesis* (Grand Rapids, MI: Baker, 1988), 154.

The narrative begins with the fact that Adam and Eve bore two sons and named the first Cain and the second Abel; they subsequently bore another son, Seth, after Cain killed Abel. It is noteworthy that the author recorded the birth of only these three sons. Is it because Adam and Eve gave birth to no other sons and daughters? It is unthinkable that they bore only these three offspring during their long lifetime. They must have had more children than these, based on the biblical record that Cain married a woman (Gen. 4:17). This woman must have been one of his sisters, if God had created only Adam and Eve. From this it can be inferred that Moses simply did not record the births of other sons and of daughters born to Adam and Eve because he purposed to focus on the births of Cain, Abel, and Seth.

Eve named her first son Cain, saying, "I have gotten a man with the help of the LORD" (Gen. 4:1). In Eve's confession of the Lord's assistance, Moses does not employ the word "son" but uses "man." In this way Moses links the divine commitment in Genesis 3:15 with this narrative and emphasizes Eve's perception that her son Cain was the man whom God sent to save her. Her excitement came from her own understanding that God's divine commitment was being realized in the birth of Cain.

Moses records the story of the offerings of Cain and Abel to position them as main characters on a stage in which the Lord of the covenant would exercise his sovereignty to elect from them the real seed of the woman. The Lord wanted the man and woman whom he created in his image to obey him from the beginning. However, they did not obey him but broke the covenant. Their disobedience brought them and his creation under his curse. Therefore, the obedience of the first seed of woman, whom God would use to fulfill his redemptive plan, is the key issue. The Lord used the offerings of Cain and Abel to test who would be loyal to his covenant of redemption and obedient to his sovereign selection of one offering over the other. Therefore, if Cain and Abel were the seed of woman, they needed to obey God's sovereign selection. This indicates that it is a matter not of whose offering was faulty or not, but of who was obedient to God's sovereign selection or not. This is why Moses did not record whose offering was faulty; he only recorded who obeyed the selection of the sovereign God. God tested who would obey him by selecting only one of their offerings out of his sovereign will. However, Cain failed to obey his sovereign choice, and he reached the height of his disobedience when he killed his brother.

In this way, it was demonstrated that Cain was not the seed of the woman from whom the eschatological Savior would arise (contrary to Eve's mistaken understanding). God the Lord made it clear that his standard for choosing between the offerings of Cain and Abel was not the quality of their offerings or (ultimately) their attitudes but he himself. The real aim of this narrative is to reveal that the sovereign God is the only standard by which he elects some to be the seed of the woman and reprobates others to be the seed of the Serpent among the descendants of Adam and Eve after the fall—and to reveal that he demands descendants of Adam and Eve to obey his sovereign choice. This point is further evidenced by the fact that he continued the line of the seed of the woman through the birth of Seth after Cain killed Abel.

This narrative, therefore, points to the inauguration of the process of fulfillment of his commitment to redeem the seed of the woman and his fallen creation.

In Hebrews 11:4

The New Testament refers to Cain and Abel in three places: Matthew 23:35; Hebrews 11:4; and 1 John 3:12. Matthew 23:35 characterizes Abel as a righteous man, and 1 John 3:12 speaks of Cain as wicked and Abel as righteous. These two biblical texts do not address their offerings at all, but Hebrews 11:4 does. Therefore, this text alone furnishes a canonical context in which our subject matter can be understood properly.

The author of Hebrews compares Abel's offering with Cain's and states that Abel's offering was superior. This adds to what we know from the Genesis account in that Genesis is silent on this point. In what sense, then, was Abel's offering superior, quantitatively or qualitatively? The text says that "by faith Abel offered to God a more acceptable sacrifice than Cain" (Heb. 11:4). The text itself does not mention the quantity or quality of the offerings at all; it only discusses whether they were offered to God in faith. The author of Hebrews judges that Abel offered his in faith, but Cain did not. Hence, to the author of Hebrews, neither the quantity nor the quality of the offering but the faith with which the offering was made must have been the crucial standard that determined the superiority of Abel's offering. Nevertheless, the author of Hebrews does not state what Abel actually believed when he offered his gift to God. The nature of faith is defined in Hebrews 11:1–3, after which it is applied to the lives of the biblical figures in the history of redemption as seen in the Old Testament. Abel is the first person in the cavalcade of faith in Hebrews 11.

How does the author of Hebrews define faith, and where did Abel get such a faith? Hebrews 11:1–2 says: "Now faith is the assurance of things hoped for, the conviction of things not seen. For by it the people of old received their commendation." George H. Guthrie put this definition another way based on his own extensive exegesis of verses 1–2: "Faith is confidence that results in action carried out in a variety of situations by ordinary people in response to the unseen God and his promises, with various earthly outcomes but always the ultimate outcome of God's commendation and reward."[32]

Faith here is not a subjective speculation, a vague and abstract imagination or meditation; faith is objective and historical because God gave faith to his people when he committed himself to fulfill his covenant. Our faith in God is a response to his commitment. Therefore, it is a realistic and concrete substance or assurance (ὑπόστασις), though not seen, that guarantees a future fulfillment and possession. Hence, this faith, founded on the commitment of God, looks forward. It is not static but a vital and dynamic force that brings its substance to its fulfillment. As God, the author of faith, works along with faith, faith brings into reality "the assurance of things hoped for, the conviction of things not seen." Thus, the fulfillment of faith is guaranteed.

This faith envisions a future reality and motivates believers to act upon it. However, faith here is not meritorious but responsive to God's grace, which is demonstrated by his commitment to his Word and deed throughout history. Believers attested to the nature and power of faith in the Old Testament period as they carried out their faith in

---

32. George H. Guthrie, *Hebrews*, NIVAC (Grand Rapids, MI: Zondervan, 1998), 390.

actual life. The author of Hebrews lists them, beginning with faith to understand that God created the universe out of nothing through his word (Heb. 11:3). Then comes the faith of Abel, who offered God a more acceptable offering than Cain's (11:4).

Where then did Abel get such a faith? It was God, the Lord of the covenant, who had planted such faith first in the hearts of Adam and Eve when God entered a covenant relationship with them after the fall, committing himself to redeem them (Gen. 3:15ff.), and demanded them to live in the faith. They must have taught faith to their sons Cain and Abel and trained them to offer God their sacrifices out of their professions of faith. This faith demanded obedience. However, Cain did not offer his sacrifice to God in this faith, but Abel did. Only God could see who had such a faith, and he alone could judge them. He chose Abel and his offering only. Abel offered his sacrifice to God in faith because he had a strong conviction of things hoped for; though not yet seen, they would become reality in the near future.

God is the sovereign Lord who gives faith to his people. It is God who gave Abel faith, but not Cain. Abel received faith only out of God's sovereign choice and grace. Although he was a passive recipient, he did not remain passive but actively exercised his faith. His faith led him to offer his sacrifice to God, and God commended him as righteous in return. But Cain, though taught the same faith by his parents, could not have faith because God did not choose to give him that gift. Therefore, Cain offered God his sacrifice, following his parent's instruction, like Abel, but he did so without faith. God rejected Cain and his offering and excluded him when choosing the first seed of the woman to fulfill his own commitment to Adam and Eve after the fall.

From this perspective, the phrase "a more acceptable sacrifice than Cain" (Heb. 11:4) does not imply any quality or quantity of the respective offerings. It does not provide any meritorious ground on which one was commended as righteous while the other was rejected. God himself alone made a sovereign choice between them. The author of Hebrews reflects the same motif as does the Genesis account in presenting the narrative of the offerings of Cain and Abel.

Conclusion

Despite attempts to answer the thorny question regarding the standard that God applied in choosing between Cain and Abel and their offerings, the narrative itself in Genesis 4:1–16 does not provide any clue to identify the standard. Hence, it was necessary to examine the context of Genesis and the biblical references to these offerings in the New Testament. Although these contexts do not provide direct clues, they offer background that helps us understand the narrative properly and a framework in which we can identify the standard.

From the perspective of this framework, the narrative is not an independent episode but a concrete instance of how God, the Lord of the covenant of redemption, inaugurated redemptive history in order to fulfill his covenant commitment to save Adam and Eve and their descendants in general, and how he formed the line of the seed of the woman against the seed of the Serpent in particular. In this narrative, God reveals his standard which he applies in electing someone for the line of the seed of the woman and in reprobating another for the line of seed of the Serpent. God used their offerings to reveal to us his standard of choice in the history of redemption.

However, the main message resides not in God's selection of an offering but in his selection of a person. This is why Moses does not specify the superiority of Abel's offering to Cain's, and why the author of Hebrews makes it clear that Abel offered his sacrifice to God by faith while Cain did not, so that not Abel's offering but Abel is commended as righteous. The biblical authors provide no reason to identify the standard in terms of the merit of the two offerings. God made a choice between Cain and Abel by his divine judgment of whose offering was made by faith, a faith given to Abel as a gift of God's love and grace by virtue of the covenant relationship he made with their parents after the fall. Calvin, noting the order of person first and the sacrifice next in the process of selection, also excludes the possibility that God selected Abel and his offering on meritorious grounds. He further emphasizes that God sovereignly implanted the faith in Abel first and then commended him as righteous by accepting his offering by faith.[33]

---

33. Calvin, *Genesis*, 194; Calvin, *Institutes*, 3.14.8.

A conclusion can be drawn that God the sovereign Lord himself is the standard by which he chose between Cain and his offering and Abel and his. God is not capricious but orderly, consistent, and faithful. He is the almighty God who sovereignly exercises his lordship over his creation and who sincerely brings to fruition the faith he affords his people as a gift.

5

Reading the Lord's Prayer Christologically

Brandon D. Crowe

Standing in the stalwart tradition of Reformed biblical theology—following such influential figures as Geerhardus Vos, John Murray, and Edmund Clowney—Vern Poythress has emphasized the Christ-centered character of Scripture throughout his more than forty-year career teaching hermeneutics and New Testament interpretation at Westminster Theological Seminary.[1] Often the challenge in reading the Bible in a faithfully Christ-centered fashion centers on the Old Testament. Reading the New Testament in a Christ-centered fashion is by all accounts much easier. My present focus may therefore be surprising. In this essay I would like to consider how we can miss the thoroughly Christ-centered nature even of the Gospels. More specifically, I will argue that the Lord's Prayer contains a rich (though implicit) Christology that comes into focus when viewed in light of the wider context of Matthew's Gospel.

---

1. See, recently, Vern S. Poythress, *Reading the Word of God in the Presence of God: A Handbook for Biblical Interpretation* (Wheaton, IL: Crossway, 2016), 33.

Of course, to claim that the Gospels are Christological documents is rather uncontroversial. The Gospels have recently been called "Christology in narrative form."[2] This statement reflects a move away from the twentieth-century albatross of form criticism, which tended to view the Gospels largely as reflections of the life settings of early Christian communities. Part of the long shadow cast by much form criticism included the downplaying of the Gospels' structures; the Gospels were often viewed as collections of discrete sayings and stories strung together by a compiler. However, form criticism's influence, while not abating entirely, has significantly waned since the last few decades of the twentieth century, and we now find more studies of the Gospels that emphasize narrative and synchronic features. These studies recognize the need to view the Gospels as integrated wholes, and seek to do justice to the plots and structures of the Gospels. This means, for example, that not only are the *contents* of the Gospels important, but so is the *order* of their contents. Similarly, many studies recognize the need to read the part in light of the whole, and give attention to the ways that the Gospel narratives progressively reveal their Christological truths. Such insights are not entirely new to Reformed biblical theology, which has long emphasized that revelation is progressively unveiled throughout Scripture.[3]

Thus, when we come to the Sermon on the Mount, we must not forget that even the didactic portions of Matthew are part of a larger, Christological narrative. It is important, therefore, to relate Jesus's teachings to his actions. Thus, in the Sermon on the Mount, not only do we read of how the disciples should live in light of the kingdom of God, but we are also pointed to the Savior who perfectly fulfills that which the disciples are called to do.[4] And in the Lord's Prayer disciples are to think not only of their own needs but also of their Savior who goes before them.

---

2. Richard A. Burridge, *What Are the Gospels? A Comparison with Graeco-Roman Biography*, 2nd ed., Biblical Resource Series (Grand Rapids, MI: Eerdmans, 2004), 289.

3. See, e.g., Geerhardus Vos, *Biblical Theology: Old and New Testaments* (Grand Rapids, MI: Eerdmans, 1948; repr., Edinburgh: Banner of Truth, 1975); G. K. Beale, *A New Testament Biblical Theology: The Unfolding of the Old Testament in the New* (Grand Rapids, MI: Baker Academic, 2011).

4. See Dale C. Allison Jr., "Structure, Biographical Impulse, and the *Imitatio Christi*," in *Studies in Matthew: Interpretation Past and Present* (Grand Rapids, MI: Baker Academic, 2005), 147–53.

Brief Sketch of the History of Interpretation

It scarcely needs to be said that studies on the Lord's Prayer are legion. As the translator of Joachim Jeremias's concise study noted some years ago, "Word for word, few creations in all the history of literature have received so much attention."[5] The Lord's Prayer is already attested in a liturgical setting in the late first or early second century, as evidenced in Didache 8, and it is apparently known to Polycarp of Smyrna (*To the Philippians* 7:1–2) in the second century. Quite intriguingly, though much less certain, evidence for the pre–AD 79 use of the Lord's Prayer might also be attested in the so-called sator word square at Pompeii, in which *pater noster* ("Our Father" in Latin) can be formed twice from the letters of the palindrome square if construed in the shape of a cross that intersects at the *N*.[6] Clement of Alexandria considered the prayer to be "the vessel of an infinite knowledge,"[7] Tertullian viewed it as "an abridgement of the entire Gospel,"[8] and Cyprian—who may have been the first to call this prayer "the Lord's Prayer"[9]—views it a "compendium of heavenly doctrine."[10] We further know that in the early church

---

5. Joachim Jeremias, *The Lord's Prayer*, trans. John Reumann, Facet Books, Biblical Series 8 (Philadelphia: Fortress, 1964), v.

6. Thus *N* is found only once, but at the center of the square. This would leave the letters *A* and *O* remaining twice, which could refer to Alpha and Omega (cf. Rev. 1:8). One of the arguments against understanding the sator square in Pompeii as early Christian material evidence is the supposed lack of evidence for the symbol of the cross before Constantine. See, e.g., Heinz Hofmann, "Sator square," in *Brill's New Pauly Encyclopedia of the Ancient World: Antiquity*, vol. 13, *Sas–Syl*, ed. Hubert Cancik and Helmuth Schneider (Leiden: Brill, 2008), 17–19. However, a number of recent studies have argued convincingly that the cross was a known Christian symbol by at least the second century, and perhaps earlier. See, e.g., Bruce W. Longenecker, *The Crosses of Pompeii: Jesus Devotion in a Vesuvian Town* (Minneapolis: Fortress, 2016). Given its difficulty, Longenecker does not consider the sator square to be possible evidence for the cross in Pompeii (see 38–39, 59), but he does make a strong argument that the cross was very likely a Christian symbol in pre–AD 79 Pompeii. Additionally, Longenecker argues that the name *Jesus* in Latin (*Iesus*) is found twice in a cross-shaped symbol from the Baths of Neptune in Ostia Antica (*Crosses of Pompeii*, 69), which is similar in principle to the possible cross-shaped *pater noster* derived from the Pompeian sator square. Indeed, Longenecker argues that the symbols from the Baths of Neptune in Ostia Antica suggest that, at least there, "the cross was the primary shape that undergirded the theological imagination of the Christians who crafted these symbols and who looked for artistic ways of depicting it" (*Crosses of Pompeii*, 70). See also Longenecker, *The Cross before Constantine: The Early Life of a Christian Symbol* (Minneapolis: Fortress, 2015). For the argument that the cross is pictorially represented in early Christian manuscripts before Constantine, see Larry W. Hurtado, *The Earliest Christian Artifacts: Manuscripts and Christian Origins* (Grand Rapids, MI: Eerdmans, 2006), 135–54, esp. 151–52.

7. As noted in Ernst Lohmeyer, *"Our Father": An Introduction to the Lord's Prayer*, trans. John Bowden (New York: Harper & Row, 1965), 19.

8. *Breviarum totius evangelii* (*Prayer* 1), as quoted in Ulrich Luz, *Matthew 1–7: A Commentary*, trans. James E. Crouch, Hermeneia (Minneapolis: Fortress, 2007), 312.

9. See Cyprian, *The Lord's Prayer*. This point is noted by Jeffrey B. Gibson, *The Disciples' Prayer: The Prayer Jesus Taught in Its Historical Setting* (Minneapolis: Fortress, 2015), 2n2.

10. *Lord's Prayer* 9, noted in Luz, *Matthew 1–7*, 312.

expositions of the Lord's Prayer were often given in association with the practice of baptism and the receiving of members into the church (see, e.g., Cyril of Jerusalem, John Chrysostom).[11]

Many valuable studies have appeared on this so-called abridgement of the gospel. Calvin's discussion in his *Institutes* continues to repay careful reading.[12] Likewise, the Westminster Larger Catechism (186–96) provides practical insights into the six petitions of the Lord's Prayer. One might also note the twentieth-century classics from Dietrich Bonhoeffer (*The Cost of Discipleship*)[13] and Martyn Lloyd-Jones (*Studies in the Sermon on the Mount*),[14] which cover the Lord's Prayer. In addition, several of Poythress's colleagues (Sinclair Ferguson,[15] Bill Edgar,[16] Kent Hughes[17]) and former students (Phil Ryken,[18] Dan Doriani[19]) have authored studies that cover the Lord's Prayer or Sermon on the Mount.

I do not desire to replace such valuable studies. Instead, I wish to supplement them by drawing more sustained attention to the Christological thrust of the prayer. To this end, we should also consider some of the more recent treatments of the prayer in New Testament scholarship. Here we might start with *"Our Father"* by Ernst Lohmeyer. Written just before his tragic death in 1946, Lohmeyer's study first appeared in English in 1965 and has proved to be a standard conversation partner for later studies. To Lohmeyer's work we could add the brief (but important) works of Joachim Jeremias[20] and Raymond E.

---

11. See T. W. Manson, "The Lord's Prayer," *Bulletin of the John Rylands Library* 38 (1955–1956): 101; Luz, *Matthew 1–7*, 312.
12. See *Institutes*, 3.20.34–49.
13. Dietrich Bonhoeffer, *The Cost of Discipleship*, trans. R. H. Fuller, rev. ed. (New York: Macmillan, 1963).
14. D. Martyn Lloyd-Jones, *Studies in the Sermon on the Mount*, 2nd ed., 2 vols. (Grand Rapids, MI: Eerdmans, 1971).
15. Sinclair B. Ferguson, *The Sermon on the Mount: Kingdom Life in a Fallen World* (Edinburgh: Banner of Truth, 1987).
16. William Edgar, *A Transforming Vision: The Lord's Prayer as a Lens for Life* (Fearn, Ross-shire, Scotland: Christian Focus, 2014).
17. R. Kent Hughes, *The Sermon on the Mount: The Message of the Kingdom*, Preaching the Word (Wheaton, IL: Crossway, 2001).
18. Philip Graham Ryken, *When You Pray: Making the Lord's Prayer Your Own* (Wheaton, IL: Crossway, 2000).
19. Daniel M. Doriani, *The Sermon on the Mount: The Character of a Disciple* (Phillipsburg, NJ: P&R, 2006).
20. Jeremias, *Lord's Prayer*. This work was later incorporated into Jeremias, *The Prayers of Jesus*, trans. John Bowden, Christoph Burchard, and John Reumann, SBT ser. 2, no. 6 (London: SCM, 1967).

Brown,[21] along with the more recent studies of N. T. Wright[22] and Jeffrey Gibson.[23] A number of commentaries are also valuable, such as those on Matthew from Ulrich Luz,[24] W. D. Davies and Dale Allison,[25] and Craig Keener,[26] as well as commentaries specifically on the Sermon on the Mount, such as the ones from Hans Dieter Betz,[27] Robert Guelich,[28] D. A. Carson,[29] Dale Allison,[30] Charles Quarles,[31] and Scot McKnight[32] (to name a few).

A key question in many of these studies is whether we should understand the Lord's Prayer to be narrowly *eschatological* in orientation. That is, should we interpret the prayer to be focused primarily on the consummation—the great end-time travail that involves the final opposition and overthrow of Satan.[33] In this essay I am not able to do justice to the debates, but I will outline my own view. In short, while much of value is to be gleaned from studies that focus on the more *narrow* eschatology of the Lord's Prayer, I believe it is more helpful to focus on the eschatology of the Lord's Prayer in a *broader* sense. In other words, the urge to read the Lord's Prayer eschatologically is a step in the right direction, but it is best to do so within the framework of an already/not-yet inaugurated eschatology. This framework recognizes that the

---

21. Raymond E. Brown, "The Pater Noster as an Eschatological Prayer," *Theological Studies* 22, no. 2 (1961): 175–208.

22. N. T. Wright, *The Lord and His Prayer* (Grand Rapids, MI: Eerdmans, 1997).

23. Gibson, *Disciples' Prayer*.

24. Luz, *Matthew 1–7*.

25. W. D. Davies and Dale C. Allison Jr., *A Critical and Exegetical Commentary on the Gospel according to Saint Matthew*, 3 vols., ICC (Edinburgh: T&T Clark, 1988–97).

26. Craig S. Keener, *The Gospel of Matthew: A Socio-Rhetorical Commentary* (Grand Rapids, MI: Eerdmans, 2009).

27. Hans Dieter Betz, *The Sermon on the Mount*, Hermeneia (Minneapolis: Fortress, 1995).

28. Robert A. Guelich, *The Sermon on the Mount: A Foundation for Understanding* (Waco, TX: Word, 1982).

29. D. A. Carson, *Jesus' Sermon on the Mount and His Confrontation with the World: An Exposition of Matthew 5–10* (Grand Rapids, MI: Baker, 1999).

30. Dale C. Allison Jr., *The Sermon on the Mount: Inspiring the Moral Imagination*, Companions to the New Testament (New York: Crossroad, 1999).

31. Charles L. Quarles, *Sermon on the Mount: Restoring Christ's Message to the Modern Church*, New American Commentary Studies in Bible and Theology 11 (Nashville: B&H, 2011).

32. Scot McKnight, *Sermon on the Mount*, The Story of God Bible Commentary (Grand Rapids, MI: Zondervan, 2013).

33. See, e.g., Brown, "Pater Noster," 175:

> By "eschatological" we refer to the period of the last days, involving the return of Christ, the destruction of the forces of evil, and the definite establishment of God's rule. We are defining the limits of our use because in a broader sense the whole Christian period can be called eschatological, since God's kingdom has already been partially established in this world through Jesus, who by His death and resurrection has won a victory over Satan.

prayer situates the disciples in a kingdom that is moving forward to a consummation, but the prayer is relevant for the entire interadventual period that marks the "latter days" anticipated in the Old Testament. And to focus on the broad eschatology of the Lord's Prayer is at the same time to recognize the need to read the Lord's Prayer *Christologically*, since the latter days are inaugurated through the promised Messiah.

The Christological Context of Matthew

In what follows I will focus particularly on the Lord's Prayer in Matthew 6:9–13. Reading the Lord's Prayer in the wider context of Matthew encourages us to see how the prayer points us to Christ himself. By the time the reader encounters the Lord's Prayer in Matthew 6, much has been established in Matthew 1–4. Already Jesus has been identified as the messianic, Davidic King. He is the Son of David and Son of Abraham (1:1–2), the Savior who will overcome the curse of exile (1:1–17). Jesus is Immanuel—"God with us"—who will "save his people from their sins" (1:21, 23), shepherd his people (2:6; cf. Mic. 5:2), and fulfill all righteousness (Matt. 3:15). Jesus is the anointed representative (3:16–17) who overcomes the Devil in the wilderness (4:1–11) and preaches the inauguration of the kingdom of God (4:17), bringing light to those who dwelled in darkness (4:14–16). This is just some of what precedes the Sermon on the Mount.

Moreover, when we read the Sermon on the Mount in light of Matthew's Gospel more broadly, we also find that Jesus himself does the things he calls his disciples to do.[34] A few examples will illustrate the correlations. In the beatitudes Jesus proclaims a blessing on the meek (5:5), and Jesus himself is demonstrated to be meek elsewhere in Matthew (11:29; 21:5). The disciples are to show mercy (5:7), as indeed Jesus himself shows mercy (9:27; 15:22). Jesus instructs his disciples to turn the other cheek (5:39), and Jesus himself does not retaliate when wronged (26:67; 27:30). Likewise, Jesus exhorts his disciples to private prayer (6:6), just as Jesus himself prays privately (14:23). It is in light of the Christological context of the Sermon on the Mount and the

---

34. See, again, Allison, "Structure, Biographical Impulse, and *Imitatio Chrsti*."

correlation of Jesus's actions with his teaching given to the disciples that we now turn to the Lord's Prayer itself.

The Christology of the Lord's Prayer

FIRST PETITION

Our Father, who art in heaven, hallowed be thy name.[35]

A Christological reading of the Lord's Prayer begins with the first words of the prayer ("Our Father"), since it is only through Jesus, the Son of God, that we are able to address God as our Father. As Calvin succinctly states, "In calling God 'Father,' we put forward the name 'Christ.'"[36] Here we should notice the difference in Jesus's own manner of speaking and praying in which God is referred to as "my Father" (e.g., Matt. 20:23; 26:29, 39, 42, 53) or simply "Father" (Matt. 11:27). On the other hand, Jesus speaks to the disciples of "your Father" (e.g., Matt. 5:16, 45, 48; 6:1) and instructs them to pray "our Father" (Matt. 6:9). The implication is that Jesus and the disciples, while they pray to the same Father, do not share an identical sort of relationship to the Father.[37] Jesus is the divine Son par excellence, who provides access to his Father for the disciples. It is a great privilege for disciples to call God Father, but we must never forget that this privilege is dependent upon Jesus's unique relationship with the Father and Jesus's role as our Mediator.[38] The phrase "our Father" thus prepares us to read the rest of the prayer with an eye to our Mediator.

When we come to the first petition ("hallowed be thy name"), we are directed to think, first of all, of God and his glory. We may be reminded here of the third commandment, that we must not take the name of the Lord our God in vain.[39] God's name is preeminently hallowed in the life of Jesus himself. Jesus never profaned the name of his Father with any word that arose from his heart, or any sinful action. He was perfectly obedient in all that he did, and demonstrated a lifelong commitment to the glory and honor of his Father, even to the point of death. Jesus therefore shows us what it means to hallow the name of God, as he prays in

---

35. In lieu of offering my own translation, I will use traditional, liturgical language.
36. *Institutes*, 3.20.36.
37. See, e.g., Richard J. Bauckham, "The Sonship of the Historical Jesus in Christology," *SJT* 31, no. 3 (1978): 245–60; Lohmeyer, *"Our Father,"* 51.
38. See Heidelberg Catechism, 120.
39. See Calvin, *Institutes*, 3.20.41; similarly, Lohmeyer, *"Our Father,"* 79.

John 17:4, "I glorified you on earth." Lloyd-Jones states it succinctly: "You cannot read the four Gospels without seeing very clearly that [the glory of God] was the consuming passion of the Lord Jesus Christ himself."[40] Thus, while the first petition does indeed call for disciples to honor appropriately the name of God, we must not lose sight of the one who honored it perfectly throughout his life.

SECOND PETITION

Thy kingdom come.

The second petition calls disciples to seek the success and the growth of the kingdom. This petition would beckon us away from worldliness,[41] and communicates "a burning desire that the whole world may bow before God in adoration, in reverence, in praise, in worship, in honor and in thanksgiving."[42] Yet as we think upon such matters, we must not lose sight of Jesus as the messianic King of the kingdom. Jesus not only preaches the kingdom but also inaugurates it through his own actions. Through Jesus the kingdom of God has come near. Thus, to pray for the advance of the kingdom is to pray specifically that the name of Christ may be made known and that all peoples throughout the world may come to know him as Lord of the kingdom. Those who take a narrowly eschatological approach view this as a prayer for the final consummation of the kingdom.[43] While we should not rule out a reference to the consummation, the second petition has relevance for the growth of the already inaugurated kingdom now. We thus pray, in the second petition, that "Christ would rule in our hearts here, and hasten the time of his second coming, and our reigning with him forever."[44]

THIRD PETITION

Thy will be done, on earth as it is in heaven.

In the third petition, which is the last of the petitions focusing more explicitly on God's name and glory, is the prayer for God's will to be

---

40. Lloyd-Jones, *Studies in the Sermon on the Mount*, 2:60.
41. Calvin, *Institutes*, 3.20.42.
42. Lloyd-Jones, *Studies in the Sermon on the Mount*, 2:61.
43. See Brown, "Pater Noster," 190.
44. WLC, 191.

done on earth as it is in heaven. This petition is also relevant for our day-to-day actions as we seek to live in conformity to God's revealed will.[45] Praying for God's will to be done is also a kingdom prayer, since God's righteousness characterizes the kingdom. And we pray this not abstractly but personally—that we might live in accord with the ethics of the kingdom in this present age.

Here again we are reminded of our Savior, who himself prayed in the garden of Gethsemane that his actions might accomplish the will of his Father (Matt. 26:42). Indeed, the phrasing is exactly the same in Matthew 6:10 and 26:42 (γενηθήτω τὸ θέλημά σου). Only Jesus perfectly lived in accord with God's revealed will throughout his life, and therefore he was uniquely suited to seal the kingdom through his death and resurrection.[46] Disciples of Jesus are indeed to follow the ethical footsteps of our Savior as citizens of the kingdom, though we (unlike Jesus) will need to ask for forgiveness where we fail (see below on the fifth petition).

Fourth Petition
Give us this day our daily bread.

With the fourth petition we come to the turning point in the Lord's Prayer. Whereas the first three petitions were given in the second person ("your"), in the fourth petition we find the first of the "we" petitions. To begin, we should recognize that the fourth petition is indeed rather straightforward; by praying for our daily bread, we are asking our heavenly Father to provide for our daily necessities. We are reminded that if our Father cares for the sparrows, he will care for us, since we are of more value than the many sparrows (Matt. 10:29–31; cf. 6:25–33). And the plural "our" reminds us that we are part of a global community of believers, whose needs we should give attention to in addition to our own.

And yet, in addition to this prayer for physical provision, the history of exegesis encourages us to consider whether there may be more

---

45. So, e.g., Calvin, *Institutes*, 3.20.43; WLC, 192.
46. Cf. Herman N. Ridderbos, *The Coming of the Kingdom*, ed. Raymond O. Zorn, trans. H. de Jongste (Philadelphia: Presbyterian and Reformed, 1962), 109, 171. See also Cyprian, *Lord's Prayer* 14.

here than we might notice at first. Perhaps the fourth petition is pointing us in a Christological direction as well. Bread serves a variety of purposes in the Gospels: it not only refers to physical bread that assuages physical hunger (and this is what we legitimately pray for in the Lord's Prayer) but also points to spiritual realities. By this point in Matthew the reader has encountered the threefold temptation of Jesus. The first of these temptations is the challenge that, if Jesus really is the Son of God, he should turn stones into bread (4:3). In response Jesus, recognizing that there is more to life than physical hunger, quotes Deuteronomy 8:3:

> Man shall not live by bread alone,
>> but by every word that comes from the mouth of God.
>>> (Matt. 4:4)

This is consistent with Jesus's response to his disciples about food in John 4:34, where Jesus states that his food is to do the will of his Father and complete his work. In both cases physical food is not as important as the need to be fully committed to God's will.

Beyond the temptation account in Matthew, bread also features prominently in the two wilderness feeding miracles of Jesus: the feeding the five thousand in Matthew 14 and of the four thousand in Matthew 15.[47] These feedings do meet the physical hunger of those present (cf. 15:32) but also point to the fulfillment of the latter-day prophetic hope in which a feast would be spread in the wilderness (cf. Isa. 25:6–8).[48] Thus these feedings serve something like a sign-act function, consistent with what we find among the Old Testament prophets.[49]

This perspective is confirmed in Matthew 16:1–12. After the Pharisees ask Jesus for a sign in 16:1–5, Jesus enters into a discussion about bread with his disciples, warning them against the leaven of the Pharisees and Sadducees (16:6). His disciples are slow to understand what

---

47. It is not to be missed how impressive these numbers are, especially when compared with cities of Galilee in Jesus's day and the likelihood that more than just the men were present. It has been estimated that Capernaum would have likely had only two thousand to three thousand citizens at this time. Cf. Joel Marcus, *Mark 1–8: A New Translation with Introduction and Commentary*, AB 27 (New Haven, CT: Yale University Press, 2000), 414.

48. See, similarly, Wright, *The Lord and His Prayer*, 38–41.

49. Similarly, Poythress has argued that Jesus's miracles should be understood as signs. See Vern S. Poythress, *The Miracles of Jesus: How the Savior's Mighty Acts Serve as Signs of Redemption* (Wheaton, IL: Crossway, 2016).

he means, since they have forgotten to bring physical bread with them (16:5, 7). Jesus then critiques his disciples for their little faith and reminds them of the miraculous provisions of bread in the wilderness (16:8–11). The disciples then understand that Jesus is warning them against the teaching of the Pharisees and Sadducees (16:12). Implicit in this exchange is the understanding that bread not only is about physical nourishment but also serves as something like a sign in Matthew. The abundant provision of bread in the wilderness points to Jesus's role in providing the blessings of eschatological life, such as we read in Isaiah 25.[50]

More clarity in this regard is found in the Last Supper account in Matthew 26, which is verbally linked with the two feedings in the wilderness. In all three accounts we find Jesus taking (λαμβάνω), breaking (κλάω), and giving (δίδωμι) bread (ἄρτος). And in each case Jesus either says a blessing (εὐλογέω, Matt. 14:19; 26:26) or gives thanks (εὐχαρι-στέω, 15:36; 26:27)[51] for God's provision. Thus, while the feedings in the wilderness are not to be taken as celebrations of the Lord's Supper, strictly speaking, readers are encouraged to view the two in similar terms. Likewise, the only other place in Matthew where we find δίδωμι and ἄρτος together is in 6:11. And we know from elsewhere in the New Testament that the sacramental supper instituted by Christ points us to Christ himself, on whom we feed by faith (cf. 1 Cor. 10:16; 11:24, 27–29). Therefore, in the feeding of the multitudes in the wilderness, along with the institution of the supper, we are encouraged to read "bread" in Matthew (including the Lord's Prayer) in a richly Christological way.

Reading "bread" in Matthew to entail a spiritual dimension also accords with the language of *daily* bread we encounter in Matthew 6:11. Understanding what is intended by *daily* (ἐπιούσιος) bread may be the most difficult exegetical decision in the entire Lord's Prayer. As Lohmeyer averred many decades ago, ἐπιούσιος "still remains to be explained and probably never will be."[52] However, perhaps we can make fruitful progress on this question if we allow for a spiritual

50. Indeed, in Isa. 25:6–8 the feast of food is linked with the abolition of death!
51. In Matthew 26 thanksgiving is offered for the wine, which is not part of the feedings in the wilderness (but is part of the Isaiah 25 imagery). Likewise, fish are present in the wilderness feedings but not at the Last Supper.
52. Lohmeyer, "*Our Father*," 15. See, more recently, McKnight, *Sermon on the Mount*, 181.

dimension to *daily* bread. One of the most ancient traditions takes ἐπιούσιος as *future* bread. This goes back at least to Jerome, who knew of
this reading in the so-called *Gospel according to the Hebrews*, which
reads *maḥar* ("tomorrow").[53] Daily bread was frequently understood
in the ancient church to refer to "future bread," "heavenly bread,"
"heavenly manna," "bread of life," or "bread of salvation."[54] It was
also commonly understood to refer to the Eucharist.[55] Calvin, on the
other hand, considers the notion that *daily* bread refers to "supersub-
stantial" bread to be "exceedingly absurd."[56] His point, apparently, is
that eucharistic superstition had replaced the simple, practical prayer
that Jesus taught his disciples to pray.

However, I believe that one can agree with Calvin against readings
that deny the simplicity of this prayer for physical bread while also
recognizing a spiritual dimension to bread in the fourth petition. For in
the biblical worldview, there is no ultimate dichotomy between physical and spiritual bread. And when we understand *daily* bread to have
a spiritual dimension, we are not denying the need to pray for physical
bread, but we are recognizing that even physical bread in Matthew's
Gospel has a kingdom dimension.[57] Thus we read that Jesus was accused of being a glutton and a drunkard for the feasts he participated
in (Matt. 11:16–19),[58] whereas Matthew makes it clear that these were
actually the messianic feasting deeds of the Messiah.[59]

It may help to consider the Gospel of John, where Jesus proclaims
that he is the Bread of Life who gives eschatological life (e.g., John
6:27, 31–33, 35, 41, 48, 54).[60] Significantly, the Johannine Bread of

53. See *The Gospel of the Nazareans* 3 in Bart D. Ehrman and Zlatko Pleše, *The Apocryphal Gospels: Texts and Translations* (Oxford: Oxford University Press, 2011), 205; cf. Origen, *Prayer* 27.13.

54. See Lohmeyer, *"Our Father,"* 142–45; Jeremias, *Lord's Prayer*, 23–25; James R. Edwards, *The Gospel according to Luke*, PNTC (Grand Rapids, MI: Eerdmans, 2015), 334.

55. See, e.g., Augustine (*Sermon on the Mount* 7.27), who understands this petition to refer to physical bread, the Eucharist, and the spiritual bread of the Word of God.

56. John Calvin, *Commentary on a Harmony of the Evangelists, Matthew, Mark, and Luke*, trans. and ed. William Pringle, 3 vols. (Grand Rapids, MI: Baker, 2003), 2:72; cf. Calvin, *Institutes*, 3.20.44. Note Jerome's translation of Matt. 6:11 in the Vulgate: *panem nostrum supersubstantialem.*

57. See also Davies and Allison, *Matthew*, 1:609; Jeremias, *Lord's Prayer*, 25–26; Lohmeyer, *"Our Father,"* 149–51.

58. See, similarly, Lohmeyer, *"Our Father,"* 149; Wright, *The Lord and His Prayer*, 37.

59. Note the *inclusio* in 11:2, 19, which focuses on the deeds (ἔργα) of the Christ.

60. Similar connections are noted in Tertullian, *Prayer* 6; Origen, *Prayer* 27.2; Cyprian, *Lord's Prayer* 18; Brown, "Pater Noster," 198.

Life discourse comes on the heels of Jesus's feeding the five thousand (6:1–15).[61] It is not difficult to argue that what John makes explicit—namely, that Jesus's feeding in the wilderness points to himself as the true Bread of Life[62]—is implicit in Matthew, where bread likewise serves multiple functions. Therefore, the fourth petition is likely worded in such a way that we should think prominently of Christ, who feeds us with the bread of eschatological life as we trust in him.[63] Significantly, in John 6 Jesus compares himself to the manna that was given through Moses, which may also provide insight into the *daily* bread of Matthew 6:11. Readers of the Old Testament will know that the manna came down from heaven *daily*. In contrast to the manna given in Moses's day, Jesus is the Bread of Life who came down from heaven that he might give eternal life for all who believe in him (John 6:29, 50–51, 58). Though many have taken John 6 to refer primarily to the Lord's Supper,[64] the primary point is the Christological reality that undergirds the supper—namely, feeding in faith on the Son of Man (cf. 6:29, 56).[65] Likewise, though the *daily bread* of Matthew 6:11 may have implications for how we understand the Lord's Supper, it is best taken as a reference to physical bread that also points in a Christological direction.[66]

In sum, the fourth petition is indeed a prayer for daily provision, but it is also a prayer for the provision of eschatological life that comes through believing in Jesus, the Bread of Life.[67]

---

61. The feeding of the five thousand is recorded in all four Gospels, underscoring its significance. Additionally, the feeding of the five thousand in John may be the fourth of seven signs arranged in a chiastic structure, which would therefore serve as the pivot emphasizing the need to believe in and abide in Christ. This would entail viewing the death and resurrection of Jesus as the seventh sign. See Brandon D. Crowe, "The Chiastic Pattern of Seven Signs in John: Revisiting a Neglected Proposal," *Bulletin for Biblical Research* (forthcoming), building on Marc Girard, "La composition structurelle des sept 'signes' dans le quatrième évangile," *Studies in Religion* 9, no. 3 (1980): 315–24.

62. See Poythress, *Miracles of Jesus*, 33–34.

63. See Tertullian, *Prayer* 6: "We may understand 'Give us this day our daily bread' *spiritually*. For *Christ* is our Bread; because Christ is Life and bread is life" (translation from ANF, 3:683, emphasis original).

64. See, already in the third century, Cyprian, *Lord's Prayer* 18.

65. See also Grant Macaskill, *Union with Christ in the New Testament* (Oxford: Oxford University Press, 2013), 216.

66. See similarly Ferguson, *Sermon on the Mount*, 129. It is noteworthy that the Lord's Prayer has historically been used in liturgical contexts. Cf. Didache 7–10 (note esp. 10:3).

67. WLC, 193 also acknowledges a spiritual dimension to this petition, noting that "in Adam, and by our own sin, we have forfeited all rights to the outward blessings of this life." The answer to our sin is the last Adam, who himself serves as the provision that overcomes our sin.

FIFTH PETITION

Forgive us our debts, as we forgive our debtors.

In the fifth petition we acknowledge the debt of our sins and ask for God's forgiveness. At least two aspects of the work of Christ in Matthew come into view at this point. First, we are reminded that though Jesus had no need for forgiveness personally (3:14–15),[68] he himself had the authority to grant forgiveness (9:2, 6; 26:28). Second, the pecuniary "debt" language reminds us not only of the parable of the unforgiving servant (18:21–35), but also of the so-called Ransom Logion in Matthew 20:28: "Even as the Son of Man came not to be served but to serve, and to give his life as a ransom for many [λύτρον ἀντὶ πολλῶν]."[69] The language of ransom (λύτρον) is significant, and while it must include Jesus's death, the term points more broadly to the entire life of Jesus given in exchange for the "many" he came to redeem.[70] The use of λύτρον thus portrays our sins as debts that need to be paid, and therefore correlates to the debts (ὀφειλήματα) of the Lord's Prayer in Matthew 6:12. Put simply, our sins create a debt to God that we cannot pay.[71] Therefore, the ransom work of Christ is described in pecuniary terms.[72] Thus, to pray "forgive us our debts" is to draw our attention to Jesus as the ransom who provides our only means of forgiveness.[73]

SIXTH PETITION

Lead us not into temptation, but deliver us from evil.

We come now to the final petition of the Lord's Prayer, which some have argued is best taken as two separate petitions. Whether one views this section as one or two petitions, the concepts in view are closely related and will be taken together here. When we pray "lead us not

68. Cf. Tertullian, *Prayer* 7.
69. Calvin seems also to note this connection. However, the Battles edition of the *Institutes* (3.20.45) supplies only Rom. 3:24 in brackets at this point and not Matt. 20:28 // Mark 10:45.
70. See Brandon D. Crowe, *The Last Adam: A Theology of the Obedient Life of Jesus in the Gospels* (Grand Rapids, MI: Baker Academic, 2017), chap. 7.
71. So Calvin, *Institutes*, 3.20.45.
72. See, further, Leon Morris, *The Apostolic Preaching of the Cross* (Grand Rapids, MI: Eerdmans, 1955), 9–59; John Murray, *Redemption Accomplished and Applied* (Grand Rapids, MI: Eerdmans, 1955), 42–50; Geerhardus Vos, *Reformed Dogmatics*, ed. and trans. Richard B. Gaffin Jr., 5 vols. (Bellingham, WA: Lexham, 2012–2016), 3:116–24.
73. See, similarly, Lloyd-Jones, *Studies in the Sermon on the Mount*, 2:75.

into temptation," we are asking to be protected from situations in which the Devil would tempt us.[74] This is consistent with the danger in view in Matthew 26:41 ("Watch and pray that you may not enter into temptation"), where the disciples are found sleeping instead of praying.[75] Much has been said about whether "temptation" or "testing" is the proper translation of πειρασμός, along with the question of whether πειρασμός is to be taken as the final, eschatological testing.[76] In my view, it is best to retain the traditional terminology of "temptation," which best accords with "evil" in the second half of the verse.[77] It must be Satan who tempts us, since God does not tempt anyone (James 1:13).[78] Instead, it is proper to speak of *testings* that God gives his people (cf. Abraham in the *Akedah* [Genesis 22]), but not of God *tempting* his people. As James 1:14 says, each person is tempted when led astray by his own desire. Indeed, we can even be *tempted* to *test* God (cf. Deut. 6:16; Pss. 78:18, 41, 56; 95:9; 1 Cor. 10:9; Heb. 3:9), which Jesus himself refused to do (Matt. 4:6–7). The sixth petition therefore is primarily a prayer that we might not be overcome by sin.[79]

The main point I wish to focus on for the present purpose, however, is the contrast between what the disciples are to pray and Jesus's own experience. Whereas disciples are to pray that God would not lead them into temptation, Jesus, as the anointed representative of his people, is led by the Spirit into the wilderness for the express purpose of being tempted by the Devil (Matt. 4:1). We therefore must read this petition in Matthew 6 in light of the temptations of Jesus in Matthew 4.[80] Thus, what was proper for Jesus, as the champion of our faith—facing the Devil's temptations in the wilderness—is not proper for those who follow him by faith.[81]

---

74. See ibid., 2:76.

75. Cf. Tertullian, *Prayer* 7.

76. See Lohmeyer, *"Our Father,"* 195; Brown, "Pater Noster," 205; Jeremias, *Lord's Prayer*, 30; Davies and Allison, *Matthew*, 1:613–14.

77. So Quarles, *Sermon on the Mount*, 216–17; cf. Ryken, *When You Pray*, 152–53. I will discuss the referent of "evil" below.

78. See the discussions in Dale C. Allison Jr., *A Critical and Exegetical Commentary on the Epistle of James*, ICC (London: T&T Clark, 2013), 135–48, 214–54.

79. See McKnight, *Sermon on the Mount*, 186; Hughes, *Sermon on the Mount*, 195. See also b. Ber. 60b.

80. This is commonly acknowledged. See McKnight, *Sermon on the Mount*, 185; Quarles, *Sermon on the Mount*, 217.

81. Additionally, as the last Adam (thus, according to his human nature), Jesus was free from the guilt and corruption of original sin and had no inclination toward evil in himself (cf. James

This approach also makes sense of the second half of the petition: "Deliver us from evil." This traditional translation, however, is open to refinement, since the articular τοῦ πονηροῦ most likely refers to the personal Devil as opposed to the more abstract "evil." When Jesus was led into temptation, he faced off with the Devil and overcame him through his obedience. Thus, we should view the temptation as an epochal moment in the history of redemption; it marked the decisive first blow of the messianic ministry of Jesus that marked the presupposition for the inauguration of the kingdom.[82] As the stronger man, Jesus bound the strong man (i.e., the Devil) throughout his entire ministry of messianic obedience, climaxing in his death and resurrection (cf. Matt. 12:22–32). In contrast, the disciples of Jesus are not called personally to overcome the strong man. Instead, the call for disciples is to be delivered from the Evil One by placing their faith in the One who is able to overcome the Devil. Calvin captures the sentiment well: "It is not in our power to engage that great warrior the devil in combat, or to bear his force and onslaught."[83]

Is there, then, any eschatological sense to the sixth petition? Yes indeed. But it is eschatological in the broad sense, not in the more narrow sense of *only* having to do with the end of the world. Instead, the sixth petition presupposes the eschatological work of Christ in facing off against the Devil in the wilderness and winning the decisive kingdom victory. Thus Jesus has, by Matthew 6, already inaugurated the kingdom as the messianic King who has begun to overcome the kingdom of Satan.[84] In light of the present reality of the messianic Kingdom, the temptations from which we may seek protection in prayer are serious

---

1:14). See Herman Bavinck, *Reformed Dogmatics*, vol. 3, *Sin and Salvation in Christ*, ed. John Bolt, trans. John Vriend (Grand Rapids, MI: Baker Academic, 2006), 314–15.

82. See Crowe, *Last Adam*, chap. 3. See also Vos, *Biblical Theology*, 320–21; Sinclair B. Ferguson, *The Holy Spirit*, Contours of Christian Theology (Downers Grove, IL: InterVarsity Press, 1996), 48; cf. Ernest Best, *The Temptation and the Passion: The Markan Soteriology*, rev. ed., SNTSMS 2 (Cambridge: Cambridge University Press, 1990), 15.

83. Calvin, *Institutes*, 3.20.46. Calvin goes on to note our need to be filled with God's Spirit to withstand the Devil. I would concur, but here I am focusing on the need for Christ to fight the Devil on our behalf. Cf. Eph. 6:10; Col. 1:13; Quarles, *Sermon on the Mount*, 220–21. Also note WLC, 195, where we pray in the sixth petition that Satan may be "trodden under our feet," which presupposes the work of Christ, who crushes the head of the Serpent (cf. Rom. 16:20).

84. Cf. Lohmeyer, *"Our Father,"* 208: "We might therefore paraphrase the [temptation] petition: 'so that we may enter thy kingdom, do not make us enter the kingdom of temptation.'" See also 225: "The existence and imminence of the kingdom of God is mirrored in the existence of the kingdom of Satan."

indeed; the goal is nothing less than final entrance into the eschatological kingdom of God. Yet the sixth petition not only envisions a final, climactic temptation, but must also include more mundane, daily temptations that may threaten to lure us into spiritual atrophy and hinder us from reaching our eschatological goal.

This is why we must be careful to relate an eschatological interpretation (broadly conceived) to everyday life in the sixth petition. There are those who say that the sixth petition has nothing to do with the peccadillos of daily living, but instead has in view the great end-time trial that could lead to apostasy.[85] However, such a view threatens to miss the continuity of the consummation of the kingdom with the real presence of the kingdom now. Put simply, there are no "trivial" sins in the already present eschatological kingdom. Because all sins potentially lead to apostasy, the stakes are eschatologically consequential.[86] Though no true apostasy is possible for those who are united by faith to Jesus Christ, the warnings to persevere are particularly relevant for the community of God's people, whose hearts may become callous to the Word of God (cf. Heb. 3:12–13). As James exhorts us: desire brings forth sin, and sin leads to death (James 1:15). We therefore must pray to be kept from sin, and trust in the One who has proved obedient on our behalf. At the end of the Lord's Prayer we are therefore reminded clearly of the Savior, who keeps us from evil[87] and who is presupposed in the entire prayer.

Conclusion[88]

It is sometimes noted that the Lord's Prayer might better be labeled "the disciples' prayer," since Jesus does not pray this prayer for himself. There is much correct about this view, though the traditional terminology does accurately communicate that Jesus *taught* this prayer.[89] Yet, since Jesus taught his *disciples* to pray this prayer, it is perhaps

---

85. See Wright, *The Lord and His Prayer*, 67; Lohmeyer, *"Our Father,"* 195, 204; Jeremias, *Lord's Prayer*, 30; Brown, "Pater Noster," 205; Davies and Allison, *Matthew*, 1:614.

86. See Simon J. Kistemaker, "The Lord's Prayer in the First Century," *JETS* 21, no. 4 (1978): 326; Guelich, *Sermon on the Mount*, 314; see also Bavinck, *Sin and Salvation in Christ*, 154.

87. See John 17:12–15 with 1 John 5:18; cf. 2 Thess. 3:2–3.

88. Given the constraints of this essay, I am not able to address the traditional liturgical ending of the Lord's Prayer.

89. So Ferguson, *Sermon on the Mount*, 121.

not surprising that the prayer encourages us to remember Christ as our Mediator. Indeed, Jesus focuses on his own mediatorial role in the intimate prayer he prays in Matthew 11:25–27.[90] It is therefore fitting that Jesus likewise features prominently in the model prayer for his disciples. Though the Lord's Prayer may evince many commonalities with traditional Jewish prayers,[91] the Lord's Prayer is distinctively Christian.[92] Christ not only teaches this prayer; he is the presupposition for the prayer.

Augustine believed we should pray the Lord's Prayer daily (*The City of God* 21.27); the Didache encourages its audience to pray the Lord's Prayer three times each day (8:3).[93] However often we pray this prayer—and we should pray it often—we do well to think not only of our own needs, but also of Christ, who gave us the prayer and provides access to the Father. In short, as often as we pray the Lord's Prayer, we do well to remember the Lord Jesus himself until he comes.

---

90. As Vos avers: "Jesus' joy and thanksgiving do not relate to something taking place outside of Himself. . . . Jesus thanks God because His own Person is the pivot, the center of the whole transaction. The glory of the Gospel dispensation with its sovereignty and wisdom is focused in His own Person." See Geerhardus Vos, *The Self-Disclosure of Jesus: The Modern Debate about the Messianic Consciousness*, ed. J. G. Vos, 2nd ed. (Grand Rapids, MI: Eerdmans, 1953; repr., Phillipsburg, NJ: P&R, 2002), 147.

91. Most notably the Kaddish. See, e.g., Quarles, *Sermon on the Mount*, 191.

92. See also Brown, "Pater Noster," 180–81.

93. See Luz, *Matthew 1–7*, 312–13.

6

Psalms Applied to Both Christ and Christians

Psalms 8, 22, 34, 118 and
Romans 15:3 // Psalm 69:9

R O B E R T J. C A R A

When a Christian reads or sings a psalm, should he apply the psalm to Christ or to himself? For example,

> Blessed is everyone who fears the LORD,
>   who walks in his ways! (Ps. 128:1)

Did God intend that the reader of this passage would conclude that it refers to Christ, who perfectly walked in the way of the Lord (Luke 24:44; Heb. 9:14) or that it refers to any Christian who walks by the Spirit (Gal. 5:16), or both?

It is now typical in the conservative Reformed tradition to emphasize that every psalm is Christological. The Reformed tradition has used a variety of arguments to make this point; however, not all agree with all of the arguments.[1] I fully affirm that all psalms are Christological, and this truth wonderfully aids our spiritual growth as we read the Psalms.

Also included currently in the conservative Reformed tradition is that every psalm relates to *both* Christ and Christians. Again, not all the arguments for this "both" view are agreed upon.[2] This "both" view probably receives less emphasis in the literature than the Christological emphasis. The emphasis on the Christological reading is understandable, given that many already assume that the Psalms are from a believer's perspective. Unfortunately, in Reformed practice, there are some who tend to be "Christological only" and others "Christians only," even though in principle they are "both-and."

To put a finer point on my view, I believe that every psalm in *some sense* refers to *both* Christ and Christians. I see some psalms as primarily about Christ and secondarily about believers; and other psalms, conversely, I see as primarily about believers and secondarily about Christ. Why do I conclude that Christ and believers are related to every

---

1. For a very good nuanced discussion of the variety of ways that Christ is part of the meaning for every psalm, see Richard P. Belcher Jr., *The Messiah and the Psalms: Preaching Christ from All the Psalms* (Fearn, Ross-shire, Scotland: Mentor, 2001). Concerning when the psalmist confesses sins (e.g., Psalm 51), Belcher argues that "in being 'answerable for our guilt' Christ vicariously confessed and repented in our behalf" (87). Mark D. Futato has interesting comments as to how the variety of genres of psalms aids us in understanding the Christological interpretations of psalms. Also he argues that the book of Psalms as a whole, in its movement from lament to praise, reflects Christ's humiliation and exaltation ("Psalms," in *A Biblical-Theological Introduction to the Old Testament: The Gospel Promised*, ed. Miles V. Van Pelt [Wheaton, IL: Crossway, 2016], 341–55). Although he overstates the case to some degree, Michael LeFebvre argues that all the psalms are the "songs of Jesus, with Jesus as your songleader" (*Singing the Songs of Jesus: Revisiting the Psalms* [Fearn, Ross-shire, Scotland: Christian Focus, 2010], 50). Bruce K. Waltke believes that the editing process of the Psalter "resignified" every psalm to point toward a future Messiah (*An Old Testament Theology: An Exegetical, Canonical, and Thematic Approach* [Grand Rapids, MI: Zondervan, 2007], 889–90). Not all fellow evangelicals agree; e.g., Walter C. Kaiser Jr. sees only thirteen psalms as messianic (*The Messiah in the Old Testament* [Grand Rapids, MI: Zondervan, 1995], 93–94). Critical scholars often see some level of messianic hope through the royal psalms, e.g., Brevard S. Childs, *Introduction to the Old Testament as Scripture* (Philadelphia: Fortress, 1979), 517.

2. Poythress argues that once individual psalms are put into the book of Psalms, they attain a "general applicability," and the psalms "apply not only to us but also to Christ, as fully human and representative for his people" (*Reading the Word of God in the Presence of God: A Handbook for Biblical Interpretation* [Wheaton, IL: Crossway, 2016], 234). Futato concludes that "once we see the book of Psalms is a portrait of the life of Christ, we can then see a portrait of our own lives in this book" ("Psalms," 345). Waltke notes that the introductory Psalms 1–2 with their emphasis on believers (Psalm 1) and the king (Psalm 2), along with the New Testament, prepare the reader "to interpret the psalms with respect to both the king and to themselves as individuals within his kingdom" (*An Old Testament Theology*, 885). Raymond B. Dillard and Tremper Longman III recommend Edmund P. Clowney's idea that the Psalms are both "prayers of Jesus (Heb. 2:12) and prayers to Jesus" (*An Introduction to the Old Testament* [Grand Rapids, MI: Zondervan, 1994], 234).

psalm? There are a variety of good arguments for this, but I want to emphasize just one of them: *The New Testament writers sometimes use the same psalm to refer to both Christ and Christians.* Since I consider the Bible an infallible hermeneutical guide, this is a strong argument that not only *these* psalms but *all* psalms are intended by God to be interpreted this way.[3]

Hence, the intention of this chapter is to emphasize just one of the many arguments to confirm that every psalm applies to both Christ and Christians. To do this, I will evaluate four psalms that are quoted by New Testament writers and applied to Christ while, in other locations, applied to believers. Then I will consider Paul's quote of Psalm 69:9 in Romans 15:3.[4] In this one New Testament verse, Christ and Christians are both included. Paul interprets Psalm 69:9 Christologically but then uses it as an example and motivation for Christians. To summarize, my overarching thesis is that *all psalms in some sense refer to both Christ and Christians*; however, in this article I will present only a truncated argument for this, which is that *the New Testament clearly uses some psalms to refer to both Christ and Christians, and Romans 15:3 (quoting Ps. 69:9) functionally does this also.*

Psalms 34, 118, 8, 22

Obviously, some psalms quoted in the New Testament refer to Christ (e.g., Ps. 110:1 // Heb. 1:13), and other quoted psalms are applied to believers (Ps. 112:9 // 2 Cor. 9:9).[5] But are there examples of a psalm quoted by a New Testament writer and applied to Christ while the same or a different New Testament writer applies the same psalm, though a different verse, to believers? In other words, is the same psalm considered from both a Christological perspective and a believer perspective, even though the exact same verse is not explicitly used for both Christ

---

3. For a broad-brush justification of using the Bible as an infallible guide for our hermeneutics in the context of typology, see Robert J. Cara, "The Use of the New Testament in the Old Testament: Trusting the New Testament's Hermeneutics," in *A Biblical-Theological Introduction to the New Testament: The Gospel Revealed*, ed. Michael J. Kruger (Wheaton, IL: Crossway, 2016), 593–602.

4. All psalm citations are from the English Bible chapter and verse notation unless explicitly noted.

5. Related to the believer category, there are also quotes that use psalms to prove that Gentiles did and would glorify God (e.g., Ps. 117:1 // Rom. 15:11). In addition, there is the question of the believer as an individual or believers as a community. This distinction does not affect the argument of this article.

and the believer? Yes, there are examples. I am going to argue that there are two clear examples, Psalms 34 and 118. In addition, there are two other, less clear examples, Psalms 8 and 22. For now, I will bracket out Psalm 69.

Of course, the definition of a quotation as opposed to an allusion or echo is fuzzy at the edges. I will simply use the quotations listed in the NA[28].[6] There are 150 psalms, and of these, at least one verse of forty-five psalms is quoted in the New Testament.[7] To get a sense of proportion of the four examples, one needs to know how many of the forty-five psalms are actually quoted twice in the New Testament. I want to filter out situations where (1) the same psalm verse is quoted in the same New Testament book with the same point (Psalms 16, 95, 146) and (2) the same psalm verse is quoted in Synoptic Gospel situations (Psalms 42, 43, 91). Given this filter and using the NA[28], there are eleven examples of the same psalm being quoted in more than one location in the New Testament (Psalms 2, 6, 8, 22, 34, 62, 69, 78, 94, 110, 118). (The UBS[5] only has six examples.[8]) This sample size of eleven is reasonable. Eleven psalms quoted at least twice in the New Testament have the possibility of evidencing that the same psalm can be applied to both Christ and believers. Of these eleven possibilities, four of them do evidence this (again, I am bracketing out Ps. 69:9 // Rom. 15:3 for the moment). My statistical point is strengthened if the UBS[5] is considered.

PSALM 34

The superscription of Psalm 34 refers to David's acting insane before Achish's men (1 Sam. 21:10–15).[9] The psalm is in acrostic form (missing a ו but adding a second פ). David thanks the Lord for rescuing him from troubles (Ps. 34:1–7), encourages believers toward wisdom and

---

6. The NA[28] quotation list is very similar to the one in the UBS[5]. When these two disagree in the Psalms, the NA[28] is more apt to consider the New Testament using a quotation.

7. Forty-five according to NA[28] and forty-one according to UBS[5].

8. For the UBS[5], Psalms 6, 42, 43, 62, 94 are not considered to be quoted twice in the New Testament.

9. I take the psalm superscriptions as part of Scripture. This superscription's use of Abimelech as opposed to Achish is explained as "Abimelech" (אבימלך, "my father the king") is used as a title for Achish. So also, William S. Plumer, *Psalms: A Critical and Expository Commentary with Doctrinal and Practical Remarks*, Geneva (1867; repr., Carlisle, PA: Banner of Truth, 1975), 417.

righteousness (Ps. 34:8–14), and reminds righteous sufferers that God cares for them (Ps. 34:15–22).

Psalm 34 is quoted three times in the New Testament. I conclude that two of the quotes are applied to believers and one to Christ.

- Psalm 34:8a: "Oh, taste and see that the Lord is good!" (quoted in 1 Pet. 2:3 and applied to believers).
- Psalm 34:12–16a: "What man is there who desires life. / ... The face of the Lord is against those who do evil" (quoted in 1 Pet. 3:10–12 and applied to believers).
- Psalm 34:20b: "Not one of them [bones] is broken" (quoted in John 19:36 and applied to Christ).

All agree with me that the two Peter quotes above refer to believers.[10] Concerning Psalm 34:20 // John 19:36, all agree that if John is referring to Psalm 34:20, then obviously it refers to Christ. It is noted that the same language as Psalm 34:20 is used in Exodus 12:10 (LXX only), 12:46, and Numbers 9:12 to refer to the Passover lamb. From my perspective, the Passover-lamb passages would be part of John's background understanding of the righteous sufferer in Psalm 34. The vast majority of scholars agree that John is referring to either only Psalm 34:20 or the Passover-lamb passages with Psalm 34:20.[11] A small minority believe, obviously, that John is referring to Christ, but they are hesitant to conclude that John is referring to Psalm 34:20 as opposed to the Passover-lamb passages. But even this small minority usually agree that at some level John is reading Psalm 34:20 as Christological.[12]

---

10. E.g., D. A. Carson, "1 Peter," in *Commentary on the New Testament Use of the Old Testament*, ed. G. K. Beale and D. A. Carson (Grand Rapids, MI: Baker, 2007), 1015–45, esp. 1023, 1036–37; and Paul J. Achtemeier, *A Commentary on First Peter*, Hermeneia (Minneapolis: Fortress, 1996), 147–48, 225–27.

11. E.g., Andreas J. Köstenberger, *John*, BECNT (Grand Rapids, MI: Baker, 2004), 553–54; Ernst Haenchen, *A Commentary on the Gospel of John Chapters 7–21*, Hermeneia (Philadelphia: Fortress, 1984), 195–96; and Herman N. Ridderbos, *The Gospel according to John: A Theological Commentary*, trans. John Vriend (Grand Rapids, MI: Eerdmans, 1997), 622–23.

12. C. K. Barrett sees it as "probable" that John's reference is "primar[ily]" to the Passover lamb, but he was also "influenced" by Ps. 34:20 (*The Gospel according to St. John: An Introduction with Commentary and Notes on the Greek Text*, 2nd ed. [Philadelphia: Westminster, 1978], 558). In Augustine's discussion of John 19:36, he implies that John is referring to the Passover lamb and does not mention Ps. 34:20 ("Tractate 120," in *Gospel of St. John* [NPNF¹, 7:435]). However, in his discussion of Ps. 34:20, Augustine connects this both to Christians and to Christ ("Psalm 34," in *Psalms* [NPNF¹, 8:78]).

Psalm 118

The context of Psalm 118 is an individual speaker who leads the congregation in thanksgiving for God's deliverance of him from enemies (118:1–5). I take the speaker to be a king who has won a military victory against his foreign enemies (118:10) and also had to deal with internal strife (118:22).[13] Psalm 118 is part of the "Egyptian Hallel" (Psalms 113–18) and is sung as part of the Passover liturgy.[14]

Psalm 118 is quoted numerous times in the New Testament. Except for one quotation, all are applied to Christ.

- Psalm 118:6: "The LORD is on my side; I will not fear. / What can man do to me?" (quoted in Heb. 13:6 and applied to believers).
- Psalm 118:22: "The stone that the builders rejected / has become the cornerstone" (quoted in Luke 20:17; Acts 4:11; 1 Pet. 2:7 and applied to Christ).
- Psalm 118:22–23: "The stone. . . . / This is the LORD's doing; / it is marvelous in our eyes" (quoted in Matt. 21:42; Mark 12:10–11 and applied to Christ).
- Psalm 118:25–26: "Save us, we pray. . . . / Blessed is he who comes in the name of the LORD!" (quoted in Matt. 21:9; Mark 11:9–10; John 12:13 and applied to Christ).
- Psalm 118:26: "Blessed is he who comes in the name of the LORD!" (quoted in Matt. 23:39; Luke 13:35; 19:38 and applied to Christ).

There is no debate in the literature concerning to whom these verses are applied. Hence, it is clear that the New Testament includes applications of Psalm 118 to both Christ and Christians.

---

13. Tremper Longman III more or less agrees: "It is possible, but not necessary, to think of the psalmist as the king or head of the army" (*Psalms: An Introduction and Commentary*, TOTC 15–16 [Downers Grove, IL: IVP Academic, 2014], 399). Artur Weiser sees Ps. 118:5–21 as a thanksgiving, "presumably" by a king; verses 22–25 are by a "choir of pilgrims," verses 26–27 are a priestly blessing, and verse 28 is the king giving a "personal word of thanks" (*The Psalms*, Old Testament Library [Philadelphia: Westminster, 1962], 724). Belcher argues that the main speaker is either a king or a priest leading the group to remember a messianic prophecy (Isa. 28:16 with Ps. 118:22) or remember the exodus event (*The Messiah and the Psalms*, 186–93). Interestingly, t. Pesahim 119a records that Rabbi Samuel bar Nahmani sees Ps. 118:21–28 rotating through various speakers: David, Jesse, Samuel, Samuel's brothers, and "all of them."

14. See Num. 10:10; Matt. 26:30; m. Pesahim 5:7; 10:6–7; t. Pesahim 10:6–9. Psalm 118 is also connected to the Feast of Tabernacles in Rabbinic literature; see m. Sukkah 3:9; 4:8; 5:1–4.

Since the Psalm 118:6 // Hebrews 13:6 quotation is the only one from Psalm 118 applied to believers, a word or two are in order. The author of Hebrews, after quoting from Joshua 1:5, states,

So we can confidently say,

> "The Lord is my helper;
>   I will not fear;
> what can man do to me?" (quoting from Ps. 118:6)

The Hebrews 13:6 quote itself follows the LXX (Ps. 117:6) virtually word for word.[15] The LXX follows closely to the Hebrew text.[16] In the context of Hebrews 13, the author is giving various exhortations, including not to love money but to be content, even in difficult times of persecution. At this point, the author quotes Joshua 1:5 and Psalm 118:6 to engender assurance and joy that God will be with his people and both aid them spiritually and bring them through physical difficulties and distress caused by adversaries of God's people.[17] Note that the author explicitly says that "we" may quote (ἡμᾶς λέγειν) Psalm 118:6, and we may use the "I" of the psalm, which at this point in Psalm 118 is the (kingly) speaker.

PSALM 8

On the surface, David in Psalm 8 extols God as Creator and King over his foes (8:1–2). Then, given this majestic God, David ponders why God would be concerned with man (8:3–4). In fact, God has given man some level of dominion (8:5–8). Psalm 8 ends in verse 9 with a repeat of verse 1, stating that God is majestic.

The New Testament clearly connects Psalm 8 to Christ.[18] Does the

---

15. The only exception is that Heb. 13:6 adds a καί to connect the two clauses. Some manuscripts do not include this καί.

16. The only substantive difference is that the Hebrew has יהוה לי ("Yahweh is to me" or "Yahweh is for me" or "Yahweh is on my side," and the LXX correctly interprets this as κύριος ἐμοὶ βοηθός ("The Lord is to me a helper").

17. George H. Guthrie, "Hebrews," in Beale and Carson, *Commentary on the New Testament Use of the Old Testament*, 919–95, esp. 991–92; Philip Edgcumbe Hughes, *A Commentary on the Epistle to the Hebrews* (Grand Rapids, MI: Eerdmans, 1977), 567–68; and Craig R. Koester, *Hebrews: A New Translation with Introduction and Commentary*, AB 36 (New York: Doubleday, 2001), 566.

18. Willem A. VanGemeren notes, "Though the psalm is not messianic in the narrow sense, it has a messianic application in that Jesus is fully man and has realized God's expectation of man in

New Testament also connect it to believers? I will answer yes based on Psalm 8:2 // Matt. 21:16:

- Psalm 8:2: "Out of the mouth of babies and infants, / you have established strength because of your foes [praise]" (quoted in Matt. 21:16 and applied to believers).
- Psalm 8:4–6: "What is man that you are mindful of him. / . . . you have put all things under his feet" (quoted in Heb. 2:6–8 and applied to Christ).
- Psalm 8:6: "You have put all things under his feet" (quoted in 1 Cor. 15:27; Eph. 1:22 and applied to Christ).

All agree that Psalm 8:6 is connected to Christ in 1 Corinthians 15:27 and Ephesians 1:22.[19] The vast majority agree that the author of Hebrews sees Psalm 8:4–6 as Christological in Hebrews 2:6–8,[20] although some interpret it anthropologically and do not see Christ in reference until Hebrews 2:9.[21] I conclude that Psalm 8:4–6 is Christological in Hebrews 2:6–8.[22] If I grant that Psalm 8 is interpreted anthropologically by the author of Hebrews, which I do not, this would actually strengthen my argument because this would be an example of Psalm 8 applied to believers that would contrast with 1 Corinthians 15:27 and Ephesians 1:22, which are clear examples of Christological interpretations. I would not have to rely on Matthew 21:16 for the believer's perspective.

---

perfect obedience and holiness" ("Psalms," in *Psalms, Proverbs, Ecclesiastes, Song of Songs*, ed. Frank E. Gaebelein et al., EBC 5 [Grand Rapids, MI: Zondervan, 1991], 1–880, esp. 110). Belcher adds other connections: Jesus "is the Creator (John 1) and his name is superior to all other names (Phil. 2:9–10)" (*The Messiah and the Psalms*, 161). Guthrie states, "The divine commission of Adam as King over God's creation ultimately has been fulfilled in Christ, the eschatological last Adam" ("Hebrews," 946).

19. E.g., Anthony C. Thiselton, *The First Epistle to the Corinthians: A Commentary on the Greek Text*, NIGTC (Grand Rapids, MI: Eerdmans, 2000), 1235; and Andrew T. Lincoln, *Ephesians*, WBC 42 (Dallas: Word, 1990), 65–66.

20. E.g., Guthrie, "Hebrews," 946; Simon Kistemaker, *The Psalm Citations in the Epistle to the Hebrews* (1961; repr., Eugene, OR: Wipf & Stock, 2010), 102–8; William L. Lane, *Hebrews 1–8*, WBC 47a (Dallas: Word, 1991), 45–47; and Harold W. Attridge, *A Commentary on the Epistle to the Hebrews*, Hermeneia (Philadelphia: Fortress, 1989), 69–73.

21. E.g., John Brown, *Hebrews*, Geneva (1862; repr., Carlisle, PA: Banner of Truth, 1961), 97–98; and Peter T. O'Brien, *The Letter to the Hebrews*, PNTC (Grand Rapids, MI: Eerdmans, 2010), 96. Although not holding this view, Paul Ellingsworth well summarizes the arguments for it (*The Epistle to the Hebrews: A Commentary on the Greek Text*, NIGTC [Grand Rapids, MI: Eerdmans, 1993], 149–50).

22. One key argument is that Psalm 110 and Psalm 8 are combined in 1 Cor. 15:24–27; Eph. 1:20–22; and Heb. 1:13–2:8.

In Matthew 21:14–17,[23] while in the temple, Jesus heals and children cry, "Hosanna to the Son of David!" This annoys the Jewish rulers, and they question Jesus about the children's comments. Jesus responds by quoting Psalm 8:2:

> Yes; have you never read,
>
> > "Out of the mouth of infants and nursing babies
> > you have prepared praise"? (Matt. 21:16)[24]

The pericope does not record the response, and Jesus goes out of the city to Bethany for the night.

By the quote, Jesus indicates that children properly praise and some leaders do not. And in fact, the Psalm 8:2 context is children praising *God*, and Jesus connects this to praise of himself as the (divine) Christ.[25] Obviously, Jesus takes Psalm 8:2 to be Christological in the sense that the praising includes praising Jesus. However, in addition to this Christological sense, Jesus clearly connects the speaking of the "infants" in Psalm 8:2 to the "children" in Matthew 21:15. This confirms that Psalm 8 also refers to believers. Therefore, a believer today is to read Psalm 8:2 and conclude that he or she should praise God/Christ. In sum, Psalm 8:2 has both a Christological and a believer perspective. More fundamentally, it is applied to believers, but part of the application is that believers should praise Christ!

In sum, Psalm 8 is an example of a psalm that is applied to Christ (Ps. 8:4–6) *and* to believers (Ps. 8:2). Admittedly, this example of a "both–and" is not as clear as Psalms 34 and 118, but it is fairly clear.

---

23. This pericope is unique to Matthew.

24. The Hebrews quote matches the LXX exactly. The LXX differs from the Hebrew in only one word; עֹז ("strength") is replaced by αἶνος ("praise"). Derek Kidner explains that the LXX paraphrased to show that the strength was an "audible bulwark" (*Psalms 1–72: An Introduction and Commentary on Books I and II of the Psalms*, TOTC 15 [Downers Grove, IL: InterVarsity Press, 1973], 67n1). Also see Ex. 15:2.

25. Seeing this also as a veiled connection to the divine Messiah is William Hendriksen, *Exposition of the Gospel according to Matthew*, New Testament Commentary (Grand Rapids, MI: Baker, 1973), 772. W. D. Davies and Dale C. Allison Jr. see the messianic connection through links between Psalm 8 and Exodus 15; this in turn connects the exodus and the Christ event (*A Critical and Exegetical Commentary on the Gospel according to Saint Matthew*, 3 vols. [Edinburgh: T&T Clark, 1988–97], 3:142). Surprisingly, D. A. Carson does not see the use of Psalm 8 in the New Testament as messianic. The use of Ps. 8:2 is simply to confirm that the "humble perceive spiritual truths more readily than the sophisticated" ("Matthew," in *Matthew, Mark, Luke*, ed. Frank E. Gaebelein et al., EBC 8 [Grand Rapids, MI: Zondervan, 1984], 1–599, esp. 443).

Psalm 22

Psalm 22 includes two movements. The first, verses 1–21, is an individual lament, and the second, verses 22–31, includes praise and thanksgiving. David's lament is related to his feeling abandoned by God as enemies attack. As is typical of most psalms, there are no specific historical details. If one wants to connect this to David's life, there are many historical occasions to chose from, especially when he is pursued by Saul.[26]

As all agree, the New Testament writers clearly see Psalm 22 as Christological. In fact, Jesus applies 22:1 to himself while on the cross (Matt. 27:46). The question for our study is whether 1 Peter 5:8 is quoting Psalm 22:13. If it is, this is another example of a psalm being applied to believers. However, before I answer, below is my summary of the use of Psalm 22 in the New Testament.

- Psalm 22:1: "My God, my God, why have you forsaken me?" (quoted in Matt. 27:46; Mark 15:34 and applied to Christ).
- Psalm 22:8: "He trusts in the LORD; let him deliver him; / . . . for he delights in him!" (quoted in Matt. 27:43 and applied to Christ).
- Psalm 22:13b: "Like a ravening and roaring lion" (quoted in 1 Pet. 5:8 and applied to believers).
- Psalm 22:18: "They divide my garments among them, / and for my clothing they cast lots" (quoted in Matt. 27:35; Mark 15:24; Luke 23:34; John 19:24 and applied to Christ).
- Psalm 22:22: "I will tell of your name to my brothers; / in the midst of the congregation I will praise you" (quoted in Heb. 2:12 and applied to Christ).

For our purposes, 1 Peter 5:8 is the focus. First Peter 5:6–11 is a unit that comforts the believer in the midst of suffering. A significant aspect of that comfort is realizing God is in control (5:6), cares for his own (5:7), and calls them to eternal glory (5:10). Also included is the knowledge that other believers are suffering (5:9). First Peter elsewhere connects Christ's sufferings to believers' sufferings (e.g., 1 Pet. 2:21; 3:17–18; 4:1, 12–13).

---

26. So also Longman, *Psalms*, 128. Theodore of Mopsuestia connects Psalm 22 to David's sin of adultery (Robert C. Hill, *Theodore of Mopsuestia: Commentary on Psalms 1–81: Translated with an Introduction and Notes* [Atlanta: SBL, 2006], 241).

Given the current difficulties, Peter exhorts his readers to "be sober-minded; be watchful. Your adversary the devil prowls around *like a roaring lion*, seeking someone to devour" (1 Pet. 5:8). Except for the omission of "ravening," "like a roaring lion" matches the wording of Psalm 22:13.[27] In Psalm 22:12–13, the enemies of David/Christ are compared to bulls that have mouths "like a ravening and roaring lion," or the lion is a separate enemy (Ps. 22:22). Lion imagery is frequent in the Old Testament, but the exact wording that Peter uses is found only in Psalm 22:13. All agree that at least at the word level for this lion imagery, Peter is using Psalm 22:13.[28] Obviously, Peter is applying Psalm 22:13 to believers at least at the imagery level, as the lion is threatening them amid their suffering.

As noted above, the key here is whether 1 Peter 5:8 is intentionally interpreting Psalm 22:13 or simply using the lion imagery from this psalm. NA[28] lists it as a quotation, and UBS[5] does not. Carson agrees that "if Peter is self-consciously alluding to any one passage, it must be [Ps. 22:13]." However, he believes that "it is not obvious that Peter is attempting any other associative transfer" than a "colorful metaphor."[29] As opposed to Carson, I do see Peter as intentionally referring to or interpreting Psalm 22:13 and applying it to believers. I base this on (1) the connections in 1 Peter between Christ's sufferings and Christians' sufferings, (2) the tendency of New Testament writers to see the Psalms as referring both to Christ and believers, and (3) the Devil is an enemy of both Christ and believers. However, I am not exegetically certain of my conclusion.

Summary of Psalms 34, 118, 8, 22

Does God intend that the Psalms apply to both Christ and believers? One aspect of the overall argument would be to determine the New Testament writers' use of particular psalms when they are quoted at

---

27. The Hebrew and LXX match: אריה טרף ושאג, ὡς λέων ὁ ἁρπάζων καὶ ὠρυόμενος. Peter takes out "ravening," but everything else is the same: ὡς λέων ὠρυόμενος. Ezek. 22:25 has similar language, although the LXX has the plural: ὡς λέοντες ὠρυόμενοι ἁρπάζοντες.
28. E.g., J. N. D. Kelly, *The Epistles of Peter and Jude*, Black's New Testament Commentary (Peabody, MA: Hendrickson, 1969), 210; Leonhard Goppelt, *A Commentary on 1 Peter*, ed. Ferdinand Hahn, trans. John E. Alsup (Grand Rapids, MI: Eerdmans, 1993), 360n11; J. Ramsey Michaels, *1 Peter*, WBC 49 (Waco, TX: Word, 1988), 298; and Peter H. Davids, *The First Epistle of Peter*, NICNT (Grand Rapids, MI: Eerdmans, 1990), 190.
29. Carson, "First Peter," 1044.

least twice in the New Testament. There are only eleven psalms that are quoted more than once in the New Testament (Psalm 69 is bracketed out for the moment). Of these, I conclude that four different psalms are applied by New Testament writers to both Christ and believers within the same psalm. I conclude that Psalms 34 and 118 are clearly applied to both Christ and believers. I further conclude that Psalms 8 and 22 also are applied to both Christ and believers; however, (1) Psalm 8 is a fairly clear example, although not as clear as Psalms 34 and 118, and (2) Psalm 22 is not clear, as it depends on 1 Peter 5:8 being an intentional interpretation of Psalm 22:13, which I believe it is, though I admit that my conclusion does not have exegetical certainty.

Romans 15:3 // Psalm 69:9

I have separated Psalm 69 from the other four psalms because, from my perspective, all of the New Testament quotations from Psalm 69 are directly applied either to Christ or to his enemies. That is, no quotation is applied directly to believers. However, it is Paul's use of his Christological interpretation of Psalm 69:9 in Romans 15:1–3 that is intriguing and pertains to this study.

This psalm by David begins with a long individual lament because of his enemies (Ps. 69:1–21). Then he asks God to give his enemies the justice they deserve (imprecatory petition[30]—69:22–29). Finally, David moves toward praise as he considers God's redemption of him and the community (69:30–36).[31]

Below are the New Testament quotations related to Psalm 69. Note that all of them relate to Christ or his enemies:

- Psalm 69:4: "Who hate me without cause"[32] (quoted in John 15:25 and applied to Christ's enemies).
- Psalm 69:9a: "For zeal for your house has consumed me" (quoted in John 2:17 and applied to Christ).

---

30. For a defense of imprecatory psalms, see Johannes G. Vos, "The Ethical Problem of the Imprecatory Psalms," *WTJ* 4, no. 2 (1942): 123–38; and James E. Adams, *War Psalms of the Prince of Peace: Lessons from the Imprecatory Psalms* (Phillipsburg, NJ: Presbyterian and Reformed, 1991).

31. Frank-Lothar Hossfeld and Erich Zenger also agree to the threefold structure of "lament-petition-praise," although, they divide it differently: lament (69:1–13b), petition (69:13c–29), and praise (69:30–36) (*A Commentary on Psalms 51–100: Translated and Interpreted*, trans. Linda M. Maloney, Hermeneia [Minneapolis: Fortress, 2005], 172–73).

32. See similar wording in Ps. 35:19.

- Psalm 69:9b: "The reproaches of those who reproach you have fallen on me" (quoted in Rom. 15:3 and applied to Christ).
- Psalm 69:22–23: "Let their own table before them become a snare. / . . . and make their loins tremble continually" (quoted in Rom. 11:9–10 and applied to portions of Israel as Christ's enemies because they stumble over the stumbling block).
- Psalm 69:25: "May their camp be a desolation; / let no one dwell in their tents" (quoted in Acts 1:20 and applied to Christ's enemy, Judas).

Romans 15:1–3 is part of the larger unit of Romans 14:1–15:13, which deals with the "weak" and the "strong."

We who are strong have an obligation to bear with the failings of the weak, and not to please ourselves. Let each of us please his neighbor for his good, to build him up. For Christ did not please himself, but as it is written, "The reproaches of those who reproached you fell on me." (15:1–3)

In a certain sense, Romans 15:1–2 is simply restating in stronger terms what Paul has already said in Romans 14.[33] The ethic for all Christians, but especially the "strong," is not to please themselves. As opposed to a pleasing-yourself-only ethic, Christians are to please their Christian neighbors for their good.[34] Then in Romans 15:3, Paul holds up Christ as an example and motive for Christians not to please themselves.[35] To prove that Christ did not please himself, Paul quotes Psalm 69:9b.[36]

---

33. So also Richard N. Longenecker, *The Epistle to the Romans: A Commentary on the Greek Text*, NIGTC (Grand Rapids, MI: Eerdmans, 2016), 1012.

34. Paul is alluding back to Rom. 13:9–10. Though not everywhere in the Bible, here in Rom. 15:2 "neighbor" (πλησίον) is restricted to believers. So also, e.g., Douglas J. Moo, *The Epistle to the Romans*, NICNT (Grand Rapids, MI: Eerdmans, 1996), 867n16; and Joseph A. Fitzmyer, *Romans: A New Translation with Introduction and Commentary*, AB 33 (New York: Doubleday, 1993), 702.

35. Charles Hodge alerted me to the "motive" aspect: "The example of Christ is constantly held up, not merely as a model, but as a motive" (*A Commentary on Romans*, Geneva [1864; repr., Carlisle, PA: Banner of Truth, 1972], 433). Also note that Paul again uses Christ as an example in Rom. 15:7. In Rom. 15:5 and 15:13, Paul connects the attributes of God to the attributes of a Christian (communicable attributes).

36. Hebrew, וחרפות חורפיך נפלו עלי; LXX, καὶ οἱ ὀνειδισμοὶ τῶν ὀνειδιζόντων σε ἐπέπεσαν ἐπ' ἐμέ; Rom. 15:3, οἱ ὀνειδισμοὶ τῶν ὀνειδιζόντων σε ἐπέπεσαν ἐπ' ἐμέ. Concerning the linguistic technicalities of the quotation, the LXX is a mechanical translation of the Hebrew of Ps. 69:9, and Rom. 15:3 is an exact match to the LXX (excepting the "and" [καί] that connects Ps. 69:9a to 69:9b). That is, this quotation is as straightforward as possible.

In Paul's reading of Psalm 69:9, Christ is the speaker of the psalm, since Paul interprets the "you" as God the Father and the "me" as Christ.[37] Paul sees that Christ's love for God the Father was such that those who were truly "reproaching" the Father were also "reproaching" him. That is, if Christ had not loved the Father and had only cared about himself, he would have avoided suffering and would not have cared about others. Hence, Christ did not have a pleasing-yourself-only ethic. Although Paul does not explicitly say, most likely he views the "reproaches" that "fell upon" Christ as culminating in the crucifixion.[38]

Now to the point of this essay, hermeneutically speaking: Paul interprets Psalm 69 Christologically, but then, having offered that interpretation, he uses Christ's actions from Psalm 69 as an example (and motive) for believers.[39] *Hence, functionally, Paul is using Psalm 69 to apply to both Christ and believers.*

Summary and Conclusion

The book of Psalms is amazing. The ultimate author, God, has so designed the book that every psalm in some sense refers both to Christ and to Christians. Currently, the conservative Reformed tradition is fairly united on this view and has a variety of biblical arguments to justify it. Admittedly, not all agree to all the arguments.

I have concentrated on only one of the many arguments. Of the forty-five psalms quoted in the New Testament, only eleven are quoted more than once so as to have the possibility of evidencing that the same psalm could be applied to both Christ and believers. Of these

---

37. Virtually all agree to this. To the contrary, W. Sanday and A. C. Headlam argued that the σε was a man, not God the Father (*A Critical and Exegetical Commentary on the Epistle to the Romans*, ICC [New York: Scribner, 1920], 395). A. T. Hanson famously argued against Sanday and Headlam with the conclusion that the σε was God the Father ("The Interpretation of the Second Person Singular in Quotations from the Psalms in the New Testament," *Hermatheua* 73 [1949]: 69–72).

38. So also, e.g., Moo, *Epistle to the Romans*, 868–69; and James D. G. Dunn, *Romans 9–16*, WBC 38b (Dallas: Word, 1988), 838. Contra Callia Rulmu, who emphasizes the suffering relative to Jew-Gentile issues ("The Use of Psalm 69:9 in Romans 15:3: Shame as Sacrifice," *Biblical Theology Bulletin* 40, no. 4 [2010]: 227–33). See Siu Fung Wu for many possible links of Psalm 69 throughout Romans ("Participating in God's Purpose by Following the Cruciform Pattern of Christ: The Use of Psalm 69:9b in Romans 15:3," *Journal for the Study of Paul and His Letters* 5, no. 1 [2015]: 1–19).

39. Although going beyond the evidence, Matthew Scott argues that Paul only uses "Christological psalmody" for "imitation." He bases this on Rom. 15:3–4, 7–9 and 2 Cor. 4:13. See *The Hermeneutics of Christological Psalmody in Paul: An Intertextual Enquiry*, SNTSMS 158 (New York: Cambridge University Press, 2014).

eleven, four exhibit the characteristic of being applied to both Christ and believers. Psalms 34 and 118 clearly do this. Psalm 8 is fairly clear. Psalm 22 exhibits this characteristic in my view, but I do not claim exegetical certainty for this. In addition to these four psalms, Psalm 69 is only applied to Christ in the New Testament; however, Paul in Romans 15:3 // Psalm 69:9 uses his Christological interpretation to present Christ as a model and motive for believers. That is, Paul uses Psalm 69 *functionally* as applied to both Christ and believers. Therefore, of the eleven psalms with at least two New Testament quotations, five (Psalms 8, 22, 34, 69, 118) refer to both Christ and Christians.

I believe that intra-biblical hermeneutics are normative for us. Given that five of the eleven possible examples refer to both Christ and believers, it is a reasonable step to conclude that all psalms are to be viewed this way. Therefore, the New Testament's use of Psalms 8, 22, 34, 69, and 118 is one of many arguments that God intends all psalms to be interpreted as referring in some sense to both Christ and Christians.

7

What Kind of Prophecy Continues?

Defining the Differences between
Continuationism and Cessationism

IAIN M. DUGUID

Vern Poythress has been a model to me in many ways, first as a teacher and now as a colleague. While holding firmly to the truth of his convictions, he always encourages his students to listen carefully to Christians with whom they disagree and to observe the biblical truths they are seeking to defend, even though we may still disagree with their conclusions. Some years ago, he wrote an article entitled "Modern Spiritual Gifts as Analogous to Apostolic Gifts: Affirming Extraordinary Works of the Spirit within Cessationist Theology."[1] Its central argument—that so-called spiritual gifts such as prophecy may function at different levels, some of which continue while

---

1. Vern S. Poythress, "Modern Spiritual Gifts as Analogous to Apostolic Gifts: Affirming Extraordinary Works of the Spirit within Cessationist Theology," *JETS* 39, no. 1 (1996): 71–102.

others cease—is reproduced and developed in his more recent booklet *What Are Spiritual Gifts?*[2] In this short piece, I intend to support Dr. Poythress's conclusion by setting the cessationist-continuationist debate in a fuller biblical-theological setting and demonstrating that the phenomenon of biblical prophecy is more multifaceted than has typically been recognized.

Delineating the Traditional Debate

For the sake of simplicity, I am going to summarize the existing debate in terms of the presentation of two representatives: Richard Gaffin[3] and Wayne Grudem.[4] Fittingly, both men have a long connection with Poythress, from the days when Vern and Wayne were students together at Westminster Theological Seminary.

Gaffin's view is as follows: Old Testament prophecy is authoritative and infallible, the very Word of God (we might call this capital-*P* prophecy). New Testament prophecy is identical to Old Testament prophecy in this respect and therefore also falls under this category of capital-*P* prophecy.[5] Such authoritative, capital-*P* prophecy, which is the only kind that the Bible knows, does not continue in the church today (hence the term "cessationist"). Graphically, we might represent Gaffin's position as shown in figure 1.

Figure 1

Old Testament		New Testament		Today
P prophecy	→	*P* prophecy	|	No *P* prophecy

Wayne Grudem agrees with Gaffin that Old Testament prophecy is authoritative and infallible (capital-*P* prophecy).[6] However, Grudem argues that in the New Testament, the men who spoke with a "Thus

---

2. Vern S. Poythress, *What Are Spiritual Gifts?* (Phillipsburg, NJ: P&R, 2010).

3. Richard B. Gaffin Jr., *Perspectives on Pentecost: New Testament Teaching on the Gifts of the Holy Spirit* (Phillipsburg, NJ: Presbyterian and Reformed, 1979). O. Palmer Robertson adopts a broadly similar position in *The Final Word: A Biblical Response to the Case for Tongues and Prophecy Today* (Edinburgh: Banner of Truth, 1993).

4. Wayne Grudem, *The Gift of Prophecy in the New Testament and Today*, 2nd ed. (Wheaton, IL: Crossway, 2000).

5. Gaffin, *Perspectives on Pentecost*, 72: "The words of the prophet are the words of God and are to be received and treated as such."

6. Grudem, *Gift of Prophecy in the New Testament and Today*, 23–25.

says the Lord" authority similar to their Old Testament counterparts were the apostles, not the prophets. This change in terminology is necessitated by two reasons. First, the spreading of the gift of prophecy to all believers means that "prophecy" is too imprecise a term to describe the more limited category of authoritative and infallible prophecy. Second, the usage of the words "prophet" and "prophesy" did not have this authoritative, infallible sense in the wider first-century Greek and Jewish context. As a result, the New Testament developed a new term, "apostles," to identify the equivalent of the Old Testament prophets.[7] Meanwhile, Grudem argues, the New Testament phenomenon denoted as "prophecy" is something quite new and distinct from the Old Testament phenomenon—a fallible human expression of the Spirit's guiding that needs to be evaluated and tested, rather than an authoritative word that must simply be received or rejected. We might call this lowercase-p prophecy.

In terms of contemporary application, Grudem believes that there is no longer any apostolic (P prophecy) in the church. No one today can authoritatively speak for God as the Old Testament prophets and the New Testament apostles did.[8] However, for Grudem there continues to be an ongoing work of the Spirit in leading, guiding, and directing his people today that is properly designated "prophecy" (with a small p). This is the *continuationist* position. Graphically, we might represent Grudem's position as shown in figure 2.

Figure 2

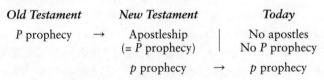

Old Testament		New Testament		Today
P prophecy	→	Apostleship (= P prophecy)	|	No apostles No P prophecy
		p prophecy	→	p prophecy

Immediately, we may notice some unexpected similarities. To begin with, Grudem and Gaffin agree about the nature of Old Testament prophecy. In addition, the contemporary application of the two positions is not as far apart as one might expect. Even though Grudem

---

7. Ibid., 34–41.
8. Ibid., 141–42.

allows for the continuation of prophecy in the contemporary church, it is a very limited kind of prophecy—the kind that is hedged around by a number of caveats and restrictions, and subject to an evaluation process by the church. Both Grudem and Gaffin agree that capital-*P* prophecy—"Thus says the Lord" prophecy—has ceased.

At the same time, many Reformed churches—including the Orthodox Presbyterian Church, of which Dr. Gaffin is a minister—insist on the continuing direction of the Spirit today in at least one area: that of a "call to ministry." Ministerial candidates are expected to have a definite and substantive sense (though not necessarily through a dramatic experience) that God, by his Spirit, is directing them into pastoral work.[9] As with Grudem's lowercase-*p* prophecy, this internal sense of call is subject to important qualifications. A man may exhibit a strong internal sense of call but may lack the gifts or character necessary for church office. Alternatively, a suitable ministry position may not present itself, even though the church affirms the man's call in general terms. But the process of evaluating and testing a man's internal sense of a call to the ministry in the Presbyterian system is broadly similar to Grudem's process of evaluating prophecies. A man whose sense of internal call is not sustained by the church is not disciplined as a false prophet. Rather, he is perceived as having simply misunderstood God's direction for his life (at least for the present).

What is more, a number of Reformed theologians are comfortable with the general concept of the Spirit's continuing role of guiding and directing his people today through intuitive promptings of various kinds. As an example, Poythress suggests someone in an American church who says, "I feel that our sister church in Shanghai is spiritually struggling and undergoing attack."[10] Such a sense is not infallible and could turn out to be mistaken, but in many cases such impressions have subsequently been confirmed, and it seems appropriate in such cases to attribute them to the work of the Spirit.

---

9. See the reference to "a man's inward call" in the OPC Form of Government, 20.3. The Form of Government of the Presbyterian Church in America says, "Ordinary vocation to office in the Church is the calling of God by the Spirit, through the inward testimony of a good conscience, the manifest approbation of God's people, and the concurring judgment of a lawful court of the Church" (16.1). Each candidate is required to "believe himself to be called to preach the Gospel" (18.1). The language of the Associate Reformed Presbyterian Form of Government, 7.1, is similar.

10. Poythress, *What Are Spiritual Gifts?*, 33.

Similar examples from Reformed church history abound.[11] Charles Spurgeon is reported to have had insights during sermons into the situations of specific members of his congregation. He once said: "There is a man sitting there who is a shoemaker; he keeps his shop open on Sundays; it was open last Sabbath morning. He took ninepence, and there was fourpence profit on it: his soul is sold to Satan for fourpence!"[12] I myself had a similar, if less dramatic, experience as a seminary student. I preached in two services on a Sunday morning at a church in Michigan where I knew no one. I delivered the exact same sermon in both services. However, on the spur of the moment, I added an illustration during the second service about a player being benched from his basketball team. After the service, a woman came to me in tears saying that this illustration had spoken directly to her son. Certainly, the Spirit is capable of giving preachers apt and specific applications during the regular sermon preparation process. Often these come simply through the knowledge a good shepherd has of his sheep, just as we might learn of the needs of the sister church in Shanghai through an email or through news reports. But on this occasion, it seems that the Spirit chose to make his role more prominent.

In addition, Reformed people have not always reserved the language of "prophecy" strictly for capital-P prophecy—an authoritative, unquestionable revelation of God. Historically, we have included other phenomena under the same rubric, especially preaching. William Perkins titled his treatise on preaching *The Art of Prophesying*, while sixteenth-century Puritan gatherings to discuss theology were called "prophesyings." The Puritans did not think that preaching or their discussions were direct revelation from God. However, they included the Spirit's broader work of leading and guiding his people through these means under the general rubric of "prophecy."[13]

The central issue of disagreement between Gaffin and Grudem, therefore, is the nature of New Testament prophecy. Is it capital-P

11. See Grudem, *Gift of Prophecy in the New Testament and Today*, 347–59.

12. Quoted in Ernest W. Bacon, *Spurgeon: Heir of the Puritans* (Grand Rapids, MI: Eerdmans, 1968), 156, cited in Poythress, *What Are Spiritual Gifts?*, 33.

13. Richard Gaffin allows that, according to the New Testament, all believers are prophets, and that we can speak of the "prophethood of believers" (*Perspectives on Pentecost*, 59). It remains unclear, however, in what sense all Christians may be said to be prophets or what specific "prophetic" activities they might engage in.

prophecy (Gaffin) or lowercase-*p* prophecy (Grudem)? The discussion is framed by the expectation that it must be one or the other.[14] Meanwhile, relatively little attention has been given to the Old Testament background.[15] In this study, I want to suggest that the Old Testament uses "prophecy" to describe both kinds of phenomena, capital-*P* ("Thus says the Lord") prophecy and lowercase-*p* prophecy (a wider range of Spirit-inspired activities), in ways that may then be reflected in the New Testament.

Prophecy in the Old Testament

It is not hard to demonstrate that the Old Testament frequently uses the words "prophecy" and "prophet" to describe what I have called capital-*P* prophecy. Classic passages such as Deuteronomy 18:9–22 and Numbers 12:4–6 clearly anticipate the work of the prophet as being the definitive delivery of divinely inspired messages. This expectation is reinforced by the work of the writing prophets, who had a divinely ordained message to deliver. Those who pretended to have access to such divinely given insights when they spoke their own words were false prophets, who were potentially subject to the death penalty.[16]

The wider use of the language of prophecy in the Old Testament has often been overlooked, however. The very first use of the Hebrew word נָבִיא in the Old Testament describes Abraham, whose "prophetic" credentials have nothing to do with a message he is to deliver from God but rather involve his ability to intercede on behalf of Abimelech (Gen. 20:7). Intercession is a regular part of the prophetic task for later capital-*P* prophets,[17] but here in Genesis, having "prophetic" ability has nothing to do with delivering a divine word; instead, it is being identified as a divinely appointed mediator.

---

14. In his published PhD thesis, Grudem allows for more than one kind of prophecy in the New Testament (*The Gift of Prophecy in 1 Corinthians* [Washington, DC: University Press of America, 1982], 3–5, 110–13), but in his later work he explicitly rejects the distinction (*Gift of Prophecy in the New Testament and Today*, 48).

15. Gaffin's treatment contains no substantive treatment of the Old Testament background of prophecy, while Grudem's 1988 edition has a bare six pages. In the 2000 edition, Grudem added a twenty-page appendix entitled "Prophets and Prophecy in the Old and New Testaments: A Biblical-Theological Study," though since the text of the book itself is unchanged, this fuller treatment can hardly be said to shape his argument.

16. For a fuller discussion of this capital-*P* aspect of Old Testament prophecy, see O. Palmer Robertson, *The Christ of the Prophets* (Phillipsburg, NJ: P&R, 2004), 31–66.

17. Most notably when that privilege is withdrawn: see Jer. 7:16; Ezek. 3:26.

There is also a class of texts in the Old Testament in which a group of people are identified as "prophets" or as "prophesying," yet there is no suggestion of anyone listening to or being instructed by authoritative pronouncements. Often these passages suggest that the "prophesying" involved some kind of ecstatic speech not readily understood by its hearers. For example, the seventy elders prophesy in Numbers 11. Here, in response to Moses's inability to lead the people alone, the Lord promises to take some of his Spirit from Moses and place it on the elders. The sign of the pouring out of the Spirit on these men is that they "prophesied" (11:25), yet none of their utterances are recorded. What is significant is not *what* they prophesied but *that* they prophesied. Nor did they continue to prophesy; their doing so was a one-time sign of the Spirit at work in them, equipping them for the administrative task of assisting Moses. Here prophecy functions not to convey divinely inspired information but to identify divinely indwelt individuals.

This is evident from the sequel. While the seventy elders were prophesying with Moses at the Tent of Meeting, two other elders, Eldad and Medad, began prophesying within the camp (Num. 11:26). Uncomfortable with this implicit challenge to Moses's authority, Joshua wanted to stop them. But Moses responded, "Would that all the LORD's people were prophets, that the LORD would put his Spirit on them!" (11:29). What is Moses requesting here? It is not clear why it would be desirable to have all Israel prophesy if prophecy is restricted to the capital-P kind. A handful of such mediators would suffice. It seems rather that Moses's desire is for some broader work of the Spirit in the hearts of all Israel, as a sign of divine indwelling. Yet such an experience could also be classified under the rubric of "prophecy."

Saul's experiences with the Spirit may be included in the same category. Twice the Spirit descended on him when Saul encountered a group of prophets, and Saul joined them in their prophesying (1 Sam. 10:6; 19:20–23). These apparently "ecstatic"[18] experiences are also called "prophesying," yet they hardly fall under the rubric of P prophecy, in which there is a word from God to be delivered to his people.

---

18. Given the presence of musical instruments in 1 Sam. 10:5, E. J. Young interprets this "prophesying" as "devout praising of God to the accompaniment of music" (*My Servants the Prophets* [Grand Rapids, MI: Eerdmans, 1962], 86). This would perhaps connect to the work of the Levites discussed below, but still distinguishes it from P prophecy.

Those who observed this activity are portrayed as uncomprehending watchers rather than engaged listeners. The point of Saul's prophesying is to mark him out as distinctly "Spirit-possessed," as was the case in the Numbers passage.

The mention of a group of prophets linked with Samuel leads to consideration of similar bands of prophets in the northern kingdom during the time of Elijah and Elisha. Ahab's steward, Obadiah, claims to have hidden a hundred prophets in two caves during the time when Jezebel was killing the Lord's prophets (1 Kings 18:4). Since this was presumably only a small proportion of those whom Jezebel sought, we gain the picture of several hundred (authentic) prophets active during this time, a situation that seems to have persisted through much of the history of Israel and Judah. What exactly was their ministry? Are we to envisage all of these prophets constantly conveying capital-P-prophecy messages directly from the Lord to their audiences? That seems unlikely.

For example, a group of men called "the sons of the prophets" appears at Bethel in 2 Kings 2, associated with Elijah. Their only re-corded "revelation" seems to convey to Elisha information he already knows, that Elijah is to be taken up to heaven that day (2:3). These men become disciples of Elisha, sitting at his feet (2 Kings 4:38) and living under his charge (2 Kings 6:1), while he appears to be the only one who "prophesies" in the P sense of the word. It is true that in 2 Kings 9:1 one of the sons of the prophets is instructed to anoint Jehu and declare him the Lord's chosen king over Israel. Yet this exception merely underlines the point, since the unnamed "son of the prophet" receives this message not directly from the Lord but from Elisha. These men function more like disciples of Elisha's regular teaching ministry than deliverers of immediate revelation from God.

The summary of the work of the prophets in 2 Kings 17:13 is sug-gestive in this regard: "Yet the LORD warned Israel and Judah by every prophet and every seer, saying, 'Turn from your evil ways and keep my commandments and my statutes, in accordance with all the Law that I commanded your fathers, and that I sent to you by my servants the prophets.'" On the one hand, this is an apt summary of the work of the writing prophets, like Isaiah, Jeremiah, and Ezekiel, whose prophecies fit into the P-prophecy mold. On the other hand, however, fulfilling this role did not necessitate direct, unmediated revelation from God, since the message was rooted and grounded in the earlier revelation of God, especially the Pentateuch. It could easily include activities closer to what we would describe as "preaching" and "teaching," not merely capital-P prophecy. That seems a more plausible regular employment for the large numbers of genuine "prophets" who seem to have operated throughout much of Old Testament history.

Perhaps the most striking broader use of the language of "prophecy" is the Chronicler's description of the work of the Levites. In 1 Chronicles 25:1, we read, "David and the chiefs of the service also set apart for the service the sons of Asaph, and of Heman, and of Jeduthun, who prophesied with lyres, with harps, and with cymbals." Asaph himself is likewise said to have prophesied in 1 Chronicles 25:2, as did the six sons of Jeduthun in 1 Chronicles 25:3, where this task is more narrowly defined as offering "thanksgiving and praise to the LORD." Prophecy is connected not merely with the design and initial ordering of the temple liturgy, or even the writing of canonical psalms, but also with its ongoing leadership by the Levites. To be sure, these men are not called prophets. Nonetheless, "prophesying" is what marks out their "Spirit-filled" ability to lead the people in thanksgiving and praise to the Lord and to declare his acceptance of Israel, something that seems more aptly located under lowercase-p prophecy than under capital-P prophecy.[19]

The Chronicler also highlights the role of prophets in writing down Israel's history. Among his historical sources, he cites "the Chronicles of Samuel the seer, the Chronicles of Nathan the prophet, and the Chronicles of Gad the seer" (1 Chron. 29:29; cf. 2 Chron. 9:29), as well as "the chronicles of Shemaiah the prophet and of Iddo the seer" (2 Chron. 12:15; cf. 13:22). He also mentions an otherwise unknown writing of Isaiah about the events of the reign of Uzziah (2 Chron. 26:22; cf. 32:32).[20] It seems that it was the responsibility of court prophets to record the events of a king's reign.

---

19. On the prophetic aspect of the Levitical ministry, see John W. Kleinig, *The Lord's Song: The Basis, Function and Significance of Choral Music in Chronicles* (Sheffield: JSOT Press, 1993), 153–57.

20. The latter reference, covering the reign of Hezekiah, could refer to the biblical book of Isaiah, but the former alludes to events during the reign of Uzziah, which are not described in the biblical book.

This raises the broader question of the writing of Israel's history. The canonical history—Joshua through 2 Kings—is termed in the Hebrew Bible "the former prophets." This title aptly highlights the role of prophets like Samuel, Elijah, and Elisha within the historical process, as well as the importance of prophecy and fulfillment in these books. Yet, the Chronicler highlights the prophetic dimension of the process of recording history as well. Its mode is different from that classically associated with capital-*P* prophecy—recording sacred history requires reflection on historical events rather than an unmediated deliverance of the Word of the Lord—yet, it is still viewed as a "prophetic" task.

Certainly, the *P* prophets such as Isaiah and Ezekiel themselves often authoritatively interpreted and applied events from Israel's history to communicate divine truth to their contemporaries, but what should we make of the noncanonical writings of prophets that acted as sources for inscripturated history? Did these sources have capital-*P* authority by virtue of their being written by prophets, so that the Chronicler could trust every word as inerrant? Or did the inspired writers of Israel's history regard these works as merely human, fallible sources? Even recognized capital-*P* prophets could err when they spoke without divine guidance, as the example of Nathan in 2 Samuel 7:3 makes clear. There are complex questions here.

To conclude, the definition of "prophecy" in the Old Testament is significantly broader than simply capital-*P* prophecy (the deliverance of unmediated authoritative oracles from God). It also covers a broader range of Spirit-inspired activities, including preaching, teaching, leading in worship, and recording history. In addition, prophesying also functions as a mark of Spirit-possession, identifying certain individuals as being singled out for particular tasks that do not necessarily include speaking with a "Thus says the Lord" authority.

Prophecy in the New Testament

This more complex portrait of prophecy in the Old Testament prepares us for a more complex understanding of the New Testament picture. The events of Pentecost, for example, are portrayed as the fulfillment of the prophecy of Joel 2:28 (see Acts 2:17). Joel anticipated that Moses's prayer that all the Lord's people would be prophets would be answered in the pouring out of the Spirit not just on all Israel but on all flesh. On the day of Pentecost, that prophecy was fulfilled in a striking way: all of the Christians prophesied—apparently all at once—and each of their hearers heard the gospel in his own tongue. Elsewhere in Acts, the apostles communicate the gospel effectively to different cultures using Greek as a common language. Here, however, to underline the universality of the good news and the reality of the gift of the Spirit, the prophetic sign was added. The key element of the prophesying was not simply the specific information being conveyed; it was especially the sign function, the proof that the Spirit had now been poured out on all who believed in Christ, from all over the world, as promised under the old covenant. In that regard, it is strongly reminiscent of the elders' experience in Numbers 11.[21]

Something similar happened when the Spirit comes to the previously uninstructed believers in Ephesus: when they receive the Spirit, all of them prophesy (Acts 19:6). The focus is not on the communication of divinely inspired information; rather, what is indicated by "prophesying" here is similar to what Luke describes as "extolling God" in the parallel event in Acts 10:46, where the Holy Spirit comes to the Gentiles for the first time.[22] These events resemble those of Numbers 11 or the empowering of the Levites in 1 Chronicles more than the inspired, inerrant utterances of Isaiah and Ezekiel.

On the other hand, at least *some* New Testament prophecies belong to the capital-*P* variety. In Luke 1:67–79, when Zechariah, the father of John the Baptist, is filled with the Spirit and prophesies, his speech is reminiscent of the language of the writing prophets, especially Isaiah. He specifically and authoritatively identifies his son as the fulfillment of the promise of a messianic forerunner. Likewise, when Agabus stands up and foretells by the Spirit that there will be a great famine over all the world (Acts 11:28), the disciples don't try to evaluate his words. Rather, they believe his prophecy and take immediate steps to

---

21. See Craig Keener, *Acts: An Exegetical Commentary*, vol. 1 (Grand Rapids, MI: Baker, 2012), 806.
22. See Gaffin, *Perspectives on Pentecost*, 82.

provide for those who will struggle financially as a result. Old Testament prophets like Ezekiel would have longed for a similar receptivity among their hearers, but their hearers would have recognized what the prophet was doing.

The same is true of Agabus's later prophecy concerning Paul in Acts 21. Here Agabus performs a sign act of the kind that Jeremiah and Ezekiel utilized, binding his own hands and feet with Paul's belt to indicate the fate that Paul will undergo in Jerusalem (21:11). He introduces his words with a version of the so-called messenger formula, "Thus says the Holy Spirit," just as Old Testament prophets introduced divine speech with "Thus says the Lord."[23] He then says, "This is how the Jews in Jerusalem will bind the man who owns this belt and deliver him into the hands of the Gentiles" (21:11). It seems hard to escape the conclusion that Agabus speaks with the same kind of authority as the Old Testament prophets whose style he evokes.

Grudem objects to these examples of capital-P prophecy. In the case of Agabus's first prediction, Grudem observes that it is said to be "through the Spirit" (διὰ τοῦ πνεύματος, Acts 11:28), which he thinks is never used in the Septuagint to describe prophetic speech.[24] This is not correct. Certainly, it is more common in the Old Testament to say that the Lord speaks "through the prophet" than that a prophet speaks "through the Spirit." However, the phrase does occur in the Septuagint of Isaiah 30:1: "'Ah, stubborn children,' declares the LORD, 'who carry out a plan, but not mine, and who make an alliance, but not of my Spirit [διὰ τοῦ πνεύματός μου], that they may add sin to sin.'" The following verse parallels "not of my Spirit" with "without inquiring of my mouth," which is a transparent reference to failing to seek capital-P prophetic direction.[25]

On the basis of parallels from Josephus and Plutarch, Grudem also thinks that the word "foretold" (σημαίνω) gives a less precise sense of something that may happen. However, in Revelation this same word is used to describe the content of the vision given to John, which is specifically described as "the things that must soon take place" (Rev. 1:1).

23. Ibid., 65.
24. Grudem, *Gift of Prophecy in the New Testament and Today*, 71.
25. See E. J. Young, *The Book of Isaiah* (Grand Rapids, MI: Eerdmans, 1969), 336–37. Compare the events of Jer. 41:17–44:7.

In the end, Grudem concedes that these objections merely "suggest" a lesser kind of authority.[26]

When it comes to Agabus's second prediction, Grudem argues that the fulfillment of the prophecy is insufficiently precise to allow it to be classed with Old Testament prophecy. He believes that Agabus had the general idea correct (Paul would be imprisoned at Jerusalem), but the specific details were wrong: the Jews did not bind Paul—the Romans did. Nor did the Jews deliver Paul over to the Romans; rather, the Romans rescued Paul from the crowd.

Richard Gaffin rightly sees this as an inappropriate insistence on pedantic precision.[27] To begin with, we do not necessarily have a full account of events in Acts: Paul could easily have been bound by the Jews, and they did in fact relinquish him ("hand him over") to the Romans, albeit unwillingly. Furthermore, if we are to insist on this level of precision, we are going to face many problems in defending the veracity of Old Testament prophecy. For example, Isaiah 53:9 declares that the suffering servant will be assigned a grave with the wicked, and with a rich man in his death. Jesus was indeed laid in the tomb of a wealthy man, Joseph of Arimethea (Matt. 27:57, which specifically notes that he was "rich"); but though the Jews intended Jesus's final resting place to be among the common criminals, he was not literally laid to rest among the wicked.[28]

An even clearer example is Ezekiel 29:17–21, widely cited in critical circles as a response to the "failure" of Ezekiel's earlier prophecy, which predicted that Tyre would be reduced to a bare rock (Ezek. 26:4). If strict and detailed literalism is the standard, then Ezekiel's earlier prophecy certainly did not come true, at least not until many centuries later, when Tyre was finally destroyed by Alexander the Great. Yet the presumption behind Ezekiel 29:17–21 is that the oracle has already been fulfilled: Nebuchadnezzar besieged Tyre for thirteen years (586–573 BC), breaking Tyre's economic and political importance and making Tyre's king his vassal.[29] All that was lacking was a proper

26. Grudem, *Gift of Prophecy in the New Testament and Today*, 72.
27. Gaffin, *Perspectives on Pentecost*, 65; so too Robertson, *Final Word*, 114.
28. See Robertson, *Final Word*, 114.
29. See Josephus, *Contra Apionem* 1.156; *Antiquities* 20.228; *Cambridge Ancient History*, 2nd ed., vol. 3, pt. 2 (Cambridge: Cambridge University Press, 1991), 235.

reward for his labors. To quibble that the prophecy was not yet fulfilled since Tyre continued to exist as a shell of its former self for several centuries afterward, and that even Alexander left some ruins intact, would seem unduly harsh. Yet, this level of precision is what Grudem insists on for Agabus. Similar examples of "imprecise" Old Testament prophecies could be multiplied.[30]

Yet if we allow for both capital-*P* and small-*p* prophecy in the New Testament, the fundamental reason for Grudem's objection is removed. His primary concern is to defend the insistence that the prophecy in 1 Corinthians is lowercase-*p* prophecy. Here he may have a point. The procedure in 1 Corinthians 14, where several prophets speak consecutively, with others evaluating their words, and where it is conceivable that a revelation would come to a second prophet, interrupting the first, does not resemble any cases of capital-*P* prophecy in the Old Testament. The only evaluation of capital-*P* prophecy in the Old Testament is whether it is genuine or false: if it is false, then the person who spoke it is supposed to be executed (Deut. 13:1–5). The category of "a fallible human expression of the Spirit's guiding" does not exist for capital-*P* prophecy. Equally, it is hard to imagine someone interrupting a capital-*P* prophet like Jeremiah or Ezekiel in full flow and asking him to sit down because the other person has something to say. Indeed, among the Spirit-given insights that Paul expected the Corinthians to bring to church with them when they met were not merely teaching, revelations, or tongues but also *psalms* (ψαλμόν, 1 Cor. 14:26 HCSB)—presumably not biblical psalms, which would hardly require a human mediator, but perhaps spiritual songs prepared for or suggested by the occasion.[31] This would resemble the work of the Levites in Chronicles rather than that of capital-*P* prophets.

In sum, if we allow the New Testament to reflect the diversity of prophetic phenomena present in the Old Testament, then the pressure

---

30. See, for example, Jeremiah's "seventy years" of exile (25:11; 29:10), which seems to be a round number that can be flexibly applied to more than one set of dates. See Mark J. Boda, *Haggai, Zechariah*, NIVAC (Grand Rapids, MI: Zondervan, 2004), 197–99. Likewise J. Alec Motyer says of Zephaniah 2: "Zephaniah preserves a certain detachment or 'distance' from historical events. With the possible exception of Assyria (2:13–15), we cannot really say that his forecasts met with this or that historical fulfillment" (*The Minor Prophets*, ed. T. E. McComiskey, vol. 3 [Grand Rapids, MI: Baker, 1998], 932).
31. See Charles Hodge, *I & II Corinthians* (repr., Edinburgh: Banner of Truth, 1974), 300.

to try to make all prophecy in the New Testament either capital-*P* prophecy or small-*p* prophecy is lifted, allowing a fairer evaluation of its manifold forms.

The Prophethood of All Believers

As mentioned earlier, one weakness of the cessationist position is that while it may affirm in a general way the prophethood of all believers, it is not clear in practice what that actually entails. Since all believers do not currently receive the gift of capital-*P* prophecy, on this view Moses's prayer in Numbers 11 and Joel's prophecy in Joel 2 seem to be barely, if at all, fulfilled. Even the Old Testament saints, who enjoyed the ministry of a multitude of unnamed prophets throughout much of their history, seem to have been better off in that regard. To be sure, New Testament Christians have the Spirit poured out upon us, and we have access to the completed Scriptures, which are no small gifts. Yet this massive extension of the work of the Spirit seems paradoxically, at the same time, to have resulted in a diminution of one key aspect of the Spirit's work, namely, prophecy.

However, if we include the lowercase-*p*-prophecy aspect of the Spirit's work, then the "prophethood of all believers" becomes a meaningful concept. In the book of Acts one of the key results of the pouring out of the Spirit on the church is the endowment of believers with the power to witness about Christ (Acts 1:8; 4:7–12, 33). Just as the Old Testament prophets confronted their compatriots with the need for repentance, so too now, empowered by the Spirit, believers can in an analogous way confront their neighbors with the truth of the gospel. Even though we do not share Paul's apostolic authority, we may still say with Paul: "We are ambassadors for Christ, God making his appeal through us. We implore you on behalf of Christ, be reconciled to God" (2 Cor. 5:20).

Second, empowered by the Spirit, believers can intercede with the Father on behalf of those with needs (Rom. 8:26–27). Unlike Old Testament saints, who needed the mediation of a prophet or priest to intercede on their behalf, under the new covenant, Jesus is the only Mediator we require (1 Tim. 2:5–6). In him, we all have direct access to the throne of grace (Heb. 4:16).

Third, we should anticipate the Spirit directing and guiding us, even though our reception of that guidance may be flawed and incomplete. Just as the Spirit directs men into pastoral ministry (subject to the evaluation of their gifts and character by the church), so too he directs our steps in many ways. Sometimes he will lead us through study of the Scriptures, reflection, and the wise counsel of others; at other times he may lead us more directly.[32] Such inner promptings do not have authority in the way that capital-*P* prophecy did; yet they are not to be despised and rejected either. They are subject to all the qualifications that Paul lays out in 1 Corinthians 12–14.

It is also important to remember that the prophethood of all believers does not eliminate the special-office aspect of the outpouring of the Spirit in the New Testament.[33] Pastors and teachers have a particular calling and spiritual gifting to declare the Word of God. In some ways, this gifting is analogous to the Old Testament capital-*P* prophetic office, while in others it is different. It is like the prophetic office insofar as the preacher is the authoritative ambassador who declares God's will and purposes to the nations. The minister stands in the pulpit as the ordained representative of Christ, appealing to his hearers to be reconciled to God. This is a very prophetic image. It is this prophetic office of the minister that the Second Helvetic Confession has in mind when it declares that "the preaching of the Word of God is the Word of God."[34] That is, the minister speaks with all of the authority of an Old Testament capital-*P* prophet when he declares, "Thus says the Lord."

On the other hand, there is also a distinction between the office of the minister and the office of the Old Testament prophet. The Old Testament prophet declared the word that came to him directly from God, while the minister's message and authority are mediated through the written Word of God. Nonetheless, there is enough point of contact that Paul can address Timothy as "man of God" (1 Tim. 6:11; 2 Tim. 3:17), a standard designation of a prophet in the Old Testament (see, e.g., 1 Sam. 2:27; 9:6; 1 Kings 17:24; 2 Kings 4:9). Paul is not claiming that Timothy is a *P* prophet; rather, he is linking his calling as a

---

32. See Poythress, *What Are Spiritual Gifts?*, 20–22.
33. See the helpful diagram in ibid., 14.
34. Second Helvetic Confession, chap. 1.

preacher and teacher to the *p*-prophetic task of the Old Testament. Our Reformed forebears were therefore right to call preaching "the art of prophesying."

One more word in conclusion. Wayne Grudem argues that the reason the New Testament adopted the language of prophecy for the broader, fallible category of lowercase-*p* prophecy rather than authoritative capital-*P* prophecy is in part the potential for misunderstanding in the wider community, where "prophecy" was generally understood to refer to the lowercase-*p* category. If this is true, it provides an excellent reason to be very cautious and guarded in using the terminology of "prophecy" in our present cultural context, where the tendency is to assume that capital-*P* prophecy is intended. In many cases, it is better to recognize the phenomena and, where appropriate, to identify them as the Spirit's working for the blessing of the church, without necessarily using the language of "prophecy," unless we are able to distinguish carefully between the different meanings of the word.

8

Christocentrism *and* Christotelism

The Spirit, Redemptive History, and the Gospel

LANE G. TIPTON

Dr. Vern Poythress has written more extensively on the hermeneutical significance of the divine nature and meaning of the Word of God in Scripture than any other Reformed theologian of our generation. A cursory reading of a bibliography of his work in this area makes the case abundantly clear. It is in deep appreciation of his insights regarding the divine authorship of Scripture and the organic character of redemptive revelation that I offer these reflections on the occasion of his Festschrift.

In this brief essay I want to bring certain features of the divine authorship of Scripture to bear on the issues of Christocentrism and so-called Christotelism in the Old Testament Scriptures, particularly in light of the recent development of the latter approach. Christotelism is a hermeneutical strategy for reading the Old Testament that in effect divests the Old Testament of a direct, per se witness to Christ and sets itself over against Christocentrism. In Christotelism, Christ is the goal toward which a "messy" Old Testament ambiguously drives. In Christocentrism, Christ is the central redemptive subject matter of the Old Testament on its own terms.

The goal of this essay is to define properly the Christocentric and Christotelic aspects of redemptive revelation and relate each to the divine (or better, pneumatological) foundation of that revelation. The two key texts I will treat in different degrees of detail are Romans 1:1–4 and 1 Peter 1:10–12, each of which helps us gain clarity on our topic.

Is the Old Testament Christotelic?

Peter Enns, in an article entitled "Apostolic Hermeneutics and an Evangelical Doctrine of Scripture: Moving beyond a Modernist Impasse,"[1] argues for a distinctive conception of how the New Testament apostles interpreted the Old Testament in light of Christ. Enns contends that there is no substantial difference between the method by which the apostles read the Old Testament and the way that Second Temple Jews read the Old Testament. What exactly is that method? Enns argues that all Second Temple methods of interpretation understand the Old Testament in light of its alleged fulfillment within the experience of the Second Temple community's reading of the Old Testament.

Bruce Waltke pinpoints the precise notion of the method Enns envisions as being utilized within Second Temple hermeneutics and, by extension, the apostles. Waltke says that if the method of the apostles is identical to the method of Second Temple hermeneutics, then this means

> that the New Testament writers used stories invented during the Second Temple period as a basis for theology; and that they employed the highly arbitrary *pesher* method of interpretation, which was used in IQpHab. According to this method of interpretation, the people who believe they are living in the eschaton impose their convictions on reluctant Old Testament texts.[2]

Hence, the Second Temple practice was to impose a series of community convictions that X is the case upon an Old Testament that, on its

---

1. *WTJ* 65, no. 2 (2003): 263–87.
2. Bruce K. Waltke, *An Old Testament Theology* (Grand Rapids, MI: Zondervan, 2007), 34n18.

own terms, does not envision that community conviction in the least. To put it in more contemporary language, the Second Temple way of reading the Old Testament is a reader-response theory of interpretation that does not care to do justice to the per se meaning of the Old Testament text as Scripture, but instead reads the interpretive concerns of the contemporary community surreptitiously back into the Old Testament.

However, while there is no difference methodologically between apostolic hermeneutics and the hermeneutics of Second Temple Judaism, there is a massive difference with regard to apostolic *goal* or *telos*. In light of Christ, his death, and his resurrection, methods in common with that Second Temple practice are utilized for an unprecedented Christotelic reading of the Old Testament and for finding Christ as its pervasive meaning.

Expanding on his 2004 article in a book entitled *Inspiration and Incarnation*, Enns affirms that for the New Testament authors, "Christ gives the Old Testament final coherence."[3] But that could happen only as they looked at the Old Testament "in a *whole new* light" that bypassed "what the Old Testament author intended."[4] The "coherence" of the Old Testament that Christ provides is one that accommodates dissonance with what the Old Testament writers intended.

What underlies Enns's viewpoint is the presupposition that the historical distance and idiosyncratic interpretive methods of the Second Temple period account entirely for the way New Testament apostles read Christ into a discordant Old Testament, whose original historical meaning was not about Christ per se. For Enns it appears that Christological categories are purely historical and coincide with the New Testament era. The historical coming of Christ confers a final coherence on the Old Testament, but it does so in a way that assumes that the Old Testament, on its own terms, is not about Christ, or at least not about him in the sense of being a text given by the Spirit of Christ that supernaturally reveals in advance to the Old Testament prophets the suffering and glory of Christ.

In summary, then, according to Enns the method of Second Temple

---

3. Peter Enns, *Inspiration and Incarnation: Evangelicals and the Problem of the Old Testament* (Grand Rapids, MI: Baker, 2005), 160.
4. Ibid., emphasis added.

Judaism is simply to reinterpret the Old Testament, not according to its own redemptive-historical terms and concerns, but around the terms and concerns of the contemporary interpretive community. The apostles appropriated this method to reinterpret the Old Testament around its "goal" in Christ. Enns himself terms his viewpoint Christotelism.[5]

Walter Brueggemann, although not himself influenced by Enns, asserts essentially the same hermeneutical practice of a Christotelic reading of the Old Testament. He says, "The Old Testament does not obviously, cleanly, or directly point to Jesus or to the New Testament."[6] He goes on to argue that the Old Testament has an "elusive quality" that invites the reader to engage in a first and second reading of the Old Testament. The first reading of the Old Testament is not Christologically regulated. But in the second reading, one can engage in interpretations that are "free, expansive, and enormously imaginative"—an activity that is "permitted and insisted on by the text."[7] With these observations in place, he states:

> It is then credible and appropriate to say that the early church, mesmerized by the person of Jesus, found it inescapable that it would draw this *elusive, polyphonic text* to its own circumstance, close to its experience, its memory, and its continuing sense of the transformed presence of Jesus. Thus as a confessing Christian, I believe that the *imaginative construal of the Old Testament toward Jesus* is a credible act and one that I fully affirm.[8]

So, by analogy, and following the trajectory of Enns, we can say that the Qumran Community construed the Old Testament as speaking of their experience and then read their experience back into the Old Testament, so that the Old Testament was imaginatively reread as though it pointed to that experience all along. We see in apostolic interpretation of the Old Testament the same method, with a different goal in place—a Christological one. But, of course, we know that just

---

5. Consult Peter Enns, "Fuller Meaning, Single Goal: A Christotelic Approach to the New Testament Use of the Old in Its First-Century Interpretive Environment," in *Three Views on the New Testament Use of the Old Testament*, ed. Kenneth Berding and Jonathan Lunde (Grand Rapids, MI: Zondervan, 2008), 167–217.
6. Walter Brueggemann, *Old Testament Theology: Testimony, Dispute, Advocacy* (Minneapolis: Fortress, 1997), 731.
7. Ibid.
8. Ibid., 732, emphasis added.

as the Old Testament is not actually and in its literal sense, on its own terms, about Qumran, nor is it about Christ. The literal sense of the Old Testament has nothing directly to do with Christ. But a second reading, a Christotelic reading, creatively imagines the Old Testament around (or toward) the apostolic experience of Christ.

With this conception of Christotelism in place—a view I will later term *historicist* Christotelism—we can now engage some biblical texts that will enable us to affirm an altogether different notion of Christotelism that exists in closest possible connection with a Christocentric history of special revelation.

Redefining Christotelism: Romans 1:1–4 and 1 Peter 1:10–12

The exegesis in the next two sections will provide the categories necessary to affirm a properly qualified notion of Christotelism, while rejecting the historicist notion of Christotelism outlined above.

ROMANS 1:1–4

The first text we will consider is Romans 1:1–4:

> Paul, a servant of Christ Jesus, called to be an apostle, set apart for the gospel of God, which he promised beforehand through his prophets in the holy Scriptures, concerning his Son, who was descended from David according to the flesh and was declared to be the Son of God in power according to the Spirit of holiness by his resurrection from the dead, Jesus Christ our Lord."

Several observations from this passage bear on the discussion above. This text, along with 1 Peter 1:10–12, is directly germane to the development of a properly qualified "Christotelic" understanding of the Old Testament Scriptures.

First, notice that this gospel that Paul proclaims is the "gospel *of God*" (Rom. 1:1). The gospel that Paul proclaims is not one that originates with Paul—or any other human being, for that matter (cf. Gal. 1:1, 11–12). The gospel has God as its subject or author. Whether the genitive phrase "of God" is to be taken in a possessive sense (the gospel belonging to God) or in a subjective sense (the gospel that comes from God), the point remains that it is first and foremost the gospel of God *before* it comes to be Paul's gospel (cf. Rom. 2:16). As such, the gospel is not the product of any creative human being or group of human beings. It has its point of origin (and ultimate authority) in the divine person and agency of God himself, and not in man, understood individually or communally.

Second, notice that Romans 1:3a clarifies that the gospel of God concerns the Son of God. The gospel has as its fundamental redemptive subject matter the divine Son, the messianic Son. It is a Son-centered gospel—a gospel that has the Redeemer of God's elect at is center or as its central redemptive subject matter. Grasping the content of the gospel, then, means that we understand that the Son of God constitutes its essential redemptive core. As Jesus says, the redemptive promises in the Old Testament—the core of the good news for Israel—centers on him (Luke 24:44–49; John 5:39, 46).

Bringing into view the history of special revelation and adding a redemptive-historical vantage point to the presentation of the gospel of God's Son, notice the language compressed into Romans 1:2. The gospel of God's Son is "promised beforehand through the prophets in the holy Scriptures."

This Son-centered gospel is presented in verse 2 from a threefold point of view: it is theological (God is the divine subject who promised it), prophetic (through the prophets), and canonical (in the Holy Scriptures of the Old Testament). And the overarching point is that what is promised beforehand by God (1:2), reaches its consummative telos in the death and resurrection of Christ (1:3–4), which gives verses 2–4 a decidedly redemptive-historical focus.

Theological. God is the subject who promised the gospel in advance. The gospel of God (Rom. 1:1) is something he promised beforehand in the Old Testament prophetic Scriptures. The reference to God as the subject who promised the gospel in advance situates the gospel in the Old Testament in terms of divine authorial intention. The reason we say that the Old Testament promises the gospel beforehand is that such is the intention of its divine author. God imbeds the gospel in the Scriptures of the Old Testament just as much as in the New.

Paul roots this gospel in the Old Testament not, first and foremost, in a "second reading" of an apostolic community of interpreters but in the intention of the divine author. Prior to and apart from any interpretive activity in the New Testament, God promised his Son-centered gospel, and this means that the gospel is deposited by God in the Old Testament in advance of the historical advent of Christ.

Prophetic. Paul also says that this divinely authored and promised gospel was given through the prophets. "Prophets" here is to be taken synecdochically of the entirety of Old Testament prophetic revelation. It includes all of the prophets, from Abel to Malachi. There is a single divine author of Scripture; yet there is a vast variety of human authors. God superintends what the prophets write in the event of divine inspiration, so that what God promises as divine author is delivered without error through the secondary human authors of the Old Testament, God's prophets.

Canonical. What the prophets wrote became canonical—the Scriptures of the Old Testament. The prophetic Scriptures contain the gospel of God's Son; this gospel is resident in the Old Testament. It does not need to be imaginatively inserted into the Old Testament; it is resident objectively within its pages by the superintending work of the Holy Spirit.

This means that Paul locates his apostolic gospel, the gospel of Jesus Christ, within the context of the prophetic Scriptures of the Old Testament as the revelation of God. This follows from the fact that there were no New Testament Scriptures, recognized as canonical, at the time Paul wrote this epistle.

Christocentrism and Christotelism. An implication of what we have observed so far is that the apostolic gospel is embedded objectively by God in the Old Testament canon, and, as such, that gospel cannot be understood as *essentially* new or creative. Granted, there is an eschatological fullness to the gospel of Christ in terms of his resurrection and Spirit-endowment (1 Cor. 15:45; 2 Cor. 3:6, 9–11, 17–18). But the gospel per se, no matter what we say (properly so) of its progressive movement toward eschatological consummation in Christ, is organically one. It is a single, unified reality that moves progressively toward a climactic fulfillment in Christ. It is critical that we gain clarity on the proper relationship between the redemptive organism (Christocentrism) and the progressive character of redemptive revelation (Christotelism).

Building on Romans 1:1–4 and moving toward theological clarification, we can begin to formulate the essential features of a properly qualified notion of Christocentrism, on the one hand, and Christotelism, on the other. The point to maintain with all the emphasis we can give it is that the Christocentric and Christotelic aspects of redemptive revelation are mutually supplementary at every point; the one does not for a moment exist apart from the other.

Christocentrism, relative to the Old Testament, is perhaps best summarized this way: *Christ, the promised Messiah, is the central redemptive subject matter of Old Testament redemptive revelation.* This entails that redemptive revelation is organic, focused on the Son of God, the Mediator of the covenant of grace. This does not mean that all of Scripture presents Christ in a monochrome way. Old Testament redemptive revelation is pluriform (cf. Heb. 1:1–2). However, that revelational pluriformity has a single redemptive subject matter that is found in Christ, humiliated and exalted (as he was promised beforehand).

The Scriptures of both Testaments know of only one gospel of God's Son. This transtestamental, Son-centered gospel constitutes the central redemptive subject matter of the Old Testament Scriptures. This is the core concern of Christocentrism, and nothing that we say about redemptive-historical progress, pluriformity of revelation, or perceived complexities within Old Testament revelation can eclipse this basic truth (cf. Luke 24:44–49; John 5:39; 2 Cor. 1:20).

In this regard, then, the Old Testament Scriptures are just as Christ-centered as the New Testament Scriptures. In fact, Romans 16:25 makes clear that Paul proclaims the gospel as a mystery that is embedded in the Old Testament itself. When viewed in this light—the light of redemptive organism—the history of redemptive revelation is substantially the same in both Testaments.

However, at the same time, the gospel of God's Son as the central redemptive subject matter of the Old Testament is qualified by Paul as being "promised beforehand [by God]" in Romans 1:2. While the gospel is the central redemptive subject matter of the Old Testament, it also exists in promise form that, by virtue of the plan of its divine author, drives toward a consummative telos in the crucified and resurrected Christ.

The gospel has a fundamentally forward-looking trajectory as it moves from promise toward eschatological fulfillment in the Son of God. The redemptive-historical movement inherent in verse 2 comes to fulfillment in verses 3–4: Jesus "descended from David according to the flesh and was declared to be the Son of God in power according to the Spirit of holiness by his resurrection from the dead." The mode of redemptive promise gives way to eschatological fulfillment in the actual historical advent of the humiliation and exaltation of the Son of God.

Put in the categories of Reformed orthodoxy, the "newness" of the gospel in the new covenant is not essential or substantial, because Christ is the central redemptive subject matter (or "substance") of the gospel in both Testaments (WCF, 7.6). The newness of the gospel in the new covenant is not substantial but administrative (or perhaps better, redemptive-historical). As the Westminster Confession of Faith delineates, "There are not therefore two covenants of grace, differing in substance, but one and the same, under various dispensations" or administrations (WCF, 7.6). The *substance* of the covenant of grace is singular, but its *administration* is a twofold redemptive-historical reality that moves from promises, types, and shadows in the old covenant to the substance or fulfillment in Christ in the new covenant (cf. WCF, 8.6).

The "substance" motif in the Westminster Confession denotes the Christocentric strand inherent in redemptive revelation; the "administration" motif denotes the Christotelic strand. Thus, from a Reformed confessional perspective, the Christocentric and the Christotelic qualify and inform one another at every point, according to the divine intention of God, the primary author of Scripture and the Lord of the history of special revelation.

The gospel, with its climactic, redemptive-historical fulfillment in Christ (Christotelism), is the *same gospel* promised beforehand through the prophets in the Holy Scriptures (Christocentrism). So, within the history of special revelation, *the gospel of God's Son is both the central redemptive subject matter of the Old Testament and its consummative telos.*

This formulation avoids polarizing the Christocentric and Christotelic strands of redemptive revelation. The Christotelic strand does not exist without the Christocentric, and the Christocentric strand does not exist without the Christotelic. Christocentrism without a telos is blind and non-eschatological. Christotelism without a center is empty and lacks redemptive substance in Christ.

Problems arise when one strand (or aspect) of redemptive revelation is set over against the other in a competitive way. On one extreme, we can stress an abstract concept of organism so strongly that eschatological movement is functionally denied. This danger leads to allegory that evacuates the genuine movement from typical to antitypical forms of revelation in redemptive history. On the other extreme, progress and movement can be stressed so strongly that the unity of the gospel of God is lost in the "messiness" of history. This is akin to a history-of-religions model in critical scholarship that reduces religion to purely human and historical conceptions and eschews a meaningful notion of revelation in history. The first extreme, one prone to more dogmatic, systematic theological forms of presentation, imposes a Parmenidean principle that is recalcitrant to historical movement. The other extreme, one prone to more historical (or historicist) principles of interpretation, loses the unity of redemptive revelation in a Heraclitean flux. Neither of these extremes can do justice to the covenantal coordination of Christocentric and Christotelic features inherent within the history of special revelation.

Geerhardus Vos on symbol and type. When set within the broader framework of the eschatology of special revelation, the Christocentric and the Christotelic comprise equally ultimate, mutually reinforcing categories of redemptive revelation. Put within a Vosian eschatological frame of reference, redemptive revelation is a single, organic, progressive, Christological reality, and it is so because behind the history of special revelation is the triune author of that revelation.

Geerhardus Vos introduced a distinction that aids in our theological grasp of the issues just considered. He argues that there is a distinction to maintain between a symbol and a type in terms of Old Testament redemptive revelation. He observes that a symbol in the Old Testament is a presentation of redemptive reality in a "lower stage of development."[9] A symbol is ordained by God to signify and communicate redemptive truth within the context of the history of Old Testament special revelation. Symbols represent the real redemptive presence of God to believers in the Old Testament era (cf. Ex. 13:21, where God's saving person and presence is in the pillar of cloud).

Vos presses on to argue that the key to understanding symbolism in relation to typology is simply this:

> The things symbolized and the things typified are not different sets of things. They are in reality the same things, only different in this respect[:] that they come first on a lower stage of development in redemption, and then again, in a later period, on a higher stage. Thus what is symbolical with regard to the already existing edition of the fact or truth becomes typical, prophetic, of the later, final edition of the same fact or truth. From this it will be perceived that a type can never be a type independently of its being first a symbol. The gateway to the house of typology is at the farther end of the house symbolism.[10]

In other words, Old and New Testament redemptive revelation constitute two editions of one basic reality, with the New bringing the Old to a stunning consummative telos in Christ—a telos that evokes wonder and is full of eschatological glory.

There is both organic unity (Christocentrism) and bona fide progress (Christotelism) in redemptive history, and both must be given all the emphasis we can give them. Failure to affirm organism will cloud the redemptive efficacy of the symbol in the Old Testament. Failure to affirm the eschatological orientation of that same revelation will sever the intrinsic connection between symbol and type.

These considerations from Romans 1:1–4, the Westminster Standards, and Geerhardus Vos help us avoid introducing a disjunction

---

9. Geerhardus Vos, *Biblical Theology: Old and New Testaments* (Carlisle, PA: Banner of Truth, 2014), 145.

10. Ibid.

between Christocentric and Christotelic strands of redemptive revelation. The two are united by the revelation of the triune personal God, the divine author of the history of special revelation. Let us probe one more text that supplements the observations up to this point.

1 Peter 1:10–12

A second text clarifies our point:

> Concerning this salvation, the prophets who prophesied about the grace that was to be yours searched and inquired carefully, inquiring what person or time the Spirit of Christ in them was indicating when he predicted the sufferings of Christ and the subsequent glories. It was revealed to them that they were serving not themselves but you, in the things that have now been announced to you through those who preached the good news to you by the Holy Spirit sent from heaven, things into which angels long to look. (1 Pet. 1:10–12)

In the opening verses of 1 Peter, especially from verses 3–8, the apostle brings into view the eschatological salvation of the church in Christ. Verse 9 is particularly instructive: the church, by faith, will receive the outcome of faith in eschatological salvation. The present salvation of the church, located in the context of the resurrection of Christ (1:3) and received by faith (1:5), is oriented toward the last time and the revelation of Jesus Christ (1:5, 8).

Verse 10 brings this salvation into view. The Petrine synopsis compresses in short compass the already and not yet of realized and future eschatology for the church in Christ. It brings into view that which *has been* realized in the life of the church, given the resurrection of Christ (1:3), and that which *will be* realized at his glorious, visible return—the parousia (1:8). The parameters established comprise the already realized redemption secured in Christ's first coming and resurrection, on the one hand, and the salvation to be revealed with the revelation of Christ at the last time, on the other hand. These points seem beyond dispute.

But immediately into verse 10, Peter brings the present salvation of the church in union with the resurrected Christ into relation to Old Testament prophecy: "the prophets who prophesied about the grace that *was to be* yours searched and inquired carefully." In a manner similar to Romans 1:2, the term "prophets" brings into view broadly the Old Testament prophets and their prophetic activity. They prophesied with respect to the grace that was to be given to the church in the age of realized eschatology. This text establishes a direct connection between the prophetic activity in the Old Testament and the salvation/grace in Christ that is given to the church in the New Testament era.

Additionally, note the verbs that qualify the prophet's role in this prophesying: "they searched and inquired carefully." The verbs together suggest the notion of a deliberate, painstaking inquiry into the substance of what was prophesied. The net effect of this is twofold. On the one hand, the prophets were aware, particularly in their role as prophets, of the salvation/grace that was to come to the church in the new covenant era. On the other hand, they searched intently and with great care concerning this salvation.

Peter makes clear that the old covenant prophets realized that they were prophesying of something on the future horizon of redemptive history. Their activity had a consummate telos in the Messiah, and they were aware of it. The prophets themselves understood that they were speaking of a future work of God—the eschatological outcome of salvation for the church. In other words, the prophets operated with an awareness that the redemptive realities with which they were involved were not the final realities to which redemptive revelation trended. They were cognizant of the fact that they operated in an age that was provisional.

The prophets realized that there was a "future grace" or, literally, an "unto you" grace in the Messiah. This much is clear: the gospel of the Messiah in its realized, new covenant fulfillment, was not something essentially hidden from the purview of the prophets. In fact, it was revealed to them. The question to ask is this: Whose agency underwrites such a supernaturalistic state of affairs that elevates the prophets beyond an ordinary time-bound perspective? The answer, in brief, is found in 1 Peter 1:11: " . . . inquiring what person or time the *Spirit of Christ* in them was indicating when he predicted the *sufferings of Christ and the subsequent glories.*"

First, the agent working in the prophets was "the Spirit of Christ." Peter uses language that is proper to a post-Pentecost situation, namely, "the Spirit of Christ," raised from the dead, to denote the activity of the Spirit in the Old Testament. Paul, in Romans 8:9, uses the exact same language to speak of the personal identification of Christ and the Spirit that results from the resurrection and ascension of Christ (cf. 1 Cor. 15:45 and 2 Cor. 3:17). What is particularly instructive is that the Spirit of Christ is the agent who "predicts in advance" (προμαρτυρόμενον) the sufferings and glory of the Christ.

Second, Peter makes it clear that the Spirit of Christ revealed in advance the sufferings and glory of the Messiah. There is a clear pneumatological and Christological circularity here as the Spirit of Christ testifies to the sufferings of Christ. The Spirit of the Son predicts in advance the sufferings and subsequent glory of the messianic Son. The third person of the Trinity, understood in closest functional proximity to the second person of the Trinity, predicts in advance the suffering and glory of the second person of the Trinity.

Third, and closely related to this, the Spirit's revelatory agency provides the context and content for the prophet's searching and inquiry. This assumes that the revelatory agency of the Spirit communicates to the prophets in such a way that the messianic focus of the primary, divine author is shared by the secondary, human author, albeit with limitations necessary to the Creator-creature distinction in place. This is true of Old Testament prophets in an Old Testament period. What is critical to note here is that while the prophets did not have the exhaustive knowledge of the Spirit, they nonetheless were made to understand what the Spirit of Christ was indicating in his predictive revelation to them. The prophets, though ordinary, time-bound human beings, were brought into the closest possible contact with the revelatory presence of the Spirit of Christ, the Spirit of the Messiah, thereby elevating their understanding as prophets beyond their ordinary, time-bound status.

Finally, and related to these points, the agency of the Spirit makes the content of the Messiah's ministry, understood in terms of suffering and glory, of central concern for the Old Testament itself. That is to say, the Christ-centered focus in the New Testament—a concern to think about the central events of humiliation and exaltation—is also an Old Testament concern, owing to the revelatory agency of the Spirit of Christ.

While there is a Christotelic concern here, a concern that makes the coming of Christ in the future a vital issue, there is also a Christocentric concern present in 1 Peter 1:10–12. That is, the coming of Christ is not merely the telos toward which prophetic revelation is oriented. Christ is also the redemptive substance of the revelation that the prophets receive. Both telos and redemptive substance are present in the Old Testament concerning the Messiah. We can overcome artificial disjunctions between Christotelism and Christocentrism precisely to the degree that we factor in at the foundation the revelatory agency of the Spirit of Christ in the Old Testament, who imbeds in both the prophets' understanding and their writing (of Scripture) the suffering and glories of the Messiah.

What this means, among other things, is that the symbolism in the Old Testament Scriptures, appropriated by the Holy Spirit and understood by the prophets, has a direct connection to the Messiah. There is a direct reference to the Messiah in the revelatory agency of the Spirit of Christ in the Old Testament and therefore, by implication, in the understanding of the Old Testament prophets to whom the Spirit of Christ revealed the Messiah's future suffering and glory. Put differently, *the Spirit of Christ rendered the suffering and glory of the Messiah typologically legible to Old Testament prophets.*

Moreover, the same Spirit who predicted in advance the sufferings and glory of the Messiah now enables apostolic preaching (1 Pet. 1:12; cf. 2 Pet. 1:19–21). Put most basically, the same Spirit of Christ reveals the same gospel of Christ to both Old Testament prophets and New Testament apostles. There is a common gospel concern, a common gospel revelation, and a common spiritual horizon between the Old and the New Testaments.

When the supernatural agency of the Spirit is given proper consideration, it becomes clear that the gospel possesses a Spirit-wrought perspicuity, as it has been pneumatically disclosed in both Testaments.

Counterbalancing this point about the clarity of the Spirit's teaching to and through the prophets and apostles, note that, from an Old Testament perspective, there is a yearning for greater revelation. There is an intent searching for the person and the time in which what the

Spirit predicted would come to its realization. There is a unified, Spirit-revealed gospel of grace and salvation that has the Messiah at its center, yet that gospel of grace and salvation in the Messiah involves movement from a time of eager searching in anticipation to consummation and fulfillment.

Concluding Observations

Perhaps at this point it will help to make explicit what we ought *not* to understand by a Christotelic approach, particularly given my emphasis that Christotelism be defined only in light of Christocentrism as a complementary limiting conception.

Enns's view, which we surveyed earlier, amounts to what I term *historicist (or critical) Christotelism*. What I have sought to set over against the historicist conception amounts to an *organic (or biblical) Christotelism*. The former has no place for redemptive organism, functional divine authorship, or the history of special revelation, and, as such, is a species of Christotelism that must be rejected. The latter, by contrast, is formulated within the context of a redemptive organism and presupposes divine authorship and the history of special revelation as the context for Christ as both the central redemptive subject matter and consummative telos of redemptive history.

Rather than setting Old and New Testament texts disjunctively over against one another and then bridging them by use of a reader-response hermeneutic that imaginatively reads the interpretive community's understanding back into a recalcitrant Old Testament (historicist Christotelism), we can affirm that Old and New Testament texts have the Spirit of Christ as their ultimate divine author, and this pneumatic consideration bears directly on the prophet's understanding of the suffering and glory of the Messiah in the Old Testament itself. This means that, by virtue of the Spirit's agency, there is an organic history of special revelation that comprises two distinct editions of one redemptive-historical reality that reaches its eschatological climax in Christ. Such an understanding, as seen in Romans 1 and 1 Peter 1, is shared by Old Testament prophets and New Testament apostles alike.

One final point needs to be made explicit. We cannot reduce Pauline or Petrine theology to a use of a *pesher* method by which both apostles read Christ into an Old Testament that, on its own terms, is recalcitrant to Christ. Rather, both speak of the objective, revelatory agency of God (Paul) or of the Spirit of Christ (Peter) as the theological ground for the gospel of the Messiah in the Old Testament prophetic Scriptures, quite apart from the New Testament. Prior to and apart from the resurrection of Christ and the writing of the New Testament, the Spirit of Christ revealed in advance the gospel of the Messiah, and it is the same Spirit who works in the preaching of the apostolic gospel in the New Testament era (cf. 1 Pet. 1:12). Neither Peter's nor Paul's gospel theology is rooted in apostolic reimagining of the Old Testament after the fact of the resurrection; rather, the theology of each is rooted in the revelatory activity of the Spirit relative to the prophets in the Old Testament, as well as the revelatory agency of the Spirit in his own writings (cf. 2 Tim. 3:16; 2 Pet. 1:19–21).

What is missing in the sorts of formulations offered by Enns and those who follow him is a thoroughgoing pneumatological understanding of the Old and New Testament Scriptures, as those Scriptures reveal the suffering and glory of Christ.

Apostolic understanding operates, to be sure, when the apostles engage in the interpretation of the Old Testament Scriptures. However, *the apostolic understanding receives an already Christ-centered and Christ-directed Word from God in the Old Testament Scriptures.* This means that the apostles did not simply borrow wholesale the methodological assumption that the Old Testament is a per se Christless document that needs subsequently to be "Christianized" by an interpretive community. Rather, they sought to expound and proclaim an Old Testament that, by virtue of its divine author, they understood to be already Christ-centered and that has now reached its eschatological climax in the humiliation and exaltation of the Son of God. Romans 1:1–4 and 1 Peter 1:10–12, properly understood, demand that such be the case.

Dr. Poythress has consistently maintained the divine authorship of Scripture, along with the proper notions of Christocentric and Christotelic strands of redemptive revelation, and he has done so with great humility and courage. May the work that he has given the church in his numerous publications continue to glorify the triune God, whom he so faithfully serves.

9

What "Symphony of Sighs"?

Reflections on the Eschatological
Future of the Creation

RICHARD B. GAFFIN JR.

Developments in biblical studies over the past century or so have led
to a broader understanding of eschatology than was generally the case
previously. These developments, stemming primarily from fresh assessments of the kingdom proclamation of Jesus in the Synoptic Gospels
and the theology of Paul, undoubtedly provide an important enhance-
ment to the traditional understanding of eschatology. For example,
typically in standard systematic theologies, "Eschatology" or "The
Last Things" is the title reserved for the final chapter, which deals
solely with those matters still future for the church concomitant with
Christ's return (along with the interim state following death). Instead—
it is now widely recognized—eschatology concerns what has already
taken place; "last things" are present for the church, not only future.
The shape of New Testament eschatology is elliptical, defined by two
foci: Christ's first as well as his second coming—the by-now-proverbial

already/not yet. Eschatology, biblically considered, is more comprehensive than was traditionally understood.

Understandably, this expanded appreciation of eschatology has prompted considerable attention and has resulted in a wide range of biblical and theological studies intent on showing its important and enriching implications for the present life and mission of the church— from a systematic-theological perspective, particularly in the areas of Christology, soteriology, and ecclesiology. A consequence of this preoccupation, no doubt often unintended, can be a diminished interest or perhaps even neglect of those issues considered in more traditional treatments of eschatology.

The eclipse of these issues must be resisted, if for no other reason than the nature of the realized or inaugurated eschatology of the New Testament itself. The dawning of the eschatological age to come in the death and resurrection of Christ is such that it does not exclude but rather anticipates its still-future consummate realization at his return. Metaphors used by Paul neatly capture this state of affairs: the "firstfruits" now present are not yet the full harvest of resurrection (Rom. 8:23; 1 Cor. 15:20, 23); the "down payment" already made is not the final inheritance still due and hoped for in its entirety (2 Cor. 1:22; 5:5; Eph. 1:14). The present life of the church is fundamentally determined within this eschatologically charged interim, bracketed by the past resurrection of Christ and his future return. Having "turned from idols to God to serve the living and true God," the church does so as it "wait[s] for his Son from heaven, whom he raised from the dead, Jesus who delivers us from the wrath to come" (1 Thess. 1:9–10).

The reflections that follow take up one aspect of this future expectation and are offered here in appreciation for the privilege of having Vern Poythress as a friend and valued colleague over many years, and for his important contributions to the cause of the gospel and the well-being of the church and its mission in and to the world.

What is the full scope of the future resurrection harvest in which believers will share bodily? What in its overall dimensions is the inheritance that awaits the church? Or, to focus the question for our purposes here, what does Scripture teach, whether "expressly" or "by good and necessary consequence" (WCF, 1.6), concerning the final future for the present creation order as a whole? What stake, if any, does the creation have in the consummate salvation of the church?

No doubt this question may be addressed from a number of different angles. The approach taken here will be oriented to the view of Geerhardus Vos as it has recently become available in English in a way it was not previously. I have chosen this approach in part because I anticipate that it will be of particular interest to many readers of this volume who are familiar with Vos's work in biblical theology.

The *Reformed Dogmatics* of Vos consists of material prepared for classroom instruction in Dutch at what is now Calvin Seminary, where Vos taught in the period 1888–1893 before moving to Princeton Seminary in the fall of 1893 to occupy its newly created chair of biblical theology until his retirement in 1932. *Reformed Dogmatics* covers the whole of systematic theology, with the exception of prolegomena (introduction), and does so under the standard major topics—from theology proper to eschatology.[1]

In its main divisions, volume 5 deals with ecclesiology, the means of grace, baptism, the Lord's Supper, and eschatology. The last of these divisions, in turn, divides into treatments first of individual eschatology and then of general eschatology. Toward its close the latter section gives some attention to the questions posed above concerning the future of the creation. A survey of this material will be followed by an assessment, giving attention to some of the pertinent biblical materials, and a brief conclusion.

The View of Vos

Vos's handling of general eschatology deals, in order, with the resurrection, the return of Christ for final judgment (including a lengthy discussion of the antichrist), the question of the millennium, hell, and heaven. Our interest here is in the four questions and answers (35–38) that make up the last of these sections, on heaven.[2]

---

1. Geerhardus Vos, *Reformed Dogmatics*, trans. and ed. Richard B. Gaffin Jr., 5 vols. (Bellingham, WA: Lexham, 2012–2016). All of its five volumes are now available in both digital and print editions. See the preface to volume 1 for further details about this work and its translation.

2. For easy reference, see the appendix at the end of this chapter, beginning on p. 161. I encourage reading it in its entirety before my survey comments.

1. Earlier, in the answer to question 1 under "General Eschatology," which lists the five topics noted in the previous paragraph, heaven is, more specifically, "the eternal beatitude of heaven."[3] Question 35, treating this topic, speaks alternatively of "the consummate salvation of the children of God."[4] In answer 35 the initial description for this bliss of heaven and final salvation is "the appearance of a new world." This focus on the new world sets the direction for everything said under the four questions about heaven with its blessings and consummate salvation.

Answer 35 immediately goes on to make clear a basic understanding one must have about this new world. With an appeal to Acts 3:21, among the other passages cited, Vos explains that the new world will be the result of and consist in the "restoration of all things," which he goes on to make clear he understands will be the restoration of the present creation. This is so because "as a matter of fact" this renovation or renewal resulting in the new world "is inherent in the relationship to the rest of creation in which man stands."

The controlling consideration here is that the church, including its future, is tethered to the creation. What will occur for believers will have corresponding effects for their present environment. Creation as a whole has been implicated in the consequences of sin. As creation is now subject to the curse on human sin, along with "the children of God it also awaits its liberation" from the effects of the curse. Salvation "is not solely about atonement for sin but about the removal of the results of sin." And that removal not only has in view the results of sin in Christians but also is such that "the last vestige of sin . . . will also need to disappear from the creation of God."

The new world will be an attendant consequence of the glorification of believers in their resurrection and following the final judgment.

2. Question and answer 36 discusses the origin of the new world and its basic relationship to the present world. In the history of theology on this issue, thought "differs greatly." These differences reduce to two basically, characterized as the Lutheran and Reformed views. The former, specifically the view of earlier Lutheran dogmaticians up

---

3. Vos, *Reformed Dogmatics*, 5:269.
4. See the appendix for this and further quotations from these four questions and answers.

through Gerhard, holds to "an absolutely new world"; the present or old world, including its substance, is annihilated and replaced by the new. The Reformed view, with a few exceptions, is the opposite: in its "substance" the present world "will be preserved but will be restored, purified in glory." Additionally, many theologians hold to some form of this Reformed view.[5]

The following four grounds are offered in support of this view:

a. The passages in 2 Peter 3 and Revelation 20 and 21 that appear decisive in supporting destruction as annihilation in fact do not. The terms used, like "passing away" and "being melted," do not describe extinction; "indeed, in our experience burning is never total annihilation."

b. The Old Testament passage from Psalm 102 cited here and those toward the close of answer 35 are clear in speaking of "change," not "annihilation." Accordingly, the cosmic shaking spoken of in Hebrews 12 should be understood to mean that, within what is shaken, "something remains that is immovable." Whether or not it will be "in the heaven of God's glory," the text likely means that "something of what is changeable will remain in order to be made unchangeable."

c. The two preceding grounds deal with specific texts. Two general grounds follow. The first is an overall interpretive observation: On the assumption of annihilation, texts speaking of change are "absolutely impossible to explain." On the assumption of change, texts apparently speaking of annihilation can be given a "very sound" explanation.

d. "Analogy speaks for change." This reiterates the inherent bond between the creation at large and the church, between believers and their environment, already expressed in answer 35, instanced now in the bodily resurrection. The present body will not be replaced by the resurrection body as a totally new creation out of nothing. The former will not be annihilated

---

5. Subsequently, in much more extensive treatments, Herman Bavinck (1918) and G. C. Berkouwer (1961), e.g., take this view, along with similar assessments of the earlier orthodox Lutheran view. See Herman Bavinck, *Reformed Dogmatics*, vol. 4, *Holy Spirit, Church, and New Creation*, ed. John Bolt, trans. John Vriend (Grand Rapids, MI: Baker Academic, 2008), 715–20; and G. C. Berkouwer, *The Return of Christ*, ed. Marlin Van Elderen, trans. James Van Oosterom (Grand Rapids, MI: Eerdmans, 1972), 211–34 (for references to Lutheran views, including Gerhard's view of annihilation and modern Lutheran rejections of this idea, see 220n18).

but changed by being glorified. Accordingly, the analogy or link noted carries with it the assumption that a corresponding change will also occur "in the wider sphere with the entire groaning creation."

3. Question and answer 37 addresses how this change will take place by commenting on the passages in 2 Peter 3 and Hebrews 12. In Vos's earlier sections on general eschatology, primarily in discussing the return of Christ for final judgment as presented in the Synoptic Gospels and elsewhere, he recognizes the presence of metaphorical elements in the apocalyptic language found in these passages.[6] Interestingly, however, here the reference to fire in 2 Peter 3 is taken literally. It cannot be figurative because of the contrast Peter makes with the past destruction of the world by the flood. As the water of the flood was literal, so the destructive fire to come "must be just as real." This fire and the cosmic shaking of Hebrews 12 are not mutually exclusive. Both prophecies would be adequately fulfilled by a worldwide inferno "with tremors and earthquakes." Also, heaven "in the celestial sense," not "as God's dwelling place," is included in this "renewal of the earth."

4. For our purposes here it will have to suffice to highlight the following in the answer to question 38. First, subpoint e (see p. 163) warns against viewing heaven "too much as an individual" and draws attention to its corporate life. Related to this undue individualism, neither should one think of heaven with its blessings "too spiritualistically." There are many who, along with failing to do justice to the resurrection of believers as bodily, do not take into consideration "that the earth, too, will be re-created. In their conception there is really no place for a new earth." This observation not only affirms bodily resurrection but also reflects the integral, inseparable bond, already noted, between the resurrection and the restoration, not the annihilation, of the present creation order as a whole.

Second, not to be overlooked is the way in which Vos frames question and answer 38. On whether it is possible to "say very much" about heaven and its blessings, the answer is immediately and decisively negative: "No, for this far surpasses our understanding." This

---

6. Vos, *Reformed Dogmatics*, 5:292.

expressed reserve sets the tone for the rest of Vos's answer, which ends in the same vein: "It should be acknowledged that we do not know what the enjoyment of God's world will be like for His children. We do not, if for no other reason because we lack any adequate comprehension of that new world itself." Vos's concern throughout has been not to overstate or speculate, but to say as much as may be said about the new world and to avoid saying more.

To round out this survey, we may note that views expressed in Vos's later writings are consistent with the *Dogmatics*. Approximately two decades later, in a lengthy encyclopedia article, "Eschatology of the New Testament,"[7] under the section heading "The Consummate State," he observes that "the eschatological kingdom" and "the present kingdom" share a common "core" of "spiritual realities and relations" but differ in that the former has "an external, visible embodiment." In this embodiment, the eschatological kingdom will have "its outward form as the doctrine of the resurrection and the *regenerated* earth plainly show."[8] Further, at the close of this section he writes, "The scene of the consummate state is the new heaven and the new earth, which are called into being by the eschatological palingenesia, 're-generation'" (with numerous passages cited in parentheses, including Matt. 19:28). "An annihilation of the substance of the present world is not taught (cf. the comparison of the future world-conflagration with the Deluge in II Pet. 3:6). The central abode of the redeemed will be in heaven, although the *renewed* earth will remain accessible to them and a part of the inheritance" (again with a number of Scripture references cited parenthetically).[9]

In Vos's view here, along with whatever differences in external form there will be between the present state of the creation and the consummate state, there will be a basic continuity in keeping with the spiritual realities of the kingdom common to both. The earth as it presently exists will not be annihilated but "regenerated," "renewed."

---

7. Geerhardus Vos, "Eschatology of the New Testament," in *Redemptive History and Biblical Interpretation: The Shorter Writings of Geerhardus Vos*, ed. Richard B. Gaffin Jr. (Phillipsburg, NJ: Presbyterian and Reformed, 1980), 25–58. The article was originally published in *The International Standard Bible Encyclopaedia*, ed. James Orr (Chicago: Howard-Severance, 1915).
8. Vos, "Eschatology of the New Testament," 54, emphasis added.
9. Ibid., 55, emphasis added.

Subsequently, shortly before his retirement, Vos wrote concerning the use of the word "regeneration" in Matthew 19:28:

> In this saying the word cannot be restricted to the more or less individualizing application of the resurrection; it covers the resurrection as a whole and even the *renewal of the universe* as is shown from the parallels in Mark and Luke which have as its equivalent descriptions of the final state, Mk. x. 29, 30; Lk. xxii. 29, 30. Thus also Josephus understands the term making it interchangeable with *apokatastasis.*[10]

With Romans 8:19–22 primarily in view, Vos comments:

> "The *creature*[11] was made subject to vanity"; it suffers from the bondage of corruption in an all-inclusive sense; it waits in eager expectation for the liberating end. That the κτίσις "the creature" is meant here in distinction from man the context clearly shows; particularly the words "itself" and "ourselves also" (vss. 21, 23) preclude all doubt concerning this.

Whether or not this "eager expectation" and other related language describing the creation are "mere personification,"

> the terms used certainly are strong; the creature manifests an ἀπο-καραδοκία for the manifestation of the sons of God. . . . The creation . . . finds itself implicated in the woeful destinies of mankind. In this fact lies, on the other hand, also the reason for its ultimate deliverance, which on account of such origin must coincide with the removal of the bondage of man to corruption and his endowment with the glorious liberty of the coming age.

Later on, Vos says concerning this eschatological liberation of the creation in reference to eschatological glory, "The 'liberty' that comes at the end to the creation, now bound to the bondage of sin through the sin-bondage of man, forms part of it [eschatological glory], because

---

10. Geerhardus Vos, *The Pauline Eschatology* (1930; repr., Grand Rapids, MI: Baker, 1979), 50, emphasis added. "There exists a certain analogy at this point between the ἀνάστασις and the *cosmical* παλιγγενεσία of Matt. xix. 28" (156, emphasis added).

11. Vos is quoting Rom. 8:20 in the KJV. As the material quoted above makes clear, he understands "creature" not as one among other created entities but as "creation" in the comprehensive sense (as do virtually all subsequent translations).

it [that glory] draws into the light whatever change has taken place: for groaning there is substituted joy"—both for the creation and the children of God.[12]

Here again, echoes of the emphases in the *Dogmatics* are clear: the present creation as a whole, along with the church specifically, awaits correlatively and inseparably not annihilation but eschatological transformation and glorification.

Assessment

In assessing this view, we may begin by recalling the general hermeneutical guideline Vos sets out in answer 36: on the supposition of annihilation, texts that speak of transformation are "absolutely impossible to explain"; supposing transformation, texts seemingly speaking of annihilation can be given a sound explanation. Specifically—it seems a fair generalization—the one approach comes to the Romans 8 passage with annihilation as a conclusion drawn primarily from the 2 Peter 3 and Hebrews 12 passages.[13] The other approach does the reverse; like

12. Vos, *Pauline Eschatology*, 84–85, 315.

13. David VanDrunen, *Living in God's Two Kingdoms: A Biblical Vision for Christianity and Culture* (Wheaton, IL: Crossway, 2010), 64–66 ("The End of the Natural Order") has been and is plausibly read as a recent instance of this approach. Following on his handling of the 2 Peter 3 and Hebrews 12 passages, he concludes from Romans 8:

> It is precisely this—*the resurrection of the believers' bodies*—that the created order is now longing for: [referring to the "eager longing" of Rom. 8:19]. Our earthly bodies are the only part of the present world that Scriptures says will be transformed and taken up into the world-to-come. *Believers themselves* are the point of continuity between this creation and the new creation. . . . Asserting that anything else in this world will be transformed and taken up into the world-to-come is speculation beyond Scripture. (66, emphasis original)

It is difficult not to conclude from such statements that, with the sole exception of believers in their bodily existence, the rest of the present natural order will be annihilated.

In personal correspondence, Dr. VanDrunen has pointed me to his view as expressed subsequently in *Divine Covenants and Moral Order: A Biblical Theology of Natural Law* (Grand Rapids, MI: Eerdmans, 2014), 442–43. There he clearly affirms that, "despite the deep discontinuity between the two," the continuity between the present creation and the new creation is also "cosmological" (with a parenthetical reference to Rom. 8:18–25, among other passages). In doing so, he also says about his view noted above: "Though some have read me here as asserting the annihilation of everything other than human bodies on the last day, I wished rather to say that the human body is the only aspect of the present creation Scripture specifically identifies as the point of continuity with the new creation" (443n35).

This later expression of his view, with its clarification of his earlier statements, approaches that of Vos. But on the continuity-discontinuity issue, it still appears to be asking the wrong question or at least to be unclear on the right question. The question to be asked is not: what in the present creation does Scripture specifically identify as continuing into the new creation? But, as the discussion that follows will note: given the ultimate destiny of the present creation, purposed already from its pre-fall, "very good" beginning, what within it as a whole does Scripture *exclude* from the new creation or say specifically is *not included* in it?

Vos, it considers the latter two passages in light of transformation as a conclusion drawn from Romans 8.

In the interests of corroborating this latter approach, some additional comment on Romans 8:18–23 will be followed by taking note of relevant considerations present in 1 Corinthians 15:44–49.[14] This will serve as well to show that views holding the only point of continuity between the present and new creation to be the resurrection body of believers do not and cannot do justice to these two key passages.

On Romans 8:18–23, reinforcing the incisive exegetical conclusions reflected in Vos's comments noted above runs the risk of belaboring them. To be sure, clearly central in these verses is the future revelation of the glory of believers to be realized in their bodily resurrection ("redemption"—8:23) as the open manifestation of their adoption, with which their present suffering is not worth comparing. But no less clearly, in distinction from believers and along with them, the rest of creation ("the whole creation"[15]—8:22) is implicated in this state of affairs—in fact, strikingly, creation even more emphatically than believers.[16]

What further is this involvement of "creation"? Verses 20 and 21 are fairly read as Paul's reflecting on the fall and its consequences for creation as a whole.[17] What presently marks the creation in a fundamental way, including the existence of believers within it, is "futility" and "bondage to corruption." But that debilitation factor, everywhere pervasive throughout the creation, is not inherent in its original makeup. Instead, it is what creation has become "subjected" to (8:20),

---

14. On 2 Peter 3, see, e.g., Christopher W. Morgan and Robert A. Peterson, eds., *Heaven* (Wheaton, IL: Crossway, 2014), in particular Peterson's helpful list of reasons in showing that verses 10 and 12 do not teach "destruction and re-creation." "In Peter's mind the governing model for the new creation is the complete perfection of the world, for redemption must reach as far as the damage of sin and its curse" (38–39, 163–64). On Heb. 12:26–27, suffice it here to say that it does not provide exegetical considerations that are decisive for annihilation or incompatible with the clear conclusion of renovation from other passages; see the comments of Vos to this effect noted above.

15. Besides believers, certain other exclusions are implied from the wider context in Paul and Scripture as a whole: angels, Satan, demons, unbelievers. "We thus see that all of *rational* creation is excluded by the terms of verses 20–23. We are restricted, therefore, to non-rational creation, animate and inanimate" (John Murray, *The Epistle to the Romans*, 2 vols., NICNT [Grand Rapids, MI: Eerdmans, 1959], 1:302).

16. Note the fivefold repetition of "creation" in 8:19–23: four times it, not believers, serves as either the grammatical or the effective subject of the actions described, and once (8:23, by implication), with believers, as the coordinate subject.

17. Noted by a number of commentators and others; e.g., Murray on verse 20: "surely Paul's commentary on Gen. 3:17, 18" (*Epistle to the Romans*, 1:303).

contrary to its original constitution and design, as we will presently see from elsewhere in Paul; its subjection to disorder and deformation is the result of God's curse on human sin. And as surely as the creation and believers share in the disintegrating effects of this curse, they both look to be delivered from those effects. Further, this deliverance for the creation will be positive on the same order that it will be for believers; it is a coordinate sharing with believers in the eschatological freedom and glory described in this passage.

That coordination is focused pointedly in the correlation of the conjoint groaning of creation, akin to birthing travail (8:22), with the groaning of believers (8:23). In view of that correlation, the former can hardly be a yearning for an outcome *for itself* radically dissimilar to the longing of believers. Rather, the groanings of the creation signal the "eager longing" (8:19) and "hope" (8:20), ascribed to creation in distinction from believers, for its own sharing along with them in "the freedom of the glory of the children of God" (8:21).[18] The longing of creation is not that it might disappear but that "the last vestige of sin . . . disappear from the creation of God" (Vos, answer 35).[19] All told, "the entire creation, as it were, sets up a grand symphony of sighs."[20] And the leitmotif of that symphony, far from being a sighing for extinction, is for eschatological glorification shared with believers.

In passing, it may be noted that this view of the passage is taken by a long list of commentators.[21] In fact, it appears that one would be hard pressed to find a recent commentary that finds the annihilation of the present creation, believers excepted, taught here. A quote from Murray may be taken as representing this consensus for its characteristic incisiveness, as well as the way it relates this to other pertinent passages, including those discussed by Vos:

> The truth set forth is not obscured by personifying what is not
> personal; non-rational creation is reserved for a regeneration that
> is correlative with "the revelation of the sons of God." It is most

---

18. "Obtain" (ESV), "brought into" (NIV) this freedom, fair renderings of the Greek text, make explicit the commensurately positive nature of creation's sharing with believers.

19. Though beyond the scope of what we are able to explore here, significantly this present groaning is also suffused with hopeful strains of joy and praise (e.g., among numerous passages, Pss. 69:34; 96:11–12; Isa. 49:13; 55:12).

20. F. A. Philippi, quoted in Murray, *Epistle to the Romans*, 1:305.

21. To mention only several: Calvin, Hodge, Murray, Ridderbos, Moo, and Schreiner.

reasonable to regard the ἀποκατάστσις πάντων of Acts 3:21 as referring to this same regeneration. In Matt. 19:28 παλιγγενεσία has frequently been interpreted in the same way. There need be no doubt that the new heavens and the new earth of II Pet. 3:13 refer to this regeneration. In this latter passage we have ultimate eschatology, and the description given in Rom. 8:19–23 of the nature of the deliverance which the creation will enjoy at the revelation of the sons of God is one that leaves room for no higher or more ultimate glory—it is defined as deliverance "into the liberty of the glory of the children of God." This liberty for the sons of God is consummate; the liberty enjoyed by the creation in its own sphere must also be consummate.[22]

Akin to Romans 8:18–23 in important respects is 1 Corinthians 15:42–49. Here too the bodily resurrection of believers is the central focus. Within the larger flow of 1 Corinthians 15 beginning at verse 12, a passage intent on refuting those who deny bodily resurrection, Paul continues in verses 42–49 to address the related questions of the mode and nature of the resurrection body of the believer (cf. 15:35).[23] A remarkable feature is the argument he develops, particularly the turn it takes within verse 44.[24]

In verses 42–44a Paul develops an antithetical parallelism, juxtaposing the dead ("sown") pre-resurrection body and the resurrection

---

22. Murray, *Epistle to the Romans*, 1:302–3, including note 26. I am unable within the confines of this chapter to survey systematic-theological or monograph treatments of this issue, though see the reference to the view of Bavinck and Berkouwer above (note 5), including the latter's documented observation of modern Lutheran rejection of views of annihilation characterizing earlier Lutheranism. To quote only from the recent work of Michael Horton, whose view I take to be fairly representative, "The resurrection of the body underscores the anticipation of the final state as the redemption of nature rather than its oblivion." And the following sentences, the final words in the volume's nearly one thousand pages of main text, provide a fitting "eschatological" ending:

> If our goal is to be liberated *from* creation rather than the liberation *of* creation, we will understandably display little concern for the world God has made. If, however, we are looking forward to "the restoration of all things" (Acts 3:21) and the participation of the whole creation in our redemption (Rom. 8:18–21), then our actions here and now pertain to the same world that will one day be finally and fully renewed. (*The Christian Faith* [Grand Rapids, MI: Zondervan, 2011], 988–89)

23. It is important to keep in mind that throughout 1 Corinthians 15 the bodily resurrection of unbelievers (see Acts 24:15) is not within Paul's purview.

24. The following comments are based largely on insights from Vos's chapter "The Eschatological Aspect of the Pauline Conception of Spirit," in the 1912 volume of essays for the centenary of Princeton Seminary, reprinted in Gaffin, *Redemptive History and Biblical Interpretation*, 91–125, and Vos, *Pauline Eschatology*, 169–70n19. Readers are encouraged to consult either or both of these references, whose content I can only sketch briefly here.

body, with their respective polar opposite predicates: "perishable" versus "imperishable," "dishonor" versus "glory," "weakness" versus "power." At verse 44b, however, the antithesis softens; he now reasons conditionally from the pre-resurrection body to the resurrection body, an argumentative move, in turn, that is supported from Scripture in verse 45.

This appeal to Genesis 2:7 functions to open up the widest possible outlook, one that covers creation from its beginning to its consummation, and the sweep of history from its inception to its eschatological conclusion. The contrasting parallelism up to this point, between bodies, is now between whole persons. Adam as a "living being" is the representative primal instance of the bodily existence that is "natural"; the last Adam, Christ, as resurrected and so become the "life-giving Spirit," is the representative initial ("firstfruits"—1 Cor. 15:20, 23) instance of the bodily existence that is "spiritual," in the sense not of its presumably immaterial composition but of being resurrected and transformed in its physicality by the work of the Holy Spirit.

Further, on the one side of this contrast, it should not be missed, is the Adam not of Genesis 3 but of Genesis 2. Adam not as fallen but as he is by virtue of creation and not yet fallen is contrasted with Christ as resurrected and exalted ("of heaven"—1 Cor. 15:48).

Whole, living persons imply an environment appropriate to each as the apostle immediately goes on to make explicit. In verse 46 the neuter singular substantives τὸ ψυχικόν and τὸ πνευματικὸν are, as Vos observes, "generalizing expressions, after which it would be a mistake to supply σῶμα"; he continues, "They designate the successive reign of two comprehensive principles in history, two successive world-orders, a first and second creation, beginning each with of Adam of its own."[25]

Here three interrelated considerations emerge. First is the tethering principle that informs the renovation of the entire creation, the essential and unbreakable bond between image-bearing creatures and the larger creation of which they are a part. Further, that bond is not the

---

25. Vos, "Eschatological Aspect," 231; elsewhere he says, "But in vs. 46 the representation widens out [beyond "the contrast between the two bodies *only*"] to a far more general, indeed cosmical one" (*Pauline Eschatology*, 167).

result of the fall but antedates the fall; it is given with the original creation. Finally, that concreated bond has in view its future consummate realization. The pre-eschatological imprimatur "very good" concerns "everything that [God] had made" (Gen. 1:31), not just his image-bearing creature. As such, it anticipates the eschatological "best" that was not yet but still to come—for image bearers as the crown of the creation, to be sure, but also for the rest of creation.[26]

The discontinuity between the present body and the resurrection body is undoubtedly radical (1 Cor. 15:42–43). But more basic than that discontinuity, no matter how far-reaching, is the underlying continuity between the two bodies. Accordingly, as that is the case for believers, likewise for creation as a whole, more basic is the continuity that underlies the radical discontinuity brought about by the transforming changes that will take place.[27] And, again, that perduring continuity will be true for both together, believers and the rest of the creation, and not for the one without the other; it will be true, moreover, as the design of God from the beginning, even before the fall. In this sense it is surely to be affirmed, "Redemption restores and perfects creation."[28]

I am unable here to explore the range of important issues that these comments bring into view, and so I end with this. As Vos reminds us

---

26. Vos explains:

> The proper solution seems to be as follows: the Apostle was intent upon showing that in the plan of God at the outset provision was made for a higher kind of body (as pertaining to a higher state of existence). From the abnormal body of sin no inference could be drawn to that effect. The abnormal and the eschatological are not so logically correlated that the one can be postulated from the other [as 1 Cor. 15:44b does]. But the world of creation [pre-fall] and the world to come *are* thus correlated, the one pointing to the other. (*Pauline Eschatology*, 169n19)

This observation entails, as Vos points out, that on the one side of the contrast, the "natural" bodies of 15:44a and 15:44b are not identical. The former with its three characteristics (15:42–43) is the body as the result of the curse on human sin (the "natural" from the vantage point of the original creation become all too "unnatural," as it might be put); the former is the body "very good," as it came from the creating hand of God.

27. Berkouwer (*Return of Christ*, 220–24) finds problematic the widespread use, traditionally, of the concept of substance (as in Vos, for instance) and the substance-accidents distinction in order to show continuity with change and to reject annihilation, both for Christians and the cosmos. It seems to me that more is made of this point and the philosophical difficulties presumably involved than need be. Whatever could be said further by way of explanation, what is essential and sufficient to affirm biblically is that for both believers and the rest of creation their present identity continues in the eschatological future. Who (not what) I am now will be raised, not someone else; the present creation will be renovated, not another created *ex nihilo*.

28. To view the disintegrating and enervating effects of the fall and the curse in the present creation as somehow reinforcing the notion that God designed its inherent, concreated expendability seriously undervalues and distorts the Bible's teaching on creation and, inevitably, in one way or another, on the full scope of redemption.

in answer 38, "because we lack any adequate comprehension of that new world itself," we are unable to "say very much" about it. We must be careful not to overstate or speculate, to go beyond what Scripture entitles us. Still, we dare not risk saying less than Scripture.

Paul's evocative use of Scripture in 1 Corinthians 2:9 particularly comes to mind in this regard:

> What no eye has seen, nor ear heard,
>   nor the heart of man imagined,
>   what God has prepared for those who love him . . .

Certainly in their immediate context (1 Cor. 1:18–2:16), these words have in view the hidden wisdom of God as already revealed in the cross of Christ and as already received and understood, however dimly (1 Cor. 13:12), by faith through the power of the Spirit. But surely they also apply by extension to what is the still future, to the yet unrealized revelation of that wisdom at the return of Christ, to the wonder of what is not yet seen, heard, or even imagined for believers as that will be given in and with their transformed resurrection bodies. And so, too, those words may be fairly applied as well to the wonder of what is not yet seen, heard, or even imagined for the entire creation consummately transformed.

> Holy, Holy, Holy, Lord God Almighty!
> All thy works shall praise thy Name, in earth and sky and sea;
> Holy, Holy, Holy, merciful and mighty!
> God in three Persons, blessed Trinity![29]

"All thy works shall praise thy Name, in earth and sky and sea." To sing that line from this well-known hymn is to confess that the present praise of creation is not merely pre-eschatological, destined in the end for the silence of eternal extinction. The present creation awaits the eschatological voice it will receive when, free at last from its "bondage to corruption," it will "obtain the freedom of the glory of the sons of God." With this obtaining together with the sons of God, creation's praise—beyond all sighing and in a manner beyond present

---

29. Reginald Heber, "Holy, Holy, Holy!," *Trinity Hymnal* (Philadelphia: Great Commission, 1990), 100, stanza 4.

comprehension—will heighten their enjoyment of that freedom and glory in the new creation of God.

Here too, as in all our theologizing, the ultimate issue is God and his glory. As "man's chief end is to glorify God and enjoy him forever" (Westminster Shorter Catechism, 1), so, too, creation's primary purpose is to display that glory, and to do so forever.

Appendix: Vos's Four Questions and Answers on Heaven[30]

35. What will precede the consummate salvation of the children of God?

The appearance of a new world. Scripture speaks of that very clearly. In Acts 3:21 Peter speaks of an ἀποκατάστασις, a "restoration of all things." And in Revelation 21:5 He who sits on the throne says: "Behold, I make all things new." As a matter of fact, all this is inherent in the relationship to the rest of creation in which man stands. It is given to him so that he would rule over it. It has been carried along with him in his fall. It has been subjected to the groaning of futility. It is in travail, since with the dawning of the glory of the children of God it also awaits its liberation [Rom. 8:19–22]. It is not solely about atonement for sin but about the removal of the results of sin. And when the devil, the demons, the lost, will be thrown "outside," then the last vestige of sin, to the extent it is "inside," will also need to disappear from the creation of God. The Old Testament in fact already speaks of this (Ps. 102:26–28; Isa. 34:4; 65:17; 66:22; 51:6, 16; 11:6–9). In the New Testament, one may also compare 2 Peter 3:7–13; Revelation 20:11; 21:1.

Scripture teaches further that this new world will follow the glorification of the children of God, that is, the glorious resurrection and the last judgment.

36. How are we to think of this bringing into being of the new world?

Thinking on this question differs greatly. Some propose an absolutely new world, so that in substance the old does not recur in the new and a new world comes in its place. The Lutheran dogmaticians

30. From Vos, *Reformed Dogmatics*, 5:308–10, quoted here with permission of the publisher.

until Gerhard were devoted to this view. But in general whenever they mention the new earth *pro forma*, they do not say much about it. The Reformed, for the most part, expressed support for the opposite view, namely that the substance of the presently existing world will be preserved but will be restored, purified in glory. Also, a host of recent theologians align themselves with the Reformed here. The grounds are:

a) Even the passages that seem to speak emphatically for the destruction of the old world are nevertheless not decisive. They are 2 Peter 3:7–13 and Revelation 20:11 and 21:1. The first passage speaks only of "passing away," "being melted," without it exactly becoming extinct; indeed, in our experience burning is never total annihilation. Revelation speaks of a "fleeing away," a "passing away," a "being no more."

b) The Old Testament passages all speak clearly of "change," not of "annihilation," for example, Psalm 102:26–27. This passage is taken up again in Hebrews 1:10–12. And accordingly, Hebrews 12:26–28 should also be so interpreted that at the shaking of the cosmos something remains that is immovable. This immovable something could be found in the heaven of God's glory, but still probably also meant is that something of what is changeable will remain in order to be made unchangeable.

c) If annihilation is assumed, then texts that speak of change are absolutely impossible to explain. If change is assumed, the texts that seem to speak of annihilation can still be explained in a very sound sense.

d) Analogy speaks for change. The body of man, too, is not annihilated and a new body created in its place. The old is changed or glorified. One should assume then that this will also take place in the wider sphere with the entire groaning creation.

37. How will that change occur?

Second Peter 3:7–12 says that it will occur "by fire." This cannot be meant figuratively. It is contrasted with the destruction that once came upon the earth by water, the water of the flood. So it must be just as real.

Hebrews 12:26–28 speaks, as we saw, of a "shaking" and "moving." But this and what Peter says do not exclude each other. A conflagration of the world with tremors and earthquakes would fulfill both prophecies.

The renewal of the earth does not affect heaven as God's dwelling place but heaven in the celestial sense.

38. Can we say very much about heaven and the blessings of heaven? No, for this far surpasses our understanding. We know only:

a) That heaven is a place. Like hell, it is to be thought of as having a locality. It may be true that someone can have heaven in his heart, but his heart must also be in heaven with his body.

b) The enjoyment of heaven is in the first place the enjoyment of God, the *visio Dei*, a "beholding of God." This is not to be understood one-sidedly in an intellectualistic manner but in all its magnitude. The nearness of God will affect every capacity of man, and every capacity will react to it. Theologians usually speak of *visio* [seeing], *amor* [love], *gaudium* [joy], *gloria* [glory]; others of knowing, serving, enjoying, and glorifying God (cf. 1 Cor. 13:9–13).

It has been asked whether this will be a seeing with physical eyes. This is not to be assumed. God is not visible to the senses. The Mediator certainly is. No one has ever seen God. This seeing follows on faith. It is thus something that is comparable with faith but that still does not necessarily need to be a perceiving with the senses. There will thus be a perception of God, yet such that it is not a material entity that appears to us.

c) The enjoyment of heaven in fellowship with God is eternal life in all its fullness.

d) Along with these enjoyments, perhaps other blessings will be bestowed on the children of God. But Scripture describes all that in images about which we cannot say to what extent they are purely metaphysical, to what extent they are metaphorical in the deeper sense of the word. Naturally, all defects and all misery will be banished from heaven.

e) Heaven will not be a world of uniformity; diversity will rule there. One is the glory of the sun, another that of the moon, another of the stars [cf. 1 Cor. 15:41]. Not all receive the same portion. The one who has sowed much receives a rich harvest.

But as already said above, diversity will not possibly function as a cause for distress.

One can think of the blessed state of heaven too much as an individual. There will be an ordering of things there. Glorified humanity will have its head in Christ and form a body under Him. In a body there are always different parts.

One can also think of the blessings of salvation too spiritualistically. Many do not reckon with the fact that the body of the believer, too, is resurrected and that the earth, too, will be re-created. In their conception there is really no place for a new earth. Still, on the other hand it should be acknowledged that we do not know what the enjoyment of God's world will be like for His children. We do not, if for no other reason because we lack any adequate comprehension of that new world itself.

Part 3

DOCTRINE OF
THE TRINITY

10

The Trinity and Monotheism

Christianity and Islam in the
Theology of Cornelius Van Til

Camden M. Bucey

It is a great privilege to celebrate my beloved professor, for his faithful service to our Lord, by writing an essay in his honor. At Westminster Theological Seminary, I learned much from Dr. Poythress. In the classroom, he prepared me to meet the diverse challenges of pastoral ministry as well as the rigors of the academy. But he also taught me many more lessons outside the classroom. Many times over, Dr. Poythress responded to requests for help with an erudition matched by grace, generosity, and patience. These qualities are often considered antithetical to the lifestyle requisite of such a prolific scholar, but Vern Poythress has never labored selfishly or for scholarship's sake. Along with the apostle Paul, he has striven to present "everyone mature in Christ" (Col. 1:28). This flows from his fundamental and uncompromising commitment to the triune God, who reveals himself in his inerrant and infallible Word. The one true God—Father, Son, and Holy Spirit—

is incomparable, and whether writing about hermeneutics, philosophy, logic, mathematics, science, or sociology, Poythress has ardently defended and advanced an explicitly *Trinitarian* theology. This places him at odds with the world and even with segments of Christendom.

While religious fundamentalists trend toward the extreme in geopolitics, others have long sought peace through shared religious values and theological principles. Many understand the Second Vatican Council's declaration *Nostra Aetate* as paving the way for a peaceful religious environment through religious dialogue.[1] In 2007, Islamic leaders wrote an open letter to Christians, calling for peace and urging a common understanding of the two religions.[2] Many prominent Christian leaders have since signed the letter, while others are convinced that such a project is misguided at best. This issue runs deeper than geopolitical front lines and the social agendas of progressive Catholicism and mainline Protestantism. It has become a contentious issue in the evangelical world as well. Conservative Christians who assumed that such matters only existed "out there" have been forced to confront them at home.

Larycia Hawkins, former professor of political science at Wheaton College, recently made the claim that Christians and Muslims worship the same God. Such a statement would have remained unnoticed in most academic institutions, but Wheaton College's response turned the issue into national news. Hawkins appealed to the theology of Miroslav Volf, who has become the champion of this issue.[3] Volf himself responded to the controversy in *The Washington Post*, arguing that the

---

1. In his essay on the Trinity and Islam, Karl Rahner minimizes the language of diversity within the Godhead, opting for a conclusion that sees Christian and Islamic monotheism as basically identical or at least compatible. He questions whether the Christian notion of diversity within the Godhead should be a significant issue for Muslims:

> As I said at the very beginning, I am aware that I have not really carried out a dialogue with Islamic theology, but only indicated a few points from the problems within Christianity with reference to monotheism and the doctrine of the Trinity, in the modest hope that it might perhaps be remotely useful for a real dialogue in which Islamic and Christian theologians would talk about a joint profession of faith in the one sole God and ask at the same time why this profession is not curtailed or threatened by the Christian doctrine of the threefoldness of this one sole God. (Karl Rahner, "Oneness and Threefoldness of God in Discussion with Islam," in *Theological Investigations*, trans. Edward Quinn, vol. 18 [New York: Crossroad, 1983], 121)

2. That letter was a response to Pope Benedict XVI, "Faith, Reason and the University—Memories and Reflections" (lecture delivered at Regensberg University, September 12, 2006).

3. Miroslav Volf, *Allah: A Christian Response* (New York: HarperOne, 2012).

issue was fundamentally a matter of bigotry toward Muslims rather than theological error.[4]

While I do not deny that religious bigotry is a strong force in the world, I reject Volf's basic claim that Muslims and Christians worship the same God. I intend to consider critically the theological methodology that establishes common ground between Christian monotheism and Muslim monotheism. Christian monotheism cannot be reduced to any metaphysical, epistemological, or ecclesiological congruity with Islam. While that position seems radical to many, even others who would not take offense to such a statement have unwittingly opened the door to a shared monotheism, because they have failed to apply rightly the Christian principle of the one and the many.

One and Many

The ecumenical creeds[5] are careful to articulate a doctrine of the Trinity that guards against the errors of tritheism and modalism. A fear of modalism causes some theologians to stress the distinctions of the persons in a way that prioritizes the persons over the essence of God, or more radically, eclipses a common essence. A fear of tritheism engenders a heavy emphasis upon what is common to the persons and the divine essence, which can lead some to prioritize the essence over the persons or, more radically, to deny meaningful personal distinctions within the Godhead. It is a short step from this latter emphasis to an identification of the essence of God with monotheism. This effectively makes the personal distinctions within the Godhead ancillary to monotheism. It is true that Christians worship one God, and God is one in essence. Yet, it is equally and foundationally true that the one God is essentially triune and commands that he be worshiped as such (Matt. 28:18–20; John 4:24; 1 Cor. 8:6; 1 Tim. 2:5). To posit that Christian monotheism can be affirmed by reference to the essence of God alone would amount to a separation between Trinity and monotheism, and this is an error.

---

4. Miroslav Volf, "Wheaton Professor's Suspension Is about Anti-Muslim Bigotry, Not Theology," *Washington Post*, December 17, 2015, https://www.washingtonpost.com/news/acts-of-faith /wp/2015/12/17/wheaton-professors-suspension-is-about-anti-muslim-bigotry-not-theology/.

5. The Councils of Nicaea (325) and Constantinople (381) are especially known for establishing Trinitarian orthodoxy. The Athanasian Creed also presents a strong Trinitarian doctrine, explicitly affirming the equality of the persons in the Godhead.

Such an error can have many contributing factors. But in this brief essay, I seek to demonstrate that the error is often rooted in a problematic theological methodology that prioritizes the unity of God over the diversity in a way that allows the essence of monotheism to be something other than Trinitarian.[6] In the larger scope of world religions, this seems appropriate, particularly when the goal is locating some common notion of monotheism. Like Islam, Christianity is monotheistic, and since adherents of each religion profess one God, it seems they share a baseline belief. But this way of construing the matter presents a major problem, for the Christian God of Scripture is essentially one *and* three.

A rich heritage of Reformed theologians has upheld this truth. Poythress is a student and defender of the theology and apologetic method of Cornelius Van Til (1895–1987), who taught at Westminster Theological Seminary from its founding in 1929 until 1979.[7] Van Til and Poythress have been equally adamant that Christian apologists must not defend bare theism, that is, anything other than Christian theism. God's identity is triune, and any defense of a generic theism is not a faithful defense of the Christian God revealed in Scripture.[8] This fundamental commitment requires any orthodox conception of monotheism to be linked inextricably with the Trinity.[9] Drawing from old Princeton and old Amsterdam, Van Til fashioned his Trinitarian theology upon three core principles: equal ultimacy, absolute personality, and *perichoresis*.[10]

---

6. Thomas Aquinas is a prime example of this general approach. His distinction between the treatises *De Deo uno* and *De Deo trino* is an application of the nature-grace distinction to Trinitarian theology and epistemology. Unaided reason may only conclude the unity of God. Only when God reveals himself in grace can humans learn that he exists as Trinity. Van Til commented, "The first point that calls for reflection here is the fact that it is, according to Scripture itself, the same God who reveals himself in nature and in grace" (Cornelius Van Til, "Nature and Scripture," in *The Infallible Word: A Symposium by the Members of the Faculty of Westminster Theological Seminary*, ed. N. B. Stonehouse and Paul Woolley, 3rd ed. [Philadelphia: Presbyterian and Reformed, 1967], 266).

7. Van Til retired in 1972 but taught at the seminary occasionally for another seven years.

8. Daniel Strange helpfully develops this idea with respect to a theology of religions in *Their Rock Is Not Like Our Rock: A Theology of Religions* (Phillipsburg, NJ: P&R, 2014).

9. Van Til was particularly sensitive to this issue because he formulated his Trinitarian theology in direct opposition to several notable personalists and absolute idealists. Lane G. Tipton skillfully surveys this context in "The Triune Personal God: Trinitarian Theology in the Thought of Cornelius Van Til" (PhD diss., Westminster Theological Seminary, 2004). B. A. Bosserman also provides a thorough discussion of Van Til's context (*The Trinity and the Vindication of Christian Paradox: An Interpretation and Refinement of the Theological Apologetic of Cornelius Van Til* [Eugene, OR: Pickwick, 2014]).

10. Van Til was indebted especially to B. B. Warfield (1851–1921) and Charles Hodge (1797–1878), who taught systematic theology at Princeton Theological Seminary. Herman Bavinck (1854–

Together these form a robust doctrine that guards against the twin heresies of tritheism and modalism.

Equal Ultimacy

Van Til incorporated a principle of equal ultimacy to address specifically the philosophical problem of the one and many. He often cast this problem, which has plagued philosophers for millennia, as a problem of predication.[11] Humans demonstrate a fundamental ability to relate objects and experiences to each other by making comparisons and contrasts. Yet, philosophers have struggled to formulate a metaphysical reality that can relate unity and diversity without ultimately capitulating toward one over the other. For example, in order for the statement "the sky is blue" to be meaningful, we must presuppose something about the sky and blue things. For predication to proceed, the sky must share some properties with blue things, though the sky must not be identical with the concept of blueness. The "problem" of the one and many lies in understanding how these two relate. If reality is ultimately unified, how can we speak meaningfully about the distinctions of seemingly different phenomena? Likewise, if reality is fundamentally diverse, how can we relate phenomena that have nothing in common? Van Til sought the metaphysical solution to this problem in the triune God, who is equally and ultimately one and three, unity and diversity.

The equal ultimacy of divine unity and diversity is encapsulated in what Van Til termed the representational principle: "The foundation of the representational principle among men is the fact that the Trinity exists in the form of a mutually exhaustive representation of the three Persons that constitute it."[12] In reference to the *ousia* (the essence, the unity of the Godhead), no single *hypostasis* (each person, the diversity of the Godhead) is privileged in its representation. Insofar as the Trinity

---

1921), who, along with Abraham Kuyper (1837–1920), largely constituted the old Amsterdam school of thought, was also a heavy influence upon Van Til, especially in his understanding of the doctrine of *perichoresis*.

11. This problem has been known by several names, including the *infima species*, the "problem of unity and diversity," and the "problem of universals." Cornelius Van Til often called it the "problem of the one-and-many."

12. Cornelius Van Til, *A Survey of Christian Epistemology*, 2nd ed. (Phillipsburg, NJ: Presbyterian and Reformed, 1980), 96. For a fuller treatment of Van Til's representational principle, see chaps. 5–6 of Tipton, "Triune Personal God."

has been revealed to men, each *hypostasis* has been equally represented. The whole of the Godhead represents each member, and each
member is an exhaustive representation of the whole. Van Til continues: "The emphasis should be placed upon the idea of *exhaustion*. This
is important because it brings out the point of the complete equality as
far as ultimacy is concerned of the principle of unity and the principle
of diversity."[13] In terms of essential ontology, no member of the Trinity is privileged over the others. The Father is no more represented in
the Godhead's unity than the Son or the Spirit. Unity and diversity are
equally ultimate. This is an important point, but it is just as important
to recognize that Van Til's concern is not with unity and diversity in
general. He locates his discussion specifically in the Godhead, the seat
of absolute personality.

Absolute Personality

Christians universally have identified God as personal. They love, worship, and commune with him personally. Yet the theological formulations meant to describe this basic truth have proved difficult to define
precisely. The varied use of the words "person" and "*hypostasis*" in
Christian theology demonstrate this challenge.[14] In his work on the
Trinity, Van Til defined "person" in the Augustinian sense, as a center
of self-consciousness. At that point, he already differed from several
contemporary theologians. In order to formulate social doctrines of the
Trinity, Catherine Mowry LaCugna[15] and Jürgen Moltmann,[16] for in-

---

13. Van Til, *Survey of Christian Epistemology*, 96.
14. The definition of *hypostasis* changed even between the Councils of Nicaea (325) and Constantinople (381).

> At Constantinople in 381, the word *hypostasis* was chosen to refer to Father, Son, and
> Spirit because it could be interpreted to the advantage of both sides [those wanting to
> emphasize the mystery of the unity and locate that mystery in diversity]. On the one
> hand, it could refer to the *ousia*, or essence of something, and be translated into Latin as
> *substantia*. On the other hand, it could be forced to refer to the face (*prosopon*) of God,
> the equivalent of *persona* in Tertullian's Latin formula, *una substantia, tres personae*.
> In sum, the term *hypostasis* equivocates. (Ted Peters, *God as Trinity: Relationality and
> Temporality in Divine Life* [Louisville: Westminster John Knox, 1993], 34).

Many contemporary theologians understand "person" in a philosophical sense. Others, such as
Karl Rahner, have lamented the divergent use of Trinitarian vocabulary. Rahner, "Oneness and
Threefoldness of God in Discussion with Islam," 110.
15. Catherine Mowry LaCugna, *God for Us: The Trinity and Christian Life* (San Francisco:
HarperSanFrancisco, 1991), 243.
16. Jürgen Moltmann, *The Trinity and the Kingdom: The Doctrine of God* (San Francisco:
Harper & Row, 1981), 150, 175, 177.

stance, defined "person" as a relation or center of activity. Others have focused on individuality, identity, or distinct manners of subsistence.[17] Van Til sympathized with the concerns of twentieth-century British and German absolute idealists, who insisted that the epistemological foundation be understood as a complete system.[18] He also interacted with the Boston personalists, who posited that ultimate reality must be absolutely personal.[19] For Van Til, the triune God, as an independent and underived self-conscious person, satisfies these requirements. Van Til maintained that "if God is left out of the picture it is up to the human mind to furnish the unity that must bind together the diversity of factual existence."[20] For him, nothing less than absolute personality is a sufficient metaphysical precondition for maintaining unity among diversity. Only God's absolute personality provides the necessary "personal atmosphere" required for human knowledge.

> The problem of the one and the many, of the universal and the particular, of being and becoming, of analytical and synthetic reasoning, of the a priori and the a posteriori must be solved by an exclusive reference to the Trinity. The only alternative to this is to assume responsibility for trying to explain the whole of reality in temporal terms, and therefore with man as the ultimate point of reference.[21]

Absolute personality constrains theologians from considering the divine essence abstractly. God is not an impersonal force. He is one tripersonal God whom we may address and worship as one triune God.

---

17. Peters provides a helpful overview of several other contemporary thinkers:

> Karl Barth believes that the modern emphasis on human individuality requires that we cease referring to Father, Son, and Spirit as persons. Robert Jenson is ready to substitute the word "identity" for "person." Karl Rahner wants to hold on to the classical formulation, but he wants to define "person" as a "distinct manner of subsisting." Leonardo Boff is happy with the word "person" (*persona*) because he believes it is equivalent to *hypostasis*. Proposals vary. Yet all seem to operate with the assumption that contemporary understandings of personhood are relevant to Trinitarian understanding. (Peters, *God as Trinity*, 35)

18. Van Til interacted primarily with the works of Bernard Bosanquet and F. H. Bradley, but was also wary of G. W. F. Hegel. For a discussion of the need for a universal epistemological foundation, see Van Til, *Survey of Christian Epistemology*, 102.

19. A. C. Knudsen and Borden Parker Bowne were the most significant personalist thinkers for Van Til.

20. Van Til, *Survey of Christian Epistemology*, 216.

21. Ibid., 96–97.

But if this reference point is to remain a *single* reference point and thus allow for meaningful communication between rational agents, Van Til needed to identify a theological means for holding the three persons of the Godhead together in one unified, yet exhaustively personal, entity. He accomplished this through his doctrine of the *perichoresis* of the persons within a common essence.

Perichoresis

Many different versions of *perichoresis* have been developed in contemporary Christianity. The Cappadocian Fathers used the term to describe the relationship of the one and the three as proper to the divinity itself and not a result of his relationship to creation. Through the history of the church, theologians have reinterpreted and appropriated the doctrine for other purposes. Though formulations differ, most incorporate the understanding that *perichoresis* is the mutual indwelling or cohering of each *hypostasis* with the other *hypostases* and the divine essence. Each person, who is identical to the essence, is conscious of himself as exhaustively indwelling the other persons, while being personally distinct from them within the unity of the Godhead.

Van Til's use of *perichoresis* allowed him to maintain that God is personal in both his unity and his diversity: "We do assert that God, that is, the whole Godhead, is one person. We have noted how each attribute is coextensive with the being of God. We are compelled to maintain this in order to avoid the notion of an uninterpreted being of some sort."[22] At this point, Van Til uses a different sense of the term "person" with reference to the "whole Godhead" than do the ecumenical creeds with reference to the individual *hypostases*. Van Til is not affirming that God is one *hypostasis* and three *hypostases*. When Van Til affirms that God is one person and three persons, he is speaking of

---

22. Cornelius Van Til, *An Introduction to Systematic Theology: Prolegomena and the Doctrines of Revelation, Scripture, and God*, 2nd ed., ed. William Edgar (Phillipsburg, NJ: P&R, 2007), 363, 363n45. Van Til was building upon the Trinitarian theology of Charles Hodge, who wrote:

> As the essence of the Godhead is common to the several persons, they have a common intelligence, will and power. There are not in God three intelligences, three wills, three efficiencies. The three are one God, and, therefore, have one mind and will. This intimate union was expressed in the Greek church by the word *perichoresis*, which the Latin words "inextentia," "inhabitatio" and "intercommunio" were used to explain. (Charles Hodge, *Systematic Theology*, vol. 1 [repr., Peabody, MA: Hendrickson, 1999], 461)

persons in a philosophical sense, as centers of consciousness. We may love, worship, and commune with the Godhead as a person even as we may do so with the Father, Son, or Spirit specifically. Van Til facilitates this by understanding the mutual, exhaustive, and self-conscious indwelling of the persons in the Godhead. Too often, Christians conceptualize the Trinity in terms of three slightly overlapping circles of partially personal relations, perhaps expressed in the bare language of subsistence. This illustration is defective in that it represents a partial indwelling and leaves co-indwelling and self-consciousness out of the picture entirely, since portions of each *hypostasis* remain private. For Van Til, there is no aspect of the divine essence that is not exhaustively indwelt by the Father, Son, and Spirit. Likewise, each *hypostasis* indwells the others with no remainder in a mutual and reciprocal bond of self-conscious fellowship.

Van Til formulated his doctrine of *perichoresis* in a way that maintained genuine distinctions in the Godhead. When Van Til is considered carefully, his conception of *perichoresis* should not be mistaken for nominalism or modalism. The *hypostases* indwell each other exhaustively but are distinguished by incommunicable personal properties. The Father is eternally unbegotten and is distinct from the Son, who is eternally begotten from the Father. The Spirit is distinct from both the Father and the Son in that he eternally proceeds from both the Father and the Son. There is no insignificant mystery here. How exactly the *hypostases* can mutually and *exhaustively* indwell one another without obliterating all real distinctions in the Godhead is perhaps ineffable, but if we maintain both exhaustive interpenetration of the persons and their incommunicable personal properties, we have the proper parameters in place to locate the mystery. Van Til attempted to formulate a doctrine of Trinitarian *perichoresis* that did justice to all of Scripture, and at this point he appeals to divine incomprehensibility.[23]

A Trinitarian Monotheism

God is essentially one God, not many gods. That is the fundamental tenet of monotheism. God is also essentially three persons. Thinking of

---

23. For a fuller discussion, see Lane G. Tipton, "The Function of Perichoresis and the Divine Incomprehensibility," *WTJ* 64, no. 2 (2002): 289–306.

the "one" God of monotheism and the "one" essence of God, theologians may be tempted to identify the two, especially if they are seeking common ground with Muslims, who judge that the Christian belief that God is three persons precludes monotheism. If, as Christians, we predicate what is true "essentially" of God, then we must say that he is essentially one and three, admitting of no priority between the two. God is just as much essentially one as he is essentially three, and vice versa. However, if we use the noun "essence" in a technical, dogmatic sense, it refers to his unity or *ousia*. It is proper to use "essence" to denote the unity of the Godhead, but at the same time, we must affirm that God is essentially both one and three, admitting of no priority of unity or diversity within the divine life.

Monotheism cannot be equated with the divine essence, and we certainly must not appeal to the essence of the one true God in such a way that undermines the complementary truth that God is essentially both one and three. The *one* true God is one in three and three in one. The essence ought not be prioritized over the *hypostases*. Divine oneness and threeness are equally ultimate. The divine *ousia* (the essence, the one) and *hypostases* (the persons, the many) cannot be isolated ontologically or epistemologically. God is simple as triune, and there is no more basic consideration of his being.[24]

Sense, Reference, and the Trinity

Our discussion brings us to a forerunner of Poythress, the brilliant mathematician Gottlob Frege (1848–1925).[25] He was accomplished in diverse fields, and he is known as the father of analytic philosophy and the greatest logician since Aristotle. Frege wrestled with several logical puzzles he recognized in language, such as how some identity statements can be informative, while others convey no such information.[26] For example, the following statement is informative:

---

24. See also K. Scott Oliphint, *Reasons for Faith: Philosophy in the Service of Theology* (Phillipsburg, NJ: P&R, 2006), 91–95, 206–7; Strange, *Their Rock Is Not Like Our Rock*, 58–61.

25. Poythress interacts with Frege in Vern Sheridan Poythress, *In the Beginning Was the Word: Language—A God-Centered Approach* (Wheaton, IL: Crossway, 2009), 350–52; Poythress, *Logic: A God-Centered Approach to the Foundation of Western Thought* (Wheaton, IL: Crossway, 2013), 420, 690.

26. Wehmeier describes these puzzles as "(1) the apparent impossibility of informative identity statements and (2) the apparent failure of substitutivity in contexts of propositional attitudes"

A. The morning star = Venus.

By identifying the morning star with Venus, we have conveyed new information. The following statement, on the other hand, is not informative:

B. The morning star = the morning star.

This sort of identity statement does not predicate anything meaningful. Statements A and B are equivalent in that their constituent terms share the same reference (the planet Venus). However, statement A seems greater or more valuable, since it conveys a genuine scientific discovery.

If the morning star is Venus (the morning star = Venus), it would seem that we could substitute "Venus" for "the morning star" without altering the value or equivalence of the statement. Frege was intrigued with the phenomenon that upon substitution, the non-informative identity statement becomes informative. We intuit that the two statements are not saying the same thing, since the denotations of the terms cannot fully account for their meaningfulness.[27] To explain this phenomenon, Frege developed what he called the *Sinn und Bedeutung*— or sense-reference—distinction.[28] He distinguished between the entity to which a term refers and how that term expresses the entity, that is, its mode of presentation.[29] Statements A and B are equivalent in identity because they share the same reference. However, statement A is informative whereas B is not because they have different senses. This is an equivocation in sense rather than reference, and it applies to our Trinitarian discussion. Consider the following statements:

C. The God of monotheism = one God.

D. The God of monotheism = one divine essence *simpliciter.*

I surmise that Volf and his sympathizers would recognize statements C and D as equivalent in identity while representing an equivocation

(Kai F. Wehmeier, "Frege, Gottlob," in *Encyclopedia of Philosophy*, ed. Donald Borchert, 2nd ed., vol. 3 [Farmington Hills, MI: Macmillan Reference USA, 2006], 728).

27. Edward N. Zalta, "Gottlob Frege," in *Stanford Encyclopedia of Philosophy*, October 29, 2016, http://plato.stanford.edu/entries/frege/.

28. Wehmeier, "Frege, Gottlob," 728.

29. Ibid.

of sense. They reason that since both Christians and Muslims affirm that God is one divine essence, they are considered monotheists of the same type. I concur that orthodox Christians affirm God is one divine essence, but this essence can never be abstracted from the persons, who eternally indwell one another and self-consciously subsist within the essence of the Godhead. This would imply that insofar as the referent in view is the essence of God *simpliciter*, it is not the Christian God who is being denoted in either C or D. In other words, neither C nor D, by reference or sense, is the Christian God. An abstract divine essence, *the divine essence simpliciter*, is a categorically different existent from the God revealed in Scripture. We must reformulate the statements:

E. The God of Christian monotheism = one God.

F. The God of Christian monotheism = three persons perichoreti-cally subsisting in one divine essence.

While statements E and F represent another equivocation of sense, they are equivalent in reference. This is a critical point. For Van Til, statement F is irreducible. The divine essence is not separate from the divine persons, an ontological as well as an epistemological truth. In each formulation, the sense of F and D prove integral for identifying the referents in view for C and E. While this is not necessarily Frege's immediate concern, the sense-reference distinction nevertheless sheds light on the topic under consideration. God is triune in his simplicity, and we cannot divide the triune, simple God into parts.[30] This truth should be reflected in our thinking, even though these epistemologi-cal dimensions stretch our abilities. Trinitarian language describes the truth as it is revealed while always reminding us of our creaturely limitations.

Sense is always colored by reference. There is no clean break be-tween the two, because there is no pure sense apart from reference. Even if a reference is purely conceptual, we cannot meaningfully speak of a bare sense apart from reference. A sense must correspond to some *quid* for it to have meaning. There is some measure of dependence between sense and reference: neither can change without altering the

---

30. Oliphint, *Reasons for Faith*, 91–95, 203n25.

other; still, there is a real distinction between the two. Gregory Na-
zianzus is a helpful exemplar when he says, "I cannot think on the
one without quickly being encircled by the splendor of the three; nor
can I discern the three without being straightway carried back to the
one."[31] Several interpreters have interacted with Gregory's well-known
statement, and others have tried to work out the implications of the
statement, but not all have done so through the lens of a robust *perichoresis* as has Van Til.[32]

This epistemological oscillation or "Nazianzen circle" is not a *dialectic*, which often suggests progress toward an eschatological resolution. The relationship between one and many in the Trinity will never be
"resolved" or otherwise overcome. The oscillation of human thoughts
from the one to the three and back again is the natural response of a
finite creature to an incomprehensible God. Van Til used *perichoresis*
as a theological means for expressing the paradox of God's equally
ultimate personal unity and diversity. We can and must positively say
certain things about the Godhead, because he has revealed himself to
us. We must rest in the mystery that God has revealed while always
striving to be transformed by the renewal of our minds according to
Scripture.

Conclusion

Christian monotheism and bare theism are different religions. The
latter category does not include the former. Trinitarianism is irreducible, and therefore it is categorically different from Islam. The *ousia*
of God cannot be identified with monotheism to the exclusion of the
hypostases. This is true also for any prioritization of the *ousia* over
the *hypostases*. Such an imbalance of the one over the many leads to

---

31. Calvin quotes Gregory in Calvin, *Institutes*, 1.13.17.
32. While I take issue with his use of "dialectic" in this matter, Colin Gunton is correct to
point out the oscillation from oneness to threeness regarding human thoughts of the Trinity as he
elaborates upon Gregory's comments:

> If there are transcendentals, they will, as we have seen, be found in the dynamic interac-
> tion of the mind and that about which it thinks. The interesting point about Gregory
> is that that is precisely what we find: a dynamic dialectic between the oneness and the
> threeness of God of such a kind that the two are both given equal weight in the pro-
> cesses of thought. Thinking about God denies his mind rest in either unity or plurality,
> in Parmenides or Heraclitus. (Colin E. Gunton, *The One, the Three, and the Many:
> God, Creation, and the Culture of Modernity. The 1992 Bampton Lectures* [Cambridge:
> Cambridge University Press, 1993], 149–50)

the belief that the *hypostases* are not "essential" to God's being. Here we must invoke Frege's sense-reference distinction again, for we have equivocated on the term "essential." Could God exist in any way other than as Trinity? No! In that sense, the *hypostases* are "essential" to God's being. Nonetheless, the *hypostases* are not the *ousia* understood according to the ecumenical creeds. It is dangerous to elide these shades of meaning, for in so doing we are at risk of fashioning an abstract monad, an object of worship for the bare theist. Worship offered to an abstract divine essence is not merely *misguided* worship offered to the God of Scripture. It is idolatry.

God desires worshipers who worship "in spirit and truth" (John 4:24). The constraints of this particular essay do not permit me to develop this idea further with regard to the concerns addressed above. Suffice it to say, proper worship is a confluence of ontology, epistemology, and ecclesiology. Ontology defines the proper object of worship. Epistemology describes our knowledge of God, which is given by revelation.[33] Ecclesiology establishes the proper context and means for worship. God is indeed "one" (Deut. 6:4), while in every respect irreducibly triune. He must be worshiped accordingly.

---

33. This should be understood with proper reference to the progressive nature of God's revelation as well. For example, prior to the giving of the New Testament Scriptures, the Jews would only have possessed knowledge of the Trinity in shadowy form, but in the fullness of time, Jesus can indict the Pharisees for failing to recognize and receive him, telling them that they are "of [their] father the devil" (John 8:44). In Pauline parlance, "the times of ignorance" have passed (Acts 17:30).

11

Language and the Trinity

A Meeting Place for the Global Church

Pierce Taylor Hibbs

I am honored and humbled to contribute a testament to the teaching and life of Vern Poythress, whose friendship and passion for a God-centered view of all things have formatively shaped me as a young scholar and Christian. His most influential work for me, as he well knows, is his work on language, particularly his attention to its divine Trinitarian roots. And in light of his heartfelt concern to serve the global church and to witness the knowledge and glory of God covering the earth "as the waters cover the sea" (Hab. 2:14), it seems fitting to apply my passion for his work to his passion for the work of the global church. That, in brief, is what I aim to do here.

• • •

In many ways, the global church is no longer a dream; it is a reality. This is not simply because the gospel has spread like wildfire to places that had never been ignited by the name of Christ, but because every wildfire sends a smoke trail into the sky. Surveying the contours of global Christianity, we can see smoke trails rising from many regions— Nigeria, Taiwan, China, Indonesia, France, Germany, India. Province and precinct, city and suburb, smoke signals are everywhere. This is not to belittle the importance of continual evangelism. Many pockets of the world have yet to hear the name and bow the knee (Phil. 2:10). I am only saying that we are aware of ourselves on the global level, perhaps in a way unprecedented in the first two thousand years of Christian history.

No doubt, the technological developments of the last thirty years or so have played a part in this. Marshall McLuhan prophesied decades ago that humanity was returning to its tribal roots. Whereas we were once concerned to expand and create distance between one another, we now desire to contract and close such spatial and temporal gaps with the various media at our disposal. McLuhan thought we were becoming a *global village*, "a metaphor for our planet reduced in all aspects of its functioning and social organization to the size of a village." For him, this was due to the effects of electricity and the redounding impact of the telegraph.[1] If when he wrote during the mid-1960s that our fragmented civilization was "experiencing an instantaneous reassembling of all its mechanized bits into an organic whole," how much more is this the case today?[2]

---

1. Marshall McLuhan, *Understanding Media: The Extensions of Man*, critical ed., ed. W. Terrence Gordon (Corte Madera, CA: Ginko, 2003), 562.

2. McLuhan suggested that our world was fragmented—people had more distance between themselves psychologically—in part because of the effects of the print medium (ibid., 117–24). Walter Ong seems to concur, arguing that print replaced a communal, sound-dominated culture with an individualist, sight-dominated one. The printed word, unlike the spoken word, was not bound by space and time. Printed words could be sent far and wide, addressing not just groups, but individuals. Ong writes:

> By removing words from the world of sound where they had first had their origin in active human interchange and relegating them definitively to visual surface, . . . print encouraged human beings to think of their own interior conscious and unconscious resources as more and more thing-like, impersonal and religiously neutral. Print encouraged the mind to sense that its possessions were held in some sort of inert mental space. (Walter J. Ong, *Orality and Literacy: The Technologizing of the Word* [New York: Routledge, 2002], 114–29)

Both Ong and McLuhan, however, seem to underestimate the "organic unity" that is fostered by print, both in space and in time, in our current global context and throughout history. God uses the printed word, we must remember, to preserve his truth for generations. So we would be reductionistic if we claimed that print led to individualism and isolation. It also led and continues to lead to unity, for receiving the written words of another "is the basis of literary knowledge

Of course, soothsayers, especially the secular sort, are usually half-right, and they always miss central biblical truths when poetically pontificating about the future. Unity is not a matter of media; it is a matter of persons: a matter of the heart and spirit being restored and united to the person of Christ by the power of the Spirit to the glory of God the Father. It matters little if we are moving toward a global village that has become blind, deaf, and dumb to the truth of the Trinity. There can be no global village, no organic unity for humanity, apart from the spiritual unity of the church.[3]

Yet, while we know biblically that our union is primarily spiritual, I do not want to say that there are no external markers of that union. Campfires of spiritual truth can be built, and those who are marked for the same destination can gather around them for warmth and strength amid the darkness and dispassion of a godless global village. In this sense, all I would like to do here is build a campfire, using the concepts of language and the Trinity as fodder.

Narrowing the Scope on "Language and the Trinity"

As topics of discussion, however, language and the Trinity are oceans in themselves, and we can easily be swept away in the current of either one if we do not tie down our anchor. What exactly do I mean when I say "language and the Trinity"?

---

that can perhaps become the basis for personal knowledge, for communion over space and time" (Kevin J. Vanhoozer, *Is There a Meaning in This Text? The Bible, the Reader, and the Morality of Literary Knowledge* [Grand Rapids, MI: Zondervan, 1998], 202). This hinges, of course, on our decision *to communicate what we read to others*, rather than storing information in the warehouse of the mind. In the latter respect, McLuhan and Ong are more correct than I would like to admit.

3. Ralph Smith points this out using the language of "harmony":

> The perfect harmony of the One and the Many in God means that men experience the harmony of the One and the Many in society when they are in conformity to God's will [i.e., living faithfully as new creatures in Christ]. Though perfect harmony never comes to fruition in this world of sin, it will characterize the social life of the resurrected society of the New Jerusalem.

He also helpfully adds that

> our self—who we are—is determined by our relationships, just as the three Persons of the Trinity are who they are in their relationships. There is no Father unless He is the Father of the Son. The Spirit is who He is because He is the Spirit of the Father and the Son. In God, relationships among the members of the Trinity are essential to the definition, or the name, of each of the three Persons. Since we are created in God's image, we, too, are defined, or named, in terms of our relationships [first to God and then to others]. (Ralph A. Smith, *Trinity and Reality: An Introduction to the Christian Faith* [Moscow, ID: Canon, 2004], 161, 163)

The short of it is that I would like us to think of these two topics *concurrently* and *conjointly*, but we still need to provide a scope for the topics themselves. By "Trinity," I want to fix us more broadly on the biblical, orthodox, and creedal definition of God as one being in three persons.[4] In this sense, our anchor is not tied to the distinction between the immanent and economic Trinity, or to how exactly we understand "person" in relation to the Godhead, or to how we can distinguish God's threeness from his oneness. These are vitally important topics, and I assume a position with regard to each of them. But I do not want to focus here on details of Trinitarian dogma. I simply want us to keep in mind the central Christian truth that God is one being in three persons, and that those persons "speak" or commune with one another in an eternal exchange of love and glory.

In terms of language, I want to focus on *what language does* for persons. Language is what I call *communion behavior*. Every instance of language can in some way be seen as drawing persons closer together—physically, socially, cognitively, or spiritually. This communion behavior is perhaps the crown jewel of the *imago Dei* and reflects the Trinity in its glorious complexity and depth.[5]

Language and the Trinity, considered in conjunction with one another, is our scope—the tri-personal God who speaks and his creatures made in his linguistic image. Admittedly, that scope is still, by any standard, far broader than most would like. But the expansive breadth is intentional, as it serves the purposes we have for union in the global church—a church doctrinally and historically variegated, not to men-

---

4. For background on this terminology, I am drawing on Cornelius Van Til, *An Introduction to Systematic Theology: Prolegomena and the Doctrines of Revelation, Scripture, and God*, 2nd ed., ed. William Edgar (Phillipsburg, NJ: P&R, 2007), 348–68; Robert Letham, *The Holy Trinity: In Scripture, History, Theology, and Worship* (Phillipsburg, NJ: P&R, 2004), 89–268; Herman Bavinck, *Reformed Dogmatics*, vol. 2, *God and Creation*, ed. John Bolt, trans. John Vriend (Grand Rapids, MI: Baker Academic, 2004), 296–304; Louis Berkhof, *Systematic Theology*, rev. ed. (Grand Rapids, MI: Eerdmans, 1996), 82–99; and John M. Frame, *Systematic Theology: An Introduction to Christian Belief* (Phillipsburg, NJ: P&R, 2013), 421–43.

5. For example, Edward Morgan explains how Augustine understands this reflection, i.e., human speech, to be analogous to the incarnation—God's internal Word manifested in the flesh and applied in the love of the Spirit—and thus how "the incarnation in fact reads as a commencement of an explicitly Trinitarian conversation between God and humanity, whereby through the incarnation humanity recognizes as Trinity the God who addresses it. Reflection on this conversation leads the human person closer to God, who is truth. Finally, the Spirit inspires this conversation" (Edward Morgan, "The Concept of Person in Augustine's De Trinitate," in *Augustine and Other Latin Writers: Papers Presented at the Fourteenth International Conference on Patristic Studies Held at Oxford*, ed. F. Young, M. Edwards, and P. Parvis, Studia Patristica 43 [Paris: Peeters, 2006], 206).

tion culturally diffuse. For such a church, union must begin at thirty thousand feet, not on the ground of nuanced dogmatics.[6]

With this in mind—the self-communing God who is three-in-one and language as a Trinitarian, image-bearing behavior—we have all the fodder we need to set the world aflame, let alone build a camp-fire. But before we strike the match, we need to remind ourselves of what caused our separation and global dispersion to begin with. What brought about our divided tongues? To answer this, we will start by revisiting the story of Babel in Genesis 11. Then, leaving off that story and portending the solution in the Trinity, we will move on to consider the Trinity and language, before once more returning to Babel and the resolution of our global dispersion.

Babel: When the Word-Made World Was Broken

Before we get to the story of Babel, a story about words, we should remind ourselves that we live in a Word-made world. Reality is pro-foundly linguistic in the sense that it was spoken into being by the Trinitarian God.[7] The Father uttered the Word in the power of the Spirit, and life took shape: dawn emerged from darkness; seas were gathered; plants and produce pushed through the soil; stars were set burning in the sky; waters teemed with life; birds whistled in the wind; and a motley multitude of land-dwelling creatures began to march and creep and climb.

And people, the image-bearing pinnacle of creation, were breathed into by the very Spirit of God (Gen. 2:7; cf. Job 27:3; 33:4) and thus endowed with the capacity to communicate and commune with one another. We were given words to function in a Word-made world. And even after the fall, when God's word was first exchanged for the

---

6. I would, at the same time, be the first to say that such nuances are critical not only to our intellectual but also to our spiritual formation.

7. On the nature of reality as Word-based, see Vern Sheridan Poythress, *In the Beginning Was the Word: Language—A God-Centered Approach* (Wheaton, IL: Crossway, 2009), 23–27. Frame notes that "nature is God's self-expression. Nature behaves as it does because God's word tells it what to do" (John M. Frame, *The Doctrine of the Word of God* [Phillipsburg, NJ: P&R, 2010], 76). Or, as Jonathan Edwards put it, "As the system of nature, and the system of revelation, are both divine works, so both are in difference senses a divine word. Both are the voice of God to intelligent creatures, a manifestation and declaration of himself to mankind" (Jonathan Edwards, "The 'Miscellanies': Number 1340," in *Christian Apologetics Past and Present*, vol. 2, *From 1500*, ed. William Edgar and K. Scott Oliphint [Wheaton, IL: Crossway, 2011], 237).

insidious words of another creature, we communed with one another using the same language (Gen. 11:1).[8] But that was soon to change.

Language had been given to us as an image-bearing reflection of the self-communing God.[9] As with everything else in creation, our language was meant to serve our relationship with him and with other people.[10] *Relational unity*—that was always the purpose for language, a purpose rooted in God himself.[11] And yet we left this behind in a selfish venture to make a name for ourselves.

> And they said to one another, "Come, let us make bricks, and burn them thoroughly." And they had brick for stone, and bitumen for mortar. Then they said, "Come, let us build ourselves a city and a tower with its top in the heavens, and let us make a name for ourselves, lest we be dispersed over the face of the whole earth." And the LORD came down to see the city and the tower, which the children of man had built. And the LORD said, "Behold, they are one people, and they have all one language, and this is only the beginning of what they will do. And nothing that they propose to do will now be impossible for them. Come, let us go down and there confuse their language, so that they may not understand one another's speech." So the LORD dispersed them from there over the face of all the earth, and they left off building the city. Therefore its name was called Babel, because there the LORD confused the language of all the earth. And from there the LORD dispersed them over the face of all the earth. (Gen. 11:3–9)

Note two critical details in this passage. First, the goal and purpose of building the tower was to make a name for themselves, perhaps a name made equal to or even higher than God's own name, and thus to preclude dispersion. The "name for ourselves" seems to point to both

8. On this linguistic tragedy, see Geerhardus Vos, *Biblical Theology: Old and New Testaments* (Carlisle, PA: Banner of Truth, 2014), 35–36; and G. K. Beale, *The Temple and the Church's Mission: A Biblical Theology of the Dwelling Place of God*, New Studies in Biblical Theology (Downers Grove, IL: InterVarsity Press, 2006), 396.

9. On speech as an essential attribute of God, see Frame, *Systematic Theology*, 522–24.

10. "The design plan of language is to serve as the medium of covenantal relations with God, with others, with the world" (Vanhoozer, *Is There a Meaning in This Text?*, 206).

11. God communes with himself in the language of love and glory. See John 17:5; Abraham Kuyper, *The Work of the Holy Spirit*, trans. Henry De Vries (Chattanooga, TN: AMG, 1995), 542; Dumitru Stăniloae, *The Holy Trinity: In the Beginning There Was Love*, trans. Roland Clark (Brookline, MA: Holy Cross Orthodox Press, 2012), 14; and Frame, *Systematic Theology*, 480–81.

their pride and an addled understanding of unity: pride in the sense that their individual names did not bring them the weight of glory they desired, unity in the sense that all people would be able to gather to one place.[12] The painful irony of sin, of course, is the twofold curse: they were left "nameless" and were scattered over the face of the earth.

Second, note the divinely endowed power of language. Because of their linguistic union, a union we noted is rooted in God himself, the Trinitarian Creator says, "Nothing that they propose to do will now be impossible for them" (11:6). *Nothing.* I do not know of another place in Scripture that so openly acknowledges the power of language.

We will return to each of these details later on. For now, we can simply note that sin scatters us. That is why we even have need of the phrase "global church." We were dispersed across the globe because of our sinful lust for glory and godless unity; this dispersion was an act of God's righteous and gracious judgment, for if God had not confused our languages, we would have succeeded in our goal (11:6) and wrested ourselves, to our own horror, from the God who speaks. Out of love and mercy, God confused our languages so that we might one day have union again, with him and with each other. But this new union was to be found not in the uplifting of "a name for ourselves," but in the communal uplifting of the greatest name (Phil. 2:9–10).

Fast forward to the New Testament, after redemption wound its way through history, in promises and punishments, grace and gratitude, orisons and answers. On one terrible and triumphant day, we were granted entrance into the name above all other names and the unity we had always longed for (Phil. 2:9; John 17:22–23). At the blood-soaked soil near the foot of the cross, people of every tribe and tongue enter into Christ, by the power of the Spirit. And each one who does so joins the glorious parade of faith, marching through time with variant voices and diverse dialects, not toward a tower (Gen. 11:4) but toward the Trinity. That is where we are headed, so let us pause here

---

12. Note that their aim was to achieve, in this sense, a godless unity that challenged God's own plans for union. The Hebrew used here, וְנַעֲשֶׂה־לָּנוּ שֵׁם, is telling, since the verb is the same as that used in reference to God's creation (Gen. 1:7, 16, 25, and, most importantly, 26), which suggests that they are "making a name" not in mimetic submission to God's creational activity but in oppositional defiance of it. The "let us make" in Gen. 11:4 seems to be a sinfully motivated parallel to God's "let us make" in Gen. 1:26; the making in 1:26 was carried out in loving communion; the making in 11:4, in prideful disunion.

to explore the Trinity and language before returning to the resolution of Babel and the union of the global church.

The Trinity

In the history of the church, the Trinity has long been recognized as the doctrine that sets Christianity apart. Consider just a few affirmations from the Reformed tradition.[13]

> [God] so proclaims himself the sole God as to offer himself to be contemplated clearly in three persons. Unless we grasp these, only the bare and empty name of God flits about in our brains, to the exclusion of the true God.[14]

> Certain things revealed in the word are of such a nature that without peril of salvation they can be unknown (although they cannot be denied without that peril). However, not only the denial, but also the simple ignorance of the Trinity is damnable.[15]

> The entire Christian belief system, all of special revelation, stands or falls with the confession of God's Trinity. It is the core of the Christian faith, the root of all its dogmas, the basic content of the new covenant.[16]

> It is a great mistake to regard [the doctrine of the Trinity] as a mere speculative or abstract truth, concerning the constitution of the Godhead, with which we have no practical concern, or which we are required to believe simply because it is revealed. On the contrary, it underlies the whole plan of salvation, and determines the character of the religion . . . of all true Christians.[17]

> In setting forth its doctrine of the Trinity the church prepared itself for its life and death struggle with the world.[18]

The doctrine of the Trinity is not an appendage to the gospel or an accolade of the early church that must be given lip service in the

---

13. This is but a sampling of what can be found across particular Christian traditions in the writings of the early church, the Scholastic period, the Reformation, and post-Reformation orthodoxy.
14. Calvin, *Institutes*, 1.13.2.
15. Francis Turretin, *Institutes of Elenctic Theology*, ed. James T. Dennison Jr., trans. George Musgrave Giger, vol. 1 (Phillipsburg, NJ: P&R, 1992), 261.
16. Bavinck, *God and Creation*, 333.
17. Charles Hodge, *Systematic Theology*, vol. 1 (repr., Peabody, MA: Hendrickson, 2013), 442–43.
18. Van Til, *Introduction to Systematic Theology*, 362; see also 30, 59.

twenty-first century by those who really only care about "Christ crucified." Christ was crucified, after all, at the behest of the Father, further
testifying to the latter's sovereign rule, and was raised by the Spirit,
proclaiming the life-giving agency of the Holy Ghost (Mark 14:36;
John 4:34; Rom. 8:11).[19] If set in isolation from the Father and the
Spirit, the interjection "Christ crucified!" is, in some ways, a misguided
avowal, for it ultimately misconstrues the object of our faith.[20] The
Trinity in its entirety—whether in conjunction with creation, fall, redemption, or consummation—is central to Christian belief, especially
to the crucifixion. This does not mean that we should not lift up the
one name of Christ for all that he has done and is doing; Scripture
compels us to do so. It simply means we can never afford to ignore the
Trinitarian context in which that work was carried out, for if we do,
we fail to understand the very nature of that work. The Trinity, then,
even in the glorious work of Christ's atonement, is central to the system
of Christian belief.

And perhaps one of the most striking attributes of the Trinity is
its internal (*ad intra*) and external (*ad extra*) communication, a fact
brought to my attention by a passage in what has become one of my
favorite works on language:

> The New Testament indicates that the persons of the Trinity speak
> to one another. . . . Not only is God a member of a language com-
> munity that includes human beings, but the persons of the Trinity
> function as members of a language community among themselves.
> Language does not have as its sole purpose human-human com-
> munication, or even divine-human communication, but also divine-
> divine communication.[21]

---

19. Wesley Hill, *Paul and the Trinity: Persons, Relations, and the Pauline Letters* (Grand Rapids, MI: Eerdmans, 2015), 92–93. Hill also notes that Jesus's reception of the "name above all
names," κύριος, which is commonly used of God in the Septuagint, "exerts a 'unitive pressure'
whereby the unique name of God in the LXX . . . becomes an assertion of oneness between the
'persons' of Father and Son in Phil. 2:6–11." Referring to the raising of Jesus by the Spirit, he further solidifies the united action of the Trinity by relating this to the identity of the persons: "God
and Jesus are who they are only in relation to this action of the Spirit, just as the Spirit is who the
Spirit is only as the Spirit of God and of Jesus" (ibid., 93–96, 163).

20. "The good news is triune: the Father shares his light, life, and love in the Son through the
Spirit" (Kevin J. Vanhoozer, *Faith Speaking Understanding: Performing the Drama of Doctrine*
[Louisville: Westminster John Knox, 2014], 75).

21. Poythress, *In the Beginning Was the Word*, 18. He goes on to cite John 16:13–15, as well
as chapter 17, in which the Son prays directly to the Father. See also Vern S. Poythress, *God-*

Along these same lines, Douglas Kelly notes, "there is—and has been from all eternity—talk, sharing and communication in the innermost life of God."[22]

There seem to be two models for our understanding of this communication. First, there is what I call the *consciousness model*: "God the Father is the speaker, God the Son is the speech, and God the Spirit is the breath carrying that speech to its destination. The Spirit is also the power who brings about its effects."[23] I use "consciousness" as a descriptor because this analogy is based upon a single person's conscious communication.

Second, there is the *interpersonal model*: "God is the Father addressing the Son, the Son responding to the Father, and the Spirit overhearing."[24] This is more along the lines of what Poythress identifies as "New Testament" revelation, in which we see the distinct persons of the Godhead communicating with one another. In this model, the

---

Centered Biblical Interpretation (Phillipsburg, NJ: P&R, 1999), 16–20; and Frame, *Systematic Theology*, 523.

22. Douglas Kelly, *Systematic Theology: Grounded in Holy Scripture and Understood in Light of the Church*, vol. 1, *The God Who Is: The Holy Trinity* (Ross-shire, Scotland: Mentor, 2008), 487. Vanhoozer adds that "it is on the basis of God's communicative presence and activity in history that we come to understand divine communicative perfection in eternity" (Kevin J. Vanhoozer, *Remythologizing Theology: Divine Action, Passion, and Authorship* [New York: Cambridge University Press, 2010], 245).

23. Poythress, *In the Beginning Was the Word*, 21.

24. Vanhoozer, *Remythologizing Theology*, 246. I am not comfortable with the language Vanhoozer takes up with regard to God having his "being" in communicative action. Though I can certainly appreciate his emphasis on God's internal communication, that wording seems dangerously close to Barth's language of God having his being "in action," a teaching that will ultimately lead to the corrosion of the distinction between the immanent and economic Trinity. See James J. Cassidy, "Election and Trinity," *WTJ* 71, no. 1 (2009): 53–81. In this regard, I find Oliphint's work on the being of God more helpful: "God, while entering into a special covenant relationship with his people, is and remains, nevertheless, *a se*. He and he alone is independent. He *is*, in a way that no one or nothing else *is*. God alone is the 'I AM'" (K. Scott Oliphint, *Reasons for Faith: Philosophy in the Service of Theology* [Phillipsburg, NJ: P&R, 2006], 174–75). Elsewhere Oliphint says:

> There are distinctions to be made between God's essential character—those properties that apply to God as God—and attributes that have in view the relationship that God as triune sustains to himself (and, secondarily, to the world). There are *personal* properties, therefore, that apply only to the respective persons of the Trinity (for example, filiation applies only to the Son, not the Spirit or the Father), and not to the oneness of God. So also, there are essential properties that serve to highlight or emphasize God's essential relational character—properties such as the love of God (directed, in the first place, to the three persons)." (Oliphint, *God with Us: Divine Condescension and the Attributes of God* [Wheaton, IL: Crossway, 2012], 40)

See also Oliphint, "Simplicity, Triunity, and the Incomprehensibility of God," in *One God in Three Persons: Unity of Essence, Distinction of Persons, Implications for Life*, ed. Bruce A. Ware and John Starke (Wheaton, IL: Crossway, 2015), 215–35. It is important to keep in view both God's triunity and his simplicity whenever we discuss his being.

Father, the Son, and Spirit are each capable of carrying out the linguistic functions of speaking and hearing.[25]

We must pause here to derogate the stale assumption that the Christian West has more affinity with the consciousness model and the East with the interpersonal model. Let us set aside exclusive reductionisms and pick up the Good Book.[26] Scripture accounts for both models; each is thus necessary to a sound understanding of the Trinity.[27] While the consciousness model draws directly on the linguistic analogy of the Son as the Word of the Father,[28] the interpersonal model synthesizes what the New Testament, in particular, says about how the persons of the Godhead interact with one another, both in time and in eternity.

Language

The above linguistic models of the Trinity are each reflected in us as God's image bearers. In analogical relation to God, we are speakers (Father), who produce speech (Son), with our God-given breath (Spirit).[29] We are also distinct *persons* who communicate with other persons.

---

25. In this respect, Vanhoozer is also right in affirming that "the gospels assign speaking parts to each of the three divine persons." The Father speaks (Matt. 3:17; 17:5; Mark 1:11); the Son obviously speaks throughout the Gospels; and the Spirit speaks through believers (Matt. 10:20). The Son also hears (John 12:49–50), as does the Spirit (John 16:13). This supplements, rather than eclipses, the order of persons in the Godhead.

26. We all have what Poythress calls "emphasizing reductionisms" because we cannot avoid choosing a focus. "Exclusive reductionisms" are the problematic sort, because they insist on "the exclusive correctness of one's own form of emphasizing reductionism" (Vern S. Poythress, *Philosophy, Science, and the Sovereignty of God* [Nutley, NJ: Presbyterian and Reformed, 1976], 48–49). This seems apropos in Trinitarian debates when there is clear scriptural support for both a consciousness and interpersonal model of divine communication.

27. While I appreciate Keith Johnson's article in which he claims that "Scripture does not call us to imitate the way in which the Father, Son, and Holy Spirit relate *to one another* in their inner life," I would contend that we have no choice but to imitate the inner Trinity according to the consciousness and interpersonal models described above. I do think that the *imitatio trinitatis* is fuller than, though certainly encompassing, the *imitatio Christi* (Keith E. Johnson, "Imitatio Trinitatis: How Should We Imitate the Trinity?," *WTJ* 75, no. 2 [2013]: 334). I also think Frame shows keen insight in noting that the mutual glorification of persons in the Godhead is also expected, derivatively, of us (Frame, *Systematic Theology*, 481).

28. On the Son as the Word of the Father, Geerhardus Vos suggests that the Son as the Word signifies the Son's rationale "inherent in the speaker," as being the "imprint of [the speaker's] personal existence," and as tied to the speaker by living on in the speaker's consciousness (Geerhardus Vos, *Reformed Dogmatics*, vol. 1, *Theology Proper*, ed. and trans. Richard B. Gaffin Jr. [Bellingham, WA: Lexham, 2014], 57).

29. This is bound up with the triad of *meaning*, *control*, and *presence*:

> The Father is closely associated with being the source of meaning. Meaning originates from the plan of the Father. As executor of the Father's will, the Son is closely associated with control. The Father speaks specific orders in his word, which is the Word of the Son. By means of the Son, the Father carries out his will. And the Holy Spirit is closely associated with the presence of God. . . .

Of course, we are not the same kind of persons as the persons of the Godhead, a topic that has, of late, drawn much discussion in Reformed circles.[30] We are, however, creaturely analogues of the tri-personal God, and all of our coherent and "good" behaviors are rooted in the Trinity.[31]

In sum, language is central to the Trinity *ad intra* and *ad extra*. God is speaker, speech, and breath, as well as distinct persons in linguistic communion with one another. Both of these elements are reflected in human language analogically.[32] Each of us is a speaker who uses speech and breath to communicate with other distinct persons. Thus, the mysterious prism of the linguistic Trinity refracts divine light onto the behavior of his embodied creatures.

But that light seems often faint in us, for sin ever works to snuff it out. As speakers, our words and the breath we use to produce them are discordant. Our hearts and minds many times mean one thing while our words another. The breath we use to speak breeds greed rather than grace, and our interpersonal relationships are laced with misunderstanding, malevolence, and misery. So, let us return to Babel now to remind ourselves why this is the case, and where our hope lies.

Reversing Babel: When the Word Made the World Anew

The chaotic disunion that was wrought at the base of Babel, an act of God's judgment and grace, was both internal and external: within each

---

Man's speech shows meaning, control, and presence. In this respect it images the meaning, control, and presence of God's speech. (Poythress, *In the Beginning Was the Word*, 25, 30)

30. Berkhof summarizes the differences between the divine persons and human persons by saying that "man is uni-personal, while God is tri-personal" (Berkhof, *Systematic Theology*, 84). With regard to "persons" in God, Bavinck suggests that "the three persons are the one divine personality brought to complete self-unfolding, a self-unfoldment arising out of, by the agency of, and within the divine being" (Bavinck, *God and Creation*, 303; on the benefits and deficiencies of the "person" analogy, see 301–4). See also Frame, *Systematic Theology*, 475–89. For a discussion of the contemporary debate on "persons" and "relations," see Wesley Hill, "Divine Persons and Their 'Reduction' to Relations: A Plea for Conceptual Clarity," *IJST* 14, no. 2 (2012): 148–60.

31. "As our being itself is derived from God (we exist because he exists), and as our knowledge is an analogue of his knowledge (we know because he knows), so, too, our capacity for language and other forms of communication is derivative of his. We speak because God speaks, because he is a speaking God; that is his nature and so, derivatively, it is ours" (Richard B. Gaffin Jr., "Speech and the Image of God: Biblical Reflections on Language and Its Uses," in *The Pattern of Sound Doctrine: Systematic Theology at the Westminster Seminaries*, ed. David VanDrunen [Phillipsburg, NJ: P&R, 2004], 182). "Finite persons are also a means of God's revelation. We are made in the image of God (Gen. 1:26–27), meaning that everything we were created to be reflects God in some way. Our bodies, minds, personalities reflect God, both individually and corporately" (Frame, *Systematic Theology*, 680).

32. Vern S. Poythress, "Reforming Ontology and Logic in the Light of the Trinity: An Application of Van Til's Idea of Analogy," *WTJ* 57, no. 1 (1995): 193–95.

person's consciousness and among interpersonal relations. In the former sense, Bavinck notes that "the confusion of languages is the result of confusion in ideas, in the mind, and in life."[33] Because language is deeply intertwined with thought, the confusion of languages was not merely an outward and phonetic curse, as if all of the people had the same idea but different sounds by which to articulate it; rather, the confusion of languages brought about contentious impressions, false premonitions, and disparate passions.

Externally, of course, this led to our scattering over the face of the earth. There can be no union where spiritual and psychic dissonance reign, and so in this sense, the physical distance between people was little more than an outworking of the distance that was already established between them internally. A warring disparity of souls brought about a lamentable dispersion of bodies. We fled to the corners of the world.

But in the person of the Word, the Logos through whom the world was created, the Trinity did not leave us to our scattered selves. As Vos wrote, "It is through the Logos that all things were made; it is also through the Logos, become flesh, that all things in redemption were accomplished."[34] By the Word, God brought us into being; in the Word, he beckoned us back to communion. The incarnate Word lifted up his voice on our behalf, so that we might "all be one, just as you, Father, are in me, and I in you, that they also may be in us" (John 17:21). "Us"—what a primal and precious pronoun! And it is the "us" not only of Father and Son but of the Spirit also.

It is the Spirit's work, mind you, that inaugurated our gathering from linguistic dispersion. On the day of Pentecost, in the brilliant light of midmorning—the very light that the Father spoke by the Son and in the Spirit (Gen. 1:3)—the curse of Babel was broken. And how fitting it was that they were communing with one another as the Trinity, the God of communion, was about to unite them (Acts 2:1)! Disparate thoughts from disparate tongues were there about to receive a language lesson from the God who speaks.

---

33. Bavinck, *God and Creation*, 525.
34. Geerhardus Vos, "The Range of the Logos Title in the Prologue to the Fourth Gospel," in *Redemptive History and Biblical Interpretation: The Shorter Writings of Geerhardus Vos*, ed. Richard B. Gaffin Jr. (Phillipsburg, NJ: Presbyterian and Reformed, 1980), 63.

> And suddenly there came from heaven a sound like a mighty rush-
> ing wind, and it filled the entire house where they were sitting.
> And divided tongues as of fire appeared to them and rested on
> each one of them. And they were all filled with the Holy Spirit and
> began to speak in other tongues as the Spirit gave them utterance.
> (Acts 2:2–4)

Divided tongues—one flame; distinct persons—the same Spirit
(cf. 1 Cor. 12:4–11). And the Devil himself could not intrude upon
that divine discourse. The Spirit who had worked in conjunction with
the Word to create the world and give life (Gen. 2:7), and who had
done the same to restore it (1 Cor. 15:45), was now translating discord
into harmony—gathering minds and hearts and voices around the in-
tractable truth that God works in history (Acts 2:11).[35] He works—
he speaks, by his Son and in the Spirit, in grace that cannot be muted.

This is how the speaking God resolved our problem of Babel in
redemptive history. We had wanted to make a name for ourselves; we
had wanted to unite in vain bravado; we had an otiose dream of independence. But now, every tongue lifts up the one name of Christ and
thus gathers to the tower of our hope (Prov. 18:10). Our shoal dream
of independence was replaced by a far deeper vision of communion.

Pentecost ushered in a gathering—a gathering of people once dispersed over the face of the earth but now united, lifting up the one
name, the Word of the Father, who created all things (Col. 1:16) and
who is recreating all things (Rev. 21:5).

We have inherited this legacy, perhaps the apex of linguistic redemption. Each of us is now part of the great gathering. And it is, as
we noted, a gathering to the Trinity: the God who is three-in-one, who
is a language community unto himself.

Meaning, Efficacy, and Presence

But, you may ask, how might we mark those heading to the same
hearth as we are? After all, many can superficially profess faith in the
Trinity and a respect for language. As we stated at the outset, these two
areas are oceans in and of themselves. What does it actually look like

---

35. I owe the emphasis of this truth to one of Lane Tipton's lectures on union with Christ,
delivered on Westminster's campus in the summer of 2015.

to treasure the Trinity and language conjointly? Perhaps we can say little more than that those who are walking toward this campfire will be marked by their *use* of words.

This involves at least three elements. First is the *communion-inspired meaning* of our words—not just that our words have meaning, since that is unavoidable, but that our semantic goal is oriented toward communion with others—socially, mentally, or spiritually.[36] Such communion is drawn from an awareness that all meaning "originates from the plan of the Father,"[37] and thus any semantic purpose aligned with that plan *can be realized*. In this sense, our words should concurrently evince a desire for communion with others and a faith in the Father's providential plan to bring about that communion *through his Word*.[38]

This leads to the second element, the cherished *efficacy* of our words, either productively (writing, speech) or receptively (reading, hearing).[39] Efficacy can take various forms—word choice, respect for elegance and form, or simply one's ability to handle words with care and precision, suggesting profound appreciation for the incarnation of a particular idea.[40] Whatever form efficacy might take, there is always a sense in which the speaker or writer holds "the fundamental presupposition that it is possible to speak truly,"[41] winsomely, and effectively. If before Babel we were capable of doing all things with our words (Gen. 11:6), how much more so is God capable and willing to do all things *through* us in his Word (Phil. 4:13)! We must cast down our communicative lethargy and practice the divine efficacy of language, as those who are both quick to listen (James 1:19) and able to speak or write a word to one who is weary (Isa. 50:4).

Third, we can identify those who are walking toward the Trinity by

---

36. This is related to Poythress's triad of meaning, control, and presence, which is built on Frame's lordship triad of authority, control, and presence. See Poythress, *In the Beginning Was the Word*, 25–31, and John M. Frame, *The Doctrine of the Knowledge of God* (Phillipsburg, NJ: Presbyterian and Reformed, 1987), 15–18. Communion-inspired meaning is also related to Dorothy Sayers's notion of the creative *idea*, which serves to unite a piece of discourse. See Dorothy L. Sayers, *The Mind of the Maker* (New York: HarperOne, 1987), 37.

37. Poythress, *In the Beginning Was the Word*, 25.

38. Or, as Vanhoozer notes, discourse "is a means of personal communication and communion" (Vanhoozer, *Is There a Meaning in This Text?*, 219).

39. This is related to the "control" aspect of language, which, in terms of the Trinity, leads us to worship the Son "as executor of the Father's will" (Poythress, *In the Beginning Was the Word*, 25).

40. See Sayers, *Mind of the Maker*, 86–92, on the incarnate "energy" of an author's idea.

41. Vanhoozer, *Is There a Meaning in This Text?*, 53.

their understanding that language evokes personal *presence*, that the linguistic expression of our desires, thoughts, and personality carries *us*.[42] This is particularly critical with our written words, which Derrida decried as dead.[43] Because "God's word and his personal presence are inseparable," analogically, our words and our personal presence are as well.[44] We are *with* our words.[45]

Most importantly, these three elements are coinherent. Referring to his triad of meaning, control, and presence, Poythress writes: "Without meaning, speech is empty. Without control, it does not accomplish anything, and makes no difference. Without presence, speech is disconnected from the speaker, and again loses its point."[46] This ectypal coinherence of our language is analogically tied to the archetypal co-inherence of the Godhead, in which "the Father as speaker, the Son as the Word spoken, and the Spirit as the 'breath' function together in producing God's speech. All three persons participate fully in the entire utterance, and the speech is, as it were, 'indwelt' by all three persons."[47] Thus, communion-inspired meaning, efficacy, and presence should all be evident in a person's use of words. Much more can and should be said here, but in the interest of brevity, these three elements will at least help us to begin working out our identity in the global church as Trinitarian image bearers of the God who speaks.

Conclusion

The global church must be looking for grounds to unite; we must be looking for places to build campfires around which we can huddle and draw strength and warmth amid a dark and cold world filled with people whose minds are still hostile toward God (Rom. 8:7) and who are often critical of language as a means of communicating truth.[48]

---

42. Poythress, *In the Beginning Was the Word*, 30.
43. Vanhoozer, *Is There a Meaning in This Text?*, 62.
44. Frame, *Doctrine of the Word of God*, 68.
45. Assuming this is part of what can make our words powerful, which is related to Sayers's triad, and to the work of the Spirit (Sayers, *Mind of the Maker*, 37–38).
46. Poythress, *In the Beginning Was the Word*, 31.
47. Ibid., 32.
48. We might call this "linguistic atheism" (Vanhoozer uses the more narrow descriptor, "literary atheism")—a lack of faith in the power and efficacy of language. Poythress notes that "some people think that language is not capable of being a channel for God to communicate with us. They conclude that the Bible's message must be *merely* human. Or if it nevertheless somehow becomes a channel for God, all kinds of hindrances in language result in poor or garbled communication"

Such people are still caught in the throes of Babel's curse and have not yet learned the Trinitarian tongue that dispels the darkness of unbelief.

Here, I hope to have gathered some embers for the global church to build upon. As the flame of the global church grows, we must keep the Trinity at the forefront of our attention. And language, as a divine behavior that we image analogically, must be there as well. We are linguistic creatures living in a linguistic world that was spoken into being by the triune linguistic God of the Bible.

Language and the Trinity: here we will gather; here we will grow into that glorious Word (Eph. 4:15–16) by whom we were made and remade. Mark yourselves, then, with the communion, efficacy, and presence of your words, and make your way toward the glow of the global church.

(Vern S. Poythress, *Inerrancy and Worldview: Answering Modern Challenges to the Bible* [Wheaton, IL: Crossway, 2012], 61). He goes on to discuss the influence of structural linguistics and the conclusions that some have drawn in secular fields that language is a contextual, significance-imprisoning medium, which would mean that God's "truth" in the Bible has significance for people in that particular time period in history, but is certainly not objectively or transcendentally true for us today. For a selected history of this in modern and contemporary theology, see Vanhoozer, *Is There a Meaning in This Text?*, 38–195. Vanhoozer's discussion of "users" and "undoers" (pragmatists and deconstructionists) is particularly helpful today.

12

Jonathan Edwards and God's Involvement in Creation

An Examination of "Miscellanies," no. 1263

JEFFREY C. WADDINGTON

It is a great privilege and pleasure to contribute to this Festschrift published in honor of my former professor and current friend and brother-in-Christ Vern Sheridan Poythress. I began reading Dr. Poythress's books more than thirty years ago, never dreaming that I would study under the man, let alone become a friend.[1] While Dr. Poythress's specialty is New Testament interpretation, he is also a well-trained mathematician and scientist. Indeed, he has published on various aspects of math and science.[2]

---

1. The first few Poythress books I read surely included *Symphonic Theology: The Validity of Multiple Perspectives in Theology* (Grand Rapids, MI: Zondervan, 1987) and *Science and Hermeneutics* (Grand Rapids, MI: Zondervan, 1988).

2. Among these are *Redeeming Science: A God-Centered Approach* (Wheaton, IL: Crossway, 2006); *Redeeming Sociology: A God-Centered Approach* (Wheaton, IL: Crossway, 2011); *Redeeming Mathematics: A God-Centered Approach* (Wheaton, IL: Crossway, 2013); and *Chance and the Sovereignty of God: A God-Centered Approach to Probability and Random Events* (Wheaton, IL:

In this chapter I would like to look at another Christian theologian with an interest in science, the highly esteemed pastor of Northampton's congregational church Jonathan Edwards.[3] In particular, I want to look at Edwards's conception of how God *relates to* this world, which he has created and *in which he has acted* to bring about redemption of his chosen through the nation of Israel, culminating in the life and ministry of Jesus Christ, and subsequently in the establishment of his church. I especially want to look at Edwards's semiprivate notebook entry "Miscellanies," no. 1263, and unpack his thinking revealed there about how God interacts with and relates to his creation. Additionally, we will consider the historical context of Edwards's thought in the rise of the "new science."[4] Finally, I will conclude by bringing insights from Poythress's article "Why Scientists Must Believe in God: Divine Attributes of Scientific Law"[5] to bear on my conclusions from the study of Edwards. My argument is twofold: First, Christian theologians (and ordinary Christians!) can be both *appreciative* of contemporary science and *critical* of how it is practiced when measured against Scripture.[6] Second, I intend to show a measure of continuity in the thinking of Edwards and Poythress. There is, as it were, a *family resemblance.*[7]

Jonathan Edwards on God's Relation to Creation

Jonathan Edwards was certainly no deist.[8] While he is often understood to share his age's fascination with the new science, he was not an uncritical observer of the anti-Christian uses that science was often

Crossway, 2014). Dr. Poythress is also an accomplished linguist. See his *In the Beginning Was the Word: Language—A God-Centered Approach* (Wheaton, IL: Crossway, 2009).

3. For helpful overviews of Edwards's life and thought, see George M. Marsden, *Jonathan Edwards: A Life* (New Haven, CT: Yale University Press, 2003) and Michael McClymond and Gerald McDermott, *The Theology of Jonathan Edwards* (New York: Oxford University Press, 2013).

4. See Avihu Zakai, *Jonathan Edwards's Philosophy of Nature: The Re-enchantment of the World in the Age of Scientific Reasoning* (London: T&T Clark; New York: Continuum, 2010).

5. Vern S. Poythress, "Why Scientists Must Believe in God: Divine Attributes of Scientific Law," *JETS* 46, no. 1 (2003): 111–23.

6. I am indebted Dr. Poythress, and the erstwhile Westminster Theological Seminary professor Cornelius Van Til for this point. Science is not the neutral discipline some present it to be. In other words, scientists are affected by the noetic effects of the fall as much as anyone else. Thomas Kuhn saliently addresses the fluctuating nature of science in his *The Structures of Scientific Revolutions*, 2nd ed. (Chicago: University of Chicago Press, 1970).

7. I intend to convey more than a shared generic orthodox Christian tradition; the two share a *Reformed* Christian community tradition.

8. For one study of how Edwards addressed the rising tide of deism in the North American British colonies, see Jeffrey C. Waddington, *The Unified Operations of the Human Soul: Jonathan Edwards' Theological Anthropology and Apologetic* (Eugene, OR: Wipf & Stock, 2015).

put to in this era of expanding knowledge of the universe.[9] We will look to the historical context in which Edwards formulated his own theological views a little later in this chapter. It is sufficient to note that Edwards was reacting to a form of *materialism* as he sought to offer a Christian alternative.

> Edwards developed his cosmological conception of real being and true substance in order, in part, to refute materialism. He rejected Hobbes' materialism, which held that the universe is a complete, autonomous, and self-sustaining system of unthinking bodies subject only to inherent, necessary, and mathematically exact laws of mechanical causation, because it ruled out the divine and providential government of the world.[10]

Edwards believed that God was both transcendent and intimately involved in his creation. Creation served as a theater in which redemption could take place.[11] Creation existed not for its own purpose but to *subserve* God's purposes in saving a people for himself. We should go back behind creation as the theater of redemption to consider the nature of God himself. Edwards conceived of God as a "communicative being" who exists in Trinitarian fellowship, and it is his nature to communicate with his sentient creatures.[12] This communication of God's goodness culminates in the work of Jesus Christ through his life, death, resurrection, and ascension. While Edwards was a fairly creative theologian, he worked within the Reformed covenant theology tradition.[13] Whatever new elements one finds in Edwards's understanding

9. Zakai, *Jonathan Edwards's Philosophy of Nature*, 207–73.
10. Specifically, Edwards was responding to Thomas Hobbes's *Leviathan*. See Zakai, *Jonathan Edwards's Philosophy of Nature*, 244–45.
11. See Craig Biehl, *The Infinite Merit of Christ: The Glory of Christ's Obedience in the Theology of Jonathan Edwards* (Jackson, MS: Reformed Academic Press, 2009) on the relation of creation and redemption in Edwards's theology.
12. See William Schweitzer, *God Is a Communicative Being: Divine Communicativeness and Harmony in the Theology of Jonathan Edwards*, Studies in Systematic Theology (New York: T&T Clark, 2012). Whether this commits Edwards to the idea of necessary creation is an important matter to ascertain but outside the purview of this chapter. Necessary creation is very problematic as it appears to require a correlation between God and the world that Scripture and the Reformed tradition as a whole have rightly rejected. See Oliver Crisp's two volumes where he deals with this matter: *Jonathan Edwards on God and Creation* (Oxford: Oxford University Press, 2012) and *Jonathan Edwards among the Theologians* (Grand Rapids, MI: Eerdmans, 2015).
13. Edwards reveals his commitment to covenant theology in his sermon "East of Eden," found in *WJE*, vol. 17, *Sermons and Discourses, 1730–1733*, ed. Mark Valeri (New Haven, CT: Yale University Press, 1999), 328–48. Carl Bogue's seminal study *Jonathan Edwards and the Covenant of Grace*, Jonathan Edwards Classic Studies (Eugene, OR: Wipf & Stock; New Haven, CT: Jonathan

of God and his relation to the world, he saw himself as expositing and defending the covenant theological tradition in which he was raised and trained and which he himself adopted as his own.

Jonathan Edwards *arguably* embraced three elements when considering God's creative, providential, and redemptive activity in the universe that cause him to stand out among covenant theologians.[14] These three elements are Trinitarian-theistic idealism, occasionalism, and continuous creation. A fourth element in Edwards's understanding of God's relation to creation is his apparent embrace of the *analogia entis* or chain of being.

> If we rise to mankind, and particularly the mind of man, by which especially he is above the inferior creatures, and consider the laws of the common operations of the mind, they are so high above such a kind of general laws of matter, and are so singular, that they are altogether untraceable. The more particular laws are the harder to be investigated and traced. And if we go from the common operations of the faculties of the mind and rise up to those that are spiritual, which are infinitely of the highest kind, and are those by which the minds are most conversant with the Creator and have their very next union with him, though these are not altogether without use made of means and some connection with antecedents and what we call (though improperly in this case) second causes, yet the operation may properly be said to be arbitrary and sovereign, the connection after the manner of the invariable laws of nature never erring from the degree and exact measure, time and precise state, of the antecedent.
>
> And if we ascend from saints on earth to angels in heaven, who always behold the face of the Father which is in heaven and constantly receive his commands on every occasion, the will of God not being made known to them by any such methods as the laws of nature but immediately given on all emergences, we shall come to greater degrees of an arbitrary intercourse.

Edwards Center of Yale University, 2009) still stands as the best work on Edwards's commitment to covenant theology.

14. I say "arguably" because whether Edwards fully embraced each of these elements is a matter of scholarly debate. For instance, Sang Hyun Lee, a leading Edwards scholar, challenges the notion that Edwards held to continuous creation, etc., in his editorial introduction to *WJE*, vol. 21, *Writings on the Trinity, Grace, and Faith*, ed. Sang Hyun Lee (New Haven, CT: Yale University Press, 2003), 1–105, esp. 52–56.

And if [we] rise to the highest step of all next to the Supreme Being himself, even the mind of the man Christ Jesus, who is united personally to the Godhead, doubtless there is a constant intercourse, as it were infinitely above the laws of nature. N.B.: When we come to the highest ranks of creatures, we come to them who themselves have the greatest image of God's arbitrary operation, who 'tis therefore most fit should be the subjects of such operations.

And if we ascend towards God, conjunctly proceeding in our ascent both according to the order of degrees and the order [of intercourse], we shall find the rule hold. Still the more arbitrary shall we find the divine influence and intercourse, and to a higher degree, than by ascending in one way singly.[15]

Edwards's embrace of the chain of being does not distinguish him from others in his era but needs to be understood as standing in the background of his theological formulations.[16]

The least controversial element of Edwards's theology proper is his Trinitarian-theistic idealism.[17] I refer to this aspect of Edwards's theology proper this way to distinguish it from other purely philosophical forms of idealism, such as those formulated by George Berkeley, Immanuel Kant, and Georg W. F. Hegel. Idealism gets its name to distinguish it from varieties of realism. Realism holds that the objects of human perception and knowledge are actually extra-mental. That is, these objects exist outside our minds and are not dependent upon them. Idealism typically makes extra-mental objects dependent in some sense on the human mind. The famous slogan of idealism *esse est percipi*, "to be is to be perceived," gets at the heart of the matter. Edwards did not

15. WJE, vol. 23, The "Miscellanies," Entry Nos. 1153–1360, ed. Douglas A. Sweeney (New Haven, CT: Yale University Press, 2004), 207.

16. See Thomas Schafer, The Concept of Being in the Thought of Jonathan Edwards (PhD diss., Duke University, 1951) about Edwards's dependence upon the chain of being. For the standard treatment of the chain of being, see Arthur O. Lovejoy, The Great Chain of Being: A Study of the History of an Idea (Cambridge, MA: Harvard University Press, 1976).

17. By this I mean not that the concept is not controversial but that most Edwards scholars recognize this feature of Edwards's theology. This is, from my perspective, an unbiblical and extra-biblical philosophical commitment embraced in reaction to the physical reductionism of materialism, which denied spiritual reality. A better ontology or metaphysic is *covenantal realism*, which recognizes the Trinitarian God of Scripture and his creation, and that God created us and our environment so that we could commune in fellowship with him, and that we are able to understand his communication with us, and all extra-mental objects are what they are (as real created entities) by virtue of their place in God's plan. When our faculties function properly, they are reliable. The entrance of sin into this picture makes things more complex but does not utterly destroy God's creation. Human faculties, once holy and righteous, are now fallen and being restored in those being saved.

think that reality depended upon the human mind. Rather, he held that the reality of the extra-mental world depended for its existence upon the mind of God. Ideas in the human mind, to be true, must conform and cohere with the ideas in God's mind. This makes Edwards's version of idealism *theistic*. Edwards's God was Trinitarian, and his formulation of the doctrine of the Trinitarian nature of God, reminiscent of Augustine and Anselm, was colored by his idealistic philosophy and theology.[18]

Edwards arguably also held forms of continuous creationism and occasionalism. Often these two ideas were fused into one notion, but they are properly distinct. Continuous creation is the concept that God continuously creates the world anew each moment. Rather than thinking of creation as one idea and providence as a related but different idea, Edwards wrote in his semiprivate notebooks that creation is the first instance of God's bringing the universe and all its elements into existence, and providence is just the additional instances of God's creating anew.[19] This would appear to undermine the ontological integrity of created things like human beings. Occasionalism is the doctrine that God is the only actor in all of creation. What appear to be secondary causes are in fact occasions for God to act.

The wedding of these two ideas would seem to produce, along with Trinitarian-theistic idealism, some form of pantheism or panentheism.[20] Neither of these is biblically appropriate. John Gerstner, using principles drawn from Charles Hodge's *Systematic Theology*, demonstrates that Edwards could not have been a pantheist but suggests that Edwards was quite possibly a panentheist.[21] Did Edwards think that God enveloped all of reality within his own being? He certainly used this kind of

---

18. For more on Edwards's Trinitarian theology, see Amy Plantinga-Pauw, *The Supreme Harmony of All: The Trinitarian Theology of Jonathan Edwards* (Grand Rapids, MI: Eerdmans, 2002); Robert N. Caldwell, *Communion in the Spirit: The Holy Spirit as the Bond of Union in the Theology of Jonathan Edwards*, Studies in Evangelical History and Thought (Eugene, OR: Wipf & Stock, 2006); Steven M. Studebaker, *Jonathan Edwards's Social Augustinian Trinitarianism in Historical and Contemporary Perspectives*, Gorgias Studies in Philosophy and Theology (Piscataway, NJ: Gorgias, 2008); and Robert N. Caldwell and Steven M. Studebaker, *The Trinitarian Theology of Jonathan Edwards: Text, Context, and Application* (London: Routledge, 2012).

19. *WJE*, vol. 1, *Freedom of the Will*, ed. Paul Ramsay (New Haven, CT: Yale University Press, 1957), 6, 451, 453.

20. John W. Cooper, in his study of panentheism, argues that Edwards was a panentheist. See Cooper, *Panentheism: The Other God of the Philosophers from Plato to the Present* (Grand Rapids, MI: Baker, 2006).

21. See John H. Gerstner, *The Rational Biblical Theology of Jonathan Edwards*, 3 vols. (Powhatan, VA: Berean; Orlando, FL: Ligonier, 1991–1993).

language as he thought Paul to have affirmed the idea in his Mars Hill address in Acts 17:28, where the apostle cites from Epimenides and Aratus that "in" God "we live and move and have our being" and that "we are indeed his offspring." Does Edwards think these citations used by Paul entail panentheism? Given his clear-throated endorsement of original sin, unvarnished pantheism would seem to be out of the question. But his apparent embrace of the classical chain-of-being doctrine may lead him astray here. Consistency would require Edwards to reject both pantheism and panentheism and also the chain-of-being doctrine. Paul's ostensible approving use of Epemenides's remark requires that it be balanced with God's aseity and Paul's affirmation of what has come to be called the Creator-creature distinction.

From this brief look at key components of Edwards's theology proper we can see that there is no room for Hobbesian materialism in his thought, nor for the embrace of the mechanicalism of the rising new science.[22] Early on Edwards mused in his "Of Atoms" notebook that laws of nature were in fact God's normal ways of acting.[23] There is no possibility of mechanistic laws of nature coming between God and his creation. For Edwards, the God of the Bible, the only God who is, is no God-of-the-gaps.

"Miscellanies," no. 1263[24]

As we turn to Jonathan Edwards's thoughts in his "Miscellanies," no. 1263, on the relation of God to his creation, we may have cause to wonder whether Edwards held to continuous creationism and occasionalism *simpliciter*.[25] Edwards gave serious thought to the relationship that God had with his creation. Like the "new science" that had arisen in the centuries before Edwards, he held to the idea of laws of nature that man could search out and discover and articulate in human language. These natural laws were not mere human inventions. Human formulations of the laws of nature discovered through the use

---

22. See *WJE*, vol. 6, *Scientific and Philosophical Writings*, ed. Wallace E. Anderson (New Haven, CT: Yale University Press, 1980), 205. Edwards notes, "From here we may see the gross mistake of those who think material things the most substantial things, and spirits more like a shadow; whereas spirits only are properly substance."

23. *WJE*, 6:213–15.

24. *WJE*, 23:201–12.

25. See especially Sang Hyun Lee's comments in his editorial introduction to *WJE*, 21:53–57.

of the empirical method actually connected to the ways things worked in the universe. What Edwards negatively reacted to was the mechanical view of nature that multiplied laws of nature and increasingly left no room for God. Potentially all of reality could be explainable in human or, more specifically, mathematical terms.

If there be a God who is truly an intelligent, voluntary, active being, what is there in reason to incline us to think that he should not act, and that he should not act upon his creatures, which, being his creatures, must have their very being from his action and must be perfectly and most absolutely subject to and dependent on his action? And if he acted once, why must he needs be still forever after and act no more? What is there in nature to disincline [us] to suppose he mayn't continue to act towards the world he made, and is under his government? And if he continues to act at all towards his creatures, then there must be some of his creatures t[hat] he continues to act upon immediately. 'Tis nonsense to say he a[cts] upon all mediately, because in so doing w[e] go back in infinitum from one thing acting on another without ever coming to a prime, present agent, and yet at the same time suppose God to be such a present agent.

There are many who allow a present, continuing, immediate operation of God on the creation (and indeed such are the late discoveries and advances which have been made in natural philosophy that all men of sense, who are also men of learning, are comp[elled] to allow it), but yet, because so many of the constant changes and events in their continued series in the external world come to pass in a certain, exact method, according to certain, fixed, invariable laws, are averse to allow that God acts any otherwise than as limiting himself by such invariable laws, fixed from the beginning of the creation, when he precisely marked out and determined the rules and paths of all his future operations, and that he never departs from those paths—so that, though they allow an immediate divine operation now, in these days, yet they sup[pose] it [is] what is limited by what we call LAWS OF NATURE, and seem averse to allow an ARBITRARY OPERATION to be continued, or ever to be expected, in these days.[26]

26. *WJE*, 23:201–2.

In "Miscellanies," no. 1263, Edwards sets out a gradation of sorts. The more spiritual and sentient a creature is, the more "arbitrary" God's interaction with it. What Edwards means by arbitrary is not irrational but what is *immediately* dependent on God's own good will.[27] The less spiritual and sentient a creature is on the grand scale of being, the more God's relation to the creature itself and the creature's function and activity is governed by laws of nature. The laws of nature are not entities that exist apart from God's knowledgeable providential care.[28] They are simply God's normal ways of doing things. In other words, God typically follows patterns that he himself has established. Creatures on the lower end of the scale of being, such as atoms and rocks, follow these laws more strictly than do creatures such as plants, animals, humans, and angels. Creatures closer in nature to God himself are less directed by laws of nature and operate or function under God's "arbitrary" care.[29]

Edwards's ruminations in "Miscellanies," no. 1263, suggest that he was not as wed to continuous creation or occasionalism as is sometimes believed. He allows for the distinction between Creator and creature, albeit on the ancient continuum of the chain of being.[30] With regard to continuous creation, Edwards certainly believed that God was the primary actor in the universe and, insofar as he upheld all of creation every moment from creation forward, he held to *divinely constituted perdurance*.[31] That is, every creature is what it is by virtue of God's

---

27. *WJE*, 23:202.

28. In his semiprivate notebook, "Of Atoms," Edwards notes that atoms are the smallest unit of reality whereby God holds things together. Atoms are indiscerptible, according to Edwards. They cannot be further divided. This was in the day before quarks and the like. Atoms were simply God's causing *resistance* (see *WJE*, 6:208–17).

29. Again, "arbitrary" does not mean irrational or unreasonable. The stress for Edwards falls on God's freedom to work in, with, or above these laws. For more discussion of these laws which God has established such that, when they intersect with one another, certain persons or events occur, see Sang Hyun Lee's treatment of habits or dispositions in his *The Philosophical Theology of Jonathan Edwards* (Princeton, NJ: Princeton University Press, 2000). More recent scholarly discussion has called Lee's influential paradigm into question. See Stephen R. Holmes, "Does Jonathan Edwards Use a Dispositional Ontology? A Response to Sang Hyun Lee," in *Jonathan Edwards, Philosophical Theologian*, ed. Paul Helm and Oliver Crisp (Burlington, VT: Ashgate, 2003), 99–114, and Oliver Crisp, "Jonathan Edwards' Ontology: A Critique of Sang Lee's Dispositional Account of Edwardsian Metaphysics," *Religious Studies* 46, no. 1 (2010): 1–20.

30. While the chain of being is an influential idea in Western philosophy and Christian theology, it does not possess the biblical support that would make its belief required. That there is a hierarchy within creation is true, but including God within the chain is an error even if it is a widely influential error.

31. See *WJE*, vol. 3, *Original Sin*, ed. Clyde A. Holbrook (New Haven, CT: Yale University Press, 1970), for how he uses divinely constituted perdurance to account for the federal headship of Adam and the relation of his sin to the sinfulness of every human being.

upholding that creature in existence and activity. Perhaps we might call this *concurrent continuous creationism* if we must retain the idea that Edwards always held to the doctrine. Edwards clearly has made room for the integrity of created entities. But these creatures are not self-creating, let alone self-sustaining. God's providential care concurs with or provides the foundation for creaturely existence and function. When spelled out in detail, this is hardly unique to Edwards.

The same can be said for occasionalism. There is such a thing as the distinction between primary and secondary causality for Edwards. Creatures do perform acts with true significance. But God upholds these creatures and their actions. Creatures behave according to their respective natures. But the higher they are on the scale of being, the more arbitrary is God's relation to them. On God's level, all creatures and all their actions are determined. On the creaturely level, there is freedom. It is not merely God acting all alone in the universe. If we were to widen our focus to include Edwards's sermons and treatises, we would immediately recognize that he fully reckoned with the reality of sin as creaturely rebellion and besottedness. If Edwards held to some strict form of occasionalism, it would appear that it was God who committed sin rather than the creature. In other words, if God is the only actor in the universe, then only God sins. There could be no such thing as human sin. Or so it would seem.

A Brief Excursus on Edwards's Historical Context[32]

Edwards was reacting against an overly mechanized view of the universe that was gaining credence in the broader republic of letters in Europe and the colonies. He was not opposed to science, as he believed the universe was searchable and could be understood by human beings using well-developed methods that had been tested. Edwards had read Sir Isaac Newton, Francis Bacon, John Locke, Thomas Hobbes, and a multitude of scientists and scientifically inclined scholars of the day.[33]

---

32. Zakai's *Jonathan Edwards's Philosophy of Nature* is a fascinating study of the conservative reaction to the rise of the "new science" in the United Kingdom and the colonies in the seventeenth and eighteenth centuries. Edwards is situated in the context of his own times, and Zakai demonstrates that Edwards was ambivalent about the uses to which science was put in his day, especially by deists.

33. See *WJE*, vol. 26, *The Reading Catalog*, ed. Peter J. Thuesen (New Haven, CT: Yale University Press, 2008).

He was familiar with the discussions of the day and accepted some aspects (the value of the empirical method properly conceived, for instance) and rejected others (the resulting God-of-the-gaps of deism).[34]

God was increasingly being defined out of existence in the scholarly conversations of the day. If every aspect of the existence and operations of the universe could be understood and delineated without reference to God, then there would be no need to refer to the God of classical Christianity. If laws of nature were self-sustaining, then God could be conceived—if thought to exist at all—as a watchmaker who wound up the universe and then stepped back and let things run on their own.

It was this trend of defining God out of existence to which Jonathan Edwards reacted in his own formulations of who God is, how God relates to his creation, and how man can know how God relates to the universe. For Edwards, theology was still the queen of the sciences and the integrating point of all knowledge—a very *medieval* idea indeed.[35] For the "new science," theology would be relegated to its own sphere of limited influence. Admittedly theologians throughout the history of the church had overstepped their competency and bounds of authority. But this was often because these theologians relied on secular philosophies and not on Scripture.

Related to this whole discussion was the question of the relationship of natural and supernatural revelation and where natural theology fit in, if at all. Edwards affirmed that natural and special revelation could never contradict one another. But he would have recognized that this was true of revelation itself and not of humanly formulated theologies *fallibly* derived from natural and supernatural revelation. Edwards recognized that scientists, like all other human beings—educated and erudite or not—are impacted by the fall and infected with sin. Redemption begins to restore the proper functioning of reason, and even unbelievers by common grace can know things in limited but often brilliant ways. So scientists suffer from the noetic effects of the fall and suppress the truth in unrighteousness (Rom. 1:18–32). Some scientists are regenerate and enjoy a reversal of some effects of the fall; and unbelieving scientists know things about this universe because God

---

34. *WJE*, 23:201.
35. Zakai, *Jonathan Edwards's Philosophy of Nature*, 4, 11–27, 52–59, 81, 87–88, 97.

provides non-saving, common grace. But no scientists are unaffected by the fall. So the fact that natural and supernatural revelation can never contradict one another does not prevent humans from misconstruing the relation of these two forms of revelation or of God's relation to his creation.

Preliminary Conclusions

Unlike some Christians who reacted to the rise the "new science,"[36] Edwards was not reactionary; but at the same time, he did not swallow everything suggested by the reigning scientists of his day. He especially rejected the mechanistic universe that in one way or another derived from the insights of Isaac Newton. God was not a watchmaker who left the universe to run on its own. God was intimately involved with his creation both in bringing it into initial existence and in upholding its continued existence. Edwards's commitment to Trinitarian-theistic idealism is a problem insofar as it compromises the Creator-creature distinction. It is not necessarily problematic that creatures exist "in" God if we understand that God exists on a wholly different plane than his creatures so that our existence does not undermine his omnipresence, as if creatures could crowd out divine space. Paul notes in Acts 17:28 that in God "we live and move and have our being." Edwards would surely understand his own view (characterized by some as panentheism) as entailed in Paul's words to the Areopagus. Edwards certainly understood creation to be real. But its reality was not self-sustaining. Creation was what it was by virtue of its constitution by the divine mind.

That Edwards assessed spiritual creatures as having greater value than merely physical creatures is true.[37] Whether his acceptance of the unbiblical chain-of-being concept is the source of this idea is debatable. God is pure uncreated spirit, angels are created spirits, and human beings are spiritual-physical creatures. The chain-of-being construct is undermined by the fact that the second person of the Trinity took to

---

36. Zakai shows various responses to the uses of science and how it was throwing many into confusion and caused great consternation. Zakai looks at the use of Newtonian science and responses by men such as John Donne and Blaise Pascal (ibid., 51–202).

37. *WJE*, 6:205, corollary 1.

himself a "true body and a reasonable soul"[38] and was and is Mediator for his elect from among the human race. So, while angels are superior in some respects to human beings, in other (most significant) respects, man is superior to angels because of redemption and the incarnation.

With regard to Edwards's acceptance of continuous creationism and occasionalism, we have seen in "Miscellanies," no. 1263, a rather major modification of the classical forms of these doctrines. Continuous creationism posits that God first creates and then recreates the universe anew every moment. While Edwards does affirm that God upholds all things, he recognizes the existence of natural laws, which are simply God's ordinary way of operating in the universe (as distinguished from his extraordinary activity in miracles). If an atom is God's causing a point of resistance or indivisibility (indiscerptibility) in the universe, this is done according to God's ordinary manner of functioning in his own universe (i.e., according to the various laws of nature). As for occasionalism, we have seen that for Edwards it is true both that, on the divine plane, God is the cause of all things and that, on the creaturely plane, creatures as secondary causes also operate at different levels of divine arbitrariness depending where they are on the chain of being and to what extent they are spiritual. Does Edwards undermine the integrity of the existence and functioning of creatures? While early formulations, in reaction to both materialism and mechanicalism, seem to suggest Edwards unknowingly stumbled into troubled territory, later formulations are much more nuanced.

Jonathan Edwards was a man of his times. We should not expect him to have held views that only later came to be articulated and embraced. Yet he, like us, had his Bible and therefore could in principle have overcome some, if not all, of these impediments. Edwards quite properly rejected a mechanistic and materialistic universe in which God was defined out of existence. He quite properly stood for a God who was intimately involved in his creation and not locked out of the universe. God was, after all, not just Creator but also providential Lord over all his creation and Redeemer of the lost. Edwards, as we earlier noted, held that creation served as the theater of God's glory

---

38. This is the language of the Westminster Shorter Catechism, 22.

most clearly revealed in redemption, culminating in the incarnation of the Son of God.[39]

Jonathan Edwards appreciated the wonders of God's world and critically appropriated many insights from modern science. He was not antiscience and, most assuredly, not anti-intellectual. But he recognized that all men are fallen and that some are regenerate and so are in the process of being restored. Some of these folk are scientists and possess insight into how God relates to and interacts with his world. Theology integrates all human knowledge, including natural scientific knowledge. What we learn from natural science must be brought to the bar of Scripture because science is conducted by fallible and sinful creatures.

Jonathan Edwards was not the only or last Christian theologian to seek to understand and learn from science. Nor was he the last to seek to understand how God relates to his world. The honoree of this Festschrift is one such contemporary Christian theologian. We now turn to briefly consider one contribution of his to this scholarly conversation.

Vern Poythress on God's Relation to Laws of Nature

In 2003 Vern Poythress published "Why Scientists Must Believe in God: Divine Attributes of Scientific Law" in the *Journal of the Evangelical Theological Society*.[40] Though Poythress did not realize he was following the path trod before him specifically by Jonathan Edwards two and half centuries before, I believe Edwards and Poythress sweetly comply. Moreover, Poythress, I believe, adds to and improves upon the insights of Edwards. This is not to suggest that they are identical in their views of things. But those familiar with the texture and contours of each theologian's work will admit a strong family resemblance beyond the obvious Reformed theological commitment they share.

Poythress's article argues that scientists typically ascribe to laws of nature divine attributes or characteristics.[41] This is inevitable in light of the reality that lies behind these laws. Laws of nature are in fact God's *acting* in nature. Poythress offers a series of thirteen points

---

39. See Biehl, *Infinite Merit of Christ*.
40. *JETS* 46, no. 1 (2003): 111–23.
41. Ibid., 112, 114.

about scientific laws and how they reveal the triune God of Scripture.[42] Poythress further argues that in light of the (quasi-) divine status ascribed to scientific laws, scientists must themselves grant that they do in fact believe in God, even if they emphatically deny it.[43]

What interests us here is that Poythress's insightful article (along with the other work he has done on a theological reckoning with science over the last forty years or so) seems to jibe well with Edwards's project even while not building upon the debatably idiosyncratic aspects of Edwards's ostensible philosophical-theological commitments already noted in this essay. Poythress builds upon the insights of theological development since the time of Jonathan Edwards, especially the work of Abraham Kuyper, Cornelius Van Til, and his colleague in arms John Frame.

Vern Poythress and Jonathan Edwards share the view that God is intimately involved in the creation he initially brought into existence and continually upholds. Both understand that God is irreducibly Trinitarian.[44] Both maintain God's transcendence and his imminence. Both understand that the laws of nature are in fact God's ordinary work of providence, which means that when he exercises extraordinary providence in his miraculous work of redemption, God is not "breaking" any laws. God is not remote in the sense of unconcerned and detached from the universe. Both Edwards and Poythress (and many, many others) have understood that God has created the theater of nature in order to assemble a cast of characters caught up in the redemption of fallen man.

Conclusion

Both Jonathan Edwards and Vern Poythress demonstrate that it is possible for a Christian theologian both to be interested in natural science and adept at it and to be able to critically appreciate it without falling

---

42. Ibid., 112–23. These include the character of scientific law, belief in scientific laws, the universal applicability of scientific law, the divine attributes of law, the power of law, the personal character of law, the incomprehensibility of law, the concern with divinizing nature, the goodness of law, the beauty of law, the rectitude of law, the Trinitarian nature of law, and how scientific laws involve God showing himself. Poythress concludes his article with five implications and conclusions.

43. Ibid., 111.

44. See Vern S. Poythress, "Reforming Ontology and Logic in the Light of the Trinity: An Application of Van Til's Idea of Analogy," *WTJ* 57, no. 1 (1995): 187–219.

into the errors of either repudiating the scientific endeavor as such or thinking it necessary to follow the methodological naturalism that is endemic in the secular academy today. A Christian, even an explicitly Christian theologian, may be able to critically appreciate and appropriate scientific insights garnered by scientists who are Christians and, because of common grace, those offered by non-Christian scientists as well.[45]

45. Whether Edwards would agree with Kuyper that there are two kinds of science because of the fall is outside the purview of this chapter. It is an interesting question in itself. I would suggest that his Bible and his theology gave him the ingredients to come to the same conclusion. I should also note explicitly that insights offered by non-Christians must be radically assessed before the bar of Scripture and Reformed theology so that the sinful aspects of such views are removed. See Augustine's discussion in *On Christian Doctrine* in NPNF[1].

Part 4

WORLDVIEW

13

Redeeming the Seminary by Redeeming Its Worldview

PETER A. LILLBACK

Abraham Kuyper (1837–1920) insisted that all of life is redeemed in Christ.[1] Professor Vern Poythress agrees and has written a series of studies that show how various disciplines of scholarship can be redeemed for the glory of Christ.[2] My purpose here is to propose that the seminary must be redeemed and that this is accomplished by redeeming the seminary's worldview.[3]

Indeed, everyone operates with presuppositions about reality.[4]

1. In Kuyper's 1898 Stone Lectures at Princeton, published in 1931 as *Lectures on Calvinism*, he argued that Calvinism is a worldview. D. Martyn Lloyd-Jones wrote in 1975: "The Christian is not only to be concerned about personal salvation. It is his duty to have a complete view of life as taught in the Scriptures. . . . We must have a world view. All of us who have ever read Kuyper, and others, have been teaching this for years" (D. M. Lloyd-Jones, "The French Revolution and After," in Graham S. Harrison et al., *The Christian and the State in Revolutionary Times* [Cambridge: Westminster Conference, 1976], 101). See also http://www.alloflliferedeemed.co.uk /introduction.htm.

2. For example, Vern S. Poythress, *Redeeming Science: A God-Centered Approach* (Wheaton, IL: Crossway, 2006). His "redeeming" series includes books on science, mathematics, philosophy, and sociology.

3. For example, Vern S. Poythress, *Inerrancy and Worldview: Answering Modern Challenges to the Bible* (Wheaton, IL: Crossway, 2012).

4. See Cornelius Van Til, *The Defense of the Faith*, 3rd ed. (Philadelphia: Presbyterian and Reformed, 1967); K. Scott Oliphint, *Reasons for Faith: Philosophy in the Service of Theology*

These beliefs or intellectual commitments about the cosmos and all that it contains have been termed worldviews. Armand Nicholi, of Harvard Medical School, explains, "All of us, whether we realize it or not, have a worldview; we have a philosophy of life—our attempt to make sense out of our existence. It contains our answers to the fundamental questions concerning the meaning of our lives, questions that we struggle with at some level all of our lives."[5] In this regard, Vern Poythress, whom we honor with these essays, has made the remarkable assertion that all thought, regardless of one's worldview or disavowal of God, inevitably leads to God:

> All scientists—including agnostics and atheists—believe in God. They have to in order to do their work. It may seem outrageous to include agnostics and atheists in this broad statement. But by their actions people sometimes show that in a sense they believe in things that they profess not to believe in.[6]

By insisting on the dependence of all thought on God, Poythress underscores the ubiquity of worldview implications for knowledge.

In the West, various worldviews have emerged that have shaped cultural development.[7] The eras of Western culture can be summarized by their prominent worldviews. The iconic spirit of specific ages in the West might be summarized as:

- Reformation: theocentric faith
- Post-Reformation: structured theocentric faith
- Enlightenment: anthropocentric knowledge
- Modernity: globalizing ideological power
- Postmodernity: narcissistic expressive individualism

Significantly, the Westminster Standards have persisted through all these epochs.

(Phillipsburg, NJ: P&R, 2006); Oliphint, *Covenantal Apologetics: Principles and Practice in Defense of Our Faith* (Wheaton, IL: Crossway, 2013); John M. Frame, *Cornelius Van Til: An Analysis of His Thought* (Phillipsburg, NJ: P&R, 1995).

5. Armand M. Nicholi, "When Worldviews Collide: C. S. Lewis and Sigmund Freud: A Comparison of Their Thoughts and Viewpoints on Life, Pain and Death, Part 1," *The Real Issue*, 16, no. 2 (1998): 9.

6. Poythress, *Redeeming Science*, 13.

7. See *Revolutions in Worldview*, ed. W. Andrew Hoffecker (Phillipsburg, NJ: P&R, 2007).

The Need to Redeem the Worldview of Western Culture

The Westminster Confession was written at the high-water mark of the Protestant Reformation in England. In the nearly four centuries of the Westminster Confession, it has passed through the enlightenment and the secular ideologies of modernity,[8] arriving at postmodernity,[9] which is often described by its expressive individualism, moral relativity, and sexual permissiveness.[10] David Wells has described this progression in worldviews as a movement from wisdom to knowledge to information.[11] In Western thought there has been a rejection of the Reformation's theism and an increasing pursuit of atheistic secular anthropocentrism.[12]

Previously, owing to biblical ethics and Reformation theology, the primary spheres of human existence in Western cultures were generally ranked in the following order of priority: (1) family, (2) church, (3) state, and (4) self. The postmodern mind, however, has turned this order upside down:

1. Self—a celebration of self-fulfillment[13]
2. State—a quest for socialism with the absolutizing of the state[14]
3. Church—where emotional hygiene eclipses biblical teaching and godliness[15]

---

8. See David F. Wells, *God in the Wasteland* (Leicester, UK: Inter-Varsity Press, 1994), 7–10.

9. For a general description of postmodernism, see http://www.spaceandmotion.com/Philosophy-Postmodernism.htm.

10. Humanist Manifesto II asserts, "The many varieties of sexual exploration should not in themselves be considered evil. . . . A civilized society should be a tolerant one" (http://americanhumanist.org/Humanism/Humanist_Manifesto_II).

11. See David Wells, "The Stupidity of Preaching and the Contemporary Moment" (paper delivered at the Richard B. Gaffin Jr. Lectures on Theology, Culture, and Mission, Westminster Theological Seminary, 2013).

12. See the fifth and sixth points of the 1933 Humanist Manifesto (http://americanhumanist.org/Humanism/Humanist_Manifesto_I). The 1973 Humanist Manifesto II proclaimed: "We believe, however, that traditional dogmatic or authoritarian religions that place revelation, God, ritual, or creed above human needs and experience do a disservice to the human species. . . . No deity will save us; we must save ourselves. . . . Promises of immortal salvation or fear of eternal damnation are both illusory and harmful. They distract humans from present concerns, from self-actualization, and from rectifying social injustices" (http://americanhumanist.org/Humanism/Humanist_Manifesto_II).

13. Cf. the eighth point of the 1933 Humanist Manifesto.

14. For a discussion of statism, see http://pages.uoregon.edu/kimball/sttism.htm. See also Peter A. Lillback, "The United Statists of America?," in *Statism: The Shadows of Another Night*, ed. Charles Rodriguez (Terre Haute, IN: Tanglewood, 2015), 109–45.

15. Cf. the ninth point of the 1933 Humanist Manifesto.

4. Family—where self-fulfillment replaces the marital covenant, which is battered by cohabitation and divorce and redefined without reference to gender[16]

To address these realities, Christian thinkers must develop an articulate worldview. As Francis Schaeffer explained:

> The basic problem of the Christians in this country . . . is that they have seen things in bits and pieces instead of totals. They have very gradually become disturbed over permissiveness, pornography, the public schools, the breakdown of the family, and finally abortion. . . . They have failed to see that all of this has come about due to a shift in worldview. . . . This shift has been away from a worldview that was at least vaguely Christian in people's memory toward something completely different.[17]

Worldviews in Conflict: The Antithetical Nature of the Christian Worldview

The Christian worldview proclaims the history of God's saving purposes. It moves from eternity past, through time, to eternity future. It might be summarized as seen in figure 3:

Figure 3

Eternal self-existing *God*

God's self-*revelation*

| *Creation* ex nihilo | Man's *fall* | *Redemption* in Christ | Eternal *hope* |

This theocentric Christian worldview begins with the self-contained, ontological, triune God who has revealed himself. The cosmos and all that it contains, including man, God's image-bearer, exist because of God's self-disclosure in creation. God has chosen to reveal himself per-

---

16. Karl Marx and Friedrich Engels wrote in section 2 of the *Communist Manifesto*, "Proletarians and Communists": "The theory of the Communists may be summed up on the single sentence: Abolition of private property. . . . Abolition of the Family! Even the most radical flare up at this infamous proposal of the Communists. On what foundation is the present family, the bourgeois family, based? On capital. . . . But, you will say, we destroy the most hallowed of relations, when we replace home education by social." For the impact of the New Age movement on the family, see Peter Jones, *Spirit Wars: Pagan Revival in America* (Enumclaw, WA: Wine Press, 1997), 15–16.

17. Francis A. Schaeffer, *A Christian Manifesto* (Wheaton, IL: Crossway, 1981), 17–18.

sonally in the covenant he established with Adam. By mankind's rejection of God's Word, all are covenant breakers. The universality of sin, death, and confusion about God are due to this broken covenant relationship.

But God as covenant keeper has restored the covenant through Christ. The covenant of grace is always the same in substance (Christ) while distinct in administration (the various epochs of salvation history).[18] Through the person and work of Christ, salvation was accomplished. Believers await its climax in the second advent of Christ and the resurrection. This accomplished salvation is applied to God's people by the regenerating work of the Holy Spirit and saving faith. This new life brings eternal life and hope. The Christian's hope is eternal and looks forward to the restoration of all things.

The Christian worldview is in radical contrast to the pessimism of atheism. Describing the despair of the atheist, Bertrand Russell wrote in 1902 that

> Man is . . . the outcome of accidental collocations of atoms; that no fire, no heroism, no intensity of thought and feeling, can preserve an individual life beyond the grave; that all the labours of the ages, all the devotion, all the inspiration, all the noonday brightness of human genius, are destined to extinction in the vast death of the solar system. . . . Man's achievement must inevitably be buried beneath the debris of a universe in ruins— . . . only on the firm foundation of unyielding despair, can the soul's habitation henceforth be safely built.[19]

The Christian worldview collides with secular atheism. And the Christian's affirmation of ultimate truth in God stands opposite postmodernism, which rejects the possibility of ultimate truth.[20] Postmodernity regards all truth claims as mere preferences. This skeptical philosophy presupposes that there are many truths, but there can be no ultimate truth, no metanarrative, no grand story to explain life.[21]

---

18. See Calvin, *Institutes*, 2.10. and 2.11.

19. Bertrand Russell, "A Free Man's Worship," in *The Basic Writings of Bertrand Russell, 1903–1959*, ed. Robert E. Egner and Lester E. Denonn (London: Routledge, 1992), 67.

20. See Allan Bloom, *The Closing of the American Mind: How Higher Education Has Failed Democracy and Impoverished the Souls of Today's Students* (New York: Simon & Schuster, 1987), 25–26.

21. Calvin argues that man's search for truth is vain, for he cannot establish the proper priorities for determining which area of the world to investigate (*Institutes*, 2.2.12).

Reformed theology is not surprised that man without divine grace denies and suppresses truth (Rom. 1:18).[22]

J. Gresham Machen, founder of Westminster Seminary, understood the importance of worldview concerns. In 1913, sixteen years before the seminary opened, he wrote:

> It would be a great mistake to suppose that all men are equally well prepared to receive the Gospel. But God usually exerts that power in connection with certain prior conditions of the human mind, and it should be ours to create, so far as we can, with the help of God, those favorable conditions for the reception of the Gospel. False ideas are the greatest obstacle to the reception of the Gospel. We may preach . . . and yet succeed only in winning a straggler . . . if we permit the whole collective thought of the nation to be controlled by ideas which prevent Christianity from being regarded as anything more than a harmless delusion.[23]

Worldview concerns were at the heart of the seminary when it launched in 1929.

Redeeming the Seminary by Redeeming the Seminary's Worldview

Worldview concerns are critical for the church as it trains leaders for ministry. The church has employed various approaches for the education of pastors. Educational methods range from pastoral apprenticeships to full residential seminaries under faculties teaching in fields of expertise. The word "seminary" means a seed bed. The seminary is where Christian seedlings, fledgling leaders, are grown and formed into leaders of the church.

Differing approaches stem not merely from pragmatic considerations but also from methods of pastoral training that are not expressly mandated by Scripture. In Scripture we discover Elisha's "sons of the prophets"—or "school of the prophets" (NIV)—(2 Kings 6:1–2); Jesus's band of disciples (Matt. 4:18–5:1) and teachers of the Law, such as Nicodemus (John 3:1–2, 10); or Paul's teacher, Gamaliel (Acts 5:34;

---

22. See ibid.
23. J. Gresham Machen, "Christianity and Culture," *PTR* 11, no. 1 (1913): 7.

22:3). Whatever method is used to educate pastors, Christ-centered and apostolic training is mandatory (Matt. 28:18–20; 2 Tim. 2:2). Through this prerequisite, the future clergyman's preparation should result in "rightly handling the word of truth" (2 Tim. 2:15; cf. Heb. 5:14).

The power of non-Christian intellectual movements to impact the seminary must not be underestimated. The history of Christianity shows that there has been a drift into liberalism. The classic examples include Harvard, Yale, Andover-Newton, and Princeton. Seminaries gradually tend to abandon orthodoxy as educators seek rapprochement with cultural trends, contemporary scholarship, and new ideologies that subtly or overtly attack "the faith that was once for all delivered to the saints" (Jude 1:3). Accommodation of liberalism often proceeds through synthesis, reflecting Hegel's dialectic of thesis, antithesis, and synthesis.

Rejecting compromise of Christian principles, Cornelius Van Til, Machen's first professor of apologetics at Westminster, identified a precognitive antithesis between Christian and non-Christian thought. This antithesis prohibited the synthesis between Christian and non-Christian worldviews.[24] However, Van Til affirmed divine common grace that enabled interaction between believers and nonbelievers, even though saving grace creates an eternal difference between them.[25]

Van Til's presuppositional approach to apologetics[26] develops themes such as (1) common grace and antithesis, (2) noetic effects of sin, (3) point of contact and regeneration, and (4) *reductio ad absurdum.*

Common Grace, Antithesis, and "Borrowed Capital"

Believers and unbelievers coexist in common grace and are separated by antithesis. The inherent antithesis between the unbeliever and the believing Christian is in their understandings of reality. The unbeliever operates without God and against his Word. Whether conscious of it

---

24. "The fight between Christianity and non-Christianity is, in modern times, no piece-meal affair. It is the life and death struggle between two mutually opposed life and world-views" (Cornelius Van Til, *An Introduction to Systematic Theology* (Philadelphia: Presbyterian and Reformed, 1952), 6. See also Greg L. Bahnsen, *Van Til's Apologetic: Readings and Analysis* (Phillipsburg, NJ: P&R, 1998), 101–2.
25. See Cornelius Van Til, *Common Grace* (Philadelphia: Presbyterian and Reformed, 1947); Van Til, *Common Grace and the Gospel* (Philadelphia: Presbyterian and Reformed, 1972).
26. See Van Til, *The Defense of the Faith*, 109.

or not, unbelievers, in Adam, live as covenant breakers (Genesis 2–3), while believers in Christ have been restored to covenant relationship. Out of the beneficence of God's common grace, he sends rain on the just and the unjust. God gives fruitful seasons to those who disregard and rebel against him. All mankind lives and moves and has its being in God as Creator. Thus all people are without excuse before God (Rom. 1:20).

Accordingly, unbelievers live by what Van Til termed "borrowed capital."[27] They have ideas, relationships, and benefits that they as unbelievers have no right to or basis for in their rebellion. They live by common grace and ungratefully borrow the blessings of the reality that only God can provide.

The Noetic Effects of Sin and "Common Ground"

While unbelievers borrows blessings from the Creator, their hostility to God creates within them intellectual darkness to divine revelation, making them blind to spiritual truth. The particular manifestations of this state of mental, spiritual darkness are the noetic effects of sin,[28] a concept developed by Kuyper.[29] This means that ethically and epistemologically there is no common ground between believer and nonbeliever. Appeals to alleged neutral spheres such as logic, reason, or natural law can never in themselves persuade an unbeliever to turn to God. The noetic effects of sin cause an unbeliever to use these intellectual tools autonomously, thus wrongly believing them to be objective realities that allow him to judge everything, including the existence of God. The unbeliever, as covenant breaker, instinctively repudiates that there is a transcendent source of life and meaning to which he is obliged. He suppresses the truth in unrighteousness (Rom. 1:18).

Point of Contact and Regeneration

The point of contact between the believer and the unbeliever is not in clearer logic or more persuasive intellectual arguments. The noetic ef-

---

27. See Van Til, *Introduction to Systematic Theology*, 81–113.
28. Calvin was keenly aware of the biblical conception of the noetic effects of sin. See John Calvin, *Concerning the Eternal Predestination of God*, trans. J. K. S. Reid (London: James Clarke, 1961), 104.
29. Abraham Kuyper developed the doctrine of the noetic effects of sin, distinguishing the weakness of human thought from the loss of knowledge of all things in unity with God. See http://biblicalphilosophy.org/Epistemology_Metaphysics/Noetic_Effects_Sin.asp.

fects of sin preempt these from making a saving impact. Ironically, the point of contact is the very knowledge of God that people suppress. Van Til explains:

> Disagreeing with the natural man's interpretation of himself as the ultimate reference-point, the Reformed apologist must seek his point of contact with the natural man in that which is beneath the threshold of his working consciousness, in the sense of deity which he seeks to suppress. And to do this the Reformed apologist must also seek a point of contact with the systems constructed by the natural man. But this point of contact must be in the nature of a head-on collision. *If there is no head-on collision with the systems of the natural man there will be no point of contact with the sense of deity in the natural man.*[30]

The ultimate means that is effective is regeneration, the work of the Holy Spirit in the new birth. This is not common but special grace, flowing from God's decree of election leading to saving faith in Christ. The point of contact with the unbeliever is the gospel and the sovereign impartation of life by the Holy Spirit. Nevertheless, all people live as divine image bearers. Thus common grace affords a point of contact in the unbeliever's soul as he is shown that he is actively suppressing the knowledge of God. But, epistemologically, there is no point of contact as the unbeliever without the gospel is unaware that he is suppressing the knowledge of God. God's general revelation and common grace are only understood through God's gift of faith. Calvin explains:

> It is therefore in vain that so many burning lamps shine for us in the workmanship of the universe to show forth the glory of its Author. Although they bathe us wholly in their radiance, yet they can of themselves in no way lead us into the right path. Surely they strike some sparks, but before their fuller light shines forth these are smothered. . . . The invisible divinity is made manifest in such spectacles, but . . . we have not the eyes to see this unless they be illumined by the inner revelation of God through faith.[31]

---

30. Van Til, *The Defense of the Faith*, 98–99, emphasis original.
31. Calvin, *Institutes*, 1.5.14.

Reductio ad Absurdum

The task of the apologist is to show the unbeliever that he cannot live without God or escape common grace. The dialogue between apologist and unbeliever seeks to show that the unbeliever has no basis for knowledge except through God. The unbeliever is confronted with the fact that he inconsistently denies God even as he unjustly and unconsciously seizes upon God to make sense of the world. This is a *reductio ad absurdum* wherein the unbeliever is confronted with the fact that he must embrace the existence of God even though he intellectually denies him. Van Til explains:

> What we shall have to do then is to try to reduce our opponent's position to an absurdity. Nothing less will do. Without God, man is completely lost in every respect; epistemologically as well as morally and religiously. . . . We must hold that the position of our opponent has in reality been reduced to self-contradiction when it is shown to be hopelessly opposed to the Christian theistic concept of God.[32]

In God's sovereignty, regeneration flows from election so that God's truth can be understood by an unbeliever.[33] The Westminster Confession of Faith, 10.1, entitles this "Effectual Calling":

> All those whom God hath predestinated unto life, and those only, he is pleased, in his appointed and accepted time, effectually to call, by his Word and Spirit, out of that state of sin and death, in which they are by nature, to grace and salvation by Jesus Christ; enlightening their minds, spiritually and savingly, to understand the things of God: taking away their heart of stone, and giving unto them an heart of flesh; renewing their wills, and by his almighty power determining them to that which is good, and effectually drawing them to Jesus Christ; yet so as they come most freely, being made willing by his grace.[34]

---

32. Cornelius Van Til, *A Survey of Christian Epistemology* (Philadelphia: Presbyterian and Reformed, 1969), 203ff.
33. Calvin teaches that the understanding of spiritual truth is only the result of divine election (*Institutes*, 1.7.5).
34. In *The Creeds of the Evangelical Protestant Churches*, vol. 3 of *The Creeds of Christendom*, ed. Philip Schaff (Grand Rapids, MI: Baker, 1977), 624.

As the seminary remains faithful to God's Word, the seminary is redeemed. The biblical theology of the Westminster Standards, fortified by Van Til's apologetic, creates a *Weltanschauung*[35] that enables Christians to redeem the seminary from the ever-present threat of drift into liberalism. The presuppositional apologetic of the Kuyper–Van Til tradition is an anchor and battle-tested starting point for Christian encounters with postmodern thought.

Redeeming the Seminary through the Contributions of Westminster Seminary

The Princeton Seminary tradition of the nineteenth century recognized that emerging worldview struggles had potential to shape the church. A. A. Hodge, professor of systematic theology at Princeton in the nineteenth century, wrote:

> The Bible, the great statute-book of the kingdom, explicitly lays down principles which . . . will regulate the action of every human being in all relations. . . . If the national life in general is organized upon non-Christian principles, the churches which are embraced within the universal assimilating power of that nation will not long be able to preserve their integrity.[36]

In the early twentieth century, the impact of what Hodge called "non-Christian principles" was recognized by Princeton's New Testament professor J. Gresham Machen. Machen determined that there was a profound difference between Christianity and theological liberalism.[37] By 1929, his concerns had grown, prompting him to establish

35. Sigmund Freud's 1933 "The Question of a Weltanschauung" defined a worldview as "an intellectual construction which solves all the problems of our existence uniformly on the basis of one overriding hypothesis" (Nicholi, "When Worldviews Collide," 9.

36. A. A. Hodge, *Popular Lectures on Theological Themes*, 119, https://theologue.files.word press.com/2014/09/popularlecturesontheologicalthemes-aahodge.pdf.

37. Machen's entry into theological conflict with "liberalism" or "modern theology" began with his address on November 3, 1921, to the Ruling Elders' Association of Chester Presbytery, which was published by *PTR* 20, no. 1 (1922): 93–117, entitled "Liberalism or Christianity." Machen explains in his preface to his subsequent book *Christianity and Liberalism*, "The interest with which the published address was received has encouraged the author to undertake a more extensive presentation of the same subject." Westminster Theological Seminary professor Carl Trueman writes in his foreword to the new edition of *Christianity and Liberalism*, "Machen summed up his thesis in a letter to *The British Weekly*, September 11, 1924: 'The truth is that the manifold religious life of the present day, despite interlocking of the branches and much interaction, does not spring from one root but from two. One root is Christianity; the other is a

Westminster Theological Seminary. Machen's efforts to redeem the seminary were theological with the goal of proclaiming "the whole counsel of God" (Acts 20:27). The theological concerns of the new seminary were captured in its name, Westminster, echoing the climactic statement of Reformed theology. The mission of the seminary was to train "specialists in the Bible" by professors who held an "*ex animo*" commitment to the Westminster Standards.[38]

The seminary was born with orthodoxy and creativity, joining old and new. Machen's commitment to the doctrine of Scripture developed by Warfield reflected the old. Van Til's departure from the rationalistic apologetic of Warfield in favor of Kuyper's world-and-life-view approach reflected a new emphasis. Machen sought to integrate varying Reformed perspectives. Machen's Presbyterianism represented the American church. Yet he exercised ecclesiastical independence by developing a Presbyterian and Reformed ecumenicity. Westminster's first faculty included Reformed theologian R. B. Kuiper, (American) Presbyterian Machen, (Scottish) Presbyterian John Murray, and ethnically Reformed but ecclesiastically Presbyterian Van Til.

Westminster is committed to classic Reformed covenant theology,[39] which presents the unity of the Bible by the progressive development of God's self-disclosure through Christ-centered covenants.[40] Biblical theology, a newer approach, emerges from this Reformed understanding of the covenant. An orthodox and covenantal biblical theology was championed at Princeton by Professor Geerhardus Vos.

Vos stated the distinctives of biblical theology in his 1894 inaugural

---

naturalistic or agnostic modernism which, despite Christian influences in detail, is fundamentally hostile to the Christian faith'" (J. Gresham Machen, *Christianity and Liberalism*, new ed. [Grand Rapids, MI: Eerdmans, 2009], ix). Also see Darryl G. Hart, *Defending the Faith: J. Gresham Machen and the Crisis of Conservative Protestantism in Modern America* (Baltimore: Johns Hopkins University Press, 1994).

38. Machen's opening address to the Westminster community, "Westminster Theological Seminary: Its Purpose and Plan," can be found in *Seeing Christ in All of Scripture*, ed. Peter A. Lillback (Glenside, PA: Westminster Seminary Press, 2016), 53–62. See also Lillback, "Confessional Subscription among the Sixteenth Century Reformers," in *The Practice of Confessional Subscription*, ed. David W. Hall (Oak Ridge, TN: Covenant Foundation, 1997).

39. This hermeneutical approach began in the early Reformation with Zwingli, Bullinger, and Calvin and continued to be perfected by Reformed theologians through the post-Reformation era. See Peter A. Lillback, *The Binding of God: Calvin's Role in the Development of Covenant Theology* (Grand Rapids, MI: Baker, 2001).

40. See Lillback, *Seeing Christ in All of Scripture*, 1–8.

lecture at Princeton.[41] He said that the theologian's task is to deal with Scripture by the principles of exegesis. By exegesis, the scholar realizes the necessity of explaining that God's revelation was not given in the definitive statements and polished definitions of systematic theology. Rather, Scripture presents dramatic episodes in the history of salvation. "Biblical Theology, rightly defined, is nothing else than the exhibition of the organic progress of supernatural revelation in its historic continuity and multiformity."[42]

The systematic theology of old Princeton was given a deeper exegetical presentation by Vos's student John Murray. As Murray taught:

> Systematic theology is tied to exegesis. It coordinates and synthesizes the whole witness of Scripture on the various topics with which it deals. But systematic theology will fail of its task to the extent to which it discards its rootage in biblical theology as properly conceived and developed. . . . The fact is that only when systematic theology is rooted in biblical theology does it exemplify its true function and achieve its purpose.[43]

Westminster's creative orthodoxy has continued with scholarly excellence within its commitment to the Westminster Standards.[44] The faculty continues to explore biblically based concepts of theology and ministry. Some fruitful faculty contributions include: redemptive-historical preaching (Edmund Clowney); biblical counseling (Jay Adams); contextual cross-cultural missions (Harvie Conn); the centrality of union with Christ and eschatology in New Testament theology (Richard B. Gaffin Jr.); biblical revelation's multiple perspectives (Vern Poythress); and the integration of technology with biblical language research (Alan Groves). Such scholarly concepts have shaped Westminster as a redeemed seminary.

---

41. Geerhardus Vos, "The Idea of Biblical Theology," in *Redemptive History and Biblical Interpretation: The Shorter Writings of Geerhardus Vos*, ed. Richard B. Gaffin Jr. (Phillipsburg, NJ: Presbyterian and Reformed, 1980), 3–24.

42. Ibid., 15.

43. John Murray, "Systematic Theology: Second Article," *WTJ* 26, no. 1 (1963): 44ff.

44. This commitment has not been without turmoil. See Peter A. Lillback, "The Infallible Rule of Interpretation of Scripture": The Hermeneutical Crisis and the Westminster Standards," in *Thy Word Is Still Truth: Essential Writings on the Doctrine of Scripture from the Reformation to Today*, ed. Peter A. Lillback and Richard B. Gaffin Jr. (Phillipsburg, NJ: P&R, 2013), 1279–1318.

Does a Redeemed Seminary Play a Role
in Redeeming the Culture?

The collision of worldviews described by Van Til intensifies.[45] This conflict was anticipated by Augustine in his seminal work *The City of God.* Augustine argued that two differing loves create two different cities. Man's love for man creates the City of Man. Man's love for God creates the City of God. These cities are in conflict as their two loves create differing worldviews. Augustine's cities evoke the concept of culture.

Culture can be conceived of as a community's religion or worldview turned outward to impact people, ideas, and things. "Culture, then, is any and all human effort and labor expended upon the cosmos, to unearth its treasures and its riches and bring them in to the service of man for the enrichment of human existence unto the glory of God."[46] If Christians are the salt of the earth and the light of the world (Matt. 5:13–16), shouldn't the seminary play a role in shaping culture?

H. Richard Niebuhr, in his work *Christ and Culture,*[47] developed a useful classification of views (with proponents shown in parentheses):

- Christ against Culture (some early church fathers, many fundamentalists)
- Christ of Culture (Clement of Alexandria, perhaps many mainline churches)
- Christ above Culture (Aquinas and other medieval thinkers)
- Christ and Culture in Paradox (Luther in his two-kingdoms view)
- Christ the Transformer of Culture (Kuyper and many in the Reformed tradition)

We could speak of the seminary's relationship to culture under similar headings:

- The Seminary against Culture
- The Seminary of Culture
- The Seminary above Culture

---

45. Van Til, *The Defense of the Faith*, 98–99.
46. Henry R. Van Til, *The Calvinistic Concept of Culture* (Grand Rapids, MI: Baker, 1972), 29–30.
47. H. Richard Niebuhr, *Christ and Culture* (New York: Harper & Row, 1951).

- The Seminary and Culture in Paradox
- The Seminary as the Transformer of Culture

Clearly, a scholarly seminary cannot be indifferent to its culture. But which of these alternatives best reflects the redeemed seminary's place in culture?

By developing apologetics from biblical theology, Van Til asserted that every fact is a God-revealing fact and so must be a God-interpreted fact. Without God, every fact devolves into a disconnected and meaningless "brute fact."[48] So if a seminary such as Westminster is to be a redeemed seminary, it must be a God-revealing and God-interpreted community. Then the seminary can become an agent in the transformation of culture.

Mainline churches and seminaries are facing dramatic decline. If they were once the seminaries of culture, it seems that postmodern culture is reducing them to near extinction by assimilation. However, Van Til's approach to epistemology and the biblical-theological understanding of the seminary are rejected by secular culture. Secularism claims that the world is composed of facts that autonomous man can correctly interpret, making the notion of God and the existence of the seminary superfluous. George M. Marsden, for example, has shown how the worldview reflected by Augustine, Kuyper, and Van Til has been banished from academia.[49] The secular mind views the biblically based seminary as a reactionary force working against culture.

The hostility of the secular worldview toward Christianity and scripturally committed seminaries has escalated. An example is the Affordable Care Act's requirement of all nonchurch employers, regardless of convictions, to provide coverage for abortion. In 2014, with its commitment to the sanctity of life, Westminster brought suit against the United States Government. The case went to the Supreme Court and was heard along with lawsuits filed by other parties such as Geneva College, Wheaton College, Houston Baptist University, and the Little Sisters of the Poor. The high court returned the case to the lower courts, and the outcome is still not clear. But what is clear is that this is not the

---

48. See Bahnsen, *Van Til's Apologetic*, 36–38.
49. George M. Marsden, *The Soul of the American University: From Protestant Establishment to Established Nonbelief* (Oxford: Oxford University Press, 1994).

last effort by the culture to require communities of faith to conform to its dictates, regardless of conscience. Whether or not the seminary wishes to adopt an adversarial stance, in the eyes of the secular culture it is the seminary against culture.

Reports reveal that the federal government, along with other leaders, has determined to advance the LGBTQ movement and the redefinition of marriage. These efforts are now aimed at state governments, schools, seminaries, and churches. Postmodern culture no longer appeals to tolerance or freedom of conscience.[50] Regardless of religious commitments, conformity is imposed.

Should the redeemed seminary engage in public theology[51] to address state coercion? Westminster's John Murray taught that it was the church's role to speak in such circumstances:

> When laws are proposed or enacted that are contrary to the Word of God, it is the duty of the church in proclamation and in official pronouncement to oppose and condemn them. . . . It is misconception of what is involved in the proclamation of the whole counsel of God to suppose or plead that the church has no concern with the political sphere. The church is concerned with every sphere and is obligated to proclaim and inculcate the revealed will of God as it bears upon every department of life.[52]

If this is the church's role, it implies that the seminary should also train its students to do so.

So, should the church and the seminary impact the culture through the cultural mandate? D. James Kennedy asserted, "We are to take all the potentialities of this world, all of its spheres and institutions, and bring them all to the glory of God."[53] However, a differing view is offered by David VanDrunen,[54] who rejects the Kuyperian conception of

50. See, for example, Robert P. George, *Conscience and Its Enemies: Confronting the Dogmas of Liberal Secularism* (Wilmington, DE: ISI, 2013).

51. The concept of public theology is widely recognized. See, for example, *Public Theology for the 21st Century*, ed. William F. Storrar and Andrew R. Morton (London: T&T Clark, 2004).

52. John Murray, "The Church, Its Identity, Function, and Resources," in *The Collected Writings of John Murray*, vol. 1, *The Claims of Truth* (Edinburgh: Banner of Truth, 1976), 241.

53. D. James Kennedy, *What If Jesus Had Never Been Born?* (Nashville: Thomas Nelson, 1994), 240.

54. David VanDrunen, *Living in God's Two Kingdoms: A Biblical Vision for Christianity and Culture* (Wheaton, IL: Crossway, 2010). VanDrunen appeals to Calvin's use of the notion of two kingdoms in support of his view. At first reading, this might suggest that Calvin also advocated

the transformation of culture by the church. Applied to the seminary, his view might be categorized as the seminary above culture, or perhaps by the more Lutheran view, the seminary and culture in paradox.

Is the way forward found in a comment written by the one we honor in this Festschrift? In a 2016 email, Dr. Poythress said:

> I would encourage you to move forward with the initiative on public theology, and to consider whether WTS might develop an institute on public theology, leadership, and proclamation.
>
> The main rationale is twofold: (1) There is and will continue to be a pressing need to inform and guide present and future leaders, and the larger Christian public, given the pressures and confusions that are surfacing in governmental activities and policies and the handling of such things by major media. In particular, civil government is on a course to dominate and control religious expression. (2) WTS is uniquely equipped by its Van Tilian, Kuyperian, and Reformed heritage to address the issues from a theologically and biblically rich framework.[55]

As one would expect from Professor Poythress, several suggestions and cautions were also provided, all of which will be taken into consideration as the exploration of the project proceeds. But whether a public theology project is realized or not, it is clear that Dr. Poythress's many years of scholarly servant leadership will have substantially contributed to the redeeming of the seminary by helping Westminster and others around the globe redeem our worldview.

---

that Christians not seek to impact the culture outside the church. However, by comparing Calvin's remarks in *Institutes*, 4.20.1 ("Differences between spiritual and civil government"), with 4.20.2 ("The two 'governments' are not antithetical"), it is evident that Calvin was not a proponent of VanDrunen's understanding of the two-kingdom model. For another non-transformationalist view of culture, see James Davison Hunter's view of the church's "faithful presence" in his *To Change the World: The Irony, Tragedy, and Possibility of Christianity in the Late Modern World* (New York: Oxford University Press, 2010).

55. Vern Poythress, email message to Peter Lillback, May 18, 2016.

14

Presuppositionalism and Perspectivalism

John M. Frame

In a previous article I indicated how Westminster Theological Seminary, though considered conservative for its stand on biblical authority and the Reformed Confessions, has actually been a fount of theological creativity.[1] One of the most impressive and enduring examples of this creativity has been the apologetics of Cornelius Van Til, sometimes called *presuppositionalism*. Presuppositionalism was, and is, not only an apologetic but also a Christian philosophical epistemology. It bears on human knowledge of God and of all aspects of God's creation.

Another fruit of Westminster's theological creativity is called *perspectivalism*. It too bears on human knowledge, both of God and of God's creation. I may be the first Westminster professor[2] to have articulated perspectival methodology, but I confess that my own confidence in this method was greatly bolstered in the early 1970s by the partnership of Vern Poythress, then a student, later and still a Westminster

---

1. John M. Frame, "In Defense of Something Close to Biblicism," *WTJ* 59, no. 2 (1997): 269–91, esp. 277–80.
2. Now I teach at Reformed Theological Seminary in Orlando, Florida.

professor, whom we honor in this volume. Initially, I thought that perspectivalism was useful primarily in the work of philosophy and theology. But Poythress saw applications of it to linguistics and other sciences. And since the early 1970s perspectivalism has been a joint project between the two of us.

So my contribution to this Festschrift will be an attempt to analyze the relationship between presuppositionalism and perspectivalism. Poythress and I emphatically endorse both positions, but that raises the question of their biblical and logical connections. It is not obvious that adherents of Van Til's apologetics should also favor perspectivalism. Indeed, a superficial look at the two ideas sometimes leads critics to think the two are inconsistent. Van Til's critics typically refer to him as an absolutist, while critics of perspectivalism often refer to it as a relativistic method. But we must get beyond superficial descriptions and look more carefully at these two developments in Westminster's theology. My thesis is that, when rightly understood, the two ideas reinforce one another. Indeed, each makes the other inevitable.

Presuppositionalism

The name "presuppositionalism" was invented not by Van Til but by one of his opponents.[3] The name was applied to Gordon H. Clark as well as Van Til, and occasionally to others. Clark seems to have liked the term better than Van Til did, but Van Til deferred to others in occasionally using it to refer to himself. My discussion here deals only with Van Til's form of presuppositionalism.

Presuppositionalism in this sense begins with two observations related to the biblical doctrines of creation and fall, respectively. The doctrine of creation establishes a distinctively biblical metaphysic. In that metaphysic, or worldview, there are two distinct levels of reality, the Creator and the creation. The Creator is the biblical God alone, described in Scripture as one God in three persons, and in the Westminster Shorter Catechism as "a Spirit, infinite, eternal, and unchangeable, in his being, wisdom, power, holiness, justice, goodness,

---

3. Most likely James Oliver Buswell, whose apologetics can be roughly described as empiricist. For the debate between Van Til and Buswell, see Cornelius Van Til, *The Defense of the Faith*, 4th ed., ed. K. Scott Oliphint (Phillipsburg, NJ: P&R, 2008), 240–64, 321.

and truth."[4] He created the universe at the beginning of time, out of nothing, by the word of his power. This creative act proceeded from God's eternal plan, so that God's knowledge of the creation is exhaustive. The universe is dependent on God for everything, including its continued existence. And it depends on God for its meaning. It is what God says it is, and its ongoing history is under God's direction.

God made human beings as part of the creation, but a part of the creation that uniquely bears his image (Gen. 1:26–27). He gave to the first couple a commission to "be fruitful and multiply and fill the earth and subdue it, and have dominion over the fish of the sea and over the birds of the heavens and over every living thing that moves on the earth" (Gen. 1:28). This commission presupposes that Adam and Eve were capable of knowing and understanding something of the world they were to explore. But to know rightly requires obedience to God. Mixed among the privileges of this commission was a prohibition: "but of the tree of the knowledge of good and evil you shall not eat, for in the day that you eat of it you shall surely die" (Gen. 2:17).

Since God has established the meaning of everything in creation, human thought is first of all a reflection on this preestablished meaning. It recognizes the authority of God to say what everything is and what role everything is to play in the God-ordained history. Human thought is secondary interpretation—a reinterpretation of God's original interpretation. The tree of the knowledge of good and evil, like everything else in the creation, is what God says it is. All human interpretations must take God's interpretation as settled.

This is another way of saying that human interpretations of creation must *presuppose* God's original interpretation of it, insofar as he has shared it with us. He has shared it through *revelation*, as in the words he spoke to Adam and Eve in Genesis 1–2. Human knowledge must presuppose God's original knowledge of the world he has made.

So, essentially, presuppositionalism is a view of knowledge that acknowledges and utilizes the truth of God's revelation to us. Presuppositionalism is the epistemology of Eden. It is the way we would all think and reason if we were not fallen. It follows necessarily from the doctrine of creation.

---

4. Question 4.

But we should also consider the doctrine of the fall. Scripture teaches that Adam and Eve did not obey God's prohibition of eating the forbidden fruit. At that point, our first parents did not think according to their original presuppositional epistemology. Satan tempted them by questioning God's revelation (Gen. 3:1–4). What followed was a different kind of reasoning: "So when the woman saw that the tree was good for food, and that it was a delight to the eyes, and that the tree was to be desired to make one wise, she took of its fruit and ate, and she also gave some to her husband who was with her, and he ate" (Gen. 3:6). As Eve reflects on the choice before her, she expresses no reverence for what God commanded, but merely accepts Satan's view that either God commanded nothing or God's word was false. She assumes that her own taste buds, eyes, and mind are sufficient to make her decision. This is what Van Til called *autonomous* thinking—thinking that rejects God's authority and imagines that the human mind is the ultimate criterion of truth and falsehood. Autonomous thought is the opposite of presuppositionalism, an epistemology that opposes God's lordship.

Apart from God's saving grace, autonomous thinking became the rule among human beings. So not only Eve's original disobedience but all the other sins of human history arose out of autonomous thought. In the Bible, God rebukes this kind of thought over and over again. Typically, he describes this thinking as "foolishness" (e.g., Pss. 14:1; 39:8; 74:22; 92:6; Prov. 1:7; 8:5) and its opposite as "wisdom" (Deut. 34:9; 1 Kings 3:28; 4:29–34). The fear of the Lord is the beginning of knowledge (Prov. 1:7) and of wisdom (Ps. 111:10), so those who do not fear God are foolish.

The apostle Paul makes much of the distinction between wisdom and foolishness, as in 1 Corinthians 1:18–3:23, and in Romans 1:18–32 he attributes foolishness to the "suppression" of the truth. What is the remedy for a sinful suppression of the truth? Only the redemption of Christ, which enables us again to serve God with our minds.

So there are two roots of presuppositionalism: (1) because we are creatures, we should serve God with our minds as well as with all our other created faculties; (2) because we are sinners, we need his salvation to receive new hearts, and therefore the mind of Christ

(1 Cor. 2:16). These are two reasons why it is necessary for us to think presuppositionally.

Since Van Til taught apologetics, presuppositionalism became known as an "apologetic method," though its applications extended beyond apologetics to cover every kind of human thinking. Presuppositional apologetics addresses the question How can we think presuppositionally in an evangelistic conversation with a non-Christian, given that the non-Christian is not willing to accept Christian presuppositions? The method answers that evangelism is no exception to the rule that we must always presuppose God's revelation. Evangelism, like all Christian speech, must be *true* in what it says, and that means true according to God's standards. Truthful reasoning requires us, even in a conversation with a non-Christian (indeed, *especially* there—1 Pet. 3:15), to honor Christ as Lord.

The most common objection to appealing to presuppositions in conversation with non-Christians is this: the procedure is circular. That is to say, the presuppositionalist, supposedly, is presupposing what he ought to be proving—namely, the truth of God's revelation. But presuppositionalists have a ready reply: in arguments over an ultimate standard of knowledge, *everyone* appeals to his own presuppositions in trying to prove them. For example, a rationalist[5] has no choice but to prove the primacy of human reason by appealing to human reason. An empiricist[6] necessarily appeals to his senses to prove the primacy of his senses.[7] Otherwise, both rationalists and empiricists are inconsistent, for they would be appealing to something other than their final criterion to prove the final criterion. If their final criterion is subject to the authority of anything other than itself, then it is not ultimate or final.

That everyone has his own presuppositions would seem to bring an end to the argument. It would seem that the Christian would make his final case by saying, "the Bible says this," and the non-Christian would conclude his argument by saying, "reason says this," or "science says this," or "the Qur'an says this," bringing an end to the dialogue. But

---

5. Rationalists believe that all knowledge is grounded in the deliverances of the human mind, our logic, science, mathematics, etc.

6. Empiricists believe that all knowledge is grounded in the deliverances of the senses, what we see, hear, etc.

7. Empiricists rarely, if ever, attempt this, because the project is so implausible. Most thinkers agree that sensation does not in itself warrant absolutes.

in fact there is more to be said, even after both parties identify their presuppositions. When Van Til argues with philosophical rationalists, for example, he points out that human reason cannot function without presupposing the biblical God. If human reason alone is the ultimate criterion of truth, then it cannot gain knowledge. From logic and reason alone, no conclusions follow. Logical arguments require premises that cannot be deduced from logic alone. And they require us to presuppose (!) that our minds are made in such a way as to gain knowledge from the empirical world.[8]

Still, we should avoid the mistaken impression that presuppositional apologetics requires us constantly to talk about presuppositions to the exclusion of other subjects. Critics sometimes say, for example, that presuppositional apologetics rejects appeal to evidence. But Van Til always insisted that evidences were an important testimony to the truth of Scripture. He only wished to remind us that appealing to evidence is never "neutral," never something we may do without presuppositions. Evidences are what they are because God has made them such. The empty tomb, for example, is evidence for Jesus's resurrection because God brought it about and communicated it to witnesses he appointed to speak truth.[9] If one tries to evaluate this evidence using a nonbiblical epistemology, such as the skepticism of David Hume,[10] then he will not find this evidence persuasive. I will say more on this issue at a later point in this essay.

Perspectivalism

BROAD MEANING

Perspectivalism is also an implication of the biblical revelation. As the doctrine of creation requires a presuppositional epistemology, so it also requires a perspectival understanding of human knowledge. "Perspectivalism" has both a broad meaning and a narrow meaning.

---

8. Evolution does not provide a sufficient explanation for the remarkable correlation between mind and universe. Evolution, if it exists, programs the mind for survival, not for discovering truth as such.

9. Note that Paul argues for the resurrection in 1 Cor. 15:1–2, 11–12 by pointing out that the resurrection was part of the apostolic preaching of the gospel.

10. Hume argued that there *cannot* be, in principle, testimony sufficient to authenticate a supernatural event; for in our experience (Hume was an empiricist) natural explanations are always more likely than supernatural ones.

The broad meaning (like that of "presuppositionalism") derives from the doctrine of creation.

Both presuppositionalism and perspectivalism teach that God's knowledge is very different from ours, because he is the Creator and we are creatures. God's knowledge is exhaustive. He knows all things by knowing himself, knowing his eternal plan, and knowing what he has done to carry out that plan. He knows every human being exhaustively as well (Psalm 139). But our knowledge is limited; we cannot know everything God knows (Ps. 139:6; Isa. 55:8–9; Rom. 11:33).

Another way of putting this point is to say that our knowledge is always from a limited *perspective*. A perspective is a *way* of knowing, a *means by which* we know something. It is the *place from which* we regard the world. God's perspective is infinite. He not only knows everything that is true but also knows everything from every perspective. He not only knows what is outside my office window but also knows how it looks to me, from my perspective. So God's perspective includes mine. He knows how everything looks to me and how everything looks to you. He knows how my office looks to a fly on the wall. Indeed, even if there is no fly on my wall, God knows what it would look like to a fly *if there were one* on my wall.[11] So God is not only omniscient; he is also omniperspectival.

As we saw earlier, God has made us able to know what we know. So, specifically, he has given us perspectives by which we gain knowledge. Most obviously, our own bodies are perspectives of knowledge. Everything I know, I know from the position my body occupies in the world. I know how the world looks through my own eyes, but not immediately through someone else's eyes. To know what the world looks like to another person, I must find out indirectly, particularly by asking the other person to describe his or her own perspective.

As I move my body around, my perspective enlarges. Looking at a tree from north, south, east, and west magnifies my knowledge of the tree, for I am including in my perspective more and more information. And as I gain testimony from others, I add their knowledge to mine. In effect, in such a case, I am adding their perspective to my own, though sometimes I have to make allowances for the other person's limitations

---

11. As many theologians have said, God knows the truth of hypotheticals as well as categoricals.

or dishonesty. Books and electronic communications enrich my perspective too, by adding to it perspectives from other people.

But ultimately, enlargements in my perspective come from God. In that sense and in others, all human knowledge comes through divine revelation. And to gain knowledge from divine revelation is, to some extent, to share in God's own perspective. Our knowledge aligns with God's perspective whenever it is true. This alignment exists in all the different locations where God reveals himself, such as nature, prophecy, and Scripture. When a human being rightly understands, say, John 3:16, and believes it, he is seeing reality from God's perspective.

Like presuppositionalism, then, perspectivalism rests on God's revelation. Indeed, these are two different ways of saying the same thing. Both understand that human beings are creatures, so that their true knowledge requires divine revelation. Presuppositionalism says that this revelation must be the starting point or criterion of our reasoning. Perspectivalism says that in learning truth we must share God's own starting point, "thinking God's thoughts after him."

Presuppositionalism addresses the *cause* that produces human knowledge and the *authority* that warrants it. Perspectivalism speaks of the *presence* of God as we share his perspective: knowledge as union with God.[12]

So perspectivalism does not succumb to the criticism that it is (unlike presuppositionalism) a relativist position. It is indeed a means of recognizing relative aspects of knowledge: the world from my perspective looks somewhat different from the world from my friend's perspective, or the perspective of the fly on the wall. So, as has often been noted, the world looks different to a poor man than it looks to a rich man, or to a sad person than to a happy person. But these differences of perspective do not imply, as with relativism, that objective knowledge is impossible. Rather, (1) typically they illumine complementary elements of the objective truth. The sad person and the happy person both understand elements of the real world as God sees it. And (2) God's perspective is available to us. It is fully objective.[13]

---

12. *Cause, authority*, and *presence* form a very important triad, which I will explore later in this chapter.
13. Or, in another sense, fully subjective, because it is identical with the content of God's own mind.

Narrow Meaning

But Poythress and I have explored further the divine perspective in its unity and complexity. Since God is one God in three persons, his perspective is singular (the one perspective that governs all others) but also threefold, including the distinct perspectives of the Father, the Son, and the Holy Spirit.

The church affirms that the three persons are equal in divinity, equal in glory, equally deserving of worship. They share, therefore, the supreme divine perspective that rules all other perspectives. God's perspective rules all others because he is himself, by very nature, *Lord* over everything other than him. So his perspective is the supreme criterion over the perspectives of creatures.

But the church also affirms that the three persons are distinct from one another. They are not mere "modes" or appearances of one divine person. Rather, they are three real persons, engaging together in a divine community of love. So each performs distinct actions. The Father sent his Son into the world to redeem sinners (Matt. 15:24; 21:37; Mark 9:37; John 3:16, 34; 4:34; 5:23–30). The Son was crucified for us (Rom. 8:32; Eph. 5:2). The Spirit was sent to empower the church (John 14:16–17; 15:26; 16:13; 20:22; Acts 1:5). These tasks are not interchangeable. Each willingly performs his allotted role.[14]

As God is both singular and differentiated, so his lordship is both singular and differentiated. In the Bible, Father, Son, and Spirit are all sometimes designated by the divine name *Yahweh*, which English translators render as "Lord." God's lordship is singular because it is the lordship of the one true God. But it is differentiated as well. The Father's lordship is seen particularly in that he originates the divine plan that all the universe obeys. Even the Son willingly subjects himself to the Father's plan (John 5:36; 12:49–50). And the Spirit bears witness not to himself but to the Son, as the Father has given him authority to speak (John 16:12–15). We may summarize this biblical teaching by speaking of the Father's lordship as *supreme authority*.

The Son's lordship is supreme as he carries out the Father's will. He carries it out perfectly, so that our salvation is certain. As such,

---

14. The origin of these allotments and their relation to the eternal generation of the Son and the eternal procession of the Spirit will have to be discussed elsewhere.

I summarize his lordship as *control* or *power*. This is not to say that he lacks authority. He shares the authority of his Father, for he perfectly conveys the Father's will, and his Father attests what he says:

> I can do nothing on my own. As I hear, I judge, and my judgment is just, because I seek not my own will but the will of him who sent me. If I alone bear witness about myself, my testimony is not true. There is another who bears witness about me, and I know that the testimony that he bears about me is true. (John 5:30–32)

But Jesus does more than speak; he translates the Father's words into actions:

> So Jesus said to them, "Truly, truly, I say to you, the Son can do nothing of his own accord, but only what he sees the Father doing. For whatever the Father does, that the Son does likewise. For the Father loves the Son and shows him all that he himself is doing. And greater works than these will he show him, so that you may marvel. For as the Father raises the dead and gives them life, so also the Son gives life to whom he will. For the Father judges no one, but has given all judgment to the Son, that all may honor the Son, just as they honor the Father. Whoever does not honor the Son does not honor the Father who sent him." (John 5:19–23)

So the Son is one with the Father in works and words. Jesus carries out the plan of the Father, so that all might equally honor both the Father and the Son. What the Father's *authority* has planned, Jesus's *power* has accomplished.

The work of the Spirit is to take these words and works and apply them to the hearts of people. Such is the teaching of the passages I quoted above in which Jesus promises that he and the Father will send the Spirit upon the church. So as the Father's work focuses on his *authority* and the Son's on his *power*, the Spirit's focuses on his *presence* in and with his people. This does not mean that Father and Son are not present with God's people. Rather, the Father and Son are *in* the Spirit, and the Spirit in them, so that the Spirit's presence carries with it the presence of the Father and the Son.

So, as I have indicated elsewhere, then, the *lordship* of God can be expressed as his authority, control, and presence in the world he has made.[15]

Here we note a continuing connection between presuppositionalism and perspectivalism. Both of these analytic tools focus our attention on the lordship of God. Presuppositionalism says that in all areas of life, including the intellectual, God is Lord. Human thinking is a moral issue: it is either belief or unbelief. For believers, it is an aspect of discipleship. We must worship our God in the intellectual sphere as in all the others. Acknowledging the authority of God's Word in the intellectual sphere is what it means to think according to God's revealed presuppositions. Apologetic conversations with nonbelievers are not occasions for setting aside the lordship of Christ; rather, they are occasions to "honor Christ the Lord as holy" (1 Pet. 3:15).

Perspectivalism explains further the nature of Christ's lordship, calling us to see all of life through his perspective—his power, authority, and presence. But there is no substantial difference between "seeing all things in the perspective of Christ's lordship" and "thinking according to the presuppositions of divine revelation." So presuppositionalism and perspectivalism coincide as descriptions of how believers should think, understand, seek knowledge, and reason.

So it is wrong to criticize perspectivalism as relativism, or to criticize presuppositionalism as an illegitimate dogmatism. Bringing these together reminds us that, yes, we should respect the legitimate diversity among perspectives but, yes, these perspectives are perspectives on something objective, which is the eternal truth of our triune God.

The Three Perspectives of Human Knowledge

Perspectivalism in the narrower sense, as we have seen, emerges from the biblical doctrine of the Trinity. It is useful to view the world alternately from the perspectives of the Father (authority), the Son (power or control), and the Spirit (presence). Ultimately the three vantage points coincide, because they are perspectives on the omniperspectival knowledge of God himself. But they are also distinct, because they are genuinely different vantage points or angles from which we may view our experience.

---

15. John M. Frame, *The Doctrine of God* (Phillipsburg, NJ: P&R, 2002), 21–119; Frame, *Systematic Theology: An Introduction to Christian Belief* (Phillipsburg, NJ: P&R, 2013), 14–52.

THE NORMATIVE PERSPECTIVE

I distinguish the *normative*, the *situational*, and the *existential* perspectives. The normative perspective derives from the *authority* of God the Father. As I said earlier, God did not make our minds to think autonomously. The mind, like every other aspect of human life, is subject to rules originating outside itself. Most thinkers understand that logic, at least, is a norm for thought. But human logic is an image of divine logic. And beyond logic, God sets many rules for human thinking and knowing. In general, the comprehensive rule for human thought is his *revelation* to us. God reveals himself in the entire creation (Ps. 19:1) including ourselves (Gen. 1:27–28), but especially in Scripture, which he has designated as sufficient for all of life: "All Scripture is breathed out by God and profitable for teaching, for reproof, for correction, and for training in righteousness, that the man of God may be complete, equipped for every good work" (2 Tim. 3:16–17). If we think according to God's Word, we will always arrive at the truth, no matter what subject matter we are inquiring about. So the normative perspective does not yield only a portion of human knowledge. It yields all of it. Thinking according to God's rules is all that we need to do. So the normative perspective is a way of viewing God and everything in the creation. To gain truth, all we need to do is think according to the rules.

THE SITUATIONAL PERSPECTIVE

Although the normative perspective is comprehensive and complete, it is not the only perspective and never functions alone. There is also a situational perspective, which derives from the *power* of God the Son: "For by him all things were created, in heaven and on earth, visible and invisible, whether thrones or dominions or rulers or authorities— all things were created through him and for him. And he is before all things, and in him all things hold together" (Col. 1:16–17). The Son has a special role in the creation of the world (John 1:3; Heb. 1:10–12) and in the ongoing processes of nature and history. When we study the *facts* of the world around us, we are studying the creative and providential work of God the Son. Of course, the Father is also active in creation and providence, so we are talking here about two perspectives, rather than exclusive domains. To study the facts is to study the

world from the situational perspective. In the end there is no difference between studying the facts of creation and studying the laws of
thought. Both perspectives include everything we would want to know.
To understand the facts and to think according to God's rules, these
are the same thing.

THE EXISTENTIAL PERSPECTIVE

We encounter a third perspective when we consider the work of the
Holy Spirit. The apostle Paul says:

> [The blessings given to believers] God has revealed to us through
> the Spirit. For the Spirit searches everything, even the depths of
> God. For who knows a person's thoughts except the spirit of that
> person, which is in him? So also no one comprehends the thoughts
> of God except the Spirit of God. Now we have received not the
> spirit of the world, but the Spirit who is from God, that we might
> understand the things freely given us by God. (1 Cor. 2:10–12)

The Spirit goes deep into the hearts of people and into the heart of God
as well. He communes with us not only by communicating rules and
facts but by communicating the very presence of God in our experience. To gain knowledge of the world around us we must know and
understand the divine presence everywhere. For God does not enlighten
us merely by teaching us rules and facts; he teaches us by revealing
himself in our midst. What I call the existential perspective focuses on
that divine presence. It also focuses on our own subjective experience,
for the Spirit enters our very hearts and souls in order to help us see
God's truth as it really is.

Even this very deep kind of revelation is nothing different from
the normative and the situational. Ultimately the three coincide. If we
understand perfectly God's norms for knowledge and follow them to
their conclusions, they will include the deepest subjective dimensions of
our thinking hearts. And if we understand perfectly the facts that God
has created, we will understand ourselves as one of those facts. So the
normative and the situational include the existential.

And the existential includes both of them. When we understand the
workings of our inner mind, we will understand that this mind must

think according to God's rules and God's facts. So it is wrong to despise the "subjective," as theologians often do. All knowledge is subjective in that it occurs in the mind. Our subjective experience, rightly understood, is a gateway to all the knowledge available to us.

Perspectivalism and Apologetic Method
The union of perspectivalism and presuppositionalism clarifies some continuing questions about apologetic method.

The Place of Evidence
I mentioned earlier in this essay the continuing controversy about the role of evidence in apologetics. Some have suggested that if we believe that all apologetic argument is governed by presuppositions, there is no place in apologetics for the use of evidences. But to appeal to evidence is nothing more than appealing to the situational perspective. For example, in 1 Corinthian 15, Paul deals with some in the church who do not believe in the resurrection of Jesus. In reply to them, he appeals to evidence: Jesus's appearances after his death to Peter (15:5), to the twelve (15:5), to five hundred brethren at once (15:6), to James (15:7), to all the apostles (15:7), and, "as to one untimely born," to Paul himself (15:8). Here Paul recites facts that are generally known in the community, facts that he hopes will persuade again those who have wavered in their faith.

But this appeal to fact does not at all compromise Paul's usual presuppositionalism. He does not appeal to the facts as if they are "brute" facts. A brute fact (as apologists understand the expression) is a fact without interpretation, or a fact available for autonomous human analysis. A brute fact, supposedly, is a fact that can be rightly understood without biblical presuppositions. But there are no brute facts in these senses, and Paul does not appeal to them.

Paul's appeal to testimony is consistent with a biblical form of reasoning. The eighteenth-century philosopher David Hume said that there was no testimony strong enough to establish a supernatural event. To Hume, when something strange took place, it was always more likely that there was a natural explanation than that there was a supernatural one. So Hume systematically disbelieved all testimony intended to validate miraculous events. But Paul did not operate with an episte-mology like Hume's. Rather, he believed in the biblical worldview, in which all nature and history proceeds according to God's plan. In that worldview, God's revelation is the ultimate interpretation of human experience. God often reveals himself, and his interpretations, through chosen representatives who testify as to what God has done. So human testimony to supernatural events is a normal part of human knowledge.

Paul himself offers such testimony. Not only does he testify to the appearance of Jesus to him personally, but he presents his whole case on his own authority as a divinely appointed church planter. In 1 Co-rinthians 15, the underlying reason why the Corinthians are to accept the testimonies of the risen Christ is that the resurrection of Jesus is part of the preaching by which Paul planted the church. He says, "Now I would remind you, brothers, of the gospel I preached to you, which you received, in which you stand, and by which you are being saved, if you hold fast to the word I preached to you—unless you believed in vain" (1 Cor. 15:1–2, cf. 3, 11, 12). Paul says that the Corinthians should believe the testimonies of those who saw the risen Jesus. And they should believe these testimonies because they are part of Paul's preaching: they are part of the Word of God. And the Word of God is the believer's presupposition.

So we appeal to facts because they are warranted by our presup-position. And (perspectivally speaking) we believe the presupposition because it is factual and because it presents the facts in their true light.

THE PLACE OF EXPERIENCE

The "argument from experience" has been part of apologetics for many years. William James, William Alston, and others have explored the claims of people to have experienced God directly and have sought to evaluate these claims. But many apologists of different schools of thought, presuppositional and otherwise, have criticized the argument from experience as subjective and vague.

Of course, it often happens that people present their subjective experience to validate their faith or even their doctrinal contentions, without any kind of cogent argument. *Fideism* is a name given to an apologetic that relies on mere feeling, without evidence or argument.

But there is a sense in which it is legitimate to appeal to one's own subjectivity in an apologetic argument. Indeed, there is a sense in which subjective evidence is the only evidence there is. For knowledge itself is a subjective event. It takes place inside us, in our minds, in our heads. When an argument appeals to presuppositions, it is to presuppositions that we have acknowledged in our hearts. When an argument appeals to facts, it is to facts that we have acknowledged subjectively.

That is to say that presuppositions, facts, and subjective experience represent the three perspectives I described earlier. Presuppositions represent the normative perspective, facts the situational, and subjective experience the existential. And these three perspectives coincide as ways to look at the world and understand it. As I have indicated, to know the normative perspective completely is to know everything. The same is true for the situational and the existential. Each of these perspectives includes the other two.

Our "subjective experience" represents the existential perspective. Rightly understood, that existential perspective is a perspective on all knowledge. As we analyze the data within our minds, we come to see that these data cannot be understood apart from biblical norms (normative perspective) and the facts of God's creation (situational perspective). Fideism ignores these necessary relationships. So when someone claims he can warrant faith by his mere subjective feelings, without norms or evidence, he has failed not only to understand the norms and evidence; he has failed to understand rightly his own subjectivity. If he had understood his own subjectivity rightly, he would have seen that he cannot understand his experience without the right norms and facts. Our subjectivity is a *perspective* on knowledge, not a stand-alone source of knowledge that conflicts with presuppositions and facts.

Summary

I have argued here four main points: (1) Presuppositionalism requires perspectivalism, for it requires us to see our own thinking as subject to God's. His thought is infinite and omniperspectival, while ours is finite and necessarily limited to our own perspectives. (2) Presuppositionalism requires perspectivalism, because it sets forth God's thought as the authoritative norm for ours and therefore as our normative perspective. (3) Perspectivalism clarifies presuppositionalism, for it shows how human thinking involves an understanding of facts and human subjectivity, as well as divine norms. (4) Perspectivalism shows the true role of evidence and subjective experience in presuppositional apologetics.

15

The Death of Tragedy

*Reflections upon a Tragic Aspect
of This Present Age*

Carl R. Trueman

Some years ago a friend of mine brought to my attention a new television adaptation of *Anna Karenina*, which was being advertised as "updated for the modern age." As my friend commented, it is impossible to update *Anna Karenina* for the modern age because today there would be no problem for Anna. She could simply obtain a divorce with a decent share of her husband's assets, custody of the child, and no social shame. We both laughed, but the point was sound. Dramatic plots hinge on certain social conventions. Once those conventions cease to exist, the tale that is told might still be comprehensible to later generations, but it cannot truly be updated.

For some forms of art, this is perhaps not a great loss. I am not sure it is of any great moment that I have no idea why anyone should consider the Three Stooges remotely funny, or disco music at all melodious. I want to suggest that for tragedy, however, the reasons why it no longer works are significant and help to highlight aspects of modern cultural shifts of which we all should be aware.

Certainly I am not alone in thinking that the death of tragedy is symptomatic of changes in our world. George Steiner wrote a famous book with that title.[1] The second volume of Philip Rieff's posthumous trilogy *Sacred Order/Social Order* bears the subtitle *The Decline of the Tragic Sensibility*.[2] That herald of the great darkness saw the loss of a sense of tragedy as emblematic of what he dubbed "the coming barbarism." The topic and the tendency are thus far from original with me, and I beg your indulgence in advance for what will be the modest nature of my contribution.

Given both the popular and technical uses of the term, I need to start by defining exactly what I mean by "tragedy" and it cognates. As has often been noted, today the word has become debased in popular usage and has really lost all technical meaning. If the death of a child from cancer can be described as a tragedy, then so can a sporting loss or a failure on an exam. Indeed, I suspect that scarcely a day goes by in this era of information overload without the *t* word being applied to some incident, whether of trivial local interest or of international significance. One might perhaps say—*pace* the title of this chapter— that, far from being absent from contemporary life, the language, if not the concept, of tragedy is all-pervasive. And if everything in general is tragic, of course, then nothing is tragic in particular.

Yet, if the language has been subject to a demotic debasement which has trivialized the term, there are also more sophisticated reasons put forward for the death of tragedy as a genre. For example, Rieff locates the loss of the tragic sensibility in the various ways modern society seeks to evade, avoid, or deny the reality and inevitability of death. Of this more later. In a similar vein, Steiner roots it in the rise of Enlightenment rationalism and the optimistic outlook of the romantics. While Enlightenment rationalism and optimism may no longer be the dominant orders of our day, postmodern irony and smirking cynicism surely undermine tragedy in another way: tragedy

---

1. George Steiner, *The Death of Tragedy* (New Haven, CT: Yale University Press, 1996).
2. Philip Rieff, *The Crisis of the Officer Class: The Decline of the Tragic Sensibility*, ed. Alan Woolfolk (Charlottesville: University of Virginia Press, 2007).

seems to need heroes, and we live in an anti-heroic age. Of course, that is not a uniquely postmodern phenomenon: we see precisely such an anticipation of the death of tragedy in the plays of Euripides, whose heroes are remarkable precisely because of their lack of classical heroism.

"Tragedy": A Working Definition

Thus, it is appropriate at the outset that I offer some working definition of how I intend to use the word in this essay. Of course, given the fact that what I intend is an argument, not simply a description, I thus render myself vulnerable to future accusations of defining "tragedy" in a way that ultimately suits my purpose. That is for the reader to judge. But, even if I prove guilty as charged, I trust what I have to say will still prove to be insightful, if only by way of provoking others to think about a more adequate or sufficient definition.

It is worth noting at the start one point upon which writers on tragedy seem to be agreed: Christianity does not offer a tragic vision, because it offers the promise of life after death. Thinkers from I. A. Richards to George Steiner to Roger Scruton have offered versions of this theme. Sometimes the case seems rather odd. Steiner, for example, denies that the book of Job is a tragedy since Job, having lost his children at the start of the book, fathers more at the very end—as if the pain of the death of one child is satisfied by the birth of another. Where there is compensation, there is justice, and where there is justice, there is no tragedy.[3] At other times, as in the cases of Scruton, the result seems implausible. Tragedy arises from living life as if it had transcendent meaning, even though it does not and to allow that death is not final is to destroy the whole possibility of tragedy.[4] Yet the step from a tragic vision conceived in those terms to absurdity seems a painful one, as evidenced by the fact that a similar advocate of the tragic sensibility, Miguel de Unamuno, chooses Don Quixote as the paradigm for the modern tragic figure. Personal passion and authenticity in the face

---

3. Steiner, *Death of Tragedy*, 4.
4. "To render the Christian idea of redemption in artistic form is automatically to move beyond the arena in which tragedies are played out, into a place where death loses its finality" (Roger Scruton, *Death-Devoted Heart: Sex and the Sacred in Wagner's Tristan and Isolde* [Oxford: Oxford University Press, 2003], 171).

of insurmountable odds becomes the hallmark of tragedy.[5] But surely when Hamlet becomes Don Quixote, it is not long before Sophocles becomes Pinter, and *Philoctetes* becomes *The Birthday Party*.

Aristotle was perhaps the most famous definer of tragedy. For him, the key lay in a tragic flaw, hubris, in the main character of the drama. Audiences benefited from the dramatic performance and from seeing how this flaw led to the character's downfall. By seeing the drama played out before them, the audience enjoyed an emotional and psychological catharsis—a remarkably difficult word to translate or understand (hence its transliteration into English).

Scholars have debated the adequacy of Aristotle's definition of tragedy, particularly the matter of the tragic flaw. It certainly seems helpful when applied to, say, Agamemnon in the *Oresteia*, or to Hamlet, Lear, Othello, and Macbeth. Yet one of the key problems is that it does not seem to cover even the limited canon of extant Greek tragedies we possess. Oedipus, for example, seems more a victim of terrible circumstances beyond his control—a pitiful plaything of the gods—than a man destroyed by some terrifying yet magnificent character flaw. I do not intend to wade into that discussion here but merely note its existence as demonstrating that the meaning of tragedy has been contested from the outset.

The key figure who turns tragedy from a discussion of dramatic dynamics into a matter of philosophy is, of course, Hegel. For him, Sophocles's *Antigone* represented the most perfect example of what constitutes tragedy. In this work we have the irreconcilable collision of worlds. Antigone is absolutely obliged both to her family and to the king. Creon is king but is also a father and husband and so also tied to the demands of kinship. The result is the death of Antigone and the related suicides of his wife and son. It was this irresolvable conflict and its conclusion only in death and suffering that led Hegel to describe Antigone as, in his judgment, "the most excellent and satisfying work of art."[6]

While Hegel's definition may well be contestable and, like Aris-

---

5. Miguel de Unamuno, *Tragic Sense of Life*, trans. J. E. Crawford Flitch (New York: Sophia-Omni, 2014).

6. See *Hegel on Tragedy*, ed. Anne Paolucci and Henry Paolucci (New York: Harper Torchbooks, 1962), 73–74.

totle's, does not cover all examples of what we would call tragedy, I am going to use it here as a serviceable working concept. Indeed, I am persuaded that Hegel is certainly right as regards the tragedy of *Antigone*. In focusing on the ethical conflict at the heart of *Antigone*, Hegel's approach points to an element of the play that sets in bold relief the difference between the Sophoclean world and ours. If *Anna Karenina* can only be understood by an act of historical imagination, so, sadly, the same is true for *Antigone*. Yet, in highlighting this, I believe we may glean insights into a number of fundamental aspects of this present age. Furthermore, and almost by accident, it also offers us grounds for arguing that Christianity does contain within it the basic elements of a tragic vision.

Seamus Heaney on *Antigone*

In 2004, Seamus Heaney translated, and to some extent expanded, Sophocles's play under the title *The Burial at Thebes*.[7] The work is interesting for precisely the reason I mentioned at the outset. It is in part an attempt to update the tragedy for the present day. Yet it is not so much the translation and the minor additions that caught my eye upon reading it. It was a comment in the afterword. Writing against the backdrop of the second Gulf War and George W. Bush's presidency, Heaney says, "Modern audiences are more sympathetic to Antigone's defiant embrace of the law of the gods, her instinctive affirmation of what we might now call a human right against the law-and-order requirements of the state."[8] This is an interesting and, for an old classics student like myself, a heartening comment—that an ancient tragedy might yet speak to contemporary audiences is surely encouraging. Indeed, we might be tempted to conclude that Sophocles breathes the very air of our own world, for if Heaney is right, Antigone is a very modern hero. Thus, the tragedy of Antigone for modern audiences lies in the conflict between the right of personal conscience, rooted in some notion of human rights, in the face of the demands of an unyielding state.

7. Seamus Heaney, *The Burial at Thebes: A Version of Sophocles' Antigone* (New York: Farrar, Straus and Giroux, 2004).
8. Ibid., 76.

Indeed, this view of Antigone is reminiscent of the famous statement of E. M. Forster that, if he had to choose between betraying his country and betraying his friend, he hoped he would have the courage to betray his country. On Heaney's reading, Antigone is thus a great exemplar of that Forsterian virtue. She defies the king out of loyalty to a beloved brother. And she becomes thereby a hero of our time.

Yet there is surely something about such a reading that is not quite right. I would argue that a more careful reflection upon the play indicates that Antigone is no paragon of Bloomsbury virtue but someone actually very alien and strange to our world. In fact, if modern audiences do read *Antigone* in the manner of Heaney, then I would suggest that they misread the play in a fundamental way. Indeed, such a reading tells us far more about the modern way of thinking than about the nature of the human self underlying Sophocles's drama. The tragedy of Antigone simply does not arise from the clash of an individual's human rights against the forces of the law of the corporate state. Rather, the tragedy derives from the perfect clash of legitimate obligations under which Antigone and her uncle Creon both operate, albeit with a perhaps unreasonable passion that accelerates their destruction. Antigone is not first and foremost an individual with rights. Rather, she is a member of society with obligations. More subtly, she is a member of several social spheres, each with obligations, some of which are incompatible with each other and yet place an equal and legitimate demand upon her.

In exploring these obligations, I want to highlight how the world in which we now operate differs from that portrayed by Sophocles, not in the simplistic way of contrasting an ancient society with an advanced modern one, but in terms of how the human self is understood. Antigone is a woman defined by family, by history, and by the presence of the dead in the land of the living.

Why is any of this of any more than antiquarian interest? I would suggest that the world of Antigone offers an alternative to the world in which we live today—an alternative not in the sense that it is a viable replacement for what we have but in the sense that it serves to set in relief the changes that have taken place in the understanding of the self. As with *Anna Karenina*, updating *Antigone* is impossible; but the reasons for such an impossibility are helpful in understanding the moral structure of our own age.

The impossibility of updating *Antigone* lies in three fundamental differences between the Sophoclean world and ours, differences that take us to the heart of what it means to be modern and of why the tragic vision has been lost—lost, I might add, to our cost. For the tragic vision embodies reality while the loss of that vision represents the arrival of a world of willful, shallow make-believe. To quote Alasdair MacIntyre, referring to the dilemma of Antigone: "Our situation is tragic in that we have to recognize the authority of both claims. There *is* an objective moral order, but our perceptions of it are such that we cannot bring rival moral truths into complete harmony with each other."[9] The tragedy of our age, by contrast, is that we have attempted to dismantle all of the structures that manifest this conflict in order to resolve it, and, in so doing, we have reduced what it really means to be human.

History, Family, the Dead: Who Is Antigone?

Three things define the person of Antigone in the play: history, family, and the dead. All three have their parts in establishing who she is and how she acts. While we might concede that there are individual, psychological aspects to her—her passion, for example—her identity is really established within the context of her family history, which combines all three of the above elements: history, family, and the dead. Let us look at each in turn. And all three make her an alien figure in this present age.

ANTIGONE AND HISTORY

Central to Antigone's personal tragedy are what we might describe as the forces of history. She is who she is because of the history that sets her in her specific place.

One of the axioms of this present age, of course, is that the past is oppressive and something from which we must be liberated. This sentiment lies deep in our modern Western mentality and has numerous

---

9. Alasdair MacIntyre, *After Virtue: A Study in Moral Theory*, 2nd ed. (London: Duckworth, 1985), 143.

sources. Indeed, it was Karl Marx who rather memorably declared in *The Eighteenth Brumaire of Louis Napoleon* that men make history but do not make the history that they choose, since the weight of all previous generations bears down upon them like a nightmare.

In more recent days, critical theory and post-structuralism have both provided sophisticated approaches to the discipline of history that have placed a premium on seeing history as a source of oppression. The focus has typically been upon the writers of history and the contemporary political use to which such history is put, whether imperialist or colonialist or other. This critical edge applies not simply to criticisms of old-style histories that pressed home the innate superiority of Western society to any other and saw the telos of history as the triumph of the Western way of doing things. It also applies to the histories that have risen in its place. It is not that black history or queer history have replaced old-style white-male history as an account of the past by demonstrating their superiority. They have rather relativized such history as a means of justifying the present. They too offer alternative narrations of the past in order to establish the legitimacy of political positions in the here and now. History is no longer history. It is contemporary politics pursued through the idiom of the past tense.

In an intriguing comment in *Fellow Teachers*, Rieff summarizes this approach: "But, for Americans, all pasts are embarrassments, beyond recall except as tactical instruments of scarcely concealed rancor against present or imagined inferiorities."[10] We can perhaps understand this when we consider that hackneyed piece of political rhetoric, the phrase "being on the right side of history." If there is one thing this phrase always means when deployed by Right or Left, it is that history has been proved to be irrelevant and to lack all authority. It speaks of the overthrowing of a particular historical narrative of which the speaker or party disapproves. And it generally means that some long-established and significant historical practice or conviction has been discarded. In short, to be on the right side of history means to occupy a position that repudiates history, to dislike history, to dismiss history.

There are not many things for which being on their right side means

---

10. Philip Rieff, *Fellow Teachers: Of Culture and Its Second Death* (Chicago: University of Chicago Press, 1985), 101.

their destruction. But the attempted elimination of history as of positive importance in the present is not restricted to the sophisticates of the New Left academy. A whole arsenal of aspects of modern culture militates against it. An economy built upon a commercial philosophy that creates desires and then offers to satisfy them is inevitably forward-looking and creative in a manner that weakens ties to history. Mass-produced architecture, the automobile, the importance of science and technology to the imagination, and high population mobility all mean that those traditional markers of memory—long-lasting possessions and distinct places tied to distinct times and a more stable form of life—are greatly weakened. Above all, perhaps, is the palace of pleasure in which we all now aspire to live. Hedonism is essentially a philosophy of the present moment. Once happiness was identified with pleasure and pleasure, via Freud, became identified with physical sex, the telos of existence became not some future goal but the intense experience of the present. History is irrelevant to the world of the sempiternal orgiast.

Now, there are certainly aspects of Antigone's story that we might see as consonant with the idea that history is something negative and to be overcome. Indeed, she might well have been a poster child for the idea that history is oppressive and damaging. The narrative in which she lives is surely not a hopeful one. She herself is the result of the incestuous coupling of Oedipus and Jocasta, and thus inevitably caught in the conflict that subsequently engulfs Thebes. She has no say in her place in the world and indeed finds herself truly in a nightmare prepared by the previous generation. She is a victim of history, if ever there was one.

It is Ismene, Antigone's sister, who articulates this so well and sees the family history as tragically oppressive. In the early speech she makes upon discovering Antigone's plan to bury Polyneices, she outlines the family history, culminating in the death of the brothers. She then calls on Antigone to obey Creon, lest she suffer the same fate. History has cursed Antigone, and the only way to overcome it, or to escape from it, is in effect to renounce her identity by refusing her obligation to her brother.

Yet Antigone's response to Ismene is to embrace her history, not to defy it or to try to overcome it. There is a simple reason for this: it is who she is. And while her history brings with it terrible and painful obligations, she will not shirk these, precisely because they define who she is. We might say that history gives her humanity, both the joys and the pain, and one cannot accept the former without risking the latter.

Thus, the first thing with which Heaney's sympathetic modern audience needs to wrestle before so closely identifying with the figure of Antigone is the role of history in defining who she is. She is the daughter of Oedipus and Jocasta, the sister of Polyneices. She cannot escape that; she cannot overcome it. She must rather accept it as the starting point for her moral agency. For it is this, with all of its demands and its risks, which makes her a human being.

Antigone and Family

Heaney's audience would no doubt instinctively find Ismene's speech problematic, for, far from encouraging Antigone to stand on her individual human rights, she is in effect calling on Antigone to do the exact opposite of E. M. Forster's aspiration. Faced with a choice between city and loved one, she is encouraging Antigone to betray her brother in favor of the state.

But careful reflection indicates that it is surely more complicated than that. Ismene is not simply suggesting an act of supine cowardice in the face of Creon's demands. It is not really Antigone's love for her brother that has imposed the obligation upon her. It is the simple fact that he *is* her brother. Love would imply choice. The blood relationship offers no choice—only a set of established obligations. That is a most alien notion to the modern audience.

Thus, Ismene is not simply offering the Forsterian choice: nation or loved one. She is surely asserting Antigone's right to decide, as an individual, how she should act in the present, over against any external, prior obligations, whether of city or of family. For her, obligation to self in the present trumps any obligation to family or to the dead. In other words, the demands of the present are all that really count. Ismene therefore speaks in a manner far more consonant with modern expressive individualism than with anything the audience will hear from Antigone. In fact, it is Antigone's acceptance of her history, along with her understanding that her history places obligations upon her from outside, that marks her off from Ismene. And that is not a modern sensibility with which Heaney's audience would be particularly sympathetic, especially in the specific way it is manifested in this play.

We noted before the role of history for Antigone, but history, of course, is not simply an abstract, general force. It is particular, and it is that which very specifically determines her identity in the present. That history is the history of her family. It is her family that is crucial in determining the circumstances in which she finds herself, the choices which lie before her, and the moral framework she must use for making those choices. And she accepts these as a given. As noted above, casting off her history is not an option for her, for to do so would be to deny, or perhaps better, to betray who she is.

Her family history sets her in place and puts her in the quandary in which she finds herself. But the family also determines who she is as a moral agent. Antigone's actions only make sense if we accept the obligations that her family ties impose upon her. If Polyneices were not her brother, and if that did not requires certain things of her, there would be no problem. In fact, so important are these obligations of family that it is perhaps wrong even to talk of them being *imposed* upon her. That implies that we can separate them from who she really is, as if we can isolate her identity from her obligations to family and to her brother. But that is not the case. Those obligations are not an external imposition upon her identity but are actually constitutive of her identity.

This family dynamic is the focal point that really should render *Antigone* the play an utterly alien experience for modern audiences. For the war against history as a determining authority has been nowhere more dramatically manifested in modern society than in the erosion of traditional family ties. Families and households have been the primary means of transmitting values from generation to generation, and of engaging in that dialogue between the living and the dead which constitutes a culture. Yet the erosion of family obligations has been a long-standing part of what now constitutes our world.

From Rousseau onward, a strong tradition of regarding the family as problematic or even tyrannical has strongly influenced Western thought. Perhaps these reached their apotheosis in the work of Wilhelm

Reich, whose book *The Sexual Revolution* presented the family unit as the single most culpable agent in the repression of sexuality and thus identity. For Reich, and for subsequent aficionados of the ongoing sexual revolution, the family is an institution of repression and is thus to be redefined, regulated, or even abolished, by the state, specifically if it seeks to hinder any child's untrammeled sexual development. Again, the sempiternal orgiast has no place for history and sees the family as a hindrance to fulfilling life's purpose of instant and constant personal gratification.[11]

Thus, while we might as moderns sympathize with Antigone in a Forsterian sort of way, assuming that it is her sentimental or emotional attachment to her brother that drives her collision with Creon, it is not that at all. Rather, it is the obligation she owes Polyneices as his sibling. *Pace* Heaney, the sympathy of modern audiences should really be toward Ismene, seeing family obligations as entirely negotiable when faced with the need for self-preservation, especially when the obligations are to someone already dead. Moderns should only have pity for Antigone, a pathetic woman driven to destruction by a deluded belief in the ideology of family.

Underlying so much of the modern antipathy to the family (as to history) is the triumph of what Rieff dubbed Psychological Man. The culture of Psychological Man is the culture of therapy. The purpose of life is the realization in practice of one's psychological identity, and external obligations or hierarchies thus always run the risk of being instruments of oppression or imposed inauthenticity. In other words, Psychological Man is one whose identity is found in being released from external constraints and obligations, or in establishing them only insofar as they comport with his inner needs and desires.[12]

Of course, a pure self-creation of this sort, one that places an absolute priority of the psychological over the social, is impossible. The notion of Psychological Man and the triumph of psychology upon which it depends are themselves historical social constructs. It is clear

---

11. Wilhelm Reich, *The Sexual Revolution: Towards a Self-Regulating Character Structure*, trans. Theodore O. Wolfe (New York: Farar, Straus and Giroux, 1986), 23–25.
12. Philip Rieff, *Freud: The Mind of the Moralist* (New York: Viking, 1959), 329–57; also Rieff, *The Triumph of the Therapeutic: Uses of Faith after Freud* (Wilmington, DE: ISI, 2006), passim.

from the work of writers as diverse as Ludwig Wittgenstein, Charles Taylor, and Roger Scruton that it is, strictly speaking, impossible to give an inner psychological identity absolute priority over the social, as Psychological Man thinks he can do. Selves are only defined in relation to other selves. Yet the idea of self-creation and of autonomy of identity grips the modern imagination. As the teenager thinks that getting a tattoo or buying clothes at Urban Outfitters is an expression of her unique individuality, Psychological Man thinks that he builds his identity from his own unique inner self, even as he needs to use prior socially constructed categories and structures so to do.

Modern audiences can only flatter themselves that they identify with the plight of Antigone if they are prepared to abandon one of the hallmarks of the modern world: that family obligations are fluid and nonbinding, to be abandoned or dissolved when convenient. For Antigone, by contrast, her history is a given, and it comes to her through her family, with specific obligations that define her actions in the present. She is Oedipus's daughter and Polyneices's sister, and that is not merely a biological fact. It is a binding, ethical relationship over which she has no control. It is determinative of her identity and her actions.

The Long Arm of the Dead

While the obligations of history and family divide Antigone from her modern audience, it is surely in the abiding presence of the dead in the land of the living that her world and identity are most obviously different from ours. As with history, the dead are increasingly absent from our notion of identity and obligation. One might respond by saying that our popular culture is full of the dead—the voices of late pop stars and movie icons are never silent on iPods and screens across the country. But such dead have merely an appearance of life. They entertain, they do not make any demands, and they place us under no obligations. They have but a pretense of presence.

Yet one might also note that the grief caused by the death of a loved one is still today a presence in the life of those left behind. This present age still knows the sadness of bereavement, a kind of negative presence that loss brings in its wake. Dylan Thomas captured this beautifully when he used the language of presence to describe the absence of his late father: "Until I die he will not leave my side."[13] Yet, as with dead movie stars, such dead make no demands upon the living, beyond the emotional trauma of their deaths and the lingering pain which their memory might bring.

Once upon a time it was not so. The dead were a palpable presence in the land of the living. To take but one example, that of Christianity, we can see how the dead exerted authority over the land of the living. Ancient Christians would meet to eat meals called *refrigerium* in *triclia*, buildings set in the midst of the tombs of the faithful departed. Thus they refreshed themselves in the company of the dead. The cult of the saints forged a close connection between this life and the next. Prayer connected this world to the world beyond, and the dead thus placed obligations of piety upon the living. The liturgical calendar marked time around the names of those who had died. Churches had graveyards so that congregants on their way to worship passed by the graves of deceased loved ones. The dead were a constant presence in the religious lives of the living.[14]

Of course, the dead often intrude into the action of tragedies. Banquo's ghost serves to precipitate Macbeth's psychological downfall. The spirit of Hamlet's father triggers the drama of the play. The dead are a dramatic presence. In Antigone's case, the ethical relationship with her brother is not severed at death. In fact, the obligation to him is intensified by his death, the point upon which the whole play turns. The difference between Ismene and Antigone is the difference in their attitude toward the dead. This becomes clear at the end of Ismene's great speech near the start of the play:

> ISMENE: In the land of the living, sister,
> The laws of the land obtain:
> And the dead know that as well.
> The dead will have to forgive me.

---

13. This is the putative last line of "Elegy," a poem left unfinished at Thomas's death in 1953. There is some debate about how best to reconstruct the poem from Thomas's notes. I here use the version in *The Poems of Dylan Thomas*, ed. Daniel Jones (New York: New Directions, 2003), 250.

14. On ritual connections between the living and the dead in ancient Christianity, see Peter Brown, *The Ransom of the Soul: Afterlife and Wealth in Early Western Christianity* (Cambridge, MA: Harvard University Press, 2015).

I'll be ruled by Creon's word.
Anything else is madness.[15]

For Ismene, the laws of the land—the land of the living—trump any obligation to the dead, and the dead know this and must set their rights aside. Yet Antigone repudiates this in one of the play's greatest speeches:

> ANTIGONE: You and the laws of the land!
> Sister, let me tell you:
> From now on, and no matter
> How your mind may change,
> I'll never accept your help.
> I will bury him myself.
> And if death comes, so be it.
> There'll be a glory in it.
> I'll go down to the underworld
> Hand in hand with a brother.
> And I'll go with my head held high.
> The gods will be proud of me.
> The land of the living, sister,
> Is neither here nor there.
> We enter it and we leave it.
> The dead in the land of the dead
> Are the ones you'll be with longest.
> And how are you going to face them,
> Ismene, if you dishonour
> Their laws and the gods' law?[16]

The laws of the land may demand one thing, but there are, for Antigone, higher courts to which she must render account—that of the dead and that of the family, here fused into one in the corpse of Polyneices. As she reminds Ismene, they will be spending an eternity with the dead, and this places any passing obligations to the city in an eternal perspective, a perspective that relativizes—though does not abolish—such.

The idea that the dead place any kind of obligation upon the living

---

15. Heaney, *Burial at Thebes*, 5.
16. Ibid.

surely sounds strange to the modern ear. This is part of a much broader shift in the cultural significance of death. Death is, of course, the one thing over which human beings know they cannot ultimately exert sovereignty. We can fly to the moon. Though we grow old, we can buy clothes and surgical procedures that make us look young. We can be born a man and legally become a woman. But we still have to die. And, as Pascal pointed out, that thought is unbearable.

The result is that we hate to be reminded of death's reality. We do our best to ignore it through a surfeit of entertainments and distractions. The great advantage of the sempiternal orgiast in such times is that he thinks only of the moment, never of the future, and thus can allow the pleasures of the present to mask the coming demand of death.

And even when death becomes unavoidable, we still pretend otherwise. We try to seize control of it by legitimating euthanasia, giving it a veneer of being just another medical procedure. More obviously, we sentimentalize it or present it as some kind of triumph. Hence the growing popularity of "celebrations of life" instead of more traditional funeral rites. Sinatra's "My Way" replaces the somber tones of the Book of Common Prayer. Death is trivialized, its reality virtually neutralized by sentimentality rather than embodied in continuing obligations. Yet this disjunction of the living from the dead is culturally of huge significance. Rieff expresses it thus:

> Cultures are constituted by the union of the living and the dead in rituals of living memory. Never before, in our late second world, has the authority of the past been sacrificed with a more conscious effort of forgetfulness. Forgetfulness is now the curricular form of our higher education. This form guarantees that we, of the transition from second to third worlds, will become the first barbarians. Barbarism is not an expression of simple technologies or of mysterious taboos; at least there were taboos and, moreover, in all first worlds, the immense authority of the past. By contrast, the coming barbarism, much of it here and now, not least to be found among our most cultivated classes, is our ruthless forgetting of the authority of the past.[17]

---

17. Philip Rieff, *Sacred Order/Social Order I: My Life among the Deathworks* (Charlottesville: University of Virginia Press, 2006), 106.

Sometimes, as we noted, these rituals have involved such things as saints' days or pilgrimages; even in the secular calendar, we mark certain days and certain places as being significant for their connection to the dead. For Antigone they involve moral obligation relative to burial. Yet what is so striking about our modern Western world is that the things that connect the living and the dead have become increasingly tenuous.

Rieff is correct, of course, in connecting this breakdown of the relationship between the living and the dead with the breakdown of history as anything more than a tool in the game of modern politics. The past has been effectively flushed down the lavatory, except as it plays to modern political sensibilities. The dead must either be remade in our image (thus the preoccupation in certain quarters with the sexuality of key historical figures) or repudiated (thus the current penchant for renaming historic buildings and even technical titles if the originals have failed to conform to the exacting standards of twenty-first-century morality or even mere linguistic connotation). We can only deal with the dead in one of two ways: as support for our political positions or as evidence of the wickedness of our political opponents. That the dead might place obligations upon us precisely at the points where they cannot be assimilated into the categories of modern politics seems to be no longer a credible option.

Thus, the idea that Antigone would herself enter the land of the dead because of obligations to one who has already gone to that realm is ridiculous to the modern mind. Society is a social contract of the living, not a covenant with the dead or the yet unborn. Heaney's audience may sympathize with Antigone, but they do so out of ignorance, not realizing how much of what she represents is what they themselves abominate.

Conclusion

Seamus Heaney's comment on modern audiences for *Antigone* reveals far more than I suspect he intended, for it takes us to the heart of the difference of our world from that of Sophocles. And yet Sophocles's world with regard to the points I have raised—history, family, and the dead—is not so different from the world that has recently passed. The world we now inhabit—one where history is taught not as history but as contemporary politics; where family is derided, denied, or dissolved;

and where the presence of the dead is increasingly absent—is of relatively recent vintage.

Part of this is because of the impact of Christianity on Western culture. I mentioned at the start that it is traditional to deny that Christianity can offer a tragic vision. I disagree. In fact, I believe Christianity helped maintain the tragic vision within Western culture. Christianity emphasizes all three of the things that underlie the tragedy of Antigone: the significance of history, family, and the dead. The hope of the resurrection does not negate those things. Rather it gives value to them in a way that they would otherwise lack. And, unlike modern society, historic forms of Christianity refuse to sentimentalize, trivialize, sanitize, or ignore death. Just compare the liturgy of Cranmer with that of Sinatra. Death is devastating, as the tears of Christ himself outside the tomb of Lazarus indicate. Whatever perspective one may have on the truth or otherwise of the Christian faith, one must acknowledge that by the standards of *Antigone*, it is consistent with a tragic vision.

Finally, I would also suggest that the loss of this tragic vision is part of the tragedy of the modern world. History is vast and, when seen as important, inevitably takes us out of ourselves, sets the present in context, and relativizes all that we experience day to day. Family shapes our identity through education and obligation in a manner that makes us who we are. And it does so by connecting us to history, both the particular and the more general, and to others in a way that makes their loss acutely painful. The freedom that comes from having a functioning family to whom one is obliged is profound, for it is the freedom to experience all that makes us human—love and loss. If you doubt this, then simply talk to somebody who lacks such a family. The modern alternative—the freedom of radical disconnectedness, whether from the past or from the family—is not really freedom at all but more often a form of free-floating confusion. And acknowledgment of the significance of the dead is part of what makes us human. These three things are crucial to all the relational complexity that makes human life so rich. As the striving for the utopianism of the eternal present increasingly captures our hedonistic mind-set, and as the three tragic elements of *Antigone* pass from the scene, I fear that the greatest tragedy of all will be a loss—or perhaps worse, a deluded denial—of what it means to be human.

16

Beholding the Glory of Jesus

How a Christ-Centered Perspective Restores
in Us the Splendor of God's Image

BRIAN COURTNEY WOOD

This essay has two primary aims. The first is to exhort believers in Jesus Christ to daily behold his glory revealed in the Holy Bible in order to become like him. The second is to underscore how doing so is the key to both living obediently and overcoming our enemy, the Devil. Finally, some brief remarks regarding the preaching of God's Word will follow.

Beholding Jesus's Glory

A daily devotion to beholding God's glory in Jesus Christ will change you. It will bring you to your knees in awestruck, reverent worship and genuine repentance. Moreover, it will motivate you to daily offer yourself to God in order for him to conform your character and conduct to his Son's likeness. Conformity to Jesus Christ in all of life should be our daily priority and preoccupation, because it is God's predestined purpose for us. He wants us all to be like Jesus. The apostle Paul said,

"For those whom he foreknew he also predestined to be conformed to the image of his Son, in order that he might be the firstborn among many brothers" (Rom. 8:29; see also Gal. 4:19; Eph. 4:13, 15).

In the four Gospel accounts, Jesus calls us to be like him. He calls us to be meek and lowly in our hearts (Matt. 11:29), humble servants of each other (Mark 10:42–45; John 13:13–15), followers of his self-less life (Luke 9:23; John 12:23–26), imitators of his sacrificial love (John 13:34; 15:12–14), and even hated and persecuted like him (Matt. 10:24–25; John 15:18–21). There are also many examples in the New Testament letters summoning us to be like Jesus. For example, in Paul's letter to the Philippians, he specifically targets our need to *think humbly* like Christ Jesus in order to serve others as he did:

> So if there is any encouragement in Christ, any comfort from love, any participation in the Spirit, any affection and sympathy, complete my joy by being of the same mind, having the same love, being in full accord and of one mind. Do nothing from selfish ambition or conceit, but in humility count others more significant than yourselves. Let each of you look not only to his own interests, but also to the interests of others. Have this mind among yourselves, which is yours in Christ Jesus. (Phil. 2:1–5)

Notice Paul's conclusion that being *in Christ* demands a certain way of thinking, or supplies believers with Christ's own mind, so we might live like him.[1] What is it, then, about Jesus Christ that summons us to be preeminently preoccupied with him as *the* pattern for our lives?

We believe that in the beginning God created us in his image, after his likeness and for his glory (Gen. 1:26–27; Rev. 4:11). There has been much written and, as Dr. Poythress might say, "a multiplicity of perspectives" given on what being created in God's image really means. When we listen to God's Word, we discover that Jesus Christ, God's Son, is *the image* of the invisible God (2 Cor. 4:4; Col. 1:15). He is the one in whom all the fullness of God is pleased to dwell (Col. 1:19; 2:9). He reveals the unknowable and invisible God (Matt. 11:27; John 1:18). All the treasures of wisdom and knowledge are found in him (Col. 2:3). Jesus Christ perfectly and comprehensively radiates the glory of God

---

1. Compare the ESV margin note for the last phrase of verse 5, "which was also in Christ Jesus."

and is exclusively the exact imprint of his nature (Heb. 1:3). He was given God's Spirit without limitation (John 3:34). He has eternally been and forever more will be in the very form of God (Phil. 2:6). Therefore, to see Jesus is to see the Father (John 12:45). To hear Jesus is to hear the Father and the Spirit (John 3:34; 12:49–50; 14:10; 17:8). To see Jesus at work is to behold God and his Spirit at work (Matt. 12:28; Luke 11:20; John 5:17, 19–20; 10:37–38). To touch Jesus is to make direct physical contact with the living and eternal triune God (John 20:27–28; Col. 1:19; 1 John 1:1–2). Once, Philip enthusiastically requested with great expectation, "Lord, show us the Father, and it is enough for us," to which Jesus chidingly responded, "Have I been with you so long, and you still do not know me, Philip? Whoever has seen me has seen the Father. How can you say, 'Show us the Father'?" (John 14:8–9). If then we have truly seen Jesus, in some sense, there really is nothing left to see.

Therefore, because Jesus *is* God's image and we are *in* God's image, we must emphasize *Jesus* as *the preeminent pattern* for our lives, as well as the central priority of thinking about Jesus and thinking like Jesus in order to become like Jesus. For Jesus reveals how those created in God's image are to live, and only when we pay attention to him are we able to see God clearly, know God genuinely, and become like God truly. Paul wrote, "Be kind to one another, tenderhearted, forgiving one another, as God in Christ forgave you. Therefore be imitators of God, as beloved children. And walk in love, as Christ loved us and gave himself up for us, a fragrant offering and sacrifice to God" (Eph. 4:32–5:2). A careful reading of these verses shows that imitating Christ is *the way* to imitate God. For through the incarnation and earthly ministry of Jesus Christ, and particularly in his sacrificial death, the kind, tenderhearted, forgiving, and loving character of God is perfectly and visibly animated in human form for us to behold and imitate (John 13:34; 15:12–13; Eph. 4:20–24; Phil. 3:10–11; 1 John 4:9–12). However, it is clear we are not being called to deity but are being called to the imitation of God's characteristics seen in Jesus's humanity that exemplify God's original design for human nature and life. Jesus shows in his incarnation and righteous life what it means to be truly human, for sin does not make us human. Sin makes us inhumane.

We learn about Jesus, his ways, and how he thinks in the Holy Bible. When we meditate on the glories of Christ revealed in Scripture, God's Holy Spirit redeems and renews our thoughts so that our character and conduct might be increasingly transformed after the beauty and glory of God's image. The apostle Paul said, "And we all, with unveiled face, beholding the glory of the Lord, are being transformed into the same image from one degree of glory to another. For this comes from the Lord who is the Spirit" (2 Cor. 3:18). Moreover, he said, "For God, who said, 'Let light shine out of darkness,' has shone in our hearts to give the light of the knowledge of the glory of God in the face of Jesus Christ" (2 Cor. 4:6).[2]

We saw in Romans 8:29 that God's *predestined purpose* is our conformity to his Son's likeness. In the passages just quoted, we see that God's *prerequisite path* for our conformity is beholding his glory revealed in Jesus Christ. We may infer that without fixating on Christ's glory, spiritual stagnation and even malformation result instead of glorious godly transformation. It is therefore imperative to understand the background of Christ's glory, of which Paul speaks, if we ever expect to experience the transformation God promises. This background, found in the book of Exodus, tells the story of Moses turning to talk with Yahweh to receive his commands and returning to speak them to Israel. When he did, the skin of his face shone with glory, and after speaking to Israel he placed a veil over his face until Yahweh spoke to him again (Ex. 34:29–35). Initially, Moses's shining face frightened Israel, and they would not approach him because Yahweh's glory was beaming from his face (Ex. 34:30). The last time Moses had come down the mountain, it had not been a pleasant experience (Ex. 32:15–29); now he was back and his face was shining like Mount Sinai! Paul appears to interpret the root cause of the people's teror as a fear of death and condemnation, given this story's proximity to the record of their idolatry and the character of the ministry that flowed from Sinai (2 Cor. 3:14–16). Moreover, they did not have Moses's friendly face-to-face fellowship with Yahweh (Ex. 33:11).

The Bible says that Moses's face shined with glory "because he

---

2. See the very helpful comments on these passages by Vern S. Poythress, *The Shadow of Christ in the Law of Moses* (Brentwood, TN: Wolgemuth & Hyatt, 1991), 5–6.

had been talking with God" (Ex. 34:29). There is, however, no record of his face shining prior to this moment. Moses talked with God at the burning bush, but nothing is said there of his face shining—only of him hiding his face for fear of looking at God (Ex. 3:6). When he initially received Yahweh's commandments (Exodus 19–23) and tabernacle instructions (Exodus 25–31), and even saw and fellowshiped with the God of Israel (Ex. 24:9–11; 33:7–11), nothing is said of his face shining. What happened in Exodus 34 that caused Moses's face to shine with glory and influenced all his subsequent encounters with Yahweh in this way? Answering this question is imperative because the temporary transformation of Moses's face foreshadows the permanent life transformation taking place in everyone beholding the Lord's glory in Jesus's face. The explanations in 2 Corinthians and Exodus 34 are illuminating.

Paul's aim in 2 Corinthians 3 is to contrast the new covenant's permanent glory with the old covenant's fading glory. The law, although given by God and therefore glorious by definition, was unable to give Israel life, justification, and transformation because of the people's sins. The law actually ministered death and condemnation, and exposed Israel's impotence for any permanent change through its ministry (3:7–11). It is important however to balance the law's *inability* to fulfill God's life-transforming purposes for us with its *ability* to lead us to Christ, in whom the law's righteous requirements are fulfilled for us and even in us (Gal. 3:24; Rom. 8:1–4; Heb. 8:8–12). In Christ and through his sacrifice we receive eternal life, justifying righteousness, access, union, and communion with the triune God, who faithfully works to transform us by his Spirit into his Son's likeness. In Christ and because of him, death is now fading (1 Cor. 15:54–55), condemnation has vanished (Rom. 8:1–4), and our inability to be like him is increasingly being transformed (2 Cor. 3:18)!

Second Corinthians 3 is rooted in Exodus 34, and it is helpful to review the story prior to Moses's shining face to understand why this happened and its relevance for this essay's aims. Exodus begins with God faithfully multiplying Israel despite extreme opposition and oppression (Exodus 1). Yahweh hears his people's cries, sees their affliction, raises Moses up, and commissions him to deliver them (Exodus 2–6).

Yahweh plagues the Egyptians, saves Israel by the blood of the lamb, and drowns their enemies in the sea (Exodus 7–15). Yahweh guides and provides for Israel in the wilderness (Exodus 15–18). Yahweh consecrates them, instructs them, and ratifies his covenant with them (Exodus 19–24). Then, Yahweh gives Israel instructions for constructing a tabernacle that he might dwell with them (Exodus 25–31). This is all a marvelous display of Yahweh's sovereign power and gracious purpose to redeem his people, advancing his agenda of filling the earth with the knowledge of his glory!

In Exodus 32 however, something terrible happens. Israel refuses to trust Yahweh or his servant Moses. The people grow impatient and purposely work to make idols to worship and praise instead of Yahweh their Redeemer (32:1–6)! Yahweh himself narrates their flagrant act of disobedience and idolatry:

> Go down, for your people, whom you brought up out of the land of Egypt, have corrupted themselves. They have turned aside quickly out of the way that I commanded them. They have made for themselves a golden calf and have worshiped it and sacrificed to it and said, "These are your gods, O Israel, who brought you up out of the land of Egypt!" (32:7–8)

Yahweh is ready to "consume" them, but Moses prays for their deliverance, only this time from Yahweh himself! Yahweh relents, but when Moses goes down to the people, he cannot contain his own anger; so he breaks Yahweh's tablets and hotly rebukes Israel, and many Israelites die. Then Moses seeks Yahweh's face for mercy, even wishing himself to be blotted out of Yahweh's book so Israel might be forgiven (Exodus 32)!

In spite of Israel's blatant sin, Yahweh is still willing to keep his covenant and bring them into the Promised Land, but now without accompanying them (Ex. 33:3). At this, Moses intercedes for Israel, pleading with Yahweh to go in their midst and reaffirm his favor. Yahweh hears Moses's prayer and promises his presence and rest (Ex. 33:12–17). Moses, wanting deeper assurance of Yahweh's favor and acceptance in view of Israel's betrayal (cf. Gen. 32:22–33:10), prays, "Please show me your glory" (Ex. 33:18).[3] However, Yahweh says, "I will make all my goodness pass before you and will proclaim before you my name 'The LORD.' And I will be gracious to whom I will be gracious, and will show mercy on whom I will show mercy. But," he said, "you cannot see my face, for man shall not see me and live" (Ex. 33:19–20).

Moses will not *see* Yahweh's glory, but he will *hear* Yahweh proclaim his glory when he proclaims his very own name. To begin to understand the glory radiating from Moses's face, we must hear Yahweh's proclamation in the immediate context of Israel's tragic idolatry (Exodus 32; 34:5–7), which in turn must be understood in the context of Yahweh redeeming Israel out of Egypt and desiring and designing to dwell with his people (Exodus 1–31). Because Yahweh has loved and redeemed Israel, their subsequent idolatry at Sinai is all the more egregious. In the same way, when Yahweh proclaims his name, subsequent to this idolatry, his self-revelation abounds with resplendent, breathtaking amazement! What is Yahweh's answer or ultimate comeback, if you will, to Israel's covenant betrayal?

> The LORD descended in the cloud and stood with him there, and proclaimed the name of the LORD. The LORD passed before him and proclaimed, "The LORD, the LORD, a God merciful and gracious, slow to anger, and abounding in steadfast love and faithfulness, keeping steadfast love for thousands, forgiving iniquity and transgression and sin, but who will by no means clear the guilty, visiting the iniquity of the fathers on the children and the children's children, to the third and fourth generation." (Ex. 34:5–7)

When Yahweh initially revealed his name to Moses at the burning bush, he highlighted his presence and power to be all that Israel needed to fulfill the promises made to Abraham, Isaac, and Jacob on their behalf (Ex. 3:13–17). In Exodus 6:2–8, Yahweh reminds Israel of his past faithfulness to their fathers, his present compassion in their own afflictions, and his plans to redeem them, judge their enemies, and bring them into the Promised Land. These statements of Yahweh highlight

---

3. Compare Philip's similar request to Jesus in John 14:8, "Lord, show us the Father, and it is enough for us." Moses's request was rejected, but Philip's request lacked perception because he failed to see the Father's glory so clearly revealed in the face of Jesus, who was standing right in front of him!

his steadfast love to his *groaning* and *suffering* people, but when Yahweh proclaims his name at Sinai, after Israel's idolatry, he is highlighting his steadfast love even to his *guilty* and *sinful* people.

This passage deserves careful consideration, because this is God's response to Moses's plea to see his glory. The glory proclaimed here, although not an exhaustive declaration, is nevertheless a foreshadowing of the mind-renewing and life-transforming glory we behold in Jesus Christ, which the Spirit increasingly uses to restore in us the beauty and glory of God's image. Additionally, the glory Yahweh proclaims here is what Paul says the "god of this world" blinds the mind from seeing (2 Cor. 4:4; 11:3). Finally, Yahweh's self-proclamation finds staggering fulfillment in his own appeal through his servants' proclamation of Jesus Christ crucified and crowned, by whom sinners are reconciled to God (1 Cor. 1:23; 2 Cor. 4:1–2, 5; 5:18–6:1). At least four things need to be underscored about the passage where Yahweh proclaims his name, four things that lie behind Paul's own preaching of Jesus Christ.

First, before Yahweh said anything, he "descended in a cloud and stood with" Moses, affirming his presence with him and Israel, whom he represented. God's presence with his people is a pervasive theme found in the Bible. We see, in this context, Yahweh's gracious desire and design to dwell with his people (cf. Ex. 29:44–46; 1 Kings 8). By Yahweh's descent and presence, the Consuming Fire graciously dwells in Israel's midst, as with the bush, not consuming them but displaying their God-given distinctiveness (Ex. 3:2–3; 33:3, 15–17; Deut. 7:6–8)! Ultimately, we are compelled to think of the incarnation of Jesus Christ, Immanuel, who came to a sinful world and dwelt among sinful people to bear our sins that we might bear his image and dwell with him forever (Matt. 1:23; John 14:3).

Second, Yahweh speaks his name twice, probably to confirm his commitment to what he reveals about himself, reinforce his name's infinite importance, and highlight Moses's need to pay close attention to his words. Yahweh's words interpret the little that Moses does see (Ex. 33:21–23), and they illuminate Yahweh's somewhat veiled, "I AM WHO I AM," initially spoken at the burning bush (Ex. 3:13–17). His self-proclamation is surprisingly being revealed *after* the disclosure of Israel's expanding depravity. God is showing Moses, Israel, and us how to think of his ways in relation to our waywardness, to stir us to worship and repentance (Ex. 33:13; 34:8; Rom. 2:4).

Third, there are at least seven, possibly nine, descriptions of Yahweh's tenderheartedness. From Yahweh's mercy to his pardoning grace, he proclaims his mercy-laden, grace-packed, and long-suffering personality to Israel, making it abundantly clear that the emphasis in *his* proclamation is on his nearness and immeasurable grace for his sinful people. Yahweh's proclamation is blessedly unbalanced, if you will, and gloriously weighed down with grace and mercy.

Fourth, the final description about visiting the iniquity of the guilty is more than justified and reasonable in light of the third point just made. When we consider the multidimensional, tenderhearted mercy and grace of Yahweh, his justness in condemning the guilty for unbelief is magnified. When the glorious presence and grace of God are rejected out of hand without repentance, condemnation is the only consequence fitting for the guilty.

Considering the above analysis, it seems clear that Moses's face shone with glory because Yahweh was proclaiming to him not simply impersonal laws but his very self, his loving and loyal character. Yahweh himself is the fountain from which the law's conduits flow. He is the bedrock on which they are founded and is himself the motivation for his people to believe in him, turn from sin, and obey him (Ex. 34:4–28). Moses's face shone with glory because Yahweh had proclaimed to him the heart of the gospel as the basis for first having communion with him so that we might be consecrated to him. However, the glory faded on Moses's face because the old covenant was temporary and incapable, even with all its meticulous legislations, of justifying us and transforming our character and conduct. These things had to wait for the coming of Jesus Christ, who unites the believing sinner to his death, burial, and resurrection (Romans 6) so that by his Spirit we are empowered to live for God (Romans 8) in ways the law alone could never provide (Romans 7).[4] Apart from Christ's work, the barrier of sin could not be removed, nor could the internal

---

4. My understanding of how these three chapters in Romans fit together was influenced in large part by a conversation I had with Dr. Poythress some years ago; see also Douglas Moo, *The Epistle to the Romans*, NICNT (Grand Rapids, MI: Eerdmans, 1996), 409–67.

transformation of the new covenant be realized (Jer. 31:31–34; Ezek. 36:24–27; Phil. 2:12–13).

Yahweh's proclaimed glory would one day be incarnated in the person and ministry of Jesus Christ. This gaze-worthy glory, this gospel, is what people must be daily devoted to beholding if they are ever to joyfully live for God's glory, gladly turn from their sins, truly bear his image, zealously proclaim his name, and experience personal, ecclesiastical, and cultural change. Yahweh makes this plain by first proclaiming to Moses the gospel, even his very self, before he ever recapitulates his specific legislation for them (Ex. 34:1–28; cf. also Gen. 3:15–19). Therefore, it is not proclaiming or emphasizing the requirements of the law detached from himself, but proclaiming and emphasizing Yahweh's glorious personality, later incarnated in Jesus Christ, that transforms Moses's face and motivates him to praise, petition, believe in, and obey Yahweh.[5]

When Moses hears Yahweh's proclamation, he unhesitatingly bows in worship (Ex. 34:8–9). He is awestruck, maybe even caught off guard by the glorious revelation of Yahweh's grace, in light of Israel's blatant sin and flagrant idolatry. Second, Moses intercedes for Israel. Previously, Yahweh said, "I will not go up among you, lest I consume you on the way, for you are a stiff-necked people" (Ex. 33:3). Moses however, now encouraged and emboldened in his faith by Yahweh's self-revelation, positively restates Yahweh's disastrous word back to him in reverent prayer: "Please let the Lord go in the midst of us, for it is a stiff-necked people" (Ex. 34:9). Israel's stubbornness is the reason for Yahweh's potential absence, but given his self-revelation, Moses prays that their stiff-necked attitude will now be the very reason for Yahweh's presence, without which they can never change or live for his glory.[6] Third, the revelation of Yahweh's name leads Moses to seek forgiveness. When Yahweh reveals how forgiving he is, it motivates honest and unhesitant confession of sin. The fact that Yahweh will "by no means clear the guilty" but

---

5. God's laws indeed reflect his character, but the emphasis must remain on his person as the living, loving covenant being who has given us his precepts to obey. He is devoted to us and not a distant, detached dictator.

6. See Edmund P. Clowney, *The Unfolding Mystery: Discovering Christ in the Old Testament* (Colorado Springs: NavPress, 1988), 110–14.

visit their iniquity is not only reasonable punishment in view of his steadfast love but also a massive motivation to confess guilt, repent of sins, and experience forgiveness. Finally, Moses asks Yahweh to take them for his inheritance. Truly, this request amplifies salvation by grace. It is beyond articulating that Yahweh would ever consider sinful, idolatrous human beings his inheritance!

In the New Testament, we see in Jesus, much more clearly and fully, what Moses longed to see. John says, "And the Word became flesh and dwelt among us, and *we have seen his glory*, glory as of the only Son from the Father, full of grace and truth" (John 1:14). In Jesus Christ, Yahweh's glorious name, character, and ways, proclaimed to Moses, are climactically incarnated. Jesus says, "'Now is my soul troubled. And what shall I say? "Father, save me from this hour"? But for this purpose I have come to this hour. Father, *glorify your name*.' Then a voice came from heaven: 'I have glorified it, and I will glorify it again'" (John 12:27–28). In the Old Testament, Yahweh's mighty works of salvation and judgment in Egypt display his power and proclaim his name in all the earth (Ex. 9:14–16; Josh. 2:8–11). In the New Testament, God's mighty works and words through the life of Christ glorify his name. In John 12, however, in light of Exodus 34, the emphasis is on how *Jesus's crucifixion* incarnates the Father's glorious name proclaimed to Moses and displays his power to judge and save. At the cross, Satan will be cast out and judged, and all who believe the gospel will be saved. Jesus proclaims, "Now is the judgment of this world; now will the ruler of this world be cast out. And I, when I am lifted up from the earth, will draw all people to myself." And John explains, "He said this to show by what kind of death he was going to die" (John 12:31–33).

Therefore, it is preeminently at the cross of Jesus Christ where we behold Yahweh's glorious name, proclaimed to Moses, incarnated. It is at the cross of Jesus—illustrated at his baptism, where he stood with sinners—that we behold Immanuel, our Savior, graciously descending by being lifted up to bear our sins (Luke 12:50)! At the cross of Jesus we behold God the Son, punished for sins, shouting God's name twice in agony (Matt. 27:46) and thereby echoing Yahweh, who, while pardoning sins, proclaimed the divine name twice in ecstasy. At the cross of Jesus we behold Yahweh's mercy, grace, and patience toward sinners (Luke 23:43). At the cross of Jesus we behold Yahweh's abounding steadfast love and faithfulness to his covenant (Acts 3:18). At the cross of Jesus we behold Yahweh's pardoning grace to lawless, perverted transgressors (Luke 23:34). At the cross of Jesus Christ we behold Yahweh by no means clearing *Jesus*, who bears our guilt and receives the consequences of our sins visited on him as he dies sacrificially as our substitute (Isa. 53:10)!

Gospel-Driven Living

By God's Spirit, we behold Yahweh's immeasurable glory revealed in the person and work of Jesus Christ in the Bible. There he reveals Yahweh's glorious name in order that we might hear, believe, and be saved (John 1:12–14; 16:14). When, by the Spirit, we increasingly comprehend this incomprehensible love (Eph. 3:19), like Moses, we too are brought to our knees in awestruck, reverent worship, genuine confession, and repentance, and are motivated to pursue all God has promised us in Christ Jesus (Rom. 12:1–2; 2 Cor. 1:20; Eph. 3:14). It is at *the cross of Christ* that we behold the greatest manifestation of God's love and therefore the greatest and most compelling motivation to love, to stop thinking and living for ourselves, but rather to start thinking like Christ and living obediently for him (Isa. 55:6–9; John 15:13; 2 Cor. 5:14–15; Phil. 2:1–17).

However, this gospel-revealing, mind-renewing, and life-transforming glory of Christ shown at his cross is the very thing the Devil blinds the unbeliever's mind from seeing. Moreover, he deceitfully aims to lead the believer's "thoughts" astray "from a sincere and pure devotion to Christ" (2 Cor. 11:3; cf. 4:3–4). The Serpent targets the minds of both unbelievers and believers, and his aim is the same. He does not want us beholding or understanding "the light of the gospel of the glory of Christ, who is the image of God" (2 Cor. 4:4). He knows that if we see this glory, we will have the greatest foundation and motivation for belief in and devotion to Christ, namely, Christ himself, who so dramatically and compellingly reveals the beauty and glory of God and his gracious gospel. When Moses chronicled for Israel humanity's initial disobedience, he further illustrates this point:

Now the serpent was more crafty than any other beast of the field
that the LORD God had made.

He said to the woman, "Did God actually say, 'You shall not
eat of any tree in the garden'?" And the woman said to the serpent,
"We may eat of the fruit of the trees in the garden, but God said,
'You shall not eat of the fruit of the tree that is in the midst of the
garden, neither shall you touch it, lest you die.'" But the serpent
said to the woman, "You will not surely die. For God knows that
when you eat of it your eyes will be opened, and you will be like
God, knowing good and evil." (Gen. 3:1–5)

Consider the structure of this passage in its context, its use of words,
and Israel, its initial audience, because it exposes the Serpent's strategy for destroying humanity. The context of Genesis 3 begins in Genesis 2:4. Note especially how God's name appears in Genesis 2:4–3:24.
The combination "LORD God" appears everywhere *except* in the
conversation between the Serpent and the woman (3:1b–5). God's
covenant name, Yahweh, with its immeasurable, grace-packed implications, which stimulate worship, obedience, and repudiation of sin, is
missing from the Serpent's lips![7] He does not want anyone beholding
Yahweh's glory proclaimed to Moses and incarnated in Jesus Christ.
It would be counterintuitive, given his aim to lead our thoughts astray
from devotion to the Lord, to speak Yahweh's name and risk reminding us of his glorious grace, motivating mercy, and compelling love
(Rom. 12:1–2; 2 Cor. 5:14–15; 1 John 4:19). The Serpent, although
a counterfeiter,[8] would not undermine his whole agenda by imitating
the Holy Spirit's intentions (Matt. 12:25–28). Among other things,
God's Spirit glorifies Jesus (John 16:14), bears witness to our adoption
(Rom. 8:14–17), and fills us with Christ, his character, and his immeasurable love (Gal. 5:22–23; Eph. 3:14–19). God's Spirit educates
us from the Holy Bible regarding God and his gospel, revealed and
fulfilled in Jesus Christ, along with its implications for our worship,

---

7. This point is also made by Edward J. Young, *Genesis 3: A Devotional and Expository Study*
(Carlisle, PA: Banner of Truth, 1966), 23–24.

8. I first heard the language of Satan being a counterfeiter from Poythress during his lectures
on the book of Revelation, at Westminster Theological Seminary, in the early 1990s; cf. also Vern
Sheridan Poythress, *The Returning King: A Guide to the Book of Revelation* (Phillipsburg, NJ:
P&R, 2000), 16–22.

transformation, obedience, and influence (2 Tim. 3:15–17; cf. Eph. 2:10; Titus 2:11–14; 3:1–7).

By contrast, the Serpent's agenda is antithetical to Moses's appeal to see Yahweh's glory, Jesus's aim to show Yahweh's glory, and Paul's ambition to announce Christ's glory. The Serpent wants humans deceived, disobedient, defeated, dominated by sin, and destroyed (Eph. 2:1–3). Genesis 3 makes plain that he succeeds in this when our minds are blinded and our thoughts are led astray from beholding the glory of Jesus Christ in the gospel. For Eve, Israel, and us, the Serpent's cunning strategy is the same (2 Cor. 2:11). It consists of proclaiming a glory-less God, if you will, by veiling Yahweh's name, tampering with his words, and slandering his character, as in Genesis 3. With the only foundation and motivation for worship and obedience hidden, we become easy prey to lead astray from devotion to the Lord.[9]

At the risk of oversimplification, our entire responsibility can be summed up as a command to love God and others, the latter love giving evidence of the former (Matt. 7:12; 22:34–40; Rom. 13:8–10; 1 John 4:7, 20–21).[10] Our life of love is motivated by the One who *is* love and whose Son has revealed to humanity the greatest love (John 15:13; 1 John 4:8, 19). It is therefore transparently clear why the Serpent's strategy is to deceive our minds and hearts from worshipfully fixating on God and his love revealed in Jesus Christ. Genesis 3 teaches us that the Serpent twists God's words and slanders his character, but his strategy begins by leading our thoughts astray from the glorious, praiseworthy, gaze-worthy, gospel-revealing character of God summed up in *Yahweh*, his covenant name, now given to Jesus Christ the Lord, who embodies all the beauty and glory of the triune God (Phil. 2:9–11; Col. 1:19; 2:9). Paul makes a similar point about the Devil's strategy:

> Finally, be strong in the Lord and in the strength of his might. Put on the whole armor of God, that you may be able to stand against the schemes of the devil. For we do not wrestle against flesh and blood, but against the rulers, against the authorities, against the

9. Consider Yahweh's indictment of his people's failure to remember his redeeming love as the reason for their fall (Ezek. 16:22, 43). They forgot where God found them and how he covenanted with them.

10. See the helpful treatment on God's law by John M. Frame, *The Doctrine of the Christian Life* (Phillipsburg, NJ: P&R, 2008), 395–401.

cosmic powers over this present darkness, against the spiritual forces of evil in the heavenly places. (Eph. 6:10–12)

Notice in this passage not only who we are and are not wrestling against but also the *location* of the battle. We fight *in the heavenly places*. This is the same realm where we have been blessed by the Father with every spiritual blessing in Christ. Moreover, it is where we have been seated with Christ Jesus, who rules over all things (Eph. 1:3, 20–21; 2:6). The Devil's agenda is to wrestle our thoughts away from beholding and blessing the Father for the innumerable blessings we have in Christ Jesus by grace, as well as from understanding our identity in Christ. In so doing, he distracts our focus from the most compelling motivation for obedience, the triune God's self-revelation in the gospel of Jesus Christ crucified and crowned. The Devil has been cast out of heaven, but he insists on wrestling in heavenly places where we behold the Father, Son, and Spirit working together for our redemption. Our response to Satan must be to bless the triune God and broadcast his glorious grace (Eph. 1:3, 6, 12, 14; 3:8–10; 2 Cor. 4:5). We conquer the Serpent by the Lamb's blood and our readiness to lay down our lives to testify to Jesus's cross and crown (Rev. 12:7–11).

As Israel heard Genesis 3, they would have recognized that Yahweh faithfully delivered them in order to be their God and dwell with them so that humanity as a whole might once again experience the incalculable blessings of Immanuel (Ex. 29:45–46; 1 Kings 7:41–43). They understood how God created Adam upright, even as his son (Luke 3:38). But in its thoughts humanity "sought out many schemes." (Eccles. 7:29). Adam and, in him, we willfully turned away from God and his word (Gen. 2:15–17; 3:1–6, 17; Rom. 5:12). We were enticed and deceived by Satan to believe we could be like God if we would only stop submitting our thoughts to his and start thinking for ourselves, but our schemes left us formless, empty, and darkened in our understanding (Eph. 4:17–19). Moses wrote that "the wickedness of man was great in all the earth, and that every intention of the thoughts of his heart was only evil continually" (Gen. 6:5). We became hostile in our minds through our evil deeds (Col. 1:21). Our minds, now set on the flesh, were even incapable of submitting to God (Rom. 8:5–7).

When Paul sums up how unredeemed humanity thinks, his portrayal is of truth-suppressing, futile-thinking, arrogant fools who refuse to acknowledge God but rather applaud what they know to be wicked and worthy of death (cf. Rom. 1:18–32). Paul concludes that even the Jews, who had the benefit of God's thoughts in written form, are no better in their understanding (Rom. 2:17–24; 3:10–12). Adam, God's son, was driven from Eden because of disobedience, and when Israel, God's national son at the time (Ex. 4:22–23), was being brought into what may be seen as a new Eden[11] (cf. Deut. 6:10–15; 8:7–10; 11:10–15), sadly Israel, like Eve, was led astray in their thoughts. Israel forgot the salvation they experienced and fell into flagrant idolatry (Ezek. 16:22, 43).

The importance of remembering God's redeeming love can be seen by Paul's interruption of the overwhelming number of indicatives in Ephesians 1–3 with one explicit imperative: to *remember* what we once were without Christ and now are in Christ (Eph. 2:11–13).[12] God uses our memory and understanding of his love to stir us to faithfulness. Paul's humble plea for the Ephesians supports this way of thinking:

> For this reason I bow my knees before the Father, from whom every family in heaven and on earth is named, that according to the riches of his glory he may grant you to be strengthened with power through his Spirit in your inner being, so that Christ may dwell in your hearts through faith—that you, being rooted and grounded in love, may have strength to comprehend with all the saints what is the breadth and length and height and depth, and to know the love of Christ that surpasses knowledge, that you may be filled with all the fullness of God. (Eph. 3:14–19)

The same Holy Spirit who powerfully came upon Mary so that God's Son might physically dwell in her (Luke 1:35) now works internally to strengthen every believer with power so Christ might spiritu-

---

11. For example, Christopher J. H. Wright, *The Mission of God: Unlocking the Bible's Grand Narrative* (Downers Grove, IL: InterVarsity Press, 2006), 333–34, 415; David Chilton, "The Holy Mountain," in *Paradise Restored: A Biblical Theology of Dominion* (Horn Lake, MS: Dominion, 2007), 28–36.

12. My first encounter with the technical terms "indicatives" and "imperatives" with regard to the pattern of our Christian living took place during the lectures of Richard B. Gaffin Jr. on the doctrine of Christ, Westminster Theological Seminary, fall 1989.

ally dwell in our hearts by faith. This strengthening, incidentally, flows from the riches of the Father's glory, which highlight his grace in Christ (cf. Eph. 1:7; 2:7; 3:8 with Ex. 34:5–7). Christ dwells in us to root and ground our lives in loving relationships, which lead us to comprehend his incomprehensible and multidimensional love, to the ultimate end of filling us with God's fullness, which is found in Christ (Col. 1:19; 2:3, 9). God's desire and design is to work powerfully in and through us in unimaginable ways for his praise (Eph. 3:19–21). Jesus's own prayer supports this same theme. He says, "I made known to them your name, and I will continue to make it known, that the love with which you have loved me may be in them, and I in them" (John 17:26; cf. Ex. 33:19; 34:5). The result of Jesus's increasing revelation of the Father's name, proclaimed long ago to Moses, is that believers are indwelt with both the Father's *love* and his *Son*, whose incarnation has revealed the Father's love and glorious name. Again, Jesus reinforces this constant emphasis on his love when he institutes the Lord's Supper. He teaches us to eat and drink in order to remember and proclaim *his death*, because the love revealed in Jesus's crucifixion is not only the greatest love known but also the constant, most compelling reminder needed to stimulate us to a life of faithful, sacrificial, Christ-like love (John 15:13; Rom. 5:6–11; 1 Cor. 11:23–25; 2 Cor. 5:14–15).[13]

Preaching Jesus Christ Crucified and Crowned

The only way for every human thought to be redeemed from demonic deception, darkness, and disobedience and taken "captive to obey Christ" so that we have the very "mind of Christ" (1 Cor. 2:16; 2 Cor. 10:3–5) is for Jesus Christ to be proclaimed (Rom. 10:14–17). What unredeemed and redeemed minds both need is a rich, robust proclamation of Jesus—his person and work—from every passage of Scripture, so that we might be empowered and motivated for a life of godly love (Matt. 7:12; Luke 24:27; 44–47; John 5:39, 46). God's Word does not return to him empty but brings regenerative transformation for his name (Isa. 55:10–13). One scarcely needs to argue for what seems

---

13. Cf. also Jesus's teaching in John 6:53–68 regarding eating his flesh and drinking his blood. Jesus illustrates the gospel-centered focus of his life-giving words and our need to digest them by faith in order to have life.

so glaringly self-evident. Jesus Christ must be the centerpiece of every sermon and teaching from God's Word if we are to truly behold God's glory and experience greater transformation into his glorious image.[14] It is primarily through Christ and his immeasurable love that we gain the motivation both for obeying his Word and for overcoming the Serpent's deceitful ways and words.

The ministry of the apostle Paul conclusively shows that Jesus Christ is the one we preach (Acts 9:15, 20, 22; 17:30–31; 28:31; Rom. 1:15; 16:25; 1 Cor. 1:17–18, 23–24; 2:2; 15:3–4; Gal. 1:16; Eph. 3:8; Phil. 1:13, 18). Doing so is the path to salvation (Rom. 10:17), to Christian maturity (Col. 1:28; 1 John 3:1–3), and to Christian security (Gal. 6:14; Phil. 3:1–10; Col. 2:6–23; Rev. 12:10–12). When Paul speaks of the "mercy" of the preaching ministry in the new covenant, he mentions his refusal "to practice cunning." Instead, he openly states the truth and exposes the Serpent's cunning when he proclaims "Jesus Christ as Lord." The "god of this world," the deceitful "serpent," "by his cunning" blinds unbelievers' minds and leads believer's thoughts astray (2 Cor. 4:1–5; 11:3). His "cunning" was manifested by his refusal to mention God's gospel-revealing, glorious name, Yahweh (Gen. 3:1b–5), now incarnated and fulfilled in Jesus Christ and his gospel. The way to godly transformation, motivation, and mortification is through proclaiming Jesus Christ crucified and crowned (1 Cor. 1:23; 2 Cor. 4:5).[15]

Without Jesus Christ and a genuine devotion to him, we cannot correctly think about, rightly interpret, or truly know God, his Word, or any aspect of his creation. It has always been through God's Word that we have come to know him. In the beginning, God's *spoken words* caused creation to supernaturally materialize (Gen. 1:3, 6, 9, 11, 14, 20, 24, 26; Ps. 33:6, 9; Prov. 8:22–31; 2 Pet. 3:5), declaring his glory

---

14. For an example of seeing Christ in all Scripture, see Clowney, *Unfolding Mystery*; Bryan Chapell, *Christ-Centered Preaching: Redeeming the Expository Sermon* (Grand Rapids, MI: Baker, 1994); Graeme Goldsworthy, *Preaching the Whole Bible as Christian Scripture* (Grand Rapids, MI: Eerdmans, 2000).

15. I don't wish to detach the cross from the incarnation, resurrection, ascension, heavenly intercession, sending of the Spirit, or return. All these things are to be held together. There does, however, seem to be an emphasis in the apostolic evangel on the death and resurrection of Christ as a matter of first importance (1 Cor. 15:3–5), as well as an emphasis on God's love revealed in Jesus's crucifixion. Christ, his cross, and his crown seem to be clearly set forth as primary in our preaching, along with the implications that flow from these realities for our living.

to humanity, and giving all people knowledge of him (Ps. 19:1–6; Rom. 1:19–20). When the *eternal Word* supernaturally materialized as Jesus of Nazareth, possessing all the treasures of wisdom and knowledge and thereby revealing the Father and his love, he received the Father's name—Lord—to command every thought of every person to be subject in every way to him (Isaiah 55; John 1:1–2, 14; 2 Cor. 10:3–5; Phil. 2:9–11). We know nothing about God apart from his creative, inscripturated, and incarnate Word. Therefore, Jesus Christ, who is uniquely honored and revealed as *the* Word who makes God known, deserves exclusive preeminence as we exegete and preach God's Word, because only as we behold Jesus's face do we gain the knowledge of the glory of God, who alone is able by his Spirit and Word to redeem every human thought and transform us into Christ's image for the glory of God's name (cf. 2 Cor. 4:6).

I thank the triune God through Jesus Christ for his servant Vern S. Poythress. His love, friendship, and continued conversations still help me handle God's Word and its testimony to the eternal Word, Jesus Christ. May this essay honor the God-given legacy of one of my most respected instructors in the faith and ultimately give glory "to him who sits on the throne and to the Lamb" (Rev. 5:13).

Part 5

HISTORY

17

Christian Missions in China

A Reformed Perspective

LUKE P. Y. LU

This brief history of Christian missions to China, a narrative of three short-lived waves followed by a fourth lasting wave still redeeming the Chinese today, is dedicated to Drs. Vern and Diane Poythress in deep appreciation of and gratitude for their missionary endeavors among our Chinese kinsmen.[1]

When did Christianity first reach China? According to tradition, the gospel was brought to China either in the first century by Thomas or Bartholomew or in the fourth century through Persian or Syrian missionaries.[2] But the earliest historical "hard evidence" we have is the Nestorian Stone Tablet, which records the first wave of Chinese Christianity in the Tang dynasty.[3]

---

1. I would like to thank my daughter An-Ting Tiffany Lu, a student of both Drs. Vern and Diane Poythress, for her editorial assistance in this essay.

2. Kenneth S. Latourette, *The History of Christian Mission in China* (London: SPCK, 1929), 48–51; Samuel Hughes Moffett, *A History of Christianity in Asia*, vol. 1, *Beginnings to 1500* (Maryknoll, NY: Orbis, 1998), 288.

3. The Nestorian Stone Tablet (大秦景教流行中國碑) was discovered in AD 1623 or 1625 (Ming dynasty) at Xi-An and is now housed in the Xi-An Monuments Museum. Its content de-

The First Wave: Nestorians in the Tang Dynasty

Nestorius became patriarch of Constantinople in AD 428. In 431, accused of teaching the heretical doctrine of two separate persons of Christ, he was condemned at the Council of Ephesus and subsequently deposed from his see. Later, his supporters, mostly bishops in Syria, gradually separated themselves from the early Catholic Church, developed the heresy we now know as Nestorianism, and formed the Nestorian church.

When the Nestorians refused to subscribe to the Chalcedonian Creed (451), they were expelled from the Roman Empire. They moved east to establish a base in Edessa, and then Nisibis of Persia, where the Persian kings welcomed and supported them for political purposes against the Roman Empire. From 498, Nestorians cut their official relationship with the early Catholic Church and called themselves the "Church in the East."

NESTORIANS IN CHINA

Nestorians enthusiastically trained and sent missionaries to central Asia, from Arabia to India. Even the Thomist church in India adopted Nestorian faith and worship liturgy. With such fruitful results, they ambitiously sent missionaries to China. The road to China, called "the Silk Road," at that time was in the hands of Turks. By the year 630, the Turks were defeated by and surrendered to Emperor Tai-Zung of the Tang dynasty, thus opening China to the Nestorians. Within a few years they were recognized and well received by the emperor; according to the Nestorian Stone Tablet, in 635 the emperor arranged a diplomatic ceremony to receive the Nestorian bishop Alopen at the western field of the capital Chang-An.

The emperors of the Tang dynasty welcomed all foreign religions. With the support of the court, Nestorian Christianity flourished in China under the name "Persian Book Religion." Later, when Persia

---

scribes the origin and development of Nestorianism in China, and records how the Nestorian bishop came to the imperial capital Xi-An (old name, Chang-An) during the Tang dynasty in AD 635. This monument was made in 781, with dimensions of 9 by 3.5 feet, and about a foot thickness, weighing two tons, with more than 1900 characters inscribed. See Chih-Hsin Wang, *History of Christianity in China* (Hong Kong: Chinese Christian Literature Council, 1959), 33; Moffett, *History of Christianity in Asia*, 1:288, 314–15; Shi-Jie Cha, Chinese Church History lecture notes, China Evangelical Seminary, Taipei, Taiwan, 1984.

was conquered by Arabian Muslims, the Nestorians decided to drop the term "Persian"; with imperial approval, they changed the name to "Jing [bright or luminous] Religion" in 745 to also differentiate themselves from the Persian Zoroastrian religion.[4]

According to the Nestorian Stone Tablet (set up in 781), Nestorianism prospered in the Tang dynasty, with its temples numbering more than a hundred in all the ten provinces of China. But Nestorianism began to decline during the reign of the Emperor Wu-Zung, who in 845 ordered the destruction of all foreign religions for political and economic considerations. Thus Nestorians were dealt a heavy setback from governmental persecution: temples were destroyed, property was confiscated, and the clergy was dissolved. Meanwhile, the Silk Road was blocked by the rise of the central Asian tribe of Turfan, so that the Nestorian headquarters in Persia could no longer send missionaries. With the fall of the Tang dynasty in 907, Nestorianism faded away in China.

THE NESTORIAN METHOD OF EVANGELISM

The Nestorians in the Tang dynasty employed the strategy of "making friends in high places," lobbying for the support of high-ranking officers in the court. They even served the emperor by being ambassadors to and collecting intelligence from central Asia, and also introduced Persian military technology. Thus, Chinese emperors found Nestorians useful and agreed to support their cause.

Nestorians also instituted widespread social services. They introduced Persian medicine, which specialized in eye and gastrointestinal clinics during that period, for the purpose of missions. According to the Nestorian Stone Tablet, they took care of suffering citizens by feeding the hungry, healing the sick, and burying the dead. Thus the Nestorians' mission strategy was twofold: associate with the upper and serve the lower. With this approach, Nestorians succeeded phenomenally until the time of Wu-Zung.

Nestorianism lasted about 210 years, through the reign of fourteen emperors. While we do not know how many Chinese converted to

---

4. Ka-Lun Liang, *Blessings upon China: Ten Talks on the Contemporary Church History of China* (Hong Kong: Tien Dao, 1988), 18; Wang, *History of Christianity in China*, 37–38.

the Nestorian faith, we do know that it did not take root in China. Chinese historical records show that Nestorianism was considered a foreign religion. All the names recorded on the Nestorian Stone Tablet are of Assyrian origin. As the Nestorian churches in Persia provided manpower and finance, foreign leaders were in control.[5]

NESTORIAN INDIGENIZATION

Even though the Nestorian mission in China did not indigenize "church order and leadership," it did seek to contextualize "worship settings and doctrinal scriptures." There are very few extant Nestorian documents—only eight manuscripts in Chinese,[6] found in the Tun-Huang Grottoes in northwestern China.[7] From the Nestorian Stone and Tun-Huang manuscripts, works of literature translated by Nestorian missionaries, we see how Nestorians indigenized their faith and doctrine by translating their scriptures and hymns with the vocabularies of Buddhism and Daoism. Using contemporary popular terms in Chinese culture to teach Nestorian doctrines, they even cooperated with Buddhist monks to translate Buddhist scriptures.[8] The Nestorian chapels in China also had the emperor's portrait and esteemed writings hanging on the walls. In fact, the Nestorian chapels looked so similar to Buddhist and Daoist temples, it was not easy for people to tell the difference. Affirming the filial piety of the Chinese, in accordance with Buddhist and Daoist practice, Nestorians also adopted the custom of praying for the dead.[9]

Thus Nestorianism came to China: absorbing some of the concepts of Buddhism and Daoism, it became syncretized in doctrines and secu-

---

5. Latourette, *History of Christian Mission in China*, 58.

6. These treat the doctrine of only one God, the doctrines and acts of the Lord Jesus, the Sermon on the Mount, the Lord Jesus's sermon at Nazareth, a hymnal, doxological hymns, a list of sacred persons and books, and a Nestorian portrait. For details, see Wang, *History of Christianity in China*, 32; Cha, Chinese Church History lecture notes.

7. The Tun-Huang Grottoes (stone caves) manuscripts were discovered in 1900. Many religious documents were stored and hidden in 1028, in fear of barbarian invasions. More than twenty thousand manuscripts and wood and tablet prints were found, and they are in Chinese and other central Asian languages, dated from 410 to 1028. The majority are Buddhist documents. See Cha, Chinese Church History lecture notes; Latourette, *History of Christian Mission in China*, 53, 56.

8. The Nestorian monk Jing Jing helped a Buddhist to translate Buddhist classics, and his collaboration was recorded in Buddhist historical records. For details, see Wang, *History of Christianity in China*, 40–41.

9. For more on the debate among scholars regarding the complex relationship between Nestorianism and Buddhism and their influences on each other, see Ralph R. Covell, *Confucius, the Buddha, and Christ* (Maryknoll, NY: Orbis, 1986), 30–31.

larized in practices. This explains why on the Nestorian Stone Tablet the cross is connected with the lotus (symbol for Buddhism) and the cloud (symbol for Daoism). This kind of indigenization and contextualization resulted in syncretism with the loss of the gospel focus on the Lord Jesus as the only way for salvation.

The Second Wave: Nestorians and Catholics in the Yuan Dynasty

THE RETURN OF NESTORIANISM

While Nestorianism disappeared from China in the fall of the Tang dynasty, it still thrived among many tribes in central Asia and the northern frontier of China. When the Mongolians invaded, conquered, and ruled all of China from 1279 to 1368 (the Yuan dynasty), Nestorianism came back to China through the officers of central Asia employed by the Mongolian court.[10] In the Mongolian language, its followers were known as Erkeun (or Arkaim), meaning "blessed people, believing blessed Gospel," and it was called "God-religion" by the Mongolians.[11]

In 1289 the Yuan government set up a religious bureau to take care of the growing population of Nestorians in China, where Nestorian temples were called the temples of the cross. Many archeological discoveries (especially tomb monuments) and Chinese government documents show the prosperous development of Nestorianism in the Yuan dynasty. Even Marco Polo reported on the Nestorian chapels and population.[12]

However, Nestorian Christians in the Yuan dynasty were foreigners from central Asia and Mongolia; there were very few indigenous Chinese (majority Han) Nestorians. In the eyes of common people, Nestorianism was a religious tool used by Mongols and their associates (the so-called color-eyed people) to rule them.[13] Unlike the Nestorians

---

10. The Keraits living close to the northern boundary of China became a Nestorian tribe; their king Unc Khan was possibly "the fabled Prester John," who Europeans believed could help against Muslim invasion. See Liang, *Blessings upon China*, 21; Covell, *Confucius, the Buddha, and Christ*, 37.

11. Latourette, *History of Christian Mission in China*, 65; Liang, *Blessings upon China*, 19.

12. Wang, *History of Christianity in China*, 49–53; Latourette, *History of Christian Mission in China*, 65.

13. The color of the irises of eyes of the Han people is dark (blackish brown). The Han people called Mongols and Central Asians "the color-eyed people" because of their significantly lighter irises.

in the Tang dynasty, Nestorians in the Yuan dynasty did not undertake the work of indigenization. They did not translate the Bible into Chinese, and continued to use Syrian languages while praying and singing during worship, which the lay people did not understand. No Chinese monasteries or seminaries were set up to train the clergy. As a result, Nestorianism appeared very different from Chinese culture. It was thought only to be for the foreign immigrants of the ruling class, and sometimes these foreigners' bad behaviors left a tainted reputation for Nestorianism. Thus Nestorianism died out with the fall of the Yuan dynasty and the retreat of the Mongols.

THE ARRIVAL OF ROMAN CATHOLICISM

In the thirteenth century, during the Mongolian Yuan dynasty, Roman Catholic missionaries came to China. When Pope Innocent IV heard the news of Mongol converts to Christianity, he sent ambassadors to visit the Mongolian emperor. In 1245–1247 the Franciscan Giovanni de Plano Carpini arrived in Holing, the capital at that time. The French king Louis IX also sent William Rubruck to Holing in 1253–1255 to enlist the support of the khan against the Muslims.[14] When they discovered Nestorians in the Mongolian court, they were given the hope that the Catholic faith also could be spread among the Chinese.

Markos and Sauma were influential Uighur Nestorian monks in China, notable for their contributions in diplomacy with Eastern and Western governments in the 1270s. Sauma and his disciple Markos journeyed together on a pilgrimage to Jerusalem. In 1281 in Baghdad, Markos became the first non-Syriac-speaking patriarch of the whole Nestorian church;[15] and in 1287, Sauma became the ambassador of Arghun Khan, the emperor of the regional Mongolian Empire. Arghun sent him to meet the pope and the Christian courts to deliver two messages: (1) the Mongols as a virtually Christian nation were worthy to

---

14. Wang, *History of Christianity in China*, 53–54; Cha, Chinese Church History lecture notes; Latourette, *History of Christian Mission in China*, 65; Covell, *Confucius, the Buddha, and Christ*, 37. For more on Rubruck's report on how disturbed he was by the Nestorians in China who did not practice their faith, see Wang, *History of Christianity in China*, 60; Moffett, *History of Christianity in Asia*, 1:411; and Latourette, *History of Christian Mission in China*, 65.

15. While Markos was relatively young and not Persian, the Nestorian leadership thought it wise for political reasons to have a Mongol patriarch in a Mongol-ruled world. See Moffett, *History of Christianity in Asia*, 1:431–32. The Chinese consider the Uighur tribe part of united China, so from this perspective Markos was also the first and only Chinese Nestorian patriarch.

be allies, and (2) the Nestorian faith had no substantial difference with Constantinople and Rome. Sauma was well received by the European leaders and given blessings.[16]

After meeting Sauma in Europe, Pope Nicholas IV sent the first Catholic missionary to China. In 1294, John of Montecorvino, the Franciscan, arrived in Beijing (the Yuan dynasty's major capital) and was permitted to preach. While converting some Nestorians to the Catholic faith, he aroused the hatred of the Nestorian church there; he also succeeded in building up churches and opening orphanages. John translated portions of the New Testament, the Old Testament, and the Psalms into Mongolian or other dialects, but not Chinese, because most of his converts were not Chinese.

In 1307, John was ordained as the archbishop of the Beijing district and was in charge of the ministry to the entire region of China. When he passed away in 1328, the number of Catholics in China had reached more than ten thousand. However, most of John's successors could not endure the hardships of life in China, thus succumbing to illness or quick departures. Though a new group of missionaries was sent, very few of them reached China, because of the treacherous sea voyages. Other setbacks included the resurgence of Muslim control in central Asia during the fourteenth century, which blocked the land route to China, and the widespread Black Death.[17] Along with the fall of the Yuan dynasty and the exit of Mongols and central Asians in 1368, this foreign religion of the rich and ruling class also had its demise.[18] Thus this Franciscan-led Catholic mission died out in China in less than a generation.

The Third Wave: Roman Catholicism in the Ming and Qing Dynasties

In the sixteenth century, a new era arrived with grand geographical discoveries, political upheavals, and economic expansion. Especially of note was the loss of Catholic territories to Protestants in the rise of the Reformation. To expand its territory, Roman Catholicism renewed an

---

16. Covell, *Confucius, the Buddha, and Christ*, 37; Moffett, *History of Christianity in Asia*, 1:433–34.

17. Cha, Chinese Church History lecture notes.

18. Wang, *History of Christianity in China*, 57–62; Liang, *Blessings upon China*, 23–24.

interest in overseas missions. With the newly founded order of Jesuits, Catholicism began a brave new mission to China.

JESUITS AS PIONEERS

In 1549 Francis Xavier came to Japan to begin the Catholic mission there, in preparation of launching a mission to China. The Ming dynasty's prohibition against foreigners kept him from entering China, and he died on an nearby island in 1552. He was succeeded by Alessandro Valignani, who in 1578 arrived in Macao. Though he also could not enter mainland China, he set up the mission strategy to China: sending self-disciplined, gentle-hearted, highly learned scholar missionaries. Michael Ruggerius was the first Jesuit to enter mainland China, in 1580, as an interpreter for merchants. Later he moved to south China in 1582 as the first Catholic father. He was also the first to write a book on Roman Catholic doctrine in Chinese.[19]

Matteo Ricci came to Macao in 1582 and moved to China in 1583. He had waited eight years to enter Beijing and finally in 1601 was allowed to meet the emperor Shen-Zung to present gifts. Shen-Zung gave him permission to live and preach at the capital. He built up churches and saw the fruit of his labor before his death in 1610: Chinese converts numbered about twenty-five hundred, and Catholic chapels were set up in several major cities. Many high-ranking officers in the court became believers.[20]

THE JESUIT MISSION STRATEGY

Ricci's strategy, "first Western scholarship, then Catholic doctrine," became the paradigm of the Jesuit mission. Jesuit fathers wrote books to introduce Western science and technology, as well as books on doctrine and ethics. Ricci observed that the dominant influence in Chinese culture was Confucian teaching, and that it was good but not enough. He proposed that Chinese intellectuals use Jesus's teaching to complete or enhance Confucius's teaching. This affirmative approach won the hearts of both Chinese scholars and the laity.

19. Latourette, *History of Christian Mission in China*, 86–91; Cha, Chinese Church History lecture notes.
20. Latourette, *History of Christian Mission in China*, 91–98; Cha, Chinese Church History lecture notes.

This synthesis method worked out very well. The success was so great that suspicion and opposition arose in the court. But it could not stop the progress of the Catholic mission. Later, Dominicans and Franciscans came to China and launched their mission works separately. By the fall of the Ming dynasty in 1644, the total number of converts had reached 150,000.[21]

THE CATHOLIC MISSION IN THE QING DYNASTY

When the Qing dynasty began its rule over China, Catholicism was treated with favor. Missionaries were still employed in the court and were allowed to continue their mission works. Despite initial opposition from court officers, Emperor Kang-Xi soon approved the doctrines of Catholicism and became the first emperor to publicly legitimize Catholicism in China.

Later the Rites Controversy brought Kang-Xi to first reprove and then ultimately prohibit Catholicism in China. Ricci and the Jesuits thought that the Chinese ancestor-worship rites were not idolatry but merely a cultural way to show filial piety. So they allowed Chinese converts to perform these rites. But the conservative Dominicans, with the support of Franciscans, contended with the Jesuits. Both sides appealed to the papacy from 1645 to 1704, and finally Pope Clement XI decreed that all the rites involved should be prohibited. This offended Kang-Xi, and in 1720 he ordered a stop to the Catholic mission in China. However, the main purpose of this decree was to show the government's displeasure, and so it was not seriously executed. He still allowed the Jesuits to conduct mission works because he desired their scientific and technological knowledge. Franciscans and Dominicans, however, were banished.[22]

In 1742, Pope Benedict XIV decreed the reconfirmation of the prohibition with no exceptions. In 1773 the order of Jesuits was dissolved by Pope Clement XIV. This was a great setback and downfall for the Catholic mission in China. The emperor after Kang-Xi was Yung-Jeng, who disliked the missionaries, and in 1724 he issued an edict

21. Liang, *Blessings upon China*, 25–26; Cha, Chinese Church History lecture notes.
22. Cha, Chinese Church History lecture notes; Latourette, *History of Christian Mission in China*, 140–48.

that totally prohibited Catholic missions. His successors continued this prohibition by expelling the missionaries and persecuting Chinese converts. While there were still Chinese Catholics, with 210,000 members reported in 1800, all churches outside Beijing had to operate underground and thus had no significant societal influence.[23]

REFLECTION

While Nestorianism in the Tang dynasty adopted Chinese customs resulting in syncretism, Catholicism in the Qing dynasty insisted on doctrinal purity in the Rites Controversy. Even when faced with the emperor's opposition and threats, the papacy did not compromise. However, in the twentieth century, the table was turned, and the ban of ancestor worship rites was lifted by the Vatican in 1939.[24] In Taiwan, the Chinese cardinal now leads the yearly public ceremony of memorializing ancestors on January 1st, showing that the rites adopted by Jesuits are recognized no longer as worship but as memorializing. Such memorializing is now encouraged.

The Jesuit accommodation of Confucianism won the hearts of Chinese intellectuals. Jesuits studied Chinese culture with perseverance, connected with elites in the court, and endured the hardships of persecutions. They conducted the foundational work of training the local Chinese to be priests from the outset of the mission, wrote Catholic doctrinal literature in Chinese, and translated the Bible into Chinese. They presented Catholicism as a holistic system to complement Confucianism and to proselytize the Chinese elites. The Jesuits had great success in the initial stage. Were it not for the Rites Controversy, Catholicism may have prospered in China indefinitely.

The Fourth Wave: Protestant Missionaries in the Qing Dynasty

The Protestant overseas mission movement, as a whole, occurred much later than Roman Catholic missionary efforts. William Carey, the fa-

---

23. Latourette, *History of Christian Mission in China*, 158–67; Liang, *Blessings upon China*, 30. For more on the Chinese Rites Controversy, see *The Chinese Rites Controversy: Its History and Meaning*, ed. David E. Mungello (Sankt Augustin: Institut Monumenta Serica; San Francisco: Ricci Institute for Chinese-Western Cultural History, 1994).

24. Mungello, *Chinese Rites Controversy*, 250.

ther of Protestant overseas missions, went to India in 1793. Then in the early nineteenth century, the Protestants began their mission to China. The troubles and hardships they faced were greater than what Nestorian and Catholic missionaries had encountered. Foreigners were forbidden to enter China, and preaching the gospel was illegal. Any Chinese who taught foreigners the Chinese language were threatened with the death penalty. The only place for Western merchants to trade was in the southern region of Guangzhou, and only for a limited season each year. And the only place for them to stay was offshore, on the island of Macao. All this made personal evangelism difficult, dangerous, and virtually impossible.

THE PREPARATION PERIOD, 1807–1842

The first Protestant missionary, Robert Morrison, a Presbyterian, was sent to China by the nondenominational London Missionary Society. In 1807 he arrived in Macao and was disliked by all; the Portuguese Catholics despised him, and the British East India Company worried that his mission effort might disturb the status quo. After two years of learning Chinese, he had to join the East India Company as an interpreter in order to stay in Macao.

Morrison spent much of his time invested in literature work. Initially, he prepared a Chinese-English dictionary and wrote gospel tracts. Most importantly, he began translating the Bible. In 1811 he published his catechism, based on the Westminster Shorter Catechism, the first piece of Reformed doctrine in Chinese.[25] Great encouragement and help came in 1812 with the arrival of William Milne, a fellow Scottish Presbyterian. With his assistance, Morrison continued to translate the Bible, finishing the New Testament in 1814 and Old Testament in 1818. The first complete Chinese Bible translated by Protestant missionaries was finally published in 1823. Morrison published his famous six-volume Chinese dictionary in 1821, which continued to be a standard reference for many generations.[26]

---

25. Michael M——, "Robert Morrison's Catechism (1811)," in *China's Reforming Churches: Mission, Polity, and Ministry in the Next Christendom*, ed. Bruce P. Baugus (Grand Rapids, MI: Reformed Heritage Books, 2014), 309–10.

26. *The Oxford Dictionary of the Christian Church*, 2nd ed., ed. F. L. Cross and E. A. Livingstone (Oxford: Oxford University Press, 1974), 942.

Morrison and Milne decided to set up a safe base in Malacca (Malaysia), and Milne moved there in 1815 to start a preparatory school to educate Chinese Christians. In 1818, the Anglo-Chinese College was officially founded there, before relocating to Hong Kong in 1843. It played a vital role in training youth for the Christianization and modernization of China.[27]

In 1814, Morrison baptized the first Chinese convert, Tsai Gau, in Macao, the first fruit of his seven years of service there. Tsai helped Morrison covertly print tracts in Macao.[28] In 1819, the printer William H. Medhurst came to join Morrison and Milne. With his help, large quantities of the Chinese Bible, tracts, and treatises were published in Malacca and sent to China secretly through Macao. Liang Afa, a printing worker brought to Malacca by Milne, was converted and baptized by Milne in 1816 and became the first Chinese minister. He returned to China as an ordained minister in 1824 and wrote and distributed tracts in a street evangelism ministry.[29]

During this early phase of Protestant missions, there were no more than 150 Chinese converts. The majority of them were located in Malacca, mostly among common and illiterate people.[30] But through literature, education, and Bible translation, Morrison and his associates built a solid foundation for the future development of Protestant missions.

THE ENTRY PERIOD, 1842–1860

The Opium War ended with the Treaty of Nanking in 1842. Five treaty ports were forced open to foreigners, and Hong Kong was ceded to Britain. Thus there were six places for missionaries to preach the gospel. Many missions moved their bases to Hong Kong or Shanghai. Schools, orphanages, and hospitals were opened for evangelism. Protestant missionaries grasped this new opportunity to proclaim the gospel with the hope of entering the inland in the future. Roman Catholics also took this opportunity to renew their missions in China.

---

27. Peter Tze Ming Ng, *Chinese Christianity: An Interplay between Global and Local Perspectives* (Leiden: Brill, 2012), 46.
28. Wang, *History of Christianity in China*, 152–53.
29. Ibid., 154–57.
30. Christopher Tang, *The First Hundred Years of Protestant Mission in China* (Hong Kong: Dao Sheng), 129; Cha, Chinese Church History lecture notes.

Passing out gospel tracts and booklets was one effective method of evangelism to the literate, though the illiteracy rate was as high as 95 percent.[31] Gospel literature was sometimes misused for political gain: a gospel booklet written by Liang Afa influenced Hong Xiu Quan, who identified a "supernatural vision" with Christian faith; from 1851 to 1864 he led the Tai Ping (Great Peace) Heavenly Kingdom movement, a political revolution eventually put down by the Qing dynasty with Western support. In the eyes of missionaries, the Tai Ping movement was not only heretical in faith but also a political movement under the disguise of religion.[32]

In this period, about 150 Protestant missionaries entered China, set up 22 chapels, and won 350 converts, mostly among nonintellectuals. Some of the initial converts were trained to be assistants to missionaries, but since they were not highly educated, they had little cultural influence. But by the next generation, young men were trained from the cradle in Western education by missionary-founded Christian schools.[33] Some were sent to America for higher education, and when they returned to China, they became leaders and specialists in many fields, including infrastructure, railroads, engineering, business, and trade. They played an important role in the modernization of China.

THE GROWING PERIOD, 1860–1900

With the signing of the Treaty of Tianjin (1858) and the Treaty of Beijing (1860), China was forced to open more ports for trade. Thanks to the "toleration clause" in these treaties, missionaries were permitted to go into inland China. But in the eyes of the Chinese, Western missionaries were associated with the unequal treaties, because they served as interpreters for drafting them. So the Chinese viewed Christianity as the tool for Western imperialism, and hatred toward missionaries grew.

From 1860 on, conflicts between Chinese community leaders and Christian missionaries and converts escalated sharply. Anti-Christian riots occurred in almost all the provinces of China and caused the martyrdom of many missionaries and converts. These conflicts reached a

---

31. Liang, *Blessings upon China*, 44.
32. For details, see Latourette, *History of Christian Mission in China*, 282–302; Wang, *History of Christianity in China*, 169–83; Covell, *Confucius, the Buddha, and Christ*, 150–81.
33. Cha, Chinese Church History lecture notes.

304   Luke P. Y. Lu

climax at the government-supported Boxers' Uprising in 1900. Though it was defeated by a united army of eight foreign countries, the uprising took many lives of missionaries and converts. Catholics lost more than 18,000 lives, and Protestants almost 7,000.[34] China lost more than 100,000 people and had to pay a huge amount of indemnity: 450 million units of silver (worth five years' income of China's national treasury) in 39 years.[35]

Yet these conflicts could not stop the progress of the Protestant mission in China. According to the records of the General Conference of Protestant Missionaries in China, the First Conference (1877) reported 13,035 communicant members, a number that grew to 37,287 by the Second Conference (1890); and by the Third Conference (1907), the centennial of the arrival of Robert Morrison, the count had reached 178,251 baptized members.[36]

MISSION STRATEGY: TAYLOR'S MODEL

Hudson Taylor (1832–1905) first came to China in 1853. He founded China Inland Mission (CIM) in 1865. The vision of CIM was to enter the unreached inland's eleven provinces and Mongolia, and not to duplicate mission works by others in coastal provinces. CIM was a nondenominational faith mission that did not solicit financial donations, a vision of Taylor shared by the missionaries who joined CIM. Later CIM became the largest mission, Protestant or Catholic, having the greatest number of missionaries.[37]

CIM's strategy was called "Taylor's Model," whereby the gospel was preached directly. Its theology was conservative and evangelical. Along with personal evangelism, CIM provided primary-school education and medical services to support this evangelism and to build up churches. Its emphasis was to save souls directly and not to focus first on cultural influence. Thus CIM worked mostly among the bottom level of society rather than targeting the elite. With this "from bottom up" strategy, CIM became the most fruitful, influential mission. Tay-

---

34. Latourette, *History of Christian Mission in China*, 501–18; Wang, *History of Christianity in China*, 231.
35. Liang, *Blessings upon China*, 116.
36. Tang, *First Hundred Years*, 644–46.
37. Ibid., 470.

lor's Model would be the mainstream method among missionaries all over China until 1890.[38]

MISSION STRATEGY: RICHARD'S MODEL

Timothy Richard (1845–1919) was sent to China in 1870 by the Baptist Missionary Society, though he left that organization and became an independent missionary in 1890. His theology was liberal, and his goal was to import Western science and democracy to transform China. Like Matteo Ricci, he compromised with Chinese culture and religions in order to influence the upper class. His emphasis was on saving China by changing the political and cultural milieu, and he worked among intellectuals in prominent positions. His strategy was called "Richard's Model" in contrast with Taylor's Model.[39]

Under Richard's Model, the first priority in China was not to practice direct evangelism but to Westernize the mind-set of the Chinese, to make it easier for them to accept Christianity eventually. In other words, Richard's method was to fulfill the cultural mandate first, not the gospel mandate. After 1890, more and more liberal missionaries came to China and adopted his model.[40]

EVALUATION OF MISSION MODELS

Since the late nineteenth century, Taylor's Model and Richard's Model have become two major competing strategies. Though Richard's goal was to transform Chinese culture through westernization, the Chinese accepted Western Christian culture to some degree yet rejected Christianity. Some intellectuals appreciated Christian culture but did not accept the Christian gospel. They believed in Christian culture only; today such people are called "Cultural Christians." Richard's dream of using Western culture to win the hearts of Chinese elite leaders was not fulfilled.[41]

Nevertheless, the fourth wave of Christian missions to China launched the first truly biblical gospel movement in China. Hudson

---

38. Cha, Chinese Church History lecture notes; Liang, *Blessings upon China*, 98.
39. Tang, *First Hundred Years*, 486; Liang, *Blessings upon China*, 98–99. For details on Timothy Richard's methodology of mission, see Ng, *Chinese Christianity*, 111–32.
40. Liang, *Blessings upon China*, 99; Cha, Chinese Church History lecture notes.
41. Liang, *Blessings upon China*, 99; Tang, *First Hundred Years*, 486.

Taylor and CIM missionaries held fast to conservative theology and preached the gospel directly. Their mission works enjoyed tremendous success in the twentieth century. Faithfully following the gospel mandate, they showed that Christian missionaries should preach the gospel, not Western culture, because the Christian gospel is the truth that transcends all human cultures, East or West.

Christianity in China in the First Half of the Twentieth Century

The Qing dynasty fell in 1911, and China became the first republic in Asia. Her founding father, Sun Yat-Sen, was a Protestant Christian. However, with the founding of the new republic, China entered a long, unstable period of internal political strife. The Nationalist Party defeated all the warlords and unified the country. Yet the Communist Party rose in 1921 and brought disunity and disorder. Then the Japanese invasion caused a war of eight years. Finally, the Communists took over China and founded the People's Republic of China in 1949.

In this new context, as China was struggling for political independence from foreign imperialism and trying to respond to all the inroads of new ideologies, the Protestant mission pressed onward. The number of Protestant communicants increased to 235,303 in 1914; and though still few in number, Protestants occupied prominent positions in political and economic arenas, as well as in education, medicine, and other fields. Their influence extended widely in this new China and its modernization challenges.[42]

ANTI-CHRISTIAN CHALLENGES

The May Fourth movement in 1919, though purportedly patriotic, was actually anti-tradition, anti-Western, and anti-religion in spirit. The anti-Christian movements in 1922–1927 among the college students and political parties created social upheaval. Christian leaders realized the urgent need for indigenization of Christianity in China. Protestant leaders took two approaches in response: one was active involvement in social reform; and the other, passive withdrawal from worldly issues in order to emphasize the spiritual alone.[43]

---

42. Covell, *Confucius, the Buddha, and Christ*, 186–87.
43. Ibid., 187.

THE SOCIAL-ACTIVIST RESPONSE

Those who were actively involved in producing a Christianized Chinese culture and society included Cheng Jingyi, Zhao Zichen (T. C. Chao), Wu Yaozong (Y. T. Wu), and Wu Leizhuan. Their failure may have stemmed from the lack of a concrete program to work out their agenda or a lack of societal influence. But perhaps the real reason was that they based their proposals on social philosophies, not uniquely Christian positions. Their efforts at indigenization were compromises with Chinese traditional culture in various degrees. While Richard's Model accommodated *Western* culture at the expense of the gospel, the social activists accommodated *Chinese* culture, also at the expense of biblical truth.

THE PIETIST-EVANGELIST RESPONSE

As mentioned above, Taylor's Model, "the Gospel and Revival Way," was to preach the gospel to save souls alone and to avoid social activism. The leaders in this camp engaged in building up indigenous churches were Watchman Nee, Wang Mingdao, and John Sung the revivalist. Nee led the Local Church movement, calling people to leave denominational churches controlled by Western missionaries.[44] The True Jesus Church was another indigenous body with Pentecostal practices. The Jesus Family was unique with its Christian farm communes. These three were the most famous of the Chinese independent church groups in the first half of the twentieth century to call for removal of Western influences.

CHURCH UNION MOVEMENT

The Chinese Church Union movement was another response to the call for removing Western influences from Chinese Christianity. The Chinese were growing increasingly averse to church operations under foreign names such as the London Missionary Society. To preserve the unity of an indigenous church amid outsider attacks and inner conflicts, smaller denominations—even of differing stripes—united to become bigger denominations with Chinese indigenous names. In 1927 a

---

44. For more on Watchman Nee and the Local Church movement, see Luke P. Y. Lu, "Watchman Nee's Doctrine of the Church with Special Reference to Its Contribution to the Local Church Movement" (PhD diss., Westminster Theological Seminary, 1992).

"Chinese Christian Church" composed of nineteen denominations had its first national assembly. While the American Laymen's Foreign Missions Inquiry of 1930 criticized this union as illegitimate and ineffective, in general this alliance was a milestone of sorts for the rise of native Chinese church leadership, progress on the road of indigenization.[45]

Even amid the turmoil of the Japanese Invasion and the Nationalist-Communist War in the 1930–1940s, the Protestant Church in China grew consistently. Before the Communists took over China in 1949, the number of Protestants reached about a million. Compared with 178,251 in 1907, this was significant growth.

Christianity in China after 1949

With the founding of the People's Republic of China in 1949, the Chinese church entered a new stage. Marxist Communism became the sole dominant ideology. The missionaries were driven out, the church leaders were persecuted, and many churches were forced to close. The Three-Self Patriotic Movement (TSPM) was instituted by Communists to control the Protestant churches. All churches were under state control. Then the Cultural Revolution (1966–1976) was a great disaster in all areas of China, and all churches were closed. After the revolution, the TSPM resumed, and the state churches reopened. Yet the underground house churches grew like mushrooms after the rain.[46]

Despite a long period of suffering, the house churches still thrive. Today the estimated number of Protestant Christians is 80–100 million. It is a miracle in the history of missions: a hundredfold growth from 1949, when the Western missionaries were driven out and Chinese church leaders imprisoned.

Conclusion

From the above historical review of the four waves of Christian missions in China, we have learned significant lessons:

---

45. Perhaps a modern analogy would be of the association of Reformed churches under the North American Presbyterian and Reformed Council (NAPARC). For more on the Church Union movement, see Liang, *Blessings upon China*, 159–60.

46. For a brief history of the origin and development of TSPM, see Jonathan Chao, *Prophetic Penetration: Critique of Chinese Communist Religions Policy and the TSPM* (Taipei: China Ministries International, 1993), 275–88.

1. The orthodox faith of the biblical gospel is the foundation of the church of Christ. Any dilution or compromise of biblical doctrines will result in a drift away from the orthodox faith, a rise in heresy, and an ineffective and short-lived mission. The Nestorian "Jing Religion" is one unfortunate example.[47]

2. The church of Christ is *in* the world, but not *of* the world. The gospel is to be preached in fallen cultures. If one treats the gospel and culture equally—without distinction, "harmonizing" them—then disaster will come. Some Chinese missions mingled the gospel with Chinese culture because they viewed the gospel as special redemptive revelation and Chinese culture as general revelation; the two were said to be in harmony such that they could be and should be united. But the problem is that Chinese Confucian culture is *not* general revelation itself but only sinners' reflection and response to it. The biblical gospel does not cooperate or integrate with culture on equal terms but instead transcends, judges, transforms, and redeems all culture. Matteo Ricci's Jesuit way of "using Jesus to complete Confucius" is an example of an unbiblical harmonization of the gospel and culture.

3. The preaching of the gospel occurs in the context of the world. Of course the text (gospel) is in the context (Chinese culture). However the context must not change the text. The so-called indigenization mission movement failed in China because the missionaries allowed Chinese culture to dominate, shape and compromise the gospel message. This kind of "contextualization" is not biblical and is syncretism at best. The true light of the gospel has shown into the dark land of China since 1807 when Robert Morrison brought Protestant and Reformed doctrines to China. Hudson Taylor continued to hold on to and proclaim the genuine gospel of Christ. Timothy Richard, as a missionary of liberalism, brought Western science and democracy to transform China. Sadly, his agenda to build the kingdom of God on earth delivered no clear biblical message of the gospel.

---

47. Luke P. Y. Lu, *The Faith of Our Fathers: Lectures on the Early Church History* (Taipei: Reformed, 2012), 287.

For the issue of contextualization of the gospel in Chinese or other cultures, the biblical doctrines of antithesis and common grace[48] can provide safeguards for sailing through the dangerous waters between Scylla and Charybdis. Antithesis (holding that special revelation of the gospel is antithetical to and above fallen cultures) guides us to maintain the purity of the gospel in the context of culture. Common grace (recognizing that general revelation is received in fallen cultures) teaches us how to approach biblical contextualization for preaching the gospel on earth. Thus the biblical worldview plays a very important role in preaching the gospel in China. The gospel mandate *includes* the cultural mandate. The cultural mandate cannot be separated from the gospel mandate. We do not have two mandates, but one, which is the Great Commission. The gospel is to transform culture. Antithesis helps us not to mingle the gospel with culture, and common grace helps us not to sever the gospel from the context of the diverse cultures it aims to redeem. So the gospel is preached *in* the culture but is not *of* the culture. And both the transcendence and the immanence of the gospel of Christ are maintained.

Concerning the prospect of Christianity and future evangelization in China, we need the holistic, full-orbed system of the Reformed doctrine of faith and life. We must give the Chinese churches the whole counsel of God and not just fragments of it.[49] Let us heed the testimony of a Western missionary who worked in China during the first half of twentieth century and, with others, confessed in retrospect:

> I have been deeply impressed with statements from China lamenting the fact that we did not in time give the Chinese church a theology and a true doctrine of the missionary obligation. The first full-orbed doctrine which the Chinese have received is Marxism. We did not give them a doctrine of the church in the purpose of God. Let us not make the same mistake in other parts of the world while there is still time."[50]

---

48. For a detailed discussion on Cornelius Van Til's view on antithesis and common grace, see John M. Frame, *Cornelius Van Til: An Analysis of His Thought* (Phillipsburg, NJ: P&R, 1995), 187–23; Greg L. Bahnsen, *Van Til's Apologetic: Readings and Analysis* (Phillipsburg, NJ: P&R, 1998), 272–311, 424–36.

49. Luke P. Y. Lu, "Why Chinese Churches Need Biblical Presbyterianism," in Baugus, *China's Reforming Churches*, 133–35.

50. John A. Mackay, "The Great Commission and the Church Today," in *Missions under the Cross*, ed. Norman Goodall (New York: Friendship, 1953), 139.

The Chinese church is in urgent need of a full-orbed doctrine of the biblical worldview on every subject.[51] By God's grace, Dr. Poythress has provided us a great help. His books on biblical inerrancy and hermeneutics form a solid foundation for preaching the biblical gospel. His books in the "Redeeming" series on subjects such as logic, science, sociology, philosophy, and mathematics are excellent cultural applications and contextualizations of each subject; they are faithful to the presupposition of seeing all of life through the lens of God's special revelation. With the aim of taking "every thought captive to obey Christ," Dr. Poythress's works on the scriptural text and the context are essential in supporting a full-orbed biblical doctrine and application. I pray that the Lord will use him mightily and raise others to continue to write and minister among the Chinese, to the praise of God's glory.

---

51. For this shared concern, see also Samuel Ling, "A Second Chance," in *Chinese Intellectuals and Gospel*, ed. Samuel Ling and Stacey Bieler (San Gabriel, CA: China Horizon, 1999), 6–8.

18

Historiography

Redeeming History

DIANE POYTHRESS

Choose one:

1. Luther was a representative of the poor, suppressed peasants.
2. Luther was a heretic.
3. Luther was driven by perceived need of a father's approval.

This is a test of worldviews, not history.[1] Yet authors write historical accounts from divergent worldviews, often without anyone critiquing them. Many historians consider history a noncreated, materialistic, self-propagating, man-made, and man-centered effect.[2] They begin

---

1. "Impersonalism corrupts sociology and social anthropology and . . . the study of history, which together would claim to offer us godless ways of understanding our situations (a situational perspective)" (Vern S. Poythress, *Inerrancy and Worldview: Answering Modern Challenges to the Bible* [Wheaton, IL: Crossway, 2012], 232).

2. See Norman F. Cantor, *Inventing the Middle Ages* (New York: William Morrow, 1991), 18. He catalogs how the lives of over twenty-eight historians affected their views. "What was wrong was not the application of powerful modern ideas to interpreting the Middle Ages but the lack of the self-critical temperament to recognize their limitations and to reexamine assumptions periodically."

with a naturalistic view, excluding God, and end with fatalistic chaos.[3] This is in direct opposition to God's Word:

> The lot is cast into the lap,
>   but its every decision is from the LORD. (Prov. 16:33)[4]

Some historians concentrate on man's motivations: psychological, economical, social, contextual, ethnic, cultural, and national. Some look at larger sweeping movements that produce "inevitable" results: the Black Death plague, drought that leads to the grabbing of another's resources, or inventions and discoveries that switch societal power bases, but with no acknowledgment of God.[5] These secondary causes often become autonomous, usurping God as the the primary cause.[6]

A Christian, however, is commanded not to be deceived by the world's views but to filter everything through the Word of God. "O Timothy, guard the deposit entrusted to you. Avoid the irreverent babble and contradictions of what is falsely called 'knowledge,' for by professing it some have swerved from the faith" (1 Tim. 6:20–21). How are Christians to interpret history? Christians are to interpret history as part of general revelation through applying special revelation.[7] We will look at (1) time/history as created and controlled by God, (2) time's significance as reflecting the person and will of God in general and special revelation, (3) the necessity of bias by the historiographer, (4) objections, and (5) applications.

---

3. See Vern S. Poythress, *The Miracles of Jesus: How the Savior's Mighty Acts Serve as Signs of Redemption* (Wheaton, IL: Crossway, 2016); Poythress, *Redeeming Science: A God-Centered Approach* (Wheaton, IL: Crossway, 2006); and Poythress, *The Lordship of Christ: Serving Our Savior All of the Time, in All of Life, with All of Our Heart* (Wheaton, IL: Crossway, 2016). "It [the position of Plato, Aristotle, Aquinas, and Kant] consists of a natural theology that must, according to the force of its interpretative principle, reduce the historic process of differentiation, as told in the Confession, to dialectical movements of a reason that is sufficient to itself" (Cornelius Van Til, "Nature and Scripture," in *The Infallible Word: A Symposium by the Members of the Faculty of Westminster Theological Seminary*, ed. N. B. Stonehouse and Paul Woolley, 3rd ed. [Philadelphia: Presbyterian and Reformed, 1967], 301, discussed 283–301).

4. See also Prov. 16:1, 3–4, 7, 9, 33.

5. See Vern Sheridan Poythress, *Redeeming Sociology: A God-Centered Approach* (Wheaton, IL: Crossway, 2011).

6. D. A. Carson points out that models of interpretation that exclude God not only examine various categories but also look to those categories as the source for solutions (resulting in idolatry) ("This Present Evil Age," in *These Last Days: A Christian View of History*, ed. Richard D. Phillips and Gabriel N. E. Fluhrer [Phillipsburg, NJ: P&R, 2011], 17–37).

7. "Just as the Confession's doctrine of Scripture may be set forth under definite notions of its necessity, its authority, its sufficiency and its perspicuity, so the Confession's doctrine of revelation in nature may be set forth under corresponding notions of necessity, authority, sufficiency and perspicuity" (Van Til, "Nature and Scripture," 264).

Time Created and Controlled

Where does a Christian begin to understand history? God is the beginning. In him are both the creational and the volitional aspects of history. He created time.

History is a subset of created time. It is past time. Therefore, it has a distinct beginning (creation) and a distinct end (now).[8] God exists outside the created reality called "time." Time obeys his will, and not just like a wound-up clock created at the beginning. He sovereignly controls its every nanosecond as the immanent, personal, omnipotent God.[9]

We know God authored time because he exists eternally, whereas the universe does not. "In the beginning, God created the heavens and the earth" (Gen. 1:1).[10] Jesus prays, "And now, Father, glorify me in your own presence with the glory that I had with you before the world existed" (John 17:5; see also Jude 25). God is independent of time, yet immanently controls it. God is eternal, but time and matter are not. Scientific law, correctly stated, says that matter cannot be created or destroyed—*apart from the will of God.*[11] God will destroy it.

> But by the same word the heavens and earth that now exist are stored up for fire, being kept until the day of judgment and destruction of the ungodly.
> . . . The heavens will pass away with a roar, and the heavenly bodies will be burned up and dissolved. (2 Pet. 3:7, 10)

Since God created matter, he can also destroy it. Since God created time, he can also destroy it. Time is a finite creation, dependent on an infinite Creator God for its existence.

We know God controls time. By this I do not mean only the existence or nonexistence of time. I also mean the contents of time. God sovereignly controls, by his free volition, what happens and when it

---

8. For an earlier view of historiography interacting with Berkouwer, see Diane Poythress, "Johannes Oecolampadius' Exposition of Isaiah, Chapters 36–37," 2 vols. (PhD diss., Westminster Theological Seminary, 1992), 1:xvi–xxxiii.

9. See Vern S. Poythress, *Chance and the Sovereignty of God: A God-Centered Approach to Probability and Random Events* (Wheaton. IL: Crossway, 2014).

10. See Vern S. Poythress, *Christian Interpretations of Genesis 1* (Phillipsburg, NJ: P&R., 2013); and Poythress, *Did Adam Exist?* (Phillipsburg, NJ: P&R, 2014).

11. See Poythress, *Redeeming Science*; Poythress, *Philosophy, Science, and the Sovereignty of God* (Nutley, NJ: Presbyterian and Reformed, 1976).

happens. This occurs at the microscopic level. "For by him [Christ] all things were created, in heaven and on earth, visible and invisible, whether thrones or dominions or rulers or authorities—all things were created through him and for him. And he is before all things, and in him all things hold together" (Col. 1:16–17). It happens on the personal level, such as the birth of a baby. So God told Abraham, "I will surely return to you about this time next year, and Sarah your wife shall have a son" (Gen. 18:10). It happens on the grander scale of kingdoms and wars. So God told Daniel, "Then a mighty king shall arise, who shall rule with great dominion and do as he wills. And as soon as he has arisen, his kingdom shall be broken and divided" (Dan. 11:3–4). The contents of time are in God's hands, and he turns them, including men's hearts, however he desires (Prov. 21:1). The exact days of a person's life, of your life and my life, have already been determined.

> Your eyes saw my unformed substance;
> in your book were written, every one of them,
>> the days that were formed for me,
>> when as yet there was none of them. (Ps. 139:16)

The Significance of Time

So we have seen that time is created and is under God's control. But what is its significance? It is twofold.

First, God's person is imaged in creation, in general revelation.[12] "For what can be known about God is plain to them, because God has shown it to them. For his invisible attributes, namely, his eternal power and divine nature, have been clearly perceived, ever since the creation of the world, in the things that have been made" (Rom. 1:19–20). We can see that God's expressed will in time, in creation, is a reflection of who he is as a person.[13] Time, and its subset of history, have been made.

---

12. "The perspicuity of God's revelation in nature depends for its very meaning upon the fact that it is an aspect of the total and totally voluntary revelation of a God who is self-contained" (Van Til, "Nature and Scripture," 277).

13. See Vern S. Poythress, *Perspectives on the Trinity* (Phillipsburg, NJ: P&R, forthcoming). "God's actions are significant, because they express who he is; God is always acting in history" (Poythress, *Theophany: A Biblical Theology of God's Appearing* [Wheaton, IL: Crossway, forthcoming]).

Therefore, we can see God's invisible attributes in them. We can see them *clearly*, according to God's Word. God's person is reflected in history. God is good. Therefore, "for those who love God all things work together for good, for those who are called according to his purpose" (Rom. 8:28). God is holy. Therefore, "those whom he predestined he also called, and those whom he called he also justified, and those whom he justified he also glorified" (Rom. 8:30). God is loving and compassionate. Therefore, he "gave himself as a ransom for all, which is the testimony given at the proper time" (1 Tim. 2:6). More could be pursued and nuances added in a longer treatment of the subject. However, we can see from Scripture that history clearly shows God's attributes.

The second significance of time/history is the accomplishment of God's will. This is spelled out in Scripture, special revelation. God made man in his image. Instead of destroying all of Adam's posterity after the first sin, in compassionate love God redeemed men. History is the time of that creation and redemption.[14] All of history would be in vain had Christ not come. Paul states, "And if Christ has not been raised, your faith is futile and you are still in your sins" (1 Cor. 15:16–22, at 17). All people would go to hell, condemned by the one sin, or the many sins, that made them unholy and separated from a holy God. Jesus alone can unroll the scroll of time, of redemptive history.[15] His will is that he will be in an eternal relationship of glory with his people, and that all things will be consummated in Christ.[16]

> . . . making known to us the mystery of his will, according to his purpose, which he set forth in Christ as a plan for the fullness of time, to unite all things in him, things in heaven and things on earth.

---

14. "The forces of nature are always at the beck and call of the power of differentiation that works toward redemption and reprobation" (Van Til, "Nature and Scripture," 268).

15. See Rev. 5:2–3, 5. See also Vern Sheridan Poythress, *The Returning King: A Guide to the Book of Revelation* (Phillipsburg, NJ: P&R, 2000). Also Poythress, *Understanding Dispensationalists* (Grand Rapids, MI: Zondervan, 1987).

16. "The reflection of glory will be realized consummately, on a cosmic scale, in the new heaven and the new earth. . . . The compressed revelation of God's glory in theophany is analogous to the more extended revelation of God in the course of history. The theophanies show us, in God himself, a pattern representing the dynamics of all of history" (Poythress, *Theophany* [forthcoming]). See Vern S. Poythress, "History of Salvation in the Old Testament: Preparing the Way for Christ," in *ESV Study Bible*, ed. Wayne Grudem et al. (Wheaton, IL: Crossway, 2008), 2635–61, which points to Christ in each chapter of the Old Testament; Poythress, *The Shadow of Christ in the Law of Moses* (Brentwood, TN: Wolgemuth & Hyatt, 1991); and Poythress, "Biblical Hermeneutics," in *Seeing Christ in All of Scripture*, ed. Peter A. Lillback (Glenside, PA: Westminster Seminary Press, 2016), 9–16.

In him, we have obtained an inheritance, having been predestined according to the purpose of him who works all things according to the counsel of his will, so that we who were the first to hope in Christ, might be to the praise of his glory. (Eph. 1:9–12)

Special revelation gives us this understanding of the goal, the telos, of creation. We can know the purpose of time and history.

The Necessity of Bias

God, the Creator and controller of history, has revealed himself within time through creation and the Word—in particular, the Word made flesh, which is Jesus Christ. However, each of us must discern this revelation in truth. We can understand God's person and will by understanding his Word.[17] But this poses the greatest problem among historians today. They think that the sinful human mind, without the aid of God, can comprehend and interpret God or his will in historical time. This is a false assumption based on the pride of the rebellious heart. "The natural person does not accept the things of the Spirit of God, for they are folly to him, and he is not able to understand them because they are spiritually discerned" (1 Cor. 2:14). We can no more understand history apart from God than we can read English literature without knowing English. By common grace, we might be able to discern certain grammatical patterns, which in and of themselves are true. But the entirety of the piece remains foolishness, open to mere subjective speculation. There must be a true communication among situational, normative, existential/personal aspects.[18] Bluntly, history can be understood only by those who know the Author.[19]

This is not a mere knowledge of facts, nor a mere assent to those facts. As Jesus told Nicodemus, "You must be born again" (John 3:7). Nicodemus was a ruler and teacher of the Jews, a member of the Sanhedrin, knowledgeable in all the laws and an expert in Scripture. But

---

17. See Vern Sheridan Poythress, *In the Beginning Was the Word: Language—A God-Centered Approach* (Wheaton, IL: Crossway, 2009).

18. See 1 Cor. 2:14–16. See also Vern S. Poythress, *God-Centered Biblical Interpretation* (Phillipsburg, NJ: P&R, 1999).

19. See Vern S. Poythress, *Reading the Word of God in the Presence of God: A Handbook for Biblical Interpretation* (Wheaton, IL: Crossway, 2016). See also the discussion by Van Til, "Nature and Scripture," 280–83.

knowledge is not salvation. We are not saved by knowing facts. We are saved by knowing the Savior in an intimate way. That does not happen through our own grasping. "That which is born of the flesh is flesh, and that which is born of the Spirit is spirit" (John 3:6). The Holy Spirit must cause us to be made into new creatures, to be given new hearts, to be born again. The result is faith to believe in Jesus as our Savior, who was punished for our sins on the cross instead of us. Then God presses our judgment upon Christ, passes over us with forgiveness, and establishes our eternal peace with him.

Being born again gives us eyes to see what was previously indiscernible. We have the Holy Spirit within us, enabling us to know God and his will.

> So also no one comprehends the thoughts of God except the Spirit of God. Now we have received not the spirit of the world, but the Spirit who is from God, that we might understand the things freely given us by God. . . .
> . . . But we have the mind of Christ. (1 Cor. 2:11–12, 16)

God enables his children to see in part what he sees and to understand what he understands, including history. Being born again is the beginning, the first step, of being able to understand history rightly. We first must intimately know the author of history. We must have minds that are freed from the chains of sin—minds remade in the likeness of the author himself. "The fear of the LORD is the *beginning* of knowledge" (Prov. 1:7).

The person who writes history, or studies those who write it, must know the Creator and controller of time in order to discern his person and purpose. He must have the Holy Spirit teaching him how to interpret history according to God's Word. A working definition for historiography might be "the application of special revelation to general revelation in the area of interpreting history." Does that mean we can find God under every rock and tree? Yes and no. Every rock, tree, or historical artifact bears the mark of the Creator. That information can be interpreted by special revelation to reflect the person and purpose of the Creator.

Let's apply this to an example from nature. A tree belongs to the created order as part of general revelation. The Bible says that we can learn from looking at a tree the invisible attributes of God. So a tree shows the Creator's wisdom, power, immanence, and beauty. If we look at the tree and say that it is twisted or diseased, and therefore God is similar, we have ignored the special revelation of Scripture, which explains the curse of sin. The Bible tells us that the disease came as a result of the judgment of the holy God against sin. We need special revelation to correctly interpret general revelation. We need the Holy Spirit to correctly interpret special revelation. Then we will see even more deeply the mystery of how the tree became simultaneously a symbol of death and of life. Jesus hung on the tree, dying for sins. The tree then became a tree of life, giving eternal life as mentioned in Genesis and Revelation.

Historiography is done by a person with a bias, either for or against God.[20] History is more than an itemized catalog of artifacts and quotes. It includes interpretation.[21] Even to list an archaeological find as a "comb" requires interpretation of the artifact which seems to resemble a toothed device. It is impossible not to interpret history. All interpretation is presuppositionally based in a heart that either loves God or does not love God. News journalism today still labors under the delusion that its reports are objective. Most historical researchers gave up such an illusion decades ago.[22] One historian is an unsaved unbeliever; one is a saved believer. One writer belongs to Augustine's City of Man; one belongs to the City of God. One is darkness; one is light. These are radically different worlds, meaning that at their *radix* (root) they are disparate. True Van Tilian presuppositionalism boils down to two perspectives: either you love God from a born-again heart, or you are in rebellion against God. Everything you conclude, observe, propose,

---

20. In the field of history, an unbiblical approach known as historical nihilism says that all history is merely a subjective project and therefore invalid, or that it is all a story to be individually appropriated and you create meaning significant for yourself.

21. Maxie B. Burch, *The Evangelical Historians: The Historiography of George Marsden, Nathan Hatch, and Mark Noll* (New York: University Press of America, 1996), critiques men for being biased by biblical presuppositions. Philip Sheldrake, *Spirituality and History: Questions of Interpretation and Method* (New York: Crossroad, 1992), promotes a Marxist position, critiquing all former historians as biased by elitist views.

22. Leopold von Ranke in the mid-1800s thought he could filter out his subjectivity. Others, such as Bernard Lategan, think that sticking to the facts could help one reach the goal of objectivity. Lategan champions the historical-critical method as helpful, but admits everyone's perspective affects his interpretation. That would leave us with as many historical accounts of an event as there are historians.

or suppose comes from your heart. There are no brute facts. Nothing is not interpreted. Or said positively, everything is interpreted by one of the two heart views. The mind is an expression of the heart: "Out of the heart of man, come evil thoughts" (Mark 7:21–23). Either you love God or you don't.[23] All historiography is biased. The only question is, In which of the two directions?

Yes, it is more complicated, because truth can be gleaned from nonbelievers through common grace. Also, believers are sinners at various stages of sanctification and subject to falsehood. Written fragments from the past could be from either category of historians. The first category might include scribes who were assigned the task of commemorating the exploits of a pagan leader. The assigned goal casts suspicion, which affects the interpretation of the recorded facts.[24] Another category might include writings of a professed Christian, for example, Wolfgang Capito, who authored a biography of Johannes Oecolampadius in 1534. Then there are opaque historians who might study other historians. So Irena Backus wrote a book in 2008 about Capito's writing a book, analyzing his motivation and context.[25]

Objections

A number of objections to writing history from an unashamedly Christian perspective sometimes come from conservative Bible professors.

---

23. Conrad Schmid unknowingly confirms this. He has done a study and found out that a person's exegesis of the Bible depends more on whether he is liberal or "positive" (conservative), than on whether he belongs to a Reformed or Lutheran denomination. What Schmid really has discovered is two worlds. The one world believes in its own rationale, whereas the other submits to God's Word as truth. One is the liberal; one the conservative. Dirk Smit writes, "Every part of the Christian tradition and community uses its own set of assumptions, whether consciously or not, and this ultimately leads to the diverse conflicts of reading and interpretations" ("Rhetoric and Ethic? A Reformed Perspective on the Politics of Reading the Bible," in *Reformed Theology: Identity and Ecumenicity II: Biblical Interpretation in the Reformed Tradition*, ed. Wallace M. Alston Jr. and Michael Welker (Grand Rapids, MI: Eerdmans, 2007), 387.

24. Speros Vryonis Jr., *Readings in Medieval Historiography* (Boston: Houghton Mifflin, 1968). He discusses the use of Suetonius's *Lives of the Twelve Caesars* as a model in the biography of Charlemagne, the use of Greek historical writing as a superior "objective" method, and the use of different perspectives, such as the three volumes on Justinian.

25. Irena Backus, *Life Writing in Reformation Europe: Lives of Reformers by Friends, Disciples and Foes* (Burlington, VT: Ashgate, 2008). Unfortunately, she guesses that Capito's motivation for writing the biography was to argue for the saintly circumstances surrounding Oecolampadius's death. Yet she ignores the fact that Capito had married Oecolampadius's widow and adopted his three children two years previously, which would have been a strong motivation to pass on a legacy to the children. See Diane Poythress, *Reformer of Basel: The Life, Thought, and Influence of Johannes Oecolampadius* (Grand Rapids, MI: Reformation Heritage, 2011). Vern Poythress, *Inerrancy and Worldview*, 48, discusses the necessity of criticism because of human fallibility.

These objections include (1) it ignores man as finite and fallen, (2) it ignores God as inscrutable, (3) it treats history as special revelation, and (4) it is unprofessional.[26] The responses to these objections require a book-length treatment. Nuances, caveats, hedges, and pitfalls need to be addressed. Only a cursory reply can be offered here. Other less Christian objections can be subsumed under these four, such as the existential, where the only authenticity in a materialistic universe is choosing your own death; the evolutionary, where meaning is apart from God and therefore constantly changes, especially at times when a historical mold must be exploded; and the humanistic, where one creates meaning out of his own subjective experience apart from God, especially ethnically.[27]

1. Objections in the first category sometimes include that we cannot know everything in history (every thought of every person, every action), and therefore we can know nothing.[28] But that is to say we must be God in order to know anything. However, God promised we can know real truth through the Holy Spirit: "When the Spirit of truth comes, he will guide you into all the truth" (John 16:13). It is not exhaustive, yet it is true.[29] We cannot see every molecule of a tree simultaneously. This does not stop us from praising God for what we do see.

This objection to man's limitations also says that the information we have is insufficient to conclude anything. Only God has all the facts.[30] The omniscient God may not have given us the information we desire; nevertheless, he has given us the parts of history that he wants

26. Could a Christian academic today write, "The Gospel's prevailing as it did against such powerful opposition [from Rome] plainly shows the hand of God"? (Jonathan Edwards, *A History of the Work of Redemption* [1774; repr., Edinburgh: Banner of Truth, 2003], 314).

27. See Vern S. Poythress, *Redeeming Philosophy: A God-Centered Approach to the Big Questions* (Wheaton, IL: Crossway, 2014); Poythress, *Redeeming Sociology*; Poythress, *Redeeming Science*. Some question the value of any historical study. But that is to doubt the value of anything in general revelation, which I have already addressed from Romans 1. An ethnic historical approach is espoused by Dale T. Irvin in *Christian Histories, Christian Traditioning: Rendering Accounts* (Maryknoll, NY: Orbis, 1998), which seems to compromise the uniqueness of Christ, the only Son of God and Savior. All principles of interpretation find their basis in God, i.e., criticism, analogy, and correlation. Secular sociology becomes a synchronic study in Poythress, *Inerrancy and Worldview*, 48, 51–55, 58.

28. For an analysis of this view, see Poythress, *In the Beginning Was the Word*, 36, 247. A broader discussion of the category of history is on 85–163.

29. "Man does not need to know exhaustively in order to know truly and certainly" (Van Til, "Nature and Scripture," 277–78).

30. "There is no discrepancy between the idea of mystery and that of perspicuity with respect either to revelation in Scripture or to revelation in nature" (ibid., 279). "For any fact to be a fact at all, it must be a revelational fact" (ibid., 280).

to make known. What he gives us is sufficient Scripture, which can be applied to the general revelation of history.

A corollary objection, originating from multicultural emphasis, is that past time cannot be understood unless you were there. That is to say, only someone living in Basel in 1516 can understand the meaning and motivations of people from that place and time.[31] However, the objection that cultural context prevents understanding by anyone in another time or place is illegitimate. God was there. God has told us about himself and his plans and the heart motives of people for all of time.[32] God is immutable. People are either redeemed or unredeemed. Again, knowledge may not be exhaustive, but it remains true knowledge.[33]

Being limited as a human being also means that any recorder or viewer of history can only see things from his own vantage point. So the objection observes that people differ in their views of history, even if they live at the same time in the same place, and therefore no one view has validity. For the Christian, however, this is too simple. God gave four Gospels. Why? Why not just one, and why don't they all say exactly the same thing?[34] We know that it is possible for a redeemed person to see genuine truth, although not necessarily exhaustively. That leaves the possibility of someone else seeing other parts of the truth from a different perspective.[35] This is not to make truth relative to each person's viewpoint. Not everyone who is looking in any and every direction speaks truth. You cannot be looking away from God, or even just looking tangentially, and maintain the right perspective. Not every view is worthy. But as each redeemed person gazes on the glory of the

---

31. Another variation is to say that history is contrived by a cultural commonality, so "all cultures are equally valid" and events are a result of the cultural belief system (Raoul Mortley, *The Idea of Universal History from Hellenistic Philosophy to Early Christian Historiography* [Lewiston, NY: Mellen, 1996], 120ff.).

32. See Poythress, *Inerrancy and Worldview*, 48–49, concerning analogy. Also for discussion on God's character revealed and remaining the same; God's universal presence establishing stability, dynamicity, and relation in history; and Christ as Mediator of creation, see Poythress, *Theophany* (forthcoming). "That is to say, man normally thinks in analogical fashion. He realizes that God's thoughts are self-contained. He knows that his own interpretation of nature must therefore be a reinterpretation of what is already fully interpreted by God" (Van Til, "Nature and Scripture," 278).

33. See Poythress, *Redeeming Sociology*; Poythress, *Redeeming Philosophy*.

34. See Vern Sheridan Poythress, *Inerrancy and the Gospels: A God-Centered Approach to the Challenges of Harmonization* (Wheaton, IL: Crossway, 2012).

35. See Vern S. Poythress, *Symphonic Theology: The Validity of Multiple Perspectives in Theology* (Grand Rapids, MI: Zondervan, 1987). Also see Poythress, *Perspectives on the Trinity* (forthcoming).

only triune Creator God, reflected in his creation, he or she is able to contribute to the one central purpose. In particular, room remains for differing genre views that explore apologetics, moral heroes, evangelism, cultural critiques, and jeremiads.[36]

The second part of the objection deals with human fallenness. Can a sinful person say anything true about history? The argument's implication is that someone must be perfectly sinless, like God, in order to deal with actual history. Sin would so thoroughly taint every endeavor, every area of study, that all efforts would be vain. If this were the case, then no true knowledge or conclusions would be possible about any subject. No one could say anything true about a tree, about history, about general revelation. It is the case that variations of historical understanding can arise from sin, immaturity, and ignorance. It is also the case that all thinking is tainted by sin, which remains in the heart. "None is righteous, no, not one" (Rom. 3:10). But the Christian is not paralyzed; rather, he is redeemed. "So then, I myself serve the law of God with my mind," says Paul (Rom. 7:25). God by salvific grace (and common grace) enables people to make just laws, raise godly children, teach wisdom and knowledge, and study his hand in history. We are sinful. God is not. We have been given God's Word, the revealed mind of God, by which to test thoughts and statements.[37]

The first objection further implies that man as sinner in his fallen state or in his earthly redeemed state is biased by that sin. And if all interpretation is biased by sin and objectivity is impossible, then historical writing is impossible. But this again is to endorse the above philosophy that all communication is meaningless since no one can correctly understand or interpret another's mind. Yet Scripture has promised that we have the mind of Christ through the work of his Holy Spirit in us. Therefore, we can see genuine truth in history, although it may not be omniscient truth.

2. The second objection is that God is not knowable. Does this refer to his person or his will? God himself has promised that he has revealed

---

36. Jay D. Green, *Christian Historiography: Five Versions* (Waco, TX: Baylor University Press, 2015). Those views include Christian, Kuyperian, providential, moralistic, and apologetic perspectives. Pros and cons of each are presented.

37. We can enjoy a redeemed use of logic. See Vern S. Poythress, *Logic: A God-Centered Approach to the Foundation of Western Thought* (Wheaton, IL: Crossway, 2013).

himself both in general revelation (his invisible attributes clearly understood as promised in Romans 1) and in special revelation. "Your word is truth," Jesus prayed (John 17:17); he also declared, "I am the way, and the truth, and the life" (John 14:6). Christ through his Spirit reveals God. "Whoever has seen me has seen the Father" he tells us (John 14:9), And "no one knows the Father except the Son and anyone to whom the Son chooses to reveal him" (Matt. 11:27). All believers would confess these points. We know that God is knowable and the Bible is knowable, but what about his will?

3. The real underlying question for the above complaint comes in the third objection. Can we correctly understand God's purpose, will, or mind in any area of study outside of the inspired, inerrant Bible? This skepticism would make science impossible. Science is the exploration of the mind of God as evidenced in general revelation. What has been created reflects God. History, as part of creation, reflects God. The fact that a deciduous tree drops its leaves around its roots, whereby nutrients are restored to the soil, shows God's intelligence and care. We see his person. But we also see his will to replenish, sustain, and continue the life of the tree, even this particular tree.

Are we able to firmly pronounce God's will concerning any given historical point? The answer is yes and no. Yes, all of history expresses God's decretive will. God's bringing to pass whatsoever he decrees is the axiomatic primary cause for all history. From the Bible, we can state that God's decreed will is to clearly reflect his attributes in creation and to accomplish his redemptive purposes for the summation of all things in Christ.[38] He has also revealed his prescriptive will. Scripture tells us what is pleasing to God and how he chooses to bless

---

38. "Meaning starts with God. The meaning of the events, within God's plan, is actually prior to the events. The events are never 'raw' events, never 'bare' events, but events that already have meaning. They have a richness of meaning in the infinity of God's mind. We as human beings can never completely plumb God's infinity, but we can appreciate some of his meaning" (Poythress, *Inerrancy and Worldview*, 104). "His plan is to fill the world with his presence—with theophany." "It is therefore the Father's purpose that the glory of his Son should be imprinted and displayed with all intensity in the entire universe" (Poythress, *Theophany* [forthcoming]). "Nature can and does reveal nothing but the one comprehensive plan of God. The psalmist does not say that the heavens possibly or probably declare the glory of God. Nor does the apostle assert that the wrath of God is probably revealed from heaven against all ungodliness and unrighteousness of men. Scripture takes the clarity of God's revelation for granted at every stage of human history" (Van Til, "Nature and Scripture," 278). "Even to the very bottom of the most complex historical situations, involving sin and all its consequences, God's revelation shines with unmistakable clarity" (279).

and curse. Both his decretive will, as seen in history and defined by consummation purposes in the Bible, and his prescriptive will are plain.

Can we derive conclusions based on concrete historical artifacts or mere speculation? Can we know why God purposed something to happen? No, not definitively, if God himself has not told us. What Christian historians can state is that God was working out his own glory and the building of his church in Christ. We know that God is working all things together for the glorious consummation of all things in Christ.[39] Can we say nothing else? Scripture gives us moral discernment. We know his person and prescriptive will by which we are enabled to make observations.[40] These are not inerrant, yet they are informed by God's Word and Spirit. "Do not be conformed to this world, but be transformed by the renewal of your mind, that by testing you may discern what is the will of God, what is good and acceptable and perfect" (Rom. 12:2).

4. Finally, some people object that writing history from a Christian perspective is unprofessional. This last objection will be viewed in principle and then in praxis. In principle, God tells us that the judgmental peer pressure or societal opinion, based on the world's standards, is worthless. "And do not fear those who kill the body but cannot kill the soul. Rather fear him who can destroy both soul and body in hell" (Matt. 10:28). We stand or fall before our Master, not men.

Applications

Standing before God means that a Christian historian in praxis must endeavor to have the most excellent motivation and method. This first means that we must be born again, for whatever is not of faith is sin (Rom. 14:23). In our new birth our eyes are opened to see God. Then our work is done in obedience to a calling from him, not from our own pride. "Whatever you do," writes Paul, "work heartily, as for the

---

39. Jeffrey K. Jue suggests themes of covenant, promise, and Sabbath in Scripture. These could be explored in post-canon literature as well ("Evangelical Eschatology: American Style," in Phillips and Fluhrer, *These Last Days*, 149–67).

40. "Man was created as an analogue of God; his thinking, his willing and his doing is therefore properly conceived as at every point analogical to the thinking, willing and doing of God" (Van Til, "Nature and Scripture," 273). "The revelation that comes to man by way of his own rational and moral nature is no less objective to him than that which comes to him through the voice of trees and animals. . . . All created reality is inherently revelational of the nature and will of God" (273–74).

Lord and not for men, knowing that from the Lord you will receive the inheritance as your reward. You are serving the Lord Christ" (Col. 3:23–24). Our motivation is to serve Christ and to do it with excellence. Elsewhere Paul says, "Do your best to present yourself to God as one approved, a worker who has no need to be ashamed" (2 Tim. 2:15). We study history for the glory of God.[41] This is our main motivation because we love our Lord, and we want to see him praised. That means that our motivation includes seeing his kingdom built and people built up in faith so that they might live to the praise of his glory.[42]

Motivation defines our method. We humbly submit to God and his inerrant Word. We pray for his words, wisdom, and guidance. We choose topics that are honorable, just, pure, lovely, commendable, excellent, and worthy of praise (Phil. 4:8). We present them in a manner that glorifies God and builds faith. We are not to write as practical atheists or deists, which would confine us to a materialistic and rationalistic worldview.[43] According to God's promise, we can see God's invisible attributes in history and declare them clearly to others. If we cannot see God, then we should delay our analysis.

We can apply knowledge of his decretive consummation purpose and his prescriptive will to history. We can definitively state that God used every epoch and item in history toward the goal of the glorious consummation of all things in Christ. We can definitively state that he directed individual believers in such a way that their lives fit this overall plan. In addition, Romans 8:28 tells us that all things in the lives of believers happened for their good and that God's will for each believer is his or her sanctification. Can we say specifically how something was used to sanctify a person? Sometimes.[44] Obviously, our opinions on

---

41. "If we leave out Jesus Christ . . . we lack the world's unifying principle. . . . Jesus Christ is the meaning of the cosmos, and Jesus Christ is the meaning of history" (Sinclair Ferguson, "The Christ of History," in Phillips and Fluhrer, *These Last Days*, 8).

42. "The Church will be able to bless nations once more with the immemorial and undreamed futuristic joys and empowerment which come from lucidly and actively seeing God, the Christ of God in history. I mean by the inescapable evidence of His presence there. Will we dare?" (Adolf Hult, *The Theology of History* [Rock Island, IL: Augustana, 1940], 29). See also discussion of Pentecost's effects on speech content and mission outreach, and personal application by Alistair Begg, "The Age of the Spirit," in Phillips and Fluhrer, *These Last Days*, 39–51.

43. See Poythress, *The Lordship of Christ*; and Poythress, *Inerrancy and Worldview*. The latter discusses the principle of criticism, analogy, and correlation as methods for interpreting history (48–49).

44. Consider the life event, the applicable biblical-referent verses, how this fits into the overall scheme of redemption universally, and how it applies personally. See Poythress, *Miracles of Jesus*.

any subject are not inerrantly inspired. Yet neither are they outside the realm of the work of glorifying God or applying special revelation to general revelation.[45] The problem in historiography today is not the overinterpretation of everything from a biblical view. The problem is the total lack of an attempt to see God, to glorify God, or to apply Scripture to the general revelation of history.

History itself as communicated to others is not morally neutral (there are no brute facts) in either its content or its transmission. Our methodology is not morally neutral. We cannot lie or obfuscate truth for the sake of reputation or any other reason.[46] Nor are we to write subjectively according to whatever emotional wave hits us, such as the current mode of writing "advocacy" history. Rather, the interpretation of history should display God in his glory and build faith. Each historian must ask, "Why am I writing this?" and "How am I writing this?" and "For whom am I writing this?"[47]

David Lotz states that the historian's purpose is "to articulate an approach to church history which is at once theological and critical, at once ecclesiastically meaningful and scientifically responsible. . . . The persistent failure to take up this challenge would be the most serious crisis of all in American church historiography" (David Lotz, "The Crisis in American Church Historiography," in *The Writing of American Religious History*, ed. Marty E. Martin, Modern American Protestantism and Its World [New York: K. G. Saur, 1992], 103).

45. D. A. Carson writes concerning

> what caused the destruction of the southern kingdom of Judah in 587 BC. One could mention the rise of the regional superpower Babylon, combined with the decline and decay of the Davidic dynasty. Or we might talk about the criminal stupidity of Zedekiah, despite Jeremiah's warnings. Or we might look at the sins of the people, sins that attracted God's judgment. Or we could simply say God caused it. Which of these answers is the most true? Well, they are equally true. (D. A. Carson, "This Present Age," in Phillips and Fluhrer, *These Last Days*, 8)

46. Irena Backus, *Historical Method and Confessional Identity in the Era of the Reformation (1378–1615)* (Leiden: Brill, 2003), suggests that some historians used history as a tool to promote their agenda, such as constructing their own identity during the Reformation (see 61, 195), or they combined special revelation with pagan stories or Greek philosophy, as in the *Centuries of Magdeburg* (see Backus, *Historical Method*, 99–100, 129, 394). Helen Parish suggests that there were a "Protestant mythology of the papacy" and new hagiography of martyrs and heroes in order to promote the Protestant cause (Helen L. Parish, *Monks, Miracles and Magic: Reformation Representation of the Medieval Church* [London: Routledge, Taylor and Francis Group, 2005], 150). The works of Heinrich Pantaleon and John Foxe have been included in the ideological use of martyrs. See Elizabeth Evenden and Thomas S. Freeman, *Religion and the Book in Early Modern England* (Cambridge: Cambridge University Press, 2011). Carl Trueman discusses recognized methods for achieving an "objective" scholarly interpretation of history, but clarifies that "objectivity is not neutrality" (Carl R. Trueman, *Histories and Fallacies: Problems Faced in the Writing of History* [Wheaton, IL: Crossway, 2010], 66).

47. John Piper asks how reason and historical scholarship relate to spiritually seeing the glory of God. "The relationship between spiritual sight and empirical observation is not antagonistic," and we depend "on the Spirit both for the right use of reason and for the gift of spiritual sight" (John Piper, *A Peculiar Glory: How the Christian Scriptures Reveal Their Complete Truthfulness* [Wheaton, IL: Crossway, 2016], 277–78).

In conclusion, we have seen that God created and controls time. History is part of general revelation, and as such it clearly communicates the invisible attributes of God. These are explained explicitly in the special revelation of the Bible. A historian must be born again in order to even begin to perceive God and his truth in history. Objections to writing from a Christian viewpoint are refuted by God's Word itself. Scripture defines the motivation and method for writing redeemed history. Because God images himself in his works, as he repeatedly teaches throughout Scripture, we are able to see him in history.[48] We are able to communicate God's attributes, his decretive will, and his prescriptive will, which includes his gospel. Anyone who pleads, "Sir, we would see Jesus," will be satisfied. Our work in history will be a pleasing sacrifice to God. Then historical studies will be the exciting story of our glorious God establishing his city. Historiography will be redeemed.

> All your works shall give thanks to you, O LORD,
>   and all your saints shall bless you!
> They shall speak of the glory of your kingdom
>   and tell of your power,
> to make known to the children of man your mighty deeds,
>   and the glorious splendor of your kingdom. (Ps. 145:10–12)

---

48. See Poythress, *Theophany* (forthcoming).

Part 6

ETHICS

19

Christians Never Have to Choose the "Lesser Sin"

WAYNE GRUDEM

I first met Vern Poythress fifty years ago, during the 1966–1967 academic year. I was a freshman at Harvard, and he was a first-year PhD student in mathematics. That meeting was significant because I think that, by God's grace, Vern has had more influence on my life and thinking than anyone else except my wife and family. Therefore, it is an honor to contribute an essay to this volume.

There were about fifty of us involved in the evangelical Christian group on campus, the Harvard-Radcliffe Christian Fellowship, and we all looked up to Vern because of his unobtrusive godliness in life and his phenomenal knowledge of Scripture (he had memorized many books of the New Testament while an undergraduate at Caltech). His commitment to prayer and to obedience to God's Word, and to the absolute truthfulness of every word of Scripture, were an inspiration to me and to many others.

I remember one brief conversation that first year that had an immense impact on my life. I had been using the King James Version of the Bible but wanted to change to a translation with more-modern

English, so I asked Vern which translation I should choose. He said, "The Revised Standard Version." So I bought one, memorized passages from it, and used it as my personal Bible for over thirty years. Little did I know, back in 1967, that in 1998 I would write a letter to the copyright holder for that same Revised Standard Version, asking permission to use that version as the basis for a new evangelical translation of the Bible, and that such permission would be granted to Crossway, and that both Vern and I would serve on the twelve-member translation committee, and that the new translation would eventually be called the English Standard Version (ESV).

Vern and I worked together on several other projects. When I was involved in controversies over evangelical feminism, he contributed a valuable chapter to the book *Recovering Biblical Manhood and Womanhood.*[1] When a controversy arose over the gender-neutral changes introduced in the TNIV, Vern and I worked together to challenge these changes, and we coauthored *The TNIV and the Gender-Neutral Bible Controversy.*[2] From 1998 to 2001, and again at our meetings in 2005, 2010, and 2015, we spent many weeks working together on details of the translation of the ESV Bible. In addition, over the last fifty years there have been countless phone conversations as I sought Vern's advice and counsel on one matter after another. He has truly been a lifelong friend.

I know from this friendship that Vern would never think it right to disobey any part of God's Word just because he could see no morally right alternative. He would rather pray for God's wisdom (James 1:5) and believe that God would enable him to see a "way of escape" (1 Cor. 10:13), a path of obedience that would not involve choosing "a lesser sin." Therefore, I am submitting this essay in Vern's honor but also, and much more importantly, for God's glory.

• • •

Some Christian writers claim that people sometimes find themselves in situations so difficult that they are faced with a choice between

---

1. John Piper and Wayne A. Grudem, *Recovering Biblical Manhood and Womanhood: A Response to Biblical Feminism* (Wheaton, IL: Crossway, 1991).
2. Vern S. Poythress and Wayne A. Grudem, *The TNIV and the Gender-Neutral Bible Controversy* (Nashville: Broadman & Holman, 2004).

disobeying one of God's moral commands or another, and in those situations they are forced by circumstances to choose the "lesser sin."

The classic example is that of a Christian in Nazi Germany who is hiding Jews in the basement of his house. What should he do when Nazi soldiers come pounding on the door, demanding to know if he is hiding Jews? The householder knows that if the Jews are discovered, they will be dragged away to a concentration camp and likely be put to death.

Is this an "impossible moral conflict," what is sometimes called a "tragic moral choice"? The dilemma is that if the householder tells the truth, he is betraying innocent life, which surely is morally wrong. But if he lies and says he has no Jews hiding in the house, he is committing the moral wrong of lying. In such a situation, isn't it better to *tell a lie* (the lesser sin) than to *betray innocent lives* so that they die (a greater sin)?

Christians Will Never Face an Impossible Moral Conflict

The position I will defend is that Christians will never be forced to choose to commit a "lesser sin," but that in every situation there will be at least one course of action open that does not involve disobedience to any of God's commands (when rightly understood and applied).

This position is sometimes called "non-conflicting moral absolutism," but I am not entirely comfortable with that label. It suggests that we are obligated to obey a handful of "moral absolutes," such as (for example) not murdering, not stealing, not lying, and loving our neighbor, and we will never find ourselves in a situation where we have to disobey one of those moral obligations in order to obey another one.

But the position I am advocating is not exactly like that. It is not based on such a list of several moral absolutes. Instead, it is based on the whole Bible. My position is more accurately called "non-conflicting biblical commands." I believe that God requires us to obey every moral command in the entire Bible that rightly applies to us in our situation.[3] It is not just a short list of "moral absolutes" that God holds us responsible to obey, but his entire Word, for *"all Scripture* [not merely a summary list of moral absolutes] is breathed out by God and *profitable*

---

3. Of course, these commands must be rightly interpreted in the contexts in which they occur.

for teaching, for reproof, for correction, and *for training in righteous-ness*" (2 Tim. 3:16). I believe that in our ethical teaching we are to do what Jesus told us to do: "teaching them to observe *all that I have commanded you*" (Matt. 28:20).

THE LIFE OF CHRIST AS PROOF

The life of Christ proves that we will never be forced to disobey one of God's commands. The New Testament gives no example anywhere of Christ disobeying any command of the Old Testament, rightly under-stood. And yet Jesus has been tempted in every way as we are: "For we do not have a high priest who is unable to sympathize with our weaknesses, but one who *in every respect has been tempted as we are*, yet without sin" (Heb. 4:15).

If we follow the reasoning of those who say we sometimes are forced to choose to commit a lesser sin, then we would have to say that there were times when Jesus committed a "lesser sin"—for example, when he affirmed a falsehood. And this implies that the one who was truly and fully God, who cannot lie (Titus 1:2; Heb. 6:18), told a lie. But this is an insurmountable difficulty for those who say there are times when God wants us to tell a lie (commit a lesser sin) in order to perform a greater good.

Where is there any convincing example of Jesus breaking a com-mand of God in any place in the Gospels? There is none. Of course, Jesus frequently healed on the Sabbath (see Mark 3:1–6; Luke 14:1–6), but he was only violating later Jewish additions to the Sabbath law, not the Old Testament law itself. Jesus's own teaching indicated that healing people was not the kind of "work" prohibited by the Sabbath commandment in Exodus 20:8–11 (see Matt. 12:12; Mark 3:4; Luke 13:15–16; 14:5; John 5:17; 7:23), nor was plucking grain to eat at once when hungry (Matt. 12:1–8).

If it was important for God to teach us that we will sometimes face impossible moral conflicts in which he wants us to disobey one of his commands in order to obey another one, would he not have made that evident in several incontrovertible examples in the life of Jesus?

By contrast, there are many examples of Jesus saying he is without sin, and of others being unable to find any sin in him.

- "Which one of you convicts me of sin?" (John 8:46).
- "If you keep my commandments, you will abide in my love, just as I have kept my Father's commandments and abide in his love" (John 15:10).
- "I find no guilt in him" (John 18:38).
- "He committed no sin, neither was deceit found in his mouth" (1 Pet. 2:22).[4]

Norman Geisler has an alternative understanding of these verses. He claims that when Jesus violated a lesser command of God, it was not actually sin because God gave him an "exemption" from one command in order that he would be able to obey a greater command. Geisler says, "When we follow the higher moral law, we are not held responsible for breaking the lower law."[5] He also says that "God does not hold a person guilty for not keeping a lower moral law so long as one keeps the higher law,"[6] and that God grants "an exemption" that eliminates the individual's culpability for not keeping the lower moral law.[7]

But Geisler's claim is supported by no explicit teaching anywhere in the New Testament. Nowhere does the apostle Paul or Peter or John write to first-century Christians and say, "When you face a difficult situation with an impossible moral conflict, God will give you an exemption for violating one of his moral laws." This idea is entirely foreign to the thought of the New Testament.

In addition, Jesus was surrounded by first-century Jewish opponents who were watching his every action and listening to his every word, trying to trap him in disobedience to some command of God, and they could find none. If Jesus had broken some moral command of God in a difficult situation, they would have pounced on him immediately and accused him of wrongdoing. But they could find in his life nothing that violated any of God's commands. Jesus repeatedly

---

4. Jesus also made the astonishing claim "I always do the things that are pleasing to him [that is, his Father]" (John 8:29). See also Luke 4:13; John 8:12; Acts 2:27; 3:14; 4:30; 7:52; 13:35; Rom. 8:3; 2 Cor. 5:21; Heb. 7:26; 1 Pet. 1:19; 3:18; 1 John 2:1; 3:5. The testimony of the New Testament to Jesus's sinlessness is overwhelming.

5. Norman Geisler, *Christian Ethics: Contemporary Issues and Options*, 2nd ed. (Grand Rapids, MI: Baker, 2010), 115.

6. Ibid., 104.

7. Ibid., 104, 110–11.

affirmed the goodness and inviolability of all of God's words in Scripture: "Scripture cannot be broken" (John 10:35).

THE PROMISE OF 1 CORINTHIANS 10:13

In writing to Christians at Corinth who were facing pressure from their non-Christian culture to participate in aspects of idol worship, Paul assures these Christians that they will never face circumstances where they are forced to do something contrary to any of God's moral standards: "No temptation has overtaken you that is not common to man. God is faithful, and he will not let you be tempted beyond your ability, but *with the temptation he will also provide the way of escape*, that you may be able to endure it" (1 Cor. 10:13).

Geisler responds that this verse applies only to situations of "temptation," not to the entire life of Christians.[8] But that is hardly a convincing argument, because situations where people claim an impossible moral conflict are by definition situations of temptation.[9] They are all situations in which Christians feel tremendous pressure from circumstances around them to disobey one of God's moral laws. And Paul says that in all those situations, God will always provide "the way of escape," a way out of the temptation, so that the Christian does not have to give in to the temptation and break one of God's moral laws.

The proper approach in such difficult situations is not to yield to the temptation and disobey, but rather to pray for God's wisdom (see James 1:5) to understand how to escape from the situation without doing something that God counts as sin.

THE CONSISTENT BIBLICAL TEACHING ON DISOBEDIENCE

It is foreign to the entire fabric of biblical moral teaching to say that God sometimes wants us to disobey one of his commandments. Where does Scripture encourage us to find out which commands we might

---

8. Ibid., 76.
9. The word Paul uses for "temptation" in 1 Cor. 10:13 is πειρασμός, "an attempt to make one do something wrong, temptation, enticement to sin" (BDAG, 793). It is used in Luke 4:13 to speak of "every *temptation*" that Satan brought against Jesus in the wilderness. But the word is also used to mean "trials," as in James 1:2: "Count it all joy, my brothers, when you meet *trials* of various kinds" (in several verses the word has the meaning "test, trial," BDAG, 793). All sorts of difficult situations are included in Paul's assurance about "no temptation" in 1 Cor. 10:13.

need to disobey in difficult times? There is nothing of that sort. Rather, the perspective of Scripture, repeated again and again, is that we are to keep *all* the commands of God:

> The law of the LORD is perfect,
>   reviving the soul;
> . . . .
> The precepts of the LORD are right,
>   rejoicing the heart;
> the commandment of the LORD is pure,
>   enlightening the eyes;
> . . . .
> The rules of the LORD are true,
>   and righteous altogether.
> . . . .
> Moreover, by them is your servant warned;
>   in keeping them there is great reward. (Ps. 19:7–11)

> Blessed are those whose way is blameless,
>   who walk in the law of the LORD!
> Blessed are those who keep his testimonies,
>   who seek him with their whole heart. (Ps. 119:1–2)

> Lead me in the path of your commandments,
>   for I delight in it. (Ps. 119:35)

> And they were both righteous before God, walking blamelessly in all the commandments and statutes of the Lord. (Luke 1:6)

> For whoever keeps the whole law but fails in one point has become guilty of all of it. (James 2:10)

The New Testament never encourages Christians to "choose the lesser sin" or to "realize they have an exemption from lesser moral laws of God in difficult situations," but rather tells believers to flee from sin and flee from temptation:

> *Flee* from sexual immorality. (1 Cor. 6:18)

> Therefore, my beloved, *flee* from idolatry. (1 Cor. 10:14)

> But as for you, O man of God, *flee* these things. Pursue righteous-
> ness, godliness, faith, love, steadfastness, gentleness. (1 Tim. 6:11)

> So *flee* youthful passions and pursue righteousness, faith, love, and
> peace, along with those who call on the Lord from a pure heart.
> (2 Tim. 2:22)

Lesser Commandments Remain Commandments

I agree that some Scripture passages distinguish between greater and
lesser commandments. But they never encourage disobedience to the
lesser commandments.

For example, Jesus rebukes the scribes and Pharisees for paying
tithes on tiny bits of spices but neglecting "*the weightier matters of
the law*: justice and mercy and faithfulness" (Matt. 23:23). But when
we read the entire verse we find that, far from encouraging disobedience to the lesser matters of the law, Jesus reminds them that they are
responsible (under the old covenant) for obeying both the greater and
lesser laws: "Woe to you, scribes and Pharisees, hypocrites! For you
tithe mint and dill and cumin, and have neglected the weightier matters
of the law: justice and mercy and faithfulness. These you ought to have
done, *without neglecting the others*" (Matt. 23:23).

In another place, Jesus talks about "the least of these commandments," implying that there are lesser and greater commandments. But,
again, he warns against teaching people that it is acceptable to disobey
even the least of the commandments:

> For truly, I say to you, until heaven and earth pass away, not an
> iota, not a dot, will pass from the Law until all is accomplished.
> Therefore *whoever relaxes one of the least of these commandments*
> and teaches others to do the same will be called least in the kingdom
> of heaven, but whoever does them and teaches them will be called
> great in the kingdom of heaven. (Matt. 5:18–19)

A Just God Does Not Give Conflicting Commands

It would be unjust of God to give us contradictory commands. But if
we in fact face situations of impossible moral conflict, and if our ulti-

mate moral obligation is to God, then this would mean that God puts us in situations where he commands us to do contradictory things, which would be inconsistent and unjust of God. As John Frame explains, "On this view, the law of God itself is contradictory, for it requires contradictory behavior. . . . Surely the consistency of Scripture is an empty concept if Scripture can command us to do contradictory things."[10]

That would not be an acceptable position. Are we to believe that God would give commands that not even Jesus himself could obey? That would be contrary to the abundant teaching of Scripture about the sinlessness of Christ.

GOD'S WISDOM AND PROVIDENCE

The "non-conflicting biblical commands" position is also consistent with the infinite wisdom of God in the moral commands he gave us, and it is consistent with his providential ordering of all the circumstances of our lives. Robert Rakestraw rightly observes:

> The character of God argues for [non-conflicting absolutism]. If God has given numerous moral absolutes, some of which genuinely conflict at times, it appears that there is conflict within the mind and moral will of God! . . . The character of God as perfect and consistent within his own moral nature appears to be jeopardized by any view which holds that God's absolutes genuinely conflict.[11]

My conclusion, based on these various considerations from Scripture, is that Christians will never face a situation of impossible moral conflict, a situation where all our choices are sinful ones. I agree with Frame when he writes, "So I must conclude that there are no tragic moral choices, no conflicts of duties."[12]

---

10. John M. Frame, *The Doctrine of the Christian Life* (Phillipsburg, NJ: P&R, 2008), 232.

11. Robert V. Rakestraw, "Ethical Choices: A Case for Non-Conflicting Absolutism," in *Readings in Christian Ethics*, vol. 1, *Theory and Method*, ed. David K. Clark and Robert V. Rakestraw (Grand Rapids, MI: Baker, 1994), 123. David W. Jones also finds that "nonconflicting absolutism" is the "least problematic" of three options advocated by Christians: conflicting absolutism, graded absolutism, and nonconflicting absolutism (*An Introduction to Biblical Ethics* [Nashville: B&H, 2013], 105).

12. Frame, *Doctrine of the Christian Life*, 233; see his longer discussion on 230–34.

The "Impossible Moral Conflict" View

A different position is supported by some Christian ethicists: the "impossible moral conflict" view. This is the view that in some situations two moral obligations conflict with each other, and we have to choose the lesser sin; or to put it another way, there are situations where we must disobey a lesser command of God in order to obey a greater command. In the rest of this chapter, I will examine the arguments of three influential ethics texts that support that view, by (1) Norman Geisler, (2) John and Paul Feinberg, and (3) David Gushee and Glen Stassen.

NORMAN GEISLER

Norman Geisler gives an extensive argument for what he calls "graded absolutism" in his 2010 book *Christian Ethics: Contemporary Issues and Options*. Geisler writes, "Some personally unavoidable moral conflicts exist in which an individual cannot obey both commands."[13] In such situations, he argues:

> God does not hold a person guilty for not keeping a lower moral law so long as one keeps the higher law. God exempts one from his duty to keep the lower law since he could not keep it without breaking a higher law.[14]

> For example, in falsifying to save a life, it is not the falsehood that is good (a lie as such is always wrong), but it is the act of mercy to save a life that is good. . . . In these cases God does not consider a person culpable for the concomitant regrettable act in view of the performance of the greater good.
>   . . . Graded absolutism does not believe there are any exceptions to absolute laws, only exemptions.[15]

> When we follow the higher moral law, we are not held responsible for breaking the lower law.[16]

Geisler explains that in "graded absolutism" certain categories of moral laws are higher than others. He gives three examples:

---

13. Geisler, *Christian Ethics*, 102.
14. Ibid., 104.
15. Ibid., 109–10.
16. Ibid., 111, 115.

1. Love for God over love for humankind
2. Obeying God over obeying government
3. Mercy over veracity[17]

Geisler clearly does not say that one should choose the lesser sin and *then ask forgiveness for sinning* (a position he calls "conflicting absolutism"), because he argues that there is *no sin involved* in breaking a lower moral law in order to obey a higher one. God does not hold the person guilty at all, so there is no need to pray for forgiveness in such cases.[18]

Geisler gives several examples from Scripture and modern life to prove that sometimes we face moral conflicts in which we cannot possibly obey both commands.

Disobeying Civil Government

Geisler claims that in some biblical cases, people had to disobey the government in order to be faithful to God, and thus they had to violate one moral obligation in order to keep a higher one. He gives these examples:

1. The Hebrew midwives Shiphrah and Puah in Exodus 1:15–22, who disobeyed when Pharaoh told them to kill the Hebrew baby boys
2. Shadrach, Meshach, and Abednego (Daniel 3), who refused to bow down to the golden image made by Nebuchadnezzar
3. Daniel, who disobeyed the king's command not to pray to anyone but the king (Daniel 6)[19]
4. The apostles, who disobeyed the Sanhedrin when they were commanded not to preach in the name of Jesus (see Acts 4:18–20; also 5:29)[20]

I agree with Geisler that the biblical narrative views with approval these actions of disobeying the government in order to be faithful to God. But I disagree with Geisler's claim that these actions constituted disobedience to any command of God.

---

17. Ibid., 104–5.
18. See Geisler's explanation and rejection of conflicting absolutism in ibid., 83–96.
19. Geisler mentions these examples especially in ibid., 102–4; see also 77.
20. Ibid., 105.

The Bible never tells people to obey every command of a secular civil government without exception. Paul does not tell Christians to "obey every command of the government," but he wisely says, "Let every person *be subject to the governing authorities*" (Rom. 13:1). To "be subject" to a government in general does not mean that one always must obey every command of that government.

An important principle here is that individual verses of Scripture should be interpreted in the light of the whole teaching of Scripture. In several passages God clearly gives approval to his people who disobey the government when the government is commanding them to carry out some sinful action.[21]

Therefore, the teaching of *all of Scripture*, when rightly understood in light of the whole, is that God tells his people to *be subject* to governing authorities, but also that we have no obligation to obey when the government commands us to sin (that is, to disobey what God commands us in Scripture).[22] No example in the Bible proves that this principle ever has to be violated.

Therefore, Geisler's list of cases where people are approved for disobeying government fails to demonstrate that there are actual moral conflicts "in which an individual cannot obey both commands."

---

21. In addition to Geisler's examples, see also Est. 4:16 (Esther) and Matt. 2:8, 12 (the wise men from the East).

22. Seeking to prove that Scripture commands believers always to obey every law of government, Geisler quotes 1 Pet. 2:13, which says we should submit to "*every ordinance* of man for the Lord's sake." Unfortunately, he has to resort to the King James Version in this verse, because the Greek word that Peter uses is not one of the common words for "law" or "ordinance" (such as νόμος or δικαίωμα). Peter instead uses κτίσις, which here has the meaning "system of established authority that is the result of some founding action, governance system, authority system" (BDAG, 573). This results in the translation "Be subject for the Lord's sake to every human *institution*" (ESV; the NASB, RSV, NRSV, and NET Bible also have "institution," while the NIV, HCSB, and NLT translate it as "authority"; the NKJV alone follows the KJV and retains "ordinance" here).

The correct meaning in 1 Pet. 2:13 is "be subject . . . to every *human institution*," because Peter goes on to give specific examples: "the emperor as supreme" (2:13) and also "governors" (2:14). Therefore, the verse does not command obedience to every "ordinance of man" but rather mandates a general submission to legitimate government authority.

The other text that Geisler uses to argue that the Bible requires us to obey every law and command of government is Titus 3:1: "Remind them to be submissive to rulers and authorities, *to be obedient*, to be ready for every good work." But such a general command to be "obedient" must be understood in light of another verse that uses this same Greek word (πειθαρχέω): "But Peter and the apostles answered, 'We must *obey* [Greek, πειθαρχέω] God rather than men'" (Acts 5:29). The teaching of the New Testament as a whole shows that Christians are to be obedient to government except when government commands them to sin against God. God does not grant an "exemption" in such cases (as Geisler claims), because God has never commanded obedience to every single law of human government in the first place.

Disobeying Parents

Another example Geisler uses is when Jesus presumably did not honor or did not obey his parents in Luke 2:41–49. Geisler says, "Jesus seemed to face real conflicts between obeying his heavenly Father and obeying his earthly parents (Luke 2)."[23] Geisler states, "At age twelve, Jesus faced a conflict between his earthly parents and his heavenly Father."[24] He speaks of a time when Jesus apparently did not keep a moral command "to obey parents,"[25] and he asserts that Jesus faced a real moral conflict "between obedience toward parents and God" (Luke 2).[26]

But once again it does not seem that Geisler is precise enough in representing what Scripture actually teaches. Nowhere does the Bible say that Jesus was disobedient to his parents. If any moral wrongdoing is suggested in the passage at all, it is on the part of Jesus's parents, who left Jerusalem without being sure that Jesus was with them:

> And when the feast was ended, as they were returning, the boy Jesus stayed behind in Jerusalem. His parents did not know it, but supposing him to be in the group they went a day's journey, but then they began to search for him among their relatives and acquaintances, and when they did not find him, they returned to Jerusalem, searching for him. After three days they found him in the temple, sitting among the teachers, listening to them and asking them questions. (Luke 2:43–46)

To claim that Jesus was disobedient to his parents in this situation is to claim something that the text simply does not say.[27]

---

23. Geisler, *Christian Ethics*, 76.
24. Ibid., 94.
25. Ibid., 104.
26. Ibid., 109.
27. Geisler also says, "If parents teach a child to hate God, the child must disobey the parents in order to obey God," and this, he argues, requires disobedience to Col. 3:20 ("Children, obey your parents in everything, for this pleases the Lord") (ibid., 104). But here Geisler mistakenly isolates "obey your parents in everything" from the context, for Paul is writing to a church where the "children" listening would have believing parents, and the very next words are "for this pleases the Lord," so that Paul's command must be understood in an overall context of seeking to please God, not hating God. The broader teaching of the whole Bible (including Matt. 19:29; Mark 10:29–30; Luke 14:26; Eph. 6:1) shows that Scripture, taken as a whole, does not teach children to always obey their parents, but teaches them to always obey their parents *except when parents tell them to disobey God*. (This is similar to the Bible's teaching on obedience to the authority of civil government.)

Working on the Sabbath

Geisler says that Jesus faced a "moral conflict" "between showing mercy and keeping the Sabbath (Mark 2:27)."[28] But again Geisler's argument is based on a misunderstanding of the scriptural passage. The New Testament points out numerous cases where Jesus broke the restrictive interpretations and rules that had been added to the Sabbath command by Jewish tradition, but there is no instance in which he broke the Sabbath commandment itself when understood correctly, in the way that God intended it in the first place. Jesus makes this very point in this passage, for he corrects the Pharisee's wrongful understanding of the Sabbath law when he says, "The Sabbath was made for man, not man for the Sabbath" (Mark 2:27).[29]

Jesus never broke the Old Testament Sabbath commandment, rightly understood. Therefore, these examples do not prove that Jesus ever faced an impossible moral conflict.

Lying

Rahab. Geisler claims that some cases in the Bible involve people who were obligated to tell a lie in order to fulfill a higher moral law. He mentions the case of Rahab, the prostitute in Jericho who hid the Jewish spies and then lied about it to the king's representatives who came to her door (Josh. 2:4–6).[30]

I have discussed the case of Rahab in some detail elsewhere,[31] and Vern Poythress has supported an important aspect of my argument with an insightful analysis of some significant differences between verbal lies and deceptive actions.[32] At this point it is sufficient to note that

---

28. Ibid., 76; he repeats this claim on 94 and 109.

29. Jesus often corrected the overly strict interpretations of the Old Testament by the Jewish rabbis of his time: "Why do you break the commandment of God for the sake of your tradition?" (Matt. 15:3; see also 15:6). Regarding the specific passage to which Geisler refers about plucking grain to eat on the Sabbath (Mark 2:23–27), D. A. Carson rightly observes (about the parallel passage in Matt. 12:1–8), "It is not even clear how they were breaking any OT law, where commandments about the Sabbath were aimed primarily at regular work. . . . Indeed, apart from Halakic interpretations, it is not at all obvious that any commandment of Scripture was being broken" (D. A. Carson, "Matthew," in *Matthew, Mark, and Luke*, ed. Frank Gaebelein et al., EBC 8 (Grand Rapids, MI: Zondervan, 1984), 281.

30. Geisler, *Christian Ethics*, 105.

31. See Wayne Grudem, "Why It Is Never Right to Lie: An Example of John Frame's Influence on My Approach to Ethics," in *Speaking the Truth in Love: The Theology of John Frame*, ed. John J. Hughes (Phillipsburg, NJ: P&R, 2009), esp. 790–92.

32. Vern S. Poythress, "Why Lying Is Always Wrong: The Uniqueness of Verbal Deceit," *WTJ* 75, no. 1 (2013): 83–95.

it is doubtful whether Scripture holds up Rahab's lie as an example for believers to imitate. This is because the context shows clearly that she was hardly an example of moral excellence, for she was a Canaanite prostitute (Josh. 2:1), and she had no previous acquaintance with the moral standards that God had given to Israel. While her faith and her courage are remarkable (and the New Testament affirms her for these things—see Heb. 11:31; James 2:25), later passages of Scripture conspicuously avoid mentioning her lie. In fact, John Calvin (1509–1564) wisely observed:

> As to the falsehood, we must admit that *though it was done for a good purpose, it was not free from fault.* For those who hold what is called a dutiful lie to be altogether excusable, do not sufficiently consider how precious truth is in the sight of God. Therefore, although our purpose be to assist our brethren . . . *it can never be lawful to lie,* because that cannot be right which is contrary to the nature of God. And God is truth.[33]

Similarly, the church father Augustine (354–430) said, "But in that she lied . . . yet not as meet [appropriate] to be imitated . . . : albeit that God hath those good things memorably honored, this evil thing mercifully overlooked."[34]

Hebrew midwives in Egypt. As mentioned above, Geisler also offers the Hebrew midwives Shiphrah and Puah in Exodus 1:15–22 as examples of lying that God commends.[35] But the text does not establish that the midwives actually lied. What is clear is that Pharaoh had commanded the midwives to kill the Hebrew babies if a son was born, "but the midwives feared God and did not do as the king of Egypt commanded them, but let the male children live" (Ex. 1:17).

When challenged by Pharaoh, the midwives told him that the Hebrew women "give birth before the midwife comes to them" (Ex. 1:19), and there is no reason to doubt that this was true. In fact, when

---

33. John Calvin, *Commentary on the Book of Joshua,* trans. Henry Beveridge (Grand Rapids, MI: Baker, 2005), 47, emphasis added.

34. Augustine, *Against Lying* 34 (*NPNF*[1], 3:497), emphasis added. John Murray comes to a similar conclusion: "Neither Scripture itself nor the theological inferences derived from Scripture provide us with any warrant for the vindication of Rahab's untruth" (*Principles of Conduct* [Grand Rapids, MI: Eerdmans, 1957], 139).

35. Geisler, *Christian Ethics,* 105.

Pharaoh's plan became known to the Hebrew people, it is entirely reasonable to think that they delayed calling the midwives until after a child's birth, perhaps using other midwives or assisting one another in the birth process. God gave favor to the midwives for preserving the children's lives, but there is no proof that they lied in what they said to Pharaoh. Augustine said many centuries ago, "That therefore which was rewarded in them was, not their deceit, but their benevolence."[36]

Lying to Nazi Soldiers

Another case where lying was supposedly morally right is the afore-mentioned example of confronting Nazi soldiers who demand to know whether you have hidden Jews in your house. Although Geisler mentions the specific case of Corrie ten Boom in Holland,[37] ethics discussions often present hypothetical situations without details.

But in actual situations, there are always other options besides lying or divulging where the Jews are hidden. Silence is one option. Inviting the soldiers to come in and look around for themselves is another option. In an actual situation, several other possible responses may present themselves, even offering hospitality and refreshments to the soldiers. In the life of Corrie ten Boom herself, there is a remarkable story of God's providential protection of people they hid, a story that Vern Poythress quotes at some length in his article on why lying is always wrong.[38]

Leaving the Lights On

Geisler mentions a modern example of people who, when they go away, leave some lights on in their home to keep burglars from entering. He says that people who do this "engage in intentional deception to save their property."[39]

But once again Geisler's argument is based on a misunderstanding of Scripture. The Bible does not prohibit *all* actions that are intended to mislead someone (see Josh. 8:3–8; 1 Sam. 21:13; 2 Sam. 5:22–25);

36. Augustine, *Against Lying* 32 (*NPNF*[1], 3:495).
37. Geisler mentions lying to Nazi soldiers in order to save Jewish people as an example of mercy being a higher moral law than truthfulness (*Christian Ethics*, 106).
38. Poythress, "Why Lying Is Always Wrong," 90–92.
39. Geisler, *Christian Ethics*, 80; see also 106.

in some cases such actions are different from lying—that is, affirming something that is false. Actions such as leaving lights on at home are neither true nor false, but they are just something that happens, and they have ambiguous meanings.[40]

What Scripture forbids is bearing "false witness against your neighbor" (Ex. 20:16), and in other cases it commands us not to lie, when lying is understood as affirming in speech or writing something we believe to be false (see Eph. 4:24; Col. 3:9–10; 1 Tim. 1:10; Rev. 14:5; 21:8; 22:15).[41] Once again, taking into account the whole of Scripture, the command is quite specific: it prohibits us from telling a lie. Leaving lights on does not violate that command. Geisler's example is not sufficient to prove that we face impossible moral conflicts.

Coming Late to Dinner

Similarly, telling your wife you will meet her for dinner at 6:00 p.m. and then stopping to help a person seriously injured in an accident[42] is not violating the command against lying. In the ordinary circumstances of life, people understand that a commitment to meet someone at a certain place and time contains the implicit qualification "unless unforeseen circumstances prevent me from doing so." In such a circumstance, no reasonable person would think that the husband who was late for dinner had done something morally wrong or violated any ethical norm.[43]

Jesus Not Testifying on His Own Behalf

Geisler claims that Jesus faced two types of moral conflict at that time of his death. First, he says that "mercy and justice came into direct and unavoidable conflict. Should he speak in defense of the innocent (himself), as the law demands (Lev. 5:1), or should he show mercy to the many (humankind) by refusing to defend himself?"[44] Geisler says

---

40. See Poythress, "Why Lying Is Always Wrong," for several differences between speech and actions.

41. See my extensive discussion of lying in Grudem, "Why It Is Never Right to Lie."

42. Geisler calls this "breaking a promise" (*Christian Ethics*, 103).

43. I would say that the husband did not break his promise because the promise contained an implied condition, "unless unforeseen circumstances prevent me from doing so." Therefore, no promise was broken. Geisler, on the other hand, would say the promise was broken but this was not sin because God gives an "exemption" where a lower moral law is broken in order to obey a higher moral law.

44. Geisler, *Christian Ethics*, 94.

that Jesus "was squeezed between the demands of justice for the innocent (himself) and mercy for humankind (the guilty). He chose mercy for the many over justice for the one. This conflict . . . dramatizes the supremacy of mercy over justice in unavoidable moral conflicts."[45]

But Geisler is incorrect in his understanding of both aspects of this situation. Leviticus 5:1 says that if someone "hears a public adjuration to testify, and though he is a witness . . . yet does not speak, he shall bear his iniquity." But Jesus obeyed this, because Matthew's Gospel explicitly tells us that when the high priest commanded Jesus under oath to testify by saying, "I adjure you by the living God, tell us if you are the Christ, the Son of God," Jesus did not remain silent but actually did reply, "You have said so" (Matt. 26:63–64, with evident allusion to the command in Lev. 5:1, which Jesus was keeping).

It is an entire misunderstanding of the nature of Jesus's trial to say that he failed to fulfill the demands of justice for the innocent, for Jesus was not the judge or the Roman governor in this case. He was the innocent victim who was wrongly condemned by Pilate. Pilate committed the injustice. Jesus did not commit this injustice—he suffered the results of it!

This example surely is inadequate evidence for Geisler's claim that we sometimes face moral conflicts in which we cannot obey both commands. Jesus disobeyed no command of Scripture when he suffered and died for us, and it is demeaning to the great glory of Christ's sacrifice on the cross to think that he violated any moral command of Scripture in his suffering for us.

Murdering

Finally, Geisler mentions two other examples, both of which, he claims violate the biblical prohibition against killing.

Samson. First, there is the example of Samson,[46] who pushed with such force against the pillars of the Philistine's stadium that it collapsed on him and killed him while also destroying thousands of the Philistine enemies of Israel (Judg. 16:28–30).

Geisler again misses the point of the passage. God never *com*

45. Ibid., 109.
46. Ibid., 102.

manded Samson to kill himself, nor was there any moral law of God that said he should kill himself. It was a heroic act of self-sacrifice on Samson's part, in some ways even prefiguring the death of Christ for us, but it is not an example of someone facing an impossible moral conflict in which he could not obey multiple commands.

Abraham and Isaac. The other example that Geisler mentions is God's command that Abraham sacrifice his son Isaac.[47] Geisler says, "The story of Abraham and Isaac (Gen. 22) contains a real moral conflict. 'Thou shall not kill' is a divine moral command (Exod. 20:13 KJV), and yet God commanded Abraham to kill his son Isaac."[48]

However, it is not necessary to believe that God commanded Abraham to kill Isaac and also commanded him not to kill Isaac at the same time. First, this would not fit Geisler's "graded absolutism" paradigm, because it would not be a case of disobeying a "lower moral law" in order to obey a "higher moral law." That is because the same moral law is involved on both sides: "Kill Isaac" versus "Don't kill Isaac." And it is not a case of obeying God over government but, as Geisler presents it, a case of obeying God ("Kill Isaac") versus obeying God ("Don't kill Isaac"). Graded absolutism therefore gives us no help in such a situation.

Every interpreter agrees that this passage about Abraham and Isaac is remarkably difficult. The resolution that I find most helpful begins with the understanding that, while we cannot rightfully murder another human being, God himself does have the right to take life, and he can rightfully take the life of any human being who has sinned ("The soul who sins shall die"—Ezek. 18:4; "The wages of sin is death"—Rom. 6:23).

God also has the right to authorize human beings to carry out this punishment for sin on another human being, as he does with civil government (see Gen. 6:5–6; Rom. 13:4).[49] Abraham's thoughts were probably in turmoil. On the one hand, he must have hoped that God would provide another solution, for he said to his servants, "Stay here with the donkey; I and the boy will go over there and worship *and*

---

47. Ibid., 102, 104.
48. Ibid., 102, see also 77, 104.
49. See discussion in Wayne Grudem, *Politics according to the Bible* (Grand Rapids, MI: Zondervan, 2010), 186–90.

come again to you" (Gen. 22:5), and the Hebrew verb for "come" is plural (וְנָשׁוּבָה, literally, "we will return").

On the other hand, he must have also realized that God in his sovereignty has the right to command even the taking of a human life, and in such a case there would be no violation of the command "You shall not murder" (Ex. 20:13).[50] But somehow Abraham also realized that God would be able to restore Isaac to life, for we read, "He considered that God was able even to raise him from the dead, from which, figuratively speaking, he did receive him back" (Heb. 11:19). In any case, this difficult passage does not support Geisler's claim that sometimes we must disobey a lower moral law in order to obey a higher moral law.

We can conclude that Geisler has not provided any convincing examples to prove his claim that "some personally unavoidable moral conflicts exist in which an individual cannot obey both commands."[51] There are simply no examples in Scripture where violating one of God's moral commands is viewed with approval.

After considering several arguments that we sometimes face impossible moral conflicts, David W. Jones wisely observes:

> One of the greatest arguments in favor of non-conflicting absolutism is a natural reading of the Bible. As was noted earlier, there are no univocal examples of moral conflict in Scripture. While proponents of both conflicting and graded absolutism cite alleged examples of moral conflict in the Bible, none of these proof-texts are presented as moral conflicts in the narrative of Scripture itself—either in their appearance or in their resolution. Indeed, it seems clear that the focus of the Bible is not on conflict between moral norms but on conflict between believers and moral norms, including the temptation to sin.[52]

JOHN AND PAUL FEINBERG

The view that we sometimes face impossible moral conflicts is also found in *Ethics for a Brave New World* by John and Paul Feinberg,[53]

---

50. Note that there was no violation of the command against murder when God later told the people of Israel to destroy the Canaanites in the conquest of Canaan (Deut. 20:16–18). In God's justice, he can require the taking of the lives of sinful human beings.

51. Geisler, *Christian Ethics*, 102.

52. David W. Jones, *An Introduction to Biblical Ethics* (Nashville: B&H, 2013), 100.

53. John S. Feinberg and Paul D. Feinberg, *Ethics for a Brave New World*, 2nd ed. (Wheaton, IL: Crossway, 2010).

a book with which I often agree. But on this issue I hold a different view. The Feinbergs say:

> As to our own view, we agree that there are *prima facie* duties and that sometimes they conflict. We agree with both Ross and Geisler that obeying one and disobeying or neglecting the other is not sin. . . . If two duties mutually exclude one another, one cannot obey both. No one is free to do the impossible.[54]

Coming late to a meeting. What evidence do the Feinbergs give to prove that sometimes our duties conflict with each other and we cannot obey both? They offer the following example:

> For example, suppose someone promises to meet someone else at 10 AM. However, while on his way he sees someone in danger whom he can help. If he stops to help, he cannot keep his promise to arrive at 10 AM. [W. D.] Ross suggests that in such a case the duty to render aid is paramount, and the duty not to break a promise appears trivial. The right course of action becomes obvious. In other cases, the actual duty will be harder to discern, but one must do so anyway.[55]

My response here echoes the one I gave earlier to Geisler's example of coming late to dinner. In ordinary societal interactions, people understand that a commitment to meet someone at a certain place and time contains the *implicit qualification* "unless unforeseen circumstances prevent me from doing so." The need to help someone in danger is just such an unforeseen circumstance, and no reasonable person would think that helping someone in danger and thereby missing a meeting involves any moral wrong.

Therefore, while I agree with Geisler and the Feinbergs that it is morally right to help the person in danger and arrive late for the 10 a.m. meeting, we would have a different moral analysis of the reason it is right. They would argue that the *higher duty* to help the person in danger takes priority over the *lower duty* not to break a promise. I would say that the helping person does not sin because his promise contained an implied condition. Both the speaker and the hearer understood the

54. Ibid., 39.
55. Ibid.

promise to imply, "I will meet you at 10 a.m. unless unforeseen circumstances prevent me."

In fact, James tells Christians that they should make clear the conditional nature of promises to do something in the future:

> Come now, you who say, "Today or tomorrow we will go into such and such a town and spend a year there and trade and make a profit"—yet you do not know what tomorrow will bring. What is your life? For you are a mist that appears for a little time and then vanishes. *Instead you ought to say, "If the Lord wills, we will live and do this or that."* (James 4:13–15)

The example of Christ. Another argument the Feinbergs make is that it is "unthinkable" that Jesus himself never faced such situations where two moral duties conflicted and it was impossible to obey both. They explain:

> Our belief that one is not guilty for failing to obey both conflicting duties also stems from an appeal to the example of Christ.[56] As Geisler argues, it is unthinkable that while on earth Christ never confronted a situation where two duties conflicted so as to make it impossible to do both. In fact, Scripture says he was tempted in all points, as we are (Heb. 4:15), and since we face such situations, he must have too. However, the same verse says that he was without sin; if that is so, it must be possible to confront such decisions, obey one duty, and not sin by neglecting or disobeying the other.[57]

The reasoning in this paragraph is as follows:

1. We face situations where two moral duties cannot both be obeyed.
2. Christ was tempted in every way we are.
3. Therefore, Christ must have faced such situations also.

But where is the argument proving step 1, that we face such situations of impossible moral conflicts? There is none, other than the example

---

56. "Also" refers to the previous paragraph, which I just quoted, in which they say: "If two duties mutually exclude one another, one cannot obey both. No one is free to do the impossible" (ibid.). But they give no further reasons and merely assert that such situations do happen.
57. Ibid.

of being late for a 10 a.m. meeting, for which there is a good alternative explanation. They give no example from Scripture where Christ disobeyed a moral law of God.

The idea of deciding among some broad general duties that sometimes conflict is not found in Scripture. The Feinbergs say that they agree with Ross that "there are certain *prima facie* duties that we all have."[58] (*Prima facie* here means "self-evident, obvious.") Ross in fact lists seven such duties:

1. Fidelity
2. Reparation (repairing or making amends for harm done)
3. Gratitude
4. Beneficence (showing kindness to others)
5. Justice
6. Self-improvement
7. Non-maleficence (not doing harm)[59]

For our purposes in studying Christian ethics, notice how far from the pattern of biblical teaching is the idea that Christians should ponder such a list of seven "self-evident duties" and then decide which one has priority in each situation. Philosophers who do not derive their standards of moral right and wrong from the Bible may speak of our moral obligations as deriving from such self-evident duties, but the Bible simply does not speak that way. Nowhere do the apostles teach people to "weigh carefully your self-evident duties and decide among them."

Rather, the biblical pattern is to teach people to obey *all* of God's commandments to us:

But his delight is in the law of the LORD,
   and *on his law he meditates day and night.* (Ps. 1:2)

Blessed are those whose way is blameless,
   who walk in the law of the LORD!
Blessed are those *who keep his testimonies,*

---

58. Ibid., 38.
59. W. D. Ross, *The Right and the Good,* ed. Philip Stratton-Lake (Oxford: Clarendon, 2002), 21.

who seek him with their whole heart,
who also do no wrong,
>   but walk in his ways! (Ps. 119:1–3)

Then I shall not be put to shame,
>   having my eyes fixed on *all* your commandments.
>   (Ps. 119:6)

With my lips I declare
>   *all* the rules of your mouth. (Ps. 119:13)

All your commandments are sure. (Ps. 119:86)

Therefore I consider *all* your precepts to be right;
>   I hate every false way. (Ps. 119:128)

My tongue will sing of your word,
>   for *all* your commandments are right (Ps. 119:172)

In the New Testament, the apostles were to teach people everything that Jesus commanded, for he told them they should be "teaching them to observe *all that I have commanded you*" (Matt. 28:20). And Paul writes that "*all Scripture* is breathed out by God and profitable . . . for training in righteousness" (2 Tim. 3:16).

DAVID GUSHEE AND GLEN STASSEN

A third "impossible moral conflict" argument comes from *Kingdom Ethics* by David Gushee and Glen Stassen.[60] They argue that ethical "rules" found in the Bible are generally to be followed, but sometimes we should disobey the rules in order to follow the deeper "principles" of Scripture. Even those principles should be disobeyed at times because of even deeper "basic convictions."

But Gushee and Stassen also speak of a more specific level for decision making than the "rules" of Scripture, and that is where rules are applied to a specific situation. They call this "the level of particular

---

60. David P. Gushee and Glen H. Stassen, *Kingdom Ethics*, 2nd ed. (Grand Rapids, MI: Eerdmans, 2016).

judgments/actions." In all, Gushee and Stassen describe "four levels of moral norms" in Christian ethics:[61]

1. The level of particular judgments/actions
2. The rules level
3. The principles level
4. The level of basic convictions[62]

With each level more general than the previous one, their system works this way: (1) At the level of particular judgments/actions we would look at *one specific action* and say, "That's wrong" or "What a good thing to do!" (2) At the rules level, broader directions apply to more than one situation, such as "go the second mile" or "do not kill."[63] Deeper than the rules are (3) principles. One of the principles that Jesus teaches is "love your enemies," which is a broader principle than just going the second mile or not killing someone. The principles "provide the basis for the rules."[64]

But there is still a deeper level than principles, (4) the level of basic convictions. These are "our most basic convictions about the character, activity, and will of God and about our nature as participants in that will."[65]

Where did Gushee and Stassen get these four levels of moral norms? They tell us, "Our approach to this issue is influenced heavily by philosophical efforts to clarify what people mean when they talk about morality," and they point especially to philosophical ethicists Henry David Aiken and James Gustafson as the source for their understanding of these four levels of moral norms in Christian ethics.[66]

The difficulty with this four-level system of Gushee and Stassen is that it provides a basis for disobeying many of the moral teachings of Scripture. Is there a rule that you are uncomfortable with? No doubt a deeper principle could be found to nullify it. Or if no principle can be found, then a deeper basic conviction rooted in the character of God could be cited. But God's character has so many attributes that people

---

61. Ibid., 65.
62. Ibid., 65–69.
63. Ibid., 67.
64. Ibid.
65. Ibid., 69.
66. Ibid., 65.

could appeal to various attributes to argue for their own subjectively preferred ethical positions.

For example, in any given situation, how can we know whether the governing basic conviction is God's love or his justice? His mercy or his truthfulness? His holiness or his grace? This system puts the professor of ethics in a position of being able to argue for a whole variety of ethical positions, even those that contradict specific rules and principles of Scripture.

Gushee and Stassen explain how this can happen:

> The rules that Jesus taught are needed, binding, and to be obeyed. Exceptions are considered as a last, not first, resort. An exception is legitimate only if it is grounded in a principle or another rule that Jesus taught or that is found in Scripture. And all actions and moral judgments must pass the basic-conviction test related to the character and will of God as revealed supremely in Jesus Christ.[67]

For example, they say, "The reasons for which the rules exist sometimes can and must override the rules themselves."[68] But they give no examples from Scripture to prove their case. Instead, they make an argument based on a parent teaching a child not to touch a pot on the stove (a rule). The parent states very firmly, "Don't ever touch pots on the stove." But, Gushee and Stassen argue, the rule does not really apply "if the pot is not hot and the stove is not turned on"; nor does it apply in the same way "when a child reaches an age in which he or she can begin to cook and work with hot pots on stoves."[69]

But this simplistic analogy is hardly persuasive. The Bible does not contain instructions intended for children such as "Don't ever touch pots on the stove." Rather, it is a product of the infinite wisdom of God, a detailed and highly complex book that requires mature wisdom to understand and apply to our situation. And because Scripture is a product of the infinite wisdom of God, we do not find in it rules that we are free to break. Gushee and Stassen's argument is unconvincing.

---

67. Ibid., 72.
68. Ibid., 68.
69. Ibid., 104.

The Harmful Results of the "Impossible Moral Conflict" View

THE SLIPPERY SLOPE TOWARD GREATER SIN

The "impossible moral conflict" view becomes a slippery slope that encourages Christians to more and more sin. Students who take ethics classes in colleges or seminaries are often persuaded to adopt this position, and then they slide downward toward moral relativism. It happens this way: A college professor challenges students with some puzzling hypothetical situations that he has honed and refined over decades of teaching (such as lying to protect the Jews in your basement from the Nazis, or stealing to feed a starving family, or fending off a drowning man in order to keep everyone else alive in an overcrowded lifeboat).[70] Many students leave the class persuaded that there are really no moral absolutes, because there are times when it is morally necessary to lie, or to steal, or even to kill in order to save lives. (It does not much matter whether they adopt an explicit hierarchy of moral laws, as in Geisler's view, or one that has to be worked out in each new situation, as in the Feinbergs' view.)

If they are convinced God's love is a "basic conviction" that can at times override the rules and principles of the Bible, then personal obligations to friends or personal attachments to a romantic relationship may easily seem more important to them than telling the truth, or staying morally pure, or honoring their parents. They need only to decide that they themselves are in a situation of impossible moral conflict where they cannot fulfill both obligations.

It can happen in the workplace, where a Christian may think it acceptable to tell his or her employer a small lie to cover up for a friend, because "mercy" is a higher moral law than "veracity,"[71] and the friend really needs to keep the job. Or a youth pastor may begin embellishing testimonies of answers to prayer, because there is a higher moral obligation to advance the kingdom of God, and these amazing stories, he thinks, will build up people's faith.

---

70. Joseph Fletcher used several such examples with great impact in his influential book *Situation Ethics* (Philadelphia: Westminster Press, 1966), esp. 37, 75, 133, 136, 143, 163–66. His goal was to convince readers that there are no absolute standards of right and wrong other than the standard of "love," which he understood to mean acting in a way that will bring the greatest good to the greatest number of people in each situation (see 59, 61, 64).

71. Geisler, *Christian Ethics*, 104–5.

Or a government official who is a Christian may conclude that it is acceptable to tell small lies and then bigger lies because the higher principle is seeking the good of the country (which, of course, is most advanced if he remains in office). In these and many other situations, such complicated rationalizations actually become a shortcut to immoral behavior.

In this way, the idea that we can face impossible moral conflicts becomes an intellectual wedge that persuades people to adopt a position that functions essentially like moral relativism—there are no absolute moral standards that must always be obeyed. And, sadly, people seeking to rationalize sin will always be able to think of some "higher moral law" they have to follow in a situation of temptation. They are convinced in a philosophy class that *sometimes* people face situations of impossible moral conflict, and then—that very week!—they suddenly find they are facing one such situation themselves, and they excuse themselves for breaking a moral command of Scripture. Then they find that they are facing another such situation the next week as well. Soon they can quietly rationalize all sorts of immoral conduct. They develop a weak moral backbone and mushy moral convictions, never being sure that any actions are absolutely wrong in all circumstances.

A Simpler Perspective: Obey God's Commands

Far better than the "impossible moral conflict" view is the simple moral principle to obey what God tells us we should do in Scripture. Our task as Scripture expresses it again and again is to obey the infinite wisdom and absolute authority of God as found in his Word.

> The *law* of the LORD is perfect,
> 　　reviving the soul;
> the *testimony* of the LORD is sure,
> 　　making wise the simple;
> the *precepts* of the LORD are right,
> 　　rejoicing the heart;
> the *commandment* of the LORD is pure,
> 　　enlightening the eyes;
> the *fear* of the LORD is clean,
> 　　enduring forever;

the *rules* of the LORD are true,
    and righteous altogether.
More to be desired are they than gold,
    even much fine gold;
sweeter also than honey
    and drippings of the honeycomb.
Moreover, by them is your servant warned;
    in keeping them there is great reward. (Ps. 19:7–11)

Therefore, our approach in difficult moral situations must be to pray for God's wisdom and for strength and courage of convictions to do what is right before God: "If any of you lacks wisdom, let him ask God, who gives generously to all without reproach, and it will be given him" (James 1:5).

I have seen the real-life benefits of such a conviction. For the last fifty years I have observed that the ethical principle I defend in this chapter has given my friend Vern Poythress both a strong moral backbone and a deep faith in God's providential direction of his life. These qualities have served as great examples and encouragement to me and many others who have had the privilege of knowing Vern.

20

Perspectives on the Kingdom of God in Romans 14:17

JOHN J. HUGHES

It is a privilege to participate in honoring Vern Poythress with this Festschrift. Vern and I were students together at Westminster Theological Seminary and the University of Cambridge. During those years and subsequently, I have profited immensely from Vern's knowledge, which is broad, deep, and focused on glorifying Christ. On numerous occasions when we were students, I had opportunities to sit down with Vern and "pick his brain" on various topics. Invariably, I came away enlightened, encouraged, and motivated to dig more deeply into the topics that we had discussed. Vern's strong Christian character, gentle disposition, scintillating intellect, deep learning, and numerous publications in the fields of linguistics, logic, mathematics, science, philosophy, hermeneutics, apologetics, and theology[1] make him a model Christian scholar who deserves to be honored.

• • •

---

1. I encourage readers to browse the bibliograpy of Vern's written works later in this book.

The 2016 presidential campaign was the dirtiest and most vicious in modern history. "Lying Hillary" and "basket of deplorables" entered the American vernacular, as the candidates attacked one another and their supporters, and as supporters (Christians and non-Christians alike) took shots at one another through articles published on the Internet and elsewhere. News cycles repeatedly focused on sexual misconduct, deception, lies, and other character-degrading revelations (whether true or false) from numerous sources (whether credible or not). Division and anger roiled our nation and rolled through the Christian community.

Watching this unfold caused me to reflect on Romans 14:15–19, where Paul's threefold list of the leading characteristics of God's kingdom shows us what the Christian community *should* look like and what the world one day *will* look like. Romans 14:15–19 says:

> For if your brother is grieved by what you eat, you are no longer walking in love. By what you eat, do not destroy the one for whom Christ died. So do not let what you regard as good be spoken of as evil. For the kingdom of God is not a matter of eating and drinking but of righteousness and peace and joy in the Holy Spirit. Whoever thus serves Christ is acceptable to God and approved by men. So then let us pursue what makes for peace and for mutual upbuilding.

These verses point us upward to God, show us the way forward with one another, and provide a firm foundation of hope for a transformed world. Righteousness, peace, and joy are three perspectives on the kingdom of God—three ways of understanding what kingdom life is supposed to be like.

The relatively slim body of literature on this verse[2] and the major

---

2. Paul H. Ballard, "The Kingdom of God Is Justice and Peace," *King's Theological Review* 8 (1985): 51–54; Steven J. Cole, "Lesson 95: Keep the Main Thing the Main Thing (Rom. 14:17–18)," accessed October 15, 2016, http://bible.org/seriespage/lesson-95-keep-main-thing-main-thing-romans-1417–18; Karl Paul Donfried, "The Kingdom of God in Paul," in *The Kingdom of God in 20th-Century Interpretation*, ed. Wendell Willis (Peabody, MA: Hendrickson, 1987), 175–90; George Johnston, "'Kingdom of God' Sayings in Paul's Letters," in *From Jesus to Paul: Studies in Honor of Francis Wright Beare*, ed. Peter Richardson and John C. Hurd (Waterloo, ON: Wilfrid Laurier University Press, 1984), 143–56; Jack P. Lewis, "'The Kingdom of God . . . Is Righteousness, Peace, and Joy in the Holy Spirit' (Rom 14:17): A Survey of Interpretation," *Restoration Quarterly* 40, no. 1 (1998): 53–68; John Piper, "The Kingdom of God Is Righteousness and Peace and Joy in the Holy Spirit," accessed October 15, 2016, http://www.desiringgod.org/messages/the

commentaries on Romans[3] do not examine in great detail (1) the theological *progression* from *righteousness* to *peace* to *joy*, (2) how *righteousness*, *peace*, *love*, and *joy* form a *summary* of Paul's ethic, and
(3) how (a) *righteousness*, (b) *peace*, and (c) *love* and *joy* form a threefold *perspective* into Paul's ethic. This essay will explore those three
topics, as well as touch briefly on metaethics.[4]

Paul's Salutation, a Cornerstone

Paul's salutation to the Romans (1:1–7) is a theologically rich explanation of the multidimensional gospel that Christ called him to
proclaim—a gospel with Trinitarian, Christological, eschatological,
redemptive, and ethical aspects. The salutation begins with Paul referring to himself as a servant of Jesus the Messiah (1:1), midway through
refers to "Jesus Christ our Lord" (1:4), and concludes by referring to
"the Lord Jesus Christ" (1:7). Jesus is the long-awaited messianic King,
and he is the *Lord*.[5] *Kingship* and *kingdom* are implicit in the first
seven verses of the epistle, thus setting the stage for Paul's sole use of
kingdom of God in Romans 14:17, which is prefaced by this "kingdom
language" (notice the fivefold use of *Lord*):

> If we live, we live to the Lord, and if we die, we die to the Lord. So
> then, whether we live or whether we die, we are the Lord's. For to

-kingdom-of-god-is-righteousness-and-peace-and-joy-in-the-holy-spirit; Gary Steven Shogren, "'Is
the Kingdom of God about Eating and Drinking or Isn't It?' (Romans 14:17)," *Novum Testamentum* 42, no. 3 (2000): 238–56; and Peter-Ben Smit, "A Symposium in Rom 14:17? A Note on Paul's
Terminology," *Novum Testamentum* 49, no. 1 (2007): 40–53.

3. For example, F. F. Bruce, *The Epistle of Paul to the Romans: An Introduction and Commen-
tary*, TNTC 6 (Grand Rapids, MI: Eerdmans, 1963); C. E. B. Cranfield, *A Critical and Exegetical
Commentary on the Epistle to the Romans: Commentary on Romans IX–XVI and Essays*, ICC
(Edinburgh: T&T Clark, 1979); Charles Hodge, *Commentary on the Epistle to the Romans* (Grand
Rapids, MI: Eerdmans, 1950); Colin G. Kruse, *Paul's Letter to the Romans*, PNTC (Grand Rapids,
MI: Eerdmans, 2012); Douglas J. Moo, *The Epistle to the Romans*, NICNT (Grand Rapids, MI:
Eerdmans, 1996); Leon Morris, *The Epistle to the Romans*, PNTC (Grand Rapids, MI: Eerdmans,
1988); John Murray, *The Epistle to the Romans*, 2 vols., NICNT (Grand Rapids, MI: Eerdmans,
1968); William Sanday and Arthur C. Headlam, *A Critical and Exegetical Commentary on the
Epistle to the Romans*, 5th ed., ICC (Edinburgh: T&T Clark, 1908); Thomas R. Schreiner, *Romans*,
BECNT (Grand Rapids, MI: Baker Academic, 1998).

4. I would like to thank my friends and former teachers John Frame and Dick Gaffin for reading
this chapter and providing a number of helpful suggestions.

5. "Jesus is Lord" is the fundamental New Testament confession. E.g., "If you confess with
your mouth that Jesus is Lord and believe in your heart that God raised him from the dead, you
will be saved" (Rom. 10:9); "Therefore I want you to understand that no one speaking in the Spirit
of God ever says 'Jesus is accursed!' and no one can say 'Jesus is Lord' except in the Holy Spirit"
(1 Cor. 12:3). Also, "Let all the house of Israel therefore know for certain that God has made him
both Lord and Christ, this Jesus whom you crucified" (Acts 2:36).

this end Christ died and lived again, that he might be Lord both of the dead and of the living.

. . . For we will all stand before the judgment seat of God; for it is written,

> "As I live, says the Lord, every knee shall bow to me,
> and every tongue shall confess to God."[6]
> (Rom. 14:8–9, 10b–11)

As Shogren notes:

> According to Rom. 14:9, Christ rose from the dead "that he might be the Lord both of the dead and of the living," that is, now in this age before the eschatological resurrection, when the categories of "living and dead" would no longer be valid. As in 1 Cor. 15:24–28, Paul here posits a vital connection between Christ's resurrection and his *lordship*: his entire mission was directed toward the *kingdom*.[7]

The good news that Paul preached is the fulfillment of what the Old Testament prophets promised. It focuses on the eternal Son,[8] who became the messianic Davidic son at his incarnation and the exalted messianic Son at his resurrection (Rom. 1:2–3).[9] The contrast in Romans 1:3–4[10] between "according to the flesh" (κατὰ σάρκα) and "according to the Spirit" (κατὰ πνεῦμα) is a contrast between this age and the age to come.[11] By virtue of his Spirit-wrought resurrection,[12] God has appointed (ὁρίζω)[13] Jesus to be Son-of-God-in-power of the age to

---

6. Isa. 45:23.

7. Shogren, "Kingdom of God," 253, emphasis added.

8. See Schreiner, *Romans*, 38, regarding "concerning his Son" in 1:3; Murray, *Romans*, 1:5.

9. This movement from eternal Son to incarnate Son to resurrected Son to exalted Son is similar to Phil. 2:6–11.

10. Regarding the origin of this couplet, see Vern S. Poythress, "Is Romans 1:3–4 a Pauline Confession After All?," *Expository Times* 87, no. 6 (1975): 180–83.

11. Schreiner, *Romans*, 44: "The age dominated by the flesh is one of weakness, while the age of the Spirit is one of power. . . . The specific point of contrast is the redemptive-historical disjunction of the old age and the new age."

12. *Of holiness* (ἁγιωσύνη) in the *hapax* "the Spirit of holiness" (Rom. 1:4) may refer to the Spirit's sanctifying role in appointing (ὁρίζω)—setting apart—Jesus as Son-of-God-in-power, as God's enthroned messianic King.

13. See Acts 10:40, 42: "God raised him on the third day. . . . He is the one *appointed* by God to be judge of the living and the dead"; and 17:31: "Because he has fixed a day on which he will judge the world in righteousness by a man whom he has *appointed*; and of this he has given assurance to all by raising him from the dead" (emphasis added). Both passages use ὁρίζω, both refer to Jesus's resurrection, and both point to Christ's *lordship*: he will judge all people, living and dead.

come who now reigns over this age as "Lord" (1:4).[14] Jesus's resurrection was nothing less than his enthronement as God's messianic King and the beginning of the age to come.

As the enthroned King, Jesus has received the Holy Spirit, by means of whom he is present and exercising his reign:

> Being therefore exalted at the right hand of God, and having received from the Father the promise of the Holy Spirit, he has poured out this that you yourselves are seeing and hearing. . . . Let all the house of Israel therefore know for certain that God has made him both Lord and Christ, this Jesus whom you crucified. (Acts 2:33, 36)

Similarly, Paul associates Christ's resurrection, his exaltation, and the work of the Holy Spirit on behalf of Christ and his kingdom in a number of places. Here is a selective sketch of an exceedingly rich topic:[15]

- By virtue of his resurrection, Christ has become a "life-giving spirit" (1 Cor. 15:45).[16]
- Paul says, "The Lord is the Spirit" and then immediately refers to "the Spirit of the Lord" (2 Cor. 3:17), because the Lord is present among his people in terms of the Spirit.
- Because we are God's sons, "God has sent the Spirit of his Son into our hearts, crying, 'Abba! Father!'" (Gal. 4:6).

---

14. Note the Trinitarian nature of 1:3–4. Acts 2:30–36, which also is Trinitarian in nature, says that "God has made him both Lord and Christ, this Jesus whom you crucified" (quoting 2:36).

15. By definition, all that the "Spirit of Christ" does among his people—e.g., empowering, revealing, giving gifts—is done on behalf of Christ and his kingdom. In his excellent discussion of the relationship between Christ's resurrection and the Spirit's work on his behalf, Murray (*Romans*, 1:10–12) says: "The only conclusion is that Christ is now by reason of the resurrection so endowed with and in control of the Holy Spirit that, without any confusion of the distinct persons, Christ is identified with the Spirit and is called 'the Lord of the Spirit' (II Cor. 3:17)," (quoting p. 11).

Richard B. Gaffin Jr. states that in Paul's writings

> the eschatological aspect of the Spirit's work is most pronounced and unmistakable. His descriptions of the Spirit as "deposit" and "firstfruits," apparently coined by him, are especially calculated, in context, to express the provisional, yet truly eschatological nature of the church's present possession of the Spirit. These single terms, *arrabōn* and *aparchē*, focus the Spirit's work within the already–not yet structure of his eschatology as a whole. In Ephesians 1:14 the Spirit is the "deposit" on the church's "inheritance," an unambiguously eschatological category (cf. esp. 1:13 with 4:30; 5:5). And in Romans 8:23 and 2 Corinthians 5:5 the Spirit is "firstfruits" and "deposit" with a view towards the future resurrection body of the believer, that is, bodily eschatological existence. ("The Holy Spirit and Eschatology," *Kerux* 4, no. 3 [1989]: 14–29, accessed October 29, 2016, http://www.kerux.com/doc/0403A2.asp.)

16. First Corinthians 15, especially in verses 20–28 and 42–49, contains Paul's most extensive correlation of Christ's resurrection and exaltation and the work of the Holy Spirit on behalf of Christ and his kingdom.

- And in Romans 8:9–11, Paul says:

  You, however, are not in the flesh but in the Spirit, if in fact the Spirit of God dwells in you. Anyone who does not have the Spirit of Christ does not belong to him. But if Christ is in you, although the body is dead because of sin, the Spirit is life because of righteousness. If the Spirit of him who raised Jesus from the dead dwells in you, he who raised Christ Jesus from the dead will also give life to your mortal bodies through his Spirit who dwells in you.[17]

As the reigning Lord, Jesus commissioned Paul to be his apostle (Rom. 1:1, 5) "to bring about the obedience of faith for the sake of his name among all the nations" (1:5). The gospel about the Son calls us to trust and obey the Son-of-God-in-power, the *Lord*. Because Christ is Lord, he calls us through the gospel to obedience.

Christ's lordship and Christian ethics are correlative. There can be no truly Christian ethic unless Christ is Lord; and because Christ is Lord, we are called to obey him. Thus Romans 1:1–7 forms the cornerstone of the foundation that Paul's long "ethical" section in Romans 12–15 rests on—a section whose coda refers back to Paul's initial thoughts in 1:1–7:

  For I will not venture to speak of anything except what Christ has accomplished through me to bring the Gentiles to obedience—by word and deed, by the power of signs and wonders, by the power of the Spirit of God—so that from Jerusalem and all the way around to Illyricum I have fulfilled the ministry of the gospel of Christ. (Rom. 15:18–19)

The Kingdom of God in Paul's Teaching

In keeping with his already/not-yet eschatological teaching, Paul portrays the kingdom of God as both present and future. Romans 14:17

---

17. Romans 8 focuses on "life in the Spirit"—"If the Spirit of him who raised Jesus from the dead dwells in you, he who raised Christ Jesus from the dead will also give life to your mortal bodies through his Spirit who dwells in you" (8:11)—and concludes with one of the strongest affirmations of Jesus's lordship and kingly reign found in the New Testament: "For I am sure that neither death nor life, nor angels nor rulers, nor things present nor things to come, nor powers, nor height nor depth, nor anything else in all creation, will be able to separate us from the love of God in Christ Jesus our Lord" (8:38–39).

and 1 Corinthians 4:20 ("For the kingdom of God does not consist in talk but in power") are the only two places in his writings where the phrase *kingdom of God* explicitly refers to a present reality. Colossians 1:13, "He has delivered us from the domain of darkness and transferred us to the kingdom of his beloved Son," is another reference to the present reality of Christ's kingdom.

In 1 Corinthians 4:20 and Romans 14:17, the disjunctive negative construction οὐ γάρ . . . ἀλλά indicates that Paul is sharply contrasting the behavior and concerns of this age (*talk* in 1 Cor. 4:20; *eating* and *drinking* in Rom. 14:17) with those of the age to come (*power* in 1 Cor. 4:20; *righteousness, peace,* and *joy in the Holy Spirit* in Rom. 14:17). His comments in both verses are expressions of his two-age eschatology. The reference to the Holy Spirit in Romans 14:17 underscores this two-age context. The ethics of the coming kingdom define the ethics of the kingdom's present manifestation.[18]

The remaining eleven references to *kingdom of God* in Paul's writings generally refer to it as a future reality, though two (1 Thess. 2:12; 2 Thess. 1:5) seem to indicate that it also exists now. It is our inheritance[19] as Christians; God has called us into it (1 Thess. 2:12). Paul worked for its coming (Col. 4:11) and trusted God to bring him safely into it (2 Tim. 4:18). Paul assured the suffering Thessalonians that they would be counted worthy of the kingdom (2 Thess. 1:5), and he looked forward to the time when Christ and the future kingdom would appear (2 Tim. 4:1). After Christ and his kingdom appear, "then comes the end, when he delivers the kingdom to God the Father after destroying

---

18. Murray (*Romans*, 2:193) says:

> The kingdom of God is that realm to which believers belong. Nothing defines their identity more characteristically than that they are members of it (*cf.* John 3:3–8; I Thess. 2:12). It should not be forgotten that the emphasis falls upon the rule of God. It is the sphere in which God's sovereignty is recognized and his will is supreme. Thus the mention of God's kingdom should always have the effect of summoning believers to that frame of mind that will make them amenable to the paramount demand of their calling, the will of God. It is in this perspective that the negation appears in its true light—it "is not eating and drinking."

Commenting on my remarks in this paragraph about Rom. 14:17, in an email to me dated November 4, 2016, Richard Gaffin said: "The most explicit correlate anthropological statement in Paul is 2 Corinthians 4:16: Therefore we do not despair, but though our outer man/self [= 'body' elsewhere in Paul; as we continue to exist in this age] is decaying, yet our inner man/self ['heart' elsewhere in Paul; as we have already entered into the age to come; 5:17, the 'new creation'] is being renewed day by day."

19. 1 Cor. 6:9–10; 15:50; Gal. 5:21; Eph. 5:5 ("the kingdom of Christ and God").

every rule and every authority and power. For he must reign until he has put all his enemies under his feet" (1 Cor. 15:24–25). Christ's reign ends with the complete defeat of "all his enemies."

There is one kingdom with two phases: the present *reign* of God through Christ by means of his Spirit in and among his people and the future *realm* where that reign will be perfected globally and "every knee shall bow" before him and "every tongue shall confess to God" (Rom. 14:11, quoting Isa. 45:23; cf. Phil. 2:9–11)—the consummation of the kingdom at the end of this age (1 Cor. 15:24–25), when "we must all appear before the judgment seat of Christ, so that each one may receive what is due for what he has done in the body, whether good or evil" (2 Cor. 5:10).

The Ethics of the Kingdom: Romans 12:1–15:13

Romans concludes with a long section of exhortations (12:1–15:13) that are closely based on (and therefore "flow from") chapters 1–11.[20] As Murray notes:

> The Holy Spirit is the Spirit of the ascended Lord (*cf.* 8:4, 9). Hence, when Paul at 12:1 enters the sphere of practical teaching, he does so on the basis of his earlier teaching. . . . Ethics must rest on the foundation of redemptive accomplishment. . . . Ethics springs from union with Christ and therefore from participation of the virtue belonging to him and exercised by him as the crucified, risen, and ascended Redeemer. Ethics consonant with the high calling of God in Christ is itself part of the application of redemption; it belongs to sanctification.[21]

Broadly speaking (and in keeping with Paul's emphasis on Christ's lordship in the salutation to the letter), Romans 12:1–15:13 is about *kingdom* behavior—God's will spelled out in specific instructions and examples.[22] Paul's arguments in this section primarily appeal to, and use as warrants for his exhortations, worship (12:1), love (12:9;

---

20. See Schreiner, *Romans*, 639: "The οὖν commencing 12:1 harks back all the way to 1:16–11:36."

21. Murray, *Romans*, 2:110.

22. As Schreiner (*Romans*, 640) and Murray (*Romans*, 2:109–10) note, Paul's ethical teaching in Romans is not limited to 12:1–15:13 but may also be found in chapters 6–8, for example. Rom. 12:1–15:13 is a presentation of various major ethical topics, not an attempt to present a systematic ethic.

13:8–10; 14:15), and the kingdom of God (righteousness, peace, and joy—14:17). Schreiner notes that

> Romans 12:1–2 serve as the paradigm for the entire exhortation section (12:1–15:13). . . . If all the exhortations contained here could be boiled down to their essence, they would be reduced to the words: Give yourselves wholly to God; do not be shaped by the old world order, but let new thought patterns transform your life. The subsequent context (12:1–15:13) fleshes out the nature of this dedication in concrete ways.[23]

Romans 12:1–2 is the language of worship, of complete submission— body and mind—to God that we might serve him by knowing and doing his will. It is language rich with "kingdom overtones." The phrase "acceptable to God" in verse 1 is used again in Romans 14:18—"Whoever thus serves Christ is acceptable to God and approved by men"—where "thus [ἐν τούτῳ] serves Christ" includes all of the kingdom of God language in Romans 14:17.[24] Both passages are concerned with our doing the will of God.

THE THEOLOGICAL PROGRESSION FROM RIGHTEOUSNESS TO PEACE TO JOY IN ROMANS 14:17

Romans 14:17 occurs in the context of Paul's discussion about "the strong" and "the weak." Schreiner does an admirable job of presenting the various views regarding their identity,[25] concluding that "the weak" primarily were Jewish Christians who observed the purity laws, and "the strong" primarily were Gentile Christians who considered the purity laws to be passé.[26]

Paul's statement in verse 17, "For the kingdom of God is not a matter of eating and drinking but of righteousness and peace and joy in the Holy Spirit,"[27] is used as a warrant to justify his argument that

23. Schreiner, *Romans*, 640.
24. Ibid., 741.
25. Ibid., 19–23, 640–41.
26. Moo, *Romans*, 828–33, reaches a similar conclusion.
27. Because *joy* is coordinated with *righteousness* and *peace*, "in the Holy Spirit" is best understood as qualifying all three terms (so Murray, *Romans*, 2:193–94; Moo, *Romans*, 857n46; and Schreiner, *Romans*, 741). All three are gifts of the Spirit—gifts given to advance the kingdom. As Schreiner puts it (*Romans*, 741), "The kingdom of God consists in his transforming power, induction into eschatological peace, and supernatural joy (cf. 1 Thess. 1:6)."

Christians should "not pass judgment on one another any longer, but rather decide never to put a stumbling block or hindrance in the way of a brother" (14:13) and "not let what you regard as good[28] be spoken of as evil" (14:16). Paul is countering one form of behavior—misusing Christian liberty—by appealing to behavior that is righteous, that leads to peace, and that results in joy.

Misusing Christian liberty raises stumbling blocks and hindrances (14:13), grieves others (14:15), destroys those for whom Christ died (14:15), and results in judging good to be evil (14:16).[29] The right use of Christian liberty is behavior that is "acceptable to God and approved by men" (14:18) and that "makes for peace and for mutual upbuilding" (14:19). So, righteousness, peace, and joy refer to Christian behavior and are to be understood ethically.[30]

But *righteousness, peace, joy,* and *Holy Spirit* in Romans 14:17 allude to *justified* (declare to be righteous), *peace, rejoice,* and *Holy Spirit* in Romans 5:1–2, 5, where *righteousness* and *peace* are used forensically and where the Holy Spirit is said to have been given to us. God's kingdom consists of the blessings of righteousness, peace, and joy that he sovereignly gives to Christians by means of the Holy Spirit (Rom. 5:1–2, 5), and these three eschatological qualities are to be manifested in Christian behavior (Rom. 14:17). The blessings that God gives by means of the Spirit are to be expressed in Christian behavior by means of the Spirit.[31]

In Romans 5:1, justification results in peace: "Therefore, since we have been justified by faith, we have peace with God through our Lord Jesus Christ." Having been declared righteous, we have peace with God. In other words:

- Righteousness is a necessary condition for peace, and righteousness results in peace.

---

28. Murray (*Romans*, 2:193) and Moo (*Romans*, 855) understand "good" (cf. 1 Cor. 10:29–30) as a reference to the liberty that the strong enjoy regarding eating and drinking. Schreiner (*Romans*, 729) understands it as "a comprehensive way of referring to the gospel and all of God's gifts." I follow Murray and Moo.

29. Schreiner (*Romans*, 733–35) has an excellent discussion of the terms used to describe the damage that can be done to "the weak," and concludes, "These terms reveal that the danger spoken of here is nothing less than eschatological judgment. . . . The very salvation of the 'weak' was at stake."

30. So Murray, *Romans*, 2:193–94.

31. Of course, we cannot justify one another, but we can treat one another righteously. We cannot establish peace in a definitive sense, but we can work for peace.

- We cannot have peace with God unless we have been declared righteous, and having been declared righteous, we have peace with God.

The same pattern is present in Romans 14:17:

- Righteousness is a necessary condition for peace, and righteousness results in peace.
- We cannot be at peace with others unless we treat them righteously, and treating others righteously results in peace.

In both cases—Romans 5 and 14—the result of righteousness and peace is joy or rejoicing. In the former case, it is rejoicing "in hope of the glory of God" (5:2), a hope that does not put us to shame because it flows from the love that God has put in our hearts by means of his Spirit (5:5). In the latter case, joy is personal and communal as Christians see the kingdom of God flourishing in their lives and in their midst by means of God's Spirit.

Not surprisingly, Paul concludes the ethical section of Romans by echoing his earlier kingdom language: "May the God of hope fill you with all joy and peace in believing, so that by the power of the Holy Spirit you may abound in hope" (Rom. 15:13).

To the extent that we practice righteousness, pursue peace, and rejoice when we see both of these in our lives and in our relationships, the kingdom of God is manifest in our midst and is visible to the world, and we are "acceptable to God and approved by men" (Rom. 14:18). Peace is the fruit of treating people righteously, on the one hand, and of pursuing it actively, on the other, which is why Paul concludes Romans 14:15–19 by saying, "So then let us pursue what makes for peace and for mutual upbuilding" (14:19).[32]

Righteousness, Peace, and Joy and Love Are a *Summary* of Paul's Ethic

Ethical teachers (and Paul was, among other things, a teacher of ethics) often employ summary statements—sometimes maxims—that capture the heart of their teaching and that help their students grasp

---

32. See Rom. 12:18: "If possible, so far as it depends on you, live peaceably with all."

the essentials. Summaries can focus on ethical standards, motives, or goals. Consider the following selective examples, some biblical and some not:

- Moses: "Hear, O Israel: The LORD our God, the LORD is one. You shall love the LORD your God with all your heart and with all your soul and with all your might" (Deut. 6:4–5).
- The Decalogue, though longer than a maxim, is another ethical summary, one that many Jews and Christians memorize.
- Micah: "He has told you, O man, what is good; / and what does the LORD require of you / but to do justice, and to love kindness, / and to walk humbly with your God?" (Mic. 6:8).
- Jesus: "You shall love the Lord your God with all your heart and with all your soul and with all your mind. This is the great and first commandment. And a second is like it: You shall love your neighbor as yourself. On these two commandments depend all the Law and the Prophets" (Matt. 22:37–40).
- Jesus: "Do to others as you would have them do to you" (Luke 6:31 NIV).
- Paul: The commandments "are summed up in this word: 'You shall love your neighbor as yourself'" (Rom. 13:9).
- Paul: "The kingdom of God is not a matter of eating and drinking but of righteousness and peace and joy in the Holy Spirit" (Rom. 14:17).
- Paul: "So, whether you eat or drink, or whatever you do, do all to the glory of God" (1 Cor. 10:31).
- Immanuel Kant: "Act only according to that maxim by which you can at the same time will that it should become a universal law."[33]
- Immanuel Kant: "Act in such a way that you treat humanity, whether in your own person or in the person of another, always at the same time as an end and never simply as a means."[34]
- Jeremy Bentham: "The greatest happiness of the greatest number is the foundation of morals and legislation."[35] This is often

---

33. "Kantian Ethics," accessed October 26, 2016, https://en.wikipedia.org/wiki/Kantian_ethics #Good_will_and_duty.

34. Ibid. Kant was a deontologist.

35. "Jeremy Bentham," accessed October 26, 2016, https://en.wikiquote.org/wiki/Jeremy _Bentham. Bentham was a utilitarian, which is a form of teleological ethics.

shortened to the pithier "the greatest good for the greatest number."

- Jean-Paul Sartre: "Act authentically."[36]

Because summary statements and maxims state general truths, fundamental principles, or basic rules of conduct, they require "unpacking"; they necessitate a certain level of exposition in order to be correctly understood and *applied*. Understanding Romans 14:17 as a Pauline ethical maxim requires that we explore what *kingdom of God*, *righteousness, peace, joy*, and *in the Holy Spirit* mean in Paul's ethic. What follows is a brief explanation of those terms.

"KINGDOM OF GOD" AND "IN THE HOLY SPIRIT"

Paul's ethic is Christological and eschatological. As we saw earlier, by virtue of his Spirit-wrought resurrection, God has appointed Jesus to be Son-of-God-in-power of the age to come who now reigns over this age as Lord (Rom. 1:4). The resurrection was Jesus's enthronement as God's messianic King. He reigns over the kingdom on God's behalf, so that the kingdom can be called "the kingdom of God" as well as "the kingdom of Christ" (Eph. 5:5; 2 Pet. 1:11; Rev. 11:15).

Paul's ethic requires the empowering presence of the Holy Spirit to be carried out (Rom. 8:1–17). We also saw earlier that as the enthroned King, Jesus has received the Holy Spirit, by means of whom he is present and exercises his reign in and among his people. The Spirit equips and empowers God's people for kingdom work in all its forms.

Because *righteousness, peace*, and *joy* in Romans 14:17 define kingdom behavior, they are to be understood Christologically, eschatologically, and pneumatically.

RIGHTEOUSNESS

Righteousness refers to right behavior toward God and people. It is a normative concept, functioning as a standard. In the Sermon on the Mount (Matt. 5:1–7:29),[37] Jesus taught that we should seek, above all

---

36. Christian J. Onof, "Jean Paul Sartre: Existentialism," accessed October 26, 2016, http://www.iep.utm.edu/sartre-ex/. Sartre was an existentialist.

37. The body of the Sermon on the Mount is demarcated by "the Law and the Prophets" in 5:17 and 7:12. Jesus pointedly related his teaching to the Old Testament.

else, God's kingdom "and his righteousness" (6:33) and that we should pray for God's kingdom to come and for his will to be done on earth as it is in heaven (6:10). He authoritatively interpreted and applied the law to his disciples, prefacing his opening remarks by saying, "Do not think that I have come to abolish the Law or the Prophets; I have not come to abolish them but to fulfill them" (5:17).[38]

Similarly, Paul "treats the basic principles of the Mosaic law as normative for Christians in passages like Romans 13:8–10; 1 Corinthians 7:19; and Galatians 5:13–14. And, like Jesus, he also sets forth ethical commands, as in Romans 12–15; Galatians 5:13–6:10; and Ephesians 4–6."[39] The basic principles of the Mosaic law, understood in terms of Christ's lordship and the realities of the new covenant, form the core of Paul's understanding of righteousness. Consider three Pauline texts:

> For neither circumcision counts for anything nor uncircumcision, but keeping the commandments of God. (1 Cor. 7:19)

> For you were called to freedom, brothers. Only do not use your freedom as an opportunity for the flesh, but through love serve one another. For the whole law is fulfilled in one word: "You shall love your neighbor as yourself." (Gal. 5:13–14)

> Owe no one anything, except to love each other, for the one who loves another has fulfilled the law. For the commandments, "You shall not commit adultery, You shall not murder, You shall not steal, You shall not covet," and any other commandment, are summed up in this word: "You shall love your neighbor as yourself." Love does no wrong to a neighbor; therefore love is the fulfilling of the law. (Rom. 13:8–10)

Paul's ethical teaching is by no means restricted to those three passages—it occurs throughout his letters—and it is not confined to the

---

38. Much has been written about the relationship of the old covenant law to our obligations in the new covenant. It is beyond the scope of this chapter to delve into this topic. For an excellent discussion, see chapter 12, "Law in Biblical Ethics," in John M. Frame, *The Doctrine of the Christian Life* (Phillipsburg, NJ: P&R, 2008), 176–99. For a helpful discussion of Matt. 5:17–20, see D. A. Carson, "Matthew," in *Matthew, Mark, Luke,* ed. Frank E. Gaebelein et al., EBC 8 (Grand Rapids, MI: Zondervan, 1984), 140–47.

39. Frame, *Doctrine of the Christian Life,* 181.

language of the Ten Commandments but includes much more. For example, in Romans 14 Paul commands us not to pass judgment on one another (14:13), not to put stumbling blocks in one another's way (14:13), not to grieve one another (14:15), and not to destroy one another (14:15). Such behaviors are incompatible with "walking in love" (14:15).

In Romans 13:8–10; 14:15; and Galatians 5:13–14, Paul defines *love* not as an emotion or a feeling but as *action*: serving one another, keeping specific commandments, doing no wrong to one's neighbor, treating one's neighbor as we would want to be treated, and not grieving our fellow Christians. Paul also defines love as *affection*, commanding us to "love one another with brotherly affection. Outdo one another in showing honor" (Rom. 12:10; cf. 15:30).[40]

Peace

Peace refers to the absence of conflict and the presence of right relationships with God and people. *Peace* is a situational concept; it functions as a goal. Paul's goal-focused language in Romans 12:18 and 14:19 is instructive: "If possible, so far as it depends on you, live peaceably with all" (12:18), and "So then let us pursue what makes for peace and for mutual upbuilding" (14:19).

Joy and Love

Joy refers to an emotion—the unmerited delight we experience when we observe or reflect on the result of the Spirit's work.[41] Joy always has a referent outside of us.[42] In the context of Romans 14:17, joy may

---

40. Frame (ibid., 333) says, "Love should be defined triperspectivally as allegiance (normative perspective), as well as action (situational perspective), and affection (existential perspective)." Chapter 12, "Law in Biblical Ethics," 176–99, focuses on love as the center of biblical ethics. In an email to me dated October 31, 2016, John said, "To use love for *allegiance* is more an OT concept than Pauline. But I think it is implicit at least in Rom. 13:8; 15:30; and elsewhere—e.g., the various references to love fulfilling the law."

41. Joy is not a mere feeling. Feelings are bodily responses to various internal and external stimuli. I feel warm or cold. I feel sleepy or alert. I feel happy or sad. I'm hungry or not. Although joy is not a *mere* feeling, it can be a response to bodily states (suggested to me by John Frame in an email, October 31, 2016). For example, if I wake up after a successful surgery and realize that I am going to be okay, I rejoice, giving God the glory. Similarly, if I wake up refreshed after a particularly restful night of sleep, I also rejoice.

42. For example, we rejoice in "hope of the glory of God" (Rom. 5:2); "in our sufferings" because they lead to hope (Rom. 5:3); in God for our reconciliation (Rom. 5:11); in seeing obedience among fellow Christians (Rom 16:19); when a fellow Christian is honored (1 Cor. 12:26); "with the truth" (1 Cor. 13:6); at the coming of Christian friends (1 Cor. 16:17); in the confidence that

refer to delighting in the peaceful state of affairs that is brought about by Spirit-empowered righteous behavior. Joy is an existential concept, and it can be individual or corporate. Interestingly, joy can be commanded; we are obligated to be joyful![43]

In the climax to his argument about "the weak" and "the strong" (Rom. 14:13–19), Paul appeals to *love*, a key ethical theme in Romans 12:10 and 13:8–10 and one of the dominant ethical themes in Romans 12:1–15:13. "Walking in love" (14:15) should control all Christian behavior, all our actions. Paul's appeal to "walking in love" in verse 15 is the overarching *motive* for serving Christ (14:18) by practicing righteousness, pursuing peace, and being joyful (14:17).

Like joy, love is an existential concept. Unlike joy, love is a *motive* for action, whereas joy is a *response* to something outside of us.

Righteousness, Peace, and Joy and Love Are *Perspectives* on Paul's Ethic

Righteousness is a normative concept; it functions as a standard. *Peace* is a situational concept; it functions as a goal. *Love* and *joy* are existential concepts; *love* functions as a motive or attitude, and *joy* functions as a response. *Righteousness*, *peace*, and *love* and *joy* are *perspectives* on Paul's ethic.[44]

---

we have in other Christians (2 Cor. 7:16). We rejoice in a beautiful sunrise or sunset; in seeing a herd of majestic antelope racing across the high plains; over the birth of a child; and so forth. For an insightful theological essay on *joy*, see Miroslav Volf, "What Is the Difference between Joy and Happiness?," accessed October 27, 2016, https://www.bigquestionsonline.com/2014/10/21/what -difference-between-joy-happiness/.

43. For example, "Rejoice in hope, be patient in tribulation, be constant in prayer" (Rom. 12:12); "Rejoice with those who rejoice, weep with those who weep" (Rom. 12:15); "rejoice in the Lord" (Phil. 3:1; 4:4); and "rejoice always" (1 Thess. 5:16). God can also command other *states* (for lack of a better term). In an email to me dated October 31, 2016, John Frame pointed out that we can also be commanded to be alert as opposed to sleepy, e.g., 1 Thess. 5:6—"So then let us not sleep, as others do, but let us keep awake and be sober"—and similar references in the Gospels, e.g., Matt. 24:42–43.

44. Much of the following discussion makes use of Frame's triperspectivalism and of Poythress's complementary concept, symphonic theology. For simplicity's sake, I will use the terms "triperspectivalism" and "perspectivalism." For more on symphonic theology, see Vern S. Poythress, *Symphonic Theology: The Validity of Multiple Perspectives in Theology* (Phillipsburg, NJ: P&R, 1987) and his *Redeeming Philosophy: A God-Centered Approach to the Big Questions* (Wheaton, IL: Crossway, 2014). For John M. Frame's development of perspectivalism, see his *The Doctrine of the Knowledge of God* (Phillipsburg, NJ: Presbyterian and Reformed, 1987); *The Doctrine of God* (Phillipsburg, NJ: P&R, 2002); *The Doctrine of the Christian Life* and *The Doctrine of the Word of God* (Phillipsburg, NJ: P&R, 2010); and *Systematic Theology: An Introduction to Christian Belief* (Phillipsburg, NJ: P&R, 2013). Many free e-books and articles by Poythress and Frame can be found on their site: http://frame-poythress.org/.

Ethical judgment "always involves the application of a *norm* to a *situation* by a *person*. These three factors can also be seen as overall perspectives on the study of ethics."[45] In discussing various ways of developing perspectives on ethics, Poythress says:

> One approach is to ask what rules and standards govern human conduct. This perspective starts with standards, or norms. . . .
> Another route to ethics starts with the goal of Christian living. The goal of Christians is to do all for the glory of God (1 Cor. 10:31). . . . We might almost call this approach to ethics "situational," "utilitarian," or "pragmatic," since Paul is saying that we must pay attention to what is useful, to what helps our situation, to what promotes God's glory in practice. . . .
> A third approach to ethics is the attitudinal perspective. In this perspective we evaluate human actions in terms of the attitudes and motives of the person doing the action. . . .
> We now have perspectives on ethics starting with standard, goal, and attitude. . . . Each perspective is obtained by expanding on an emphasis and a focus embodied in Scripture. In each case this focus becomes the starting point for a perspective on the whole field of ethics.[46]

Frame makes the same points this way:

> (1) Christian ethics is normative, applying the moral laws of God given in Scripture and nature. (2) It is also situational, in that it analyzes the world that God has made to know how best to apply God's norms to a given situation. And (3) it is existential, in that it deals with the ethical agent to understand his role in making ethical decisions, how he takes the norms of God and applies them to his situation. In making decisions, the Christian goes round and round the triangle [see fig. 4], interpreting the situation by the moral law, applying the moral law by investigating the situation, and understanding both of these through his subjective faculties.[47]

---

45. Frame, *Systematic Theology*, 1109. I will refer to this group of three concepts, along with other "threesomes," as a *triad*. See John M. Frame, *Salvation Belongs to the Lord: An Introduction to Christian Theology* (Phillipsburg, NJ: P&R, 2006), 330.
46. Poythress, *Symphonic Theology*, 34–36.
47. John M. Frame, *A History of Western Philosophy and Theology* (Phillipsburg, NJ: P&R, 2015), 34–35.

ETHICAL PERSPECTIVES IN ROMANS 14:15, 17

Figure 4 shows what this ethical triad looks like in Romans 14:15, 17.

Figure 4. Ethical perspectives in Romans 14:15, 17

Normative Perspective: *Righteousness*
(Standard)

Situational Perspective: *Peace*
(Goal)

Existential Perspective: *Love, Joy*
(Motive/Attitude, Response)

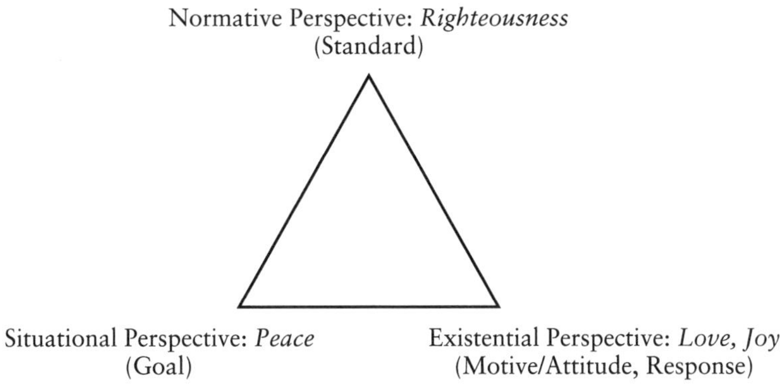

Righteousness refers to right conduct. It is the norm that we are to apply to every situation. *Peace* refers to the right relationships that result from treating one another righteously. It is the situation we are to strive to bring about. *Love* refers to an attitude (and to action), while *joy* refers to the heartfelt emotion of true delight in the peaceful state of affairs brought about by righteous behavior. *Love* and *joy* refer to what our attitudes, motives, and responses should be like.

The righteousness, peace, and love and joy of which Paul speaks are possible only by means of the empowering presence of the Holy Spirit, on the one hand, and our decision to serve Christ "in this way" (Rom. 14:18 NIV), on the other. Paul's righteousness-peace-love/joy triad is a significant definition of what the kingdom of God looks like, both now and in the future.

ETHICAL PERSPECTIVES IN ROMANS 14:17

Romans 14:17 contains another triad, one that envelops the verse as a whole. Figure 5 shows what this ethical triad looks like.

The kingdom of God can be seen as normative; righteousness, peace, and joy as situational; and the Holy Spirit as existential—God's presence with us.

Figure 5. Ethical perspectives in Romans 14:17

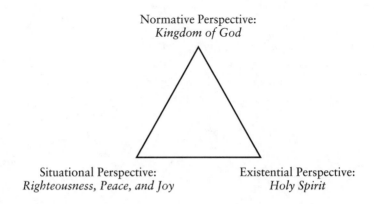

Normative Perspective:
Kingdom of God

Situational Perspective: Existential Perspective:
Righteousness, Peace, and Joy   *Holy Spirit*

THE INTERDEPENDENCE AND INCLUSIVITY OF PERSPECTIVES

How do the perspectives in these ethical triads relate to one another? Poythress offers an instructive summary:

1. Each perspective has a separate focus of interest.
2. Each perspective is, in the end, dependent on the others and intelligible only in the context of the others.
3. Each perspective is, in principle, harmonizable with the others.
4. Any one perspective, when expanded far enough, involves the others and, in fact, encompasses the others. Each can be viewed as an aspect of the others.
5. Because of the tendency to human oversight or one-sided emphasis, each perspective is useful in helping us to notice facts and relationships that tend to be further in the background in the other perspectives.[48]

Poythress concludes: "The perspectives are like facets of a jewel. The whole jewel—the whole of ethics—can be seen through any *one* of the facets, if we look carefully enough. But not everything can be seen equally easily through only one facet."[49] Later he writes: "We use what we have gained from one perspective to reinforce, correct, or improve what we understand through another. I call this procedure *symphonic*

---

48. Poythress, *Symphonic Theology*, 36.
49. Ibid.

theology because it is analogous to the blending of various musical instruments to express the variations of a symphonic theme."[50]

Put another way, the perspectives in a given triad (e.g., ethical) are *interdependent* and *inclusive*. These are foundational concepts for triperspectivalism. In "A Primer on Perspectivalism," Frame says:

> All finite perspectives are *interdependent*. God's perspective is independent in a way that ours are not, for God governs all perspectives. But even his knowledge, as we have seen, includes a knowledge of all finite perspectives. And all finite perspectives must, to attain truth, "think God's thoughts after him." So in one sense, all perspectives coincide. Each, when fully informed, includes all the knowledge found in every other. There is one truth, and each perspective is merely an angle from which that truth can be viewed.[51]

For our purposes, we may define *interdependence* and *inclusivity* as follows:[52] Two (or more) perspectives are *interdependent* if each is necessary for properly understanding the other.[53] No one has made this point more clearly than John Calvin in his opening statements in the *Institutes*. At the beginning of book 1, chapter 1, under the heading "The Knowledge of God and That of Ourselves Are Connected. How They Are Interrelated," Calvin's first and second points are "1. Without knowledge of self there is no knowledge of God," and "2. Without knowledge of God there is no knowledge of self"; each is a necessary

50. Ibid., 43.
51. Accessed October 27, 2016, http://frame-poythress.org/a-primer-on-perspectivalism-revised-2008/. Also see Frame, *Doctrine of the Knowledge of God*, 18–40, and John M. Frame, *Cornelius Van Til: An Analysis of His Thought* (Phillipsburg, NJ: P&R, 1995), 97–113. C. S. Lewis offers a similar insight about perspectives in his essay "Meditation in a Toolshed," in *God in the Dock: Essays on Theology and Ethics*, ed. Walter Hooper (Grand Rapids, MI: Eerdmans, 1994), 212–15. Lewis distinguishes between "looking at" and "looking along." To "look along" is to see something from the inside, rather than analytically from without—to experience it subjectively, not just objectively. As Lewis stood in a dark toolshed, he *looked at* a sunbeam coming in. He saw the beam itself and nothing more. Then he moved and *looked along* the beam. The previous picture vanished, and he saw the world outside the toolshed. He stepped outside of one experience and into another. Instead of seeing the beam, he was seeing the world as the beam revealed it. Stepping out of one experience and into another is equivalent to looking at something from a new perspective.
52. Some of the material in the following pages is taken, in modified form, from my chapter "The Heart of John Frame's Theology," in *Speaking the Truth in Love: The Theology of John M. Frame*, ed. John J. Hughes (Phillipsburg, NJ: P&R, 2009), 31–74.
53. *Reciprocity* and *correlativity* are other terms sometimes used to describe the interdependence of perspectives in triperspectivalism.

but not a sufficient condition for the other.[54] Immediately after making the first point, Calvin says, "Nearly all the wisdom we possess, that is to say, true and sound wisdom, consists of two parts: the knowledge of God and of ourselves. But, while joined by many bonds, which one precedes and brings forth the other is not easy to discern."[55]

The inclusivity of perspectives is a function of their interdependence. If two (or more) perspectives—knowledge of God and knowledge of man—are interdependent, they also are mutually inclusive, because studying one perspective *necessarily* requires studying the other to gain a full understanding of either perspective. I believe that when Calvin says, "Which one precedes and brings forth the other is not easy to discern," "brings forth" is a way of talking about the inclusiveness of interdependent perspectives. Studying one perspective—knowledge of God—"brings forth" a study of the other—knowledge of man, and vice versa. Inclusivity, then, presupposes interdependence, is a function of it, and addresses how studying one perspective in a set of interdependent perspectives brings forth a study of the other perspectives. Additionally, Calvin's acknowledgment that he could not discern which is more fundamental and which entails the other—knowledge of God or knowledge of self—shows that he believed either perspective to be equally valid as a starting point for investigating both perspectives, since both perspectives are interdependent and inclusive.

Because of the triadic dynamics of interdependence and inclusivity, perspectives in any given triad are not *parts* of knowledge but different entrances into the *whole* object of knowledge. Each perspective represents a different emphasis, a different initial question. Thus, in the end, the three perspectives in each triad coincide so that "a true understanding of each will include true understandings of the others."[56] Therefore, the perspectives in a given triad "are ultimately identical."[57]

---

54. *Institutes*, 1.1.1, 1.1.2. See 36n2 in the McNeill and Battles edition, where they note that prior to the 1559 edition of the *Institutes*, Calvin had separate chapters on "knowledge of God" and "knowledge of man." Beginning with the 1559 edition, Calvin combined these two topics to show more clearly their close interrelationship, "emphasizing, both in title and content, 'how they are interrelated.'"

55. *Institutes*, 1.1.1.

56. Frame, *Salvation*, 324.

57. Ibid.

INTERDEPENDENCY AND INCLUSIVENESS OF
PERSPECTIVES IN ROMANS 14:15–19

How are the perspectives in the ethical triad in Romans 14:15–19 (*righteousness, peace,* and *love* and *joy*)—see figure 4, p. 377—*interdependent* and *inclusive*? To simplify things, pretend that you are one of the original recipients of Romans and that you do not have the other sixty-five books of the Bible. To understand Paul's use of *righteousness* (normative perspective, standard) in this context, you would need to study everything in Romans that Paul has said about righteousness and related concepts like law keeping (e.g., 12:10 and 13:8–10). Studying *righteousness* would lead to a study of *love* (existential perspective, motive/attitude), because Paul explicitly relates the two ideas in 12:10 and 13:8–10. Righteousness in Romans is not mere law keeping; it is law keeping motivated by the attitude of love; it is affectionate love in action. But what is the goal of such affectionate action? Is it mere kindness? Your study now would lead you to study *peace* (situational perspective, goal) in Romans, because Paul correlates righteousness with peace (14:17) and exhorts us to pursue peace (12:18; 14:19). And what should your response be to pursuing peace and seeing it take root in the Christian community by virtue of your practicing righteousness in a loving manner? Should you say to yourself, "That's nice"? Should you breathe a sigh of relief and say, "Glad that's done"? No, you should be filled with joy (existential perspective, response); you should rejoice because Paul correlates joy with righteousness and peace (14:17).

That was a brief (and incomplete) sketch of Frame's notion of going "round and round the triangle"[58] and of Poythress's idea of using "what we have gained from one perspective to reinforce, correct, or improve what we understand through another."[59] Since we have all sixty-six books of the Bible, the exercise of going round and round the triangle becomes exponentially more involved but also exponentially richer, more informative, and more rewarding. We went around the triangle from normative to existential to situational and back to existential. We could just as easily have gone from situational to normative

---

58. Frame, *Western Philosophy and Theology*, 35.
59. Poythress, *Symphonic Theology*, 43.

to existential. Any of the three perspectives is a valid starting point for studying the others.

INTERDEPENDENCY AND INCLUSIVENESS OF PERSPECTIVES IN ROMANS 14:17

How are the perspectives in the ethical triad in Romans 14:17 (*kingdom of God*; *righteousness, peace, and joy*; and *Holy Spirit*)—see figure 5, p. 378—*interdependent* and *inclusive*? Again, imagine that Romans is the only book of the Bible you have. Your study of *the kingdom of God* (normative perspective) per se would not get you far (since this phrase only occurs in 14:17). You would need to understand how it is tied to Jesus's messianic lordship (as we saw at the beginning of this chapter). But what is the kingdom of God? Now you would need to study *righteousness*, *peace*, and *joy* (situational perspective); they define what Paul means by *kingdom of God* in 14:17. That study would lead you to ask, "How can I practice righteousness, pursue peace, and be joyful?"—a question that would push you to study what Paul means by "in the Holy Spirit" (existential perspective). Thus:

- Righteousness is a perspective on peace and joy.
- Peace is a perspective on righteousness and joy.
- Joy is a perspective on righteousness and peace.

Metaethics and Romans 14

Metaethics is a "general *method* for approaching ethical problems," rather than a discussion of specific ethical issues.[60] There are three basic metaethical tendencies: existential ethics, teleological ethics, and deontological ethics. Each of these tendencies, or trajectories, tends toward absolutizing one of the three ethical perspectives—existential, situational, or normative.

Existential ethics focuses on the *role* of the decision maker in the ethical process. According to existential ethics, says Frame, "ethical behavior is an expression of what a person is."[61] Teleological ethics

---

60. John M. Frame, "Perspectives on the Word of God. Part 3 of 3: 'The Word of God and Christian Ethics,'" accessed October 28, 2016, http://www.thirdmill.org/files/english/html/th/TH.h.Frame.Perspectives.Word.3.html.
61. Ibid.

focuses on the *goal* of the decision maker in the ethical process, usually expressing the goal as "happiness" or "pleasure," and thus affirming an ethical standard external to the decision maker.[62] Deontological ethics focuses on the decision maker's *duty*. "A good person does his duty simply because it is his duty," *duty* being a self-attesting and supremely authoritative concept.[63]

As Frame explains, a Christian metaethic

> accepts as final only God's Word. That Word is found pre-eminently in Scripture, the covenant constitution of the people of God (Deut. 6:6–9; Matt. 5:17–20; 2 Tim. 3:15–17; 2 Pet. 1:21), but is also revealed in the world (Ps. 19:1ff.; Rom. 1:18ff.) and in the self (Gen. 1:27ff.; 9:6; Eph. 4:24; Col. 3:10). A Christian will study these three realms presupposing their coherence and therefore seeking at each point to integrate each source of knowledge with the other two.[64]

Like existentialist ethicists, Christians seek a metaethic that will realize human nature and human freedom, *but only as these are revealed in Scripture* (the normative perspective). The Bible teaches that we are made in God's image and therefore unique in all creation, but that we are sinful, rebellious, proud, slaves to sin, and blinded by the Devil to God's truth. We need forgiveness of sin, liberation from the Devil, and transformation of our hearts, minds, and wills if we are to become the people God created us to be.[65] In short, we need Christ—crucified, risen, exalted, and indwelling us by means of his Spirit.

Like teleological ethicists, Christians seek a metaethic that will bring about the greatest good for the greatest number of people, *but only as this concept is defined in Scripture*. The Bible teaches us to extend God's kingdom of "righteousness and peace and joy in the Holy Spirit" (Rom. 14:17) by loving our fellow man with Christlike love

---

62. Ibid
63. Ibid.
64. Ibid.
65. Our three enemies—the world, the flesh, and the Devil—may be seen as an adversarial triad: World is situational; flesh is existential; and the Devil is, in an evil way, normative—"the prince of the power of the air" (Eph. 2:2), "the ruler of this world" (John 12:31; 14:30; 16:11). On "the world, the flesh, and the devil," see the Book of Common Prayer, "The Great Litany," which includes this petition: "From all inordinate and sinful affections; and from all the deceits of the world, the flesh, and the devil, *Good Lord, deliver us.*"

(Rom. 14:15), and it illustrates this doctrine concretely (e.g., in terms of what we eat and drink—Rom. 14:15).

Like deontological ethicists, Christians seek a metaethic that will help us know our duty, *but only as this is defined in Scripture.* The Bible teaches that we are to love God with all our heart, mind, soul, and strength and to love our neighbors as ourselves (Matt. 22:37–40). In other words, we are to be perfect as our heavenly Father is perfect (Matt. 5:43–48). The Bible defines Christian love concretely in terms of attitudes, actions, and laws, illustrates this love clearly, and teaches that loving God and loving our neighbors are covenant obligations.

Unlike secular metaethical systems, a Christian metaethic must be unashamedly multiperspectival, always using the existential, situational, and normative perspectives to analyze and understand each ethical issue. Romans 14 is an excellent example of this principle. We are to use our freedom in Christ (existential perspective) to extend God's kingdom (situational perspective) by loving people as Christ does (normative perspective)—another triadic way of looking at Romans 14. Although stronger Christians may eat anything (existential perspective), if doing so distresses a weaker brother (situational perspective), they should refrain from doing so out of love for that brother (normative perspective)—another triad. Each perspective is a vantage point from which to view the issue at hand, and answering the questions raised by one perspective requires answering the questions raised by the other two perspectives.[66] Frame says:

> Put in more practical terms, all of this means that when we face an ethical problem, or when we are counseling someone else, we need to ask three questions, (1) what is the problem? (situational perspective), (2) what does Scripture say about it? (normative perspective), and (3) what changes are needed in me (him, her), so that I (he, she) may do the right thing? (existential perspective). Each of those questions must be asked and answered seriously and carefully. And it should be evident that none of those three questions can be fully answered unless we have some answer to the others.[67]

---

66. As we saw earlier, perspectives are interdependent and include one another.

67. Frame, "Perspectives on the Word of God." Also John M. Frame, *Perspectives on the Word of God: An Introduction to Christian Ethics* (Eugene, OR: Wipf & Stock, 1999).

In the Romans 14 example, the questions and answers would be these:

1. What is the problem (situational perspective)? Weaker Christians are stumbling in their faith and distressed in their hearts because of the meat-eating behavior of stronger Christians.
2. What does Scripture say about it (normative perspective)? Love leads to peace and mutual edification (14:19); it does not distress a brother or destroy God's work (14:15, 19–20a); and it extends God's kingdom of righteousness, peace, and joy (14:17).
3. What changes are needed in the stronger Christian so that he can do the right thing (existential perspective)? It is better to stop eating meat than to cause a brother to stumble (14:2–21). Presumably, we could also argue that it would be a good thing for weaker brothers, by studying and understanding Scripture more fully, to grow stronger in their opinions about such matters, even if they choose not to become meat-eaters.

In this manner, Christian metaethics avoids the rotten fruit of skepticism and relativity that result from seeking an absolute root in creation—human subjectivity (existentialism), the world (teleologism), and logic or reason (deontologism)—by being firmly rooted and grounded in the objective revelation of God's written Word, the Bible, and by viewing ethical issues perspectivally.

Conclusion

The bitter election campaign of 2016 should serve to remind us that as Christians our *defining identity* is not American, Democrat, Independent, or Republican (or Baptist, or Presbyterian, etc.). We are sons of God and servants of the risen King, the Lord Jesus Christ. God has "delivered us from the domain of darkness and transferred us to the kingdom of his beloved Son" (Col. 1:13). We are members of a kingdom of "righteousness and peace and joy in the Holy Spirit" (Rom. 14:17). "Our citizenship is in heaven, and from it we await a Savior, the Lord Jesus Christ" (Phil. 3:20).

Upon Christ's return, his present *reign* among his people will be expanded to a global *realm* where "every knee shall bow" before him and "every tongue shall confess to God" (Rom. 14:11; cf. Phil. 2:9–11)—the consummation of the kingdom at the end of this age (1 Cor. 15:24–25). Not only will this mark the end of political campaigns; it will usher in a world where "righteousness and peace and joy in the Holy Spirit" will characterize our lives. As together we look forward to that day, "may the God of hope fill you with all joy and peace in believing, so that by the power of the Holy Spirit you may abound in hope" (Rom. 15:13).

Appendix

Scripture Versions Cited

Writings of Vern Poythress

This bibliography is adapted from http://frame-poythress.org/vern -poythress-bibliography/. Entries are chronological by years and arranged alphabetically within the same year.

1960s

"The Baptism of the Holy Spirit: What Does It Mean?" *Torch and Trumpet*, February 1969, 8–10; March 1969, 18–19; April 1969, 7–9.

"The Structure of Truth: SDS and the Harvard Establishment." Paper distributed at Harvard University after the Harvard strike, spring 1969.

1970s

"Partial Algebras." PhD diss., Harvard University, 1970.

"From Three Fuddlers." In Eutychus and His Kin. *Christianity Today*, May 12, 1972, 756–57.

"A Method to Construct Convex, Connected Venn Diagrams for Any Finite Number of Sets." Coauthored with Hugo Sun. *The Pentagon* 31, no. 2 (1972): 80–82.

"Unconditional Election." *Synapse II*, 1972, 6.

"A Formalism for Describing Rules of Conversation." *Semiotica* 7, no. 4 (1973): 285–99.

"Partial Morphisms on Partial Algebras." *Algebra Universalis* 3, no. 2 (1973): 182–202.

"An Approach to Evangelical Philosophy of Science." ThM thesis, Westminster Theological Seminary, 1974.

"Creation and Mathematics; or What Does God Have to Do with Numbers?" *The Journal of Christian Reconstruction* 1, no. 1 (1974): 128–40.

"Embedded Pronoun Reference." *Information and Control* 24, no. 4 (1974): 336–57.

"Ezra 3, Union with Christ, and Exclusive Psalmody." *WTJ* 37, no. 1 (1974): 74–94.

"Is God's Sovereignty Antagonistic to Human Responsibility?" *Synapse III*, 1974, 4–5.

"The Scope and Character of Godly Living." *Synapse III*, 1974, 6.

"Baptism in the Holy Spirit." *The Outlook*, May 1975, 11–15.

"Ezra 3, Union with Christ, and Exclusive Psalmody (Sequel)." *WTJ* 37, no. 2 (1975): 218–35.

"Is Romans 1:3–4 a *Pauline* Confession After All?" *Expository Times* 87, no. 6 (1975): 180–83.

"Problems for Limited Inerrancy." *JETS* 18, no. 2 (1975): 93–104. Reprinted in *Evangelicals and Inerrancy*, edited by Ronald Youngblood, 174–85. Nashville: Thomas Nelson, 1984.

Review of *The Distinction between Power-Word and Text-Word in Recent Reformed Thought: The View of Scripture Set Forth by Some Representatives of the Philosophy of the Law-Idea*, by Harry L. Downs. *WTJ* 37, no. 3 (1975): 410–13.

"Baptism in the Holy Spirit." *Journal of Korean Theological Seminary, Pusan* 3 (1976): 116–27.

"A Biblical View of Mathematics." In *Foundations of Christian Scholarship: Essays in the Van Til Perspective*, edited by Gary North, 159–88. Vallecito, CA: Ross House, 1976.

"The Holy Ones of the Most High in Daniel VII." *Vetus Testamentum* 26, no. 2 (1976): 208–13.

"Mathematical Representations of Sociolinguistic Restraints on Three-Person Conversations." *Information and Control* 30, no. 3 (1976): 234–46.

Philosophy, Science, and the Sovereignty of God. Nutley, NJ: Presbyterian and Reformed, 1976.

Review of *Das Ende der historisch-critischen Methode*, by Gerhard Maier. *WTJ* 38, no. 3 (1976): 415–17.

Review of *The Historical-Critical Method*, by Edgar Krentz. *JETS* 19, no. 3 (1976): 260.

"Structural Relations in Pauline Expressions for the Application of Redemption (with Special Reference to Holiness)." MLitt thesis, University of Cambridge, 1976.

"Tagmemic Analysis of Elementary Algebra." *Semiotica* 17, no. 2 (1976): 131–51.

"The Nature of Corinthian Glossolalia: Possible Options." *WTJ* 40, no. 1 (1977): 130–35.

Review of *Above the Battle? The Bible and Its Critics*, by Harry Boer. *WTJ* 40, no. 1 (1977): 195–97.

Review of *Interpreting the Word of God*, edited by Samuel J. Schultz and Morris A. Inch. *WTJ* 39, no. 2 (1977): 408–9.

Review of *Theological Dictionary of the New Testament*. Vol. 10, index volume, edited by Ronald E. Pitkin. *WTJ* 39, no. 2 (1977): 418–20.

Review of *Two Testaments, One Bible*, by D. L. Baker. *WTJ* 40, no. 1 (1977): 194–95.

Review of *What Is Structural Exegesis?*, by Daniel Patte, and of *Semiology and Parables: Exploration of the Possibilities Offered by Structuralism for Exegesis*, by Daniel Patte. *WTJ* 40, no. 1 (1977): 181–82.

"Ground Rules of New Testament Interpretation: A Review Article." *WTJ* 41, no. 1 (1978): 190–201.

Review of *Story, Sign, and Self: Phenomenology and Structuralism as Literary-Critical Methods*, by Robert Detweiler. *WTJ* 41, no. 1 (1978): 210–11.

"Structuralism and Biblical Studies." *JETS* 21, no. 3 (1978): 221–37.

"Thirteen-Box Tagmemic Theory as a Method for Displaying Semi-independent Language Variables." *Studies in Language* 2, no. 1 (1978): 71–85.

"Analysing a Biblical Text: Some Important Linguistic Distinctions." *SJT* 32, no. 2 (1979): 113–37.

"Analysing a Biblical Text: What Are We After?" *SJT* 32, no. 4 (1979): 319–31.

"Philosophical Roots of Phenomenological and Structuralist Literary Criticism." *WTJ* 41, no. 1 (1979): 165–71.

1980s

"Linguistic and Sociological Analyses of Modern Tongues-Speaking: Their Contributions and Limitations." *WTJ* 42, no. 2 (1980): 367–88. Reprinted in *Speaking in Tongues: A Guide to Research on Glossolalia*, edited by Watson E. Mills, 469–89. Grand Rapids, MI: Eerdmans, 1986.

Review of *The Gospel of Luke: A Commentary on the Greek Text*, by
I. Howard Marshall. *WTJ* 42, no. 2 (1980): 438–40.

Review of *Structural Analysis of Acts 6:8–8:3*, by H. J. B. Combrink. *WTJ* 42, no. 2 (1980): 440–41.

Review of *Structural Exegesis: From Theory to Practice. Exegesis of Mark 15 and 16. Hermeneutical Implications*, by Daniel Patte and Aline Patte. *WTJ* 42, no. 2 (1980): 441–44.

Review of *Textentfaltungen. Semiotische Experimente mit einer biblischen Geschichte*, by Alex Stock. *WTJ* 43, no. 1 (1980): 189.

Review of *The Two Horizons: New Testament Hermeneutics and Philosophical Description with Special Reference to Heidegger, Bultmann, Gadamer, and Wittgenstein*, by Anthony C. Thiselton. *WTJ* 43, no. 1 (1980): 178–80.

Review of *Essays on Biblical Interpretation*, by Paul Ricoeur. *WTJ* 43, no. 2 (1981): 378–80.

Review of *The Parables of Jesus*, by Simon J. Kistemaker. *WTJ* 43, no. 2 (1981): 380–82.

"Structural Approaches to Understanding the Theology of the Apostle Paul." DTh diss., University of Stellenbosch, 1981.

"A Framework for Discourse Analysis: The Components of a Discourse, from a Tagmemic Viewpoint." *Semiotica* 38, no. 3/4 (1982): 277–98.

"Hierarchy in Discourse Analysis: A Revision of Tagmemics." *Semiotica* 40, no. 1/2 (1982): 107–37.

"Preparing to Pray." *The Bulletin of Westminster Theological Seminary* 21 (Summer 1982): 1–2.

"Propositional Relations." In *The New Testament Student and His Field*. Vol. 5 of *The New Testament Student*. Edited by John H. Skilton and Curtiss A. Ladley, 159–212. Phillipsburg, NJ: Presbyterian and Reformed, 1982.

Review of *The Formation of Christian Understanding*, by Charles M. Wood. *WTJ* 44, no. 1 (1982): 140–43.

Review of *Hermeneutics*, by Henry A. Virkler. *WTJ* 44, no. 1 (1982): 143–46.

Review of *An Introduction to the Parables of Jesus*, by Robert H. Stein. *WTJ* 44, no. 1 (1982): 158–60.

Review of *The Overcomers*, by Chuck Colclasure. *WTJ* 44, no. 1 (1982): 163–64.

"Mathematics as Rhyme." *JASA* 35, no. 4 (1983): 196–203.

"Newton's Laws as Allegory." *JASA* 35, no. 3 (1983): 156–61.

"Science as Allegory." *JASA* 35, no. 2 (1983): 65–71.

"Adequacy of Language and Accommodation." In *Hermeneutics, Inerrancy, and the Bible*, edited by Earl D. Radmacher and Robert D. Preus, 351–76. Grand Rapids, MI: Zondervan, 1984.

"Problems for Limited Inerrancy." In *Evangelicals and Inerrancy*, edited by Ronald Youngblood, 174–85. Nashville: Thomas Nelson, 1984. Reprint of an article in *JETS* 18, no. 2 (1975): 93–104.

"Testing for Johannine Authorship by Examining the Use of Conjunctions." *WTJ* 46, no. 2 (1984): 350–69.

"The Use of the Intersentence Conjunctions *De, Oun, Kai,* and *Asyndeton* in the Gospel of John." *Novum Testamentum* 26, no. 4 (1984): 312–40.

"Cosa c'entra Dio con i numeri?" *Studi di teologia* 8, no. 16 (1985): 242–69. Italian translation of "Creation and Mathematics; or What Has God to Do with Numbers?" *The Journal of Christian Reconstruction* 1, no. 1 (1974): 128–40.

"Hermeneutical Factors in Determining the Beginning of the Seventy Weeks (Daniel 9:25)." *Trinity Journal,* n.s., 6 (1985): 131–49.

"Johannine Authorship and the Use of Intersentence Conjunctions in the Book of Revelation." *WTJ* 47, no. 2 (1985): 329–36.

"Redaction Criticism: Is It Worth the Risk?" With other panelists. *Christianity Today,* October 18, 1985, 1–12 (insert).

Review of *Daniel and Revelation: Riddles or Realities?,* by A. Berkeley Mickelsen. *WTJ* 47, no. 2 (1985): 350–51.

Review of *A Hermeneutic Critique of Structuralist Exegesis, with Specific Reference to Luke 10:29–37,* by Sandra Wachman Perpich. *JETS* 28, no. 3 (1985): 343–44.

Review of *Interpreting the Bible in Theology and the Church,* by Henry Vander Goot. *WTJ* 47, no. 2 (1985): 337–40.

Review of *The Use of Daniel in Jewish Apocalyptic Literature and in the Revelation of St. John,* by G. K. Beale. *WTJ* 47, no. 2 (1985): 348–50.

"Divine Meaning of Scripture." *WTJ* 48, no. 2 (1986): 241–79.

"Linguistic and Sociological Analyses of Modern Tongues-Speaking: Their Contributions and Limitations." In *Speaking in Tongues: A Guide to Research on Glossolalia,* edited by Watson E. Mills, 469–89. Grand Rapids, MI: Eerdmans, 1986. Reprint of an article in *WTJ* 42, no. 2 (1980): 367–88.

Review of *Power Healing*, by John Wimber. *Eternity*, October 1987, 46–47.

Symphonic Theology: The Validity of Multiple Perspectives in Theology. Grand Rapids, MI: Zondervan, 1987.

Understanding Dispensationalists. Grand Rapids, MI: Zondervan, 1987.

"Understanding the Miracles of Jesus." *Evangelical Times*, October 1987, 8.

"Christ the Only Savior of Interpretation." *WTJ* 50, no. 2 (1988): 305–21. Reprinted in *The Best in Theology* 4 (1990): 161–73.

"God's Lordship in Interpretation." *WTJ* 50, no. 1 (1988): 27–64.

Science and Hermeneutics: Implications of Scientific Method for Biblical Interpretation. Foundations of Contemporary Interpretation 6. Grand Rapids, MI: Zondervan, 1988.

"What Does God Say through Human Authors?" In *Inerrancy and Hermeneutic: A Tradition, a Challenge, a Debate,* edited by Harvie M. Conn, 81–99. Grand Rapids, MI: Baker, 1988.

"Response to Paul S. Karleen's Paper 'Understanding Covenant Theologians.'" *GTJ* 10, no. 2 (1989): 147–55.

"Response to Robert L. Saucy's Paper." *GTJ* 10, no. 2 (1989): 157–59.

1990s

"Christian-Theistic Transfiguration of Science." *The Bulletin of Westminster Theological Seminary* 29, no. 5 (1990): 6.

"A Christian-Theistic View of the Age of the Universe." *The Bulletin of Westminster Theological Seminary* 29, no. 6 (1990): 3.

The Church as a Family: Why Male Leadership in the Family Requires Male Leadership in the Church as Well. Wheaton, IL: Council on Biblical Manhood and Womanhood, 1990.

"Effects of Interpretive Frameworks on the Application of Old Testament Law." In *Theonomy: A Reformed Critique,* edited by William S. Barker and W. Robert Godfrey, 103–23. Grand Rapids, MI: Zondervan, 1990.

Review of *Christianity and the Nature of Science,* by J. P. Moreland. *WTJ* 52, no. 1 (1990): 173–75.

Review of *Linguistics and Biblical Interpretation,* by Peter Cotterell and Max Turner. *Christian Scholars Review* 20, no. 2 (1990): 194–95.

"The Church as Family: Why Male Leadership in the Family Requires Male Leadership in the Church." In *Recovering Biblical Manhood and Womanhood*, edited by John Piper and Wayne Grudem, 237–50. Wheaton, IL: Crossway, 1991.

The Shadow of Christ in the Law of Moses. Brentwood, TN: Wolgemuth & Hyatt, 1991.

"L'église, une famille: la responsabilité que l'homme exerce dans la famille lui revient également dans l'église: pourquoi?" *La revue réformée* 43, no. 175–1992, no. 5 (1992): 21–38.

"Genre and Hermeneutics in Rev. 20:1–6." *JETS* 36, no. 1 (1993): 41–54.

Review of *New Horizons in Hermeneutics*, by Anthony Thiselton. *WTJ* 55, no. 2 (1993): 343–46.

Review of *Revelation: A Book for the Rest of Us*, by Scott Gambrill Sinclair; *Interpreting the Book of Revelation*, by J. Ramsey Michaels; *Revelation 1–7*, by Robert L. Thomas; and *Revelation*, by Robert W. Wall. *WTJ* 55, no. 1 (1993): 164–66.

Symphonic Theology. Korean ed. Seoul: Compass House, 1993. Translation of the same title published by Zondervan, 1987.

"Divine Meaning of Scripture." In *The Right Doctrine from the Wrong Texts? Essays on the Use of the Old Testament in the New*, edited by G. K. Beale, 82–113. Grand Rapids, MI: Baker, 1994. Reprint of an article in *WTJ* 48, no. 2 (1986): 241–79.

"2 Thessalonians 1 Supports Amillennialism." *JETS* 37, no. 4 (1994): 529–38.

Understanding Dispensationalists. 2nd ed. Phillipsburg, NJ: P&R, 1994.

Notes on Revelation. Contributor. In *New Geneva Study Bible*. Edited by R. C. Sproul, Bruce Waltke, and Moisés Silva. Nashville: Thomas Nelson, 1995.

"Reforming Ontology and Logic in the Light of the Trinity: An Application of Van Til's Idea of Analogy." *WTJ* 57, no. 1 (1995): 187–219.

Review of *Text, Church and World: Biblical Interpretation in Theological Perspective*, by Francis Watson. *WTJ* 57, no. 2 (1995): 475–78.

The Shadow of Christ in the Law of Moses. Phillipsburg, NJ: P&R, 1995. Reprint of the same title published by Wolgemuth & Hyatt, 1991.

"Territorial Spirits: Some Biblical Perspectives." *Urban Mission* 13, no. 2 (1995): 37–49.

"Modern Spiritual Gifts as Analogous to Apostolic Gifts: Affirming Extraordinary Works of the Spirit within Cessationist Theology." *JETS* 39, no. 1 (1996): 71–101.

Review of *Models for Interpretation of Scripture*, by John Goldingay. *WTJ* 58, no. 2 (1996): 316–19.

"Science and Hermeneutics." In *Foundations of Contemporary Interpretation: Six Volumes in One*, edited by Moisés Silva, 431–531. Grand Rapids, MI: Zondervan, 1996. Reprint of *Science and Hermeneutics*. Grand Rapids, MI: Zondervan, 1988.

"Counterfeiting in the Book of Revelation as a Perspective on Non-Christian Culture." *JETS* 40, no. 3 (1997): 411–18.

"Indifferentism and Rigorism in the Church: With Implications for Baptizing Small Children." *WTJ* 59, no. 1 (1997): 13–29.

"Linking Small Children with Infants in the Theology of Baptizing." *WTJ* 59, no. 2 (1997): 143–58.

Review of *Interpreting God and the Postmodern Self: On Meaning, Manipulation and Promise*, by Anthony C. Thiselton. *WTJ* 59, no. 1 (1997): 131–33.

"Gender in Bible Translation: Exploring a Connection with Male Representatives." *WTJ* 60, no. 2 (1998): 225–53.

"Gender in Bible Translation: How Fallacies Distort Understanding of the New Testament Gender Passages." *JBMW* 3, no. 4 (1998): 1, 5–7, 12. An adaptation of an article in *WTJ* 60, no. 2 (1998): 225–54.

"Keep On Praying!" *Decision*, October 1998, 31–35.

Review of *Jesus and the Angels: Angelology and the Christology of the Apocalypse of John*, by Peter R. Carrell. *WTJ* 60, no. 1 (1998): 159–62.

"Searching Instead for an Agenda-Neutral Bible." Review of *The Inclusive Language Debate: A Plea for Realism*, by D. A. Carson; and *Distorting Scripture? The Challenge of Bible Translation and Gender Accuracy*, by Mark L. Strauss. *World*, November 21, 1998, 24–25.

God-Centered Biblical Interpretation. Phillipsburg, NJ: P&R, 1999.

"Out of the Frying Pan and into the. . . . " *Tabletalk* 23, no. 3 (1999): 8–10, 56.

"Response to Paul Nelson and John Mark Reynolds"; "Response to Robert C. Newman"; "Response to Howard J. Van Till." In *Three Views on Creation and Evolution*, edited by J. P. Moreland and John Mark Reynolds, 90–94; 148–52; 236–39. Grand Rapids, MI: Zondervan, 1999.

Review of *Is There a Meaning in This Text? The Bible, the Reader, and the Morality of Literary Knowledge*, by Kevin J. Vanhoozer. *WTJ* 61, no. 1 (1999): 125–28.

2000s

"Currents within Amillennialism." *Presbyterion: Covenant Seminary Review* 26, no. 1 (2000): 21–25.

The Gender-Neutral Bible Controversy: Muting the Masculinity of God's Words. Coauthored with Wayne A. Grudem. Nashville, TN: Broadman and Holman, 2000.

The Returning King: A Guide to the Book of Revelation. Phillipsburg, NJ: P&R, 2000.

Review of *The Book of Revelation: A Commentary on the Greek Text*, by G. K. Beale; and *John's Use of the Old Testament in Revelation*, by G. K. Beale. *WTJ* 62, no. 1 (2000): 143–46.

"The Ten Commandments: The Greatest Commandment: The Very Heart of the Matter." *Decision*, December 2000, 31–34.

"The Greatest Commandment: The Very Heart of the Matter." In *The Ten Commandments: A Bible Study.* Minneapolis: World Wide Publications, 2001.

"Greek Lexicography and Translation: Comparing Bauer's and Louw-Nida's Lexicons." *JETS* 44, no. 2 (2001): 285–96.

"Avoiding Generic 'He' in the TNIV." *JBMW* 7, no. 2 (2002): 21–30.

"Extended Definitions in the Third Edition of Bauer's *Greek-English Lexicon.*" *JETS* 45, no. 1 (2002): 125–31.

"'Hold Fast' versus 'Hold Out' in Philippians 2:16." *WTJ* 64, no. 1 (2002): 45–53.

"The Meaning of μάλιστα in 2 Timothy 4:13 and Related Verses." *Journal of Theological Studies*, n.s., 53, no. 2 (2002): 523–32.

"Presbyterianism and Dispensationalism." In *The Practical Calvinist: An Introduction to the Presbyterian and Reformed Heritage*, edited by Peter A. Lillback, 415–24. Fearn, Ross-shire, Scotland: Christian Focus, 2002.

The Returning King: A Guide to the Book of Revelation. Korean ed. Translated by Sang Sub Yoo. Seoul: Christian Publishing House, 2002.

Review of *New Testament Commentary: Exposition of the Book of Revelation*, by Simon J. Kistemaker. *WTJ* 64, no. 1 (2002): 201–2.

"Systematic Pattern in TNIV." *WTJ* 64, no. 1 (2002): 185–92.

"The TNIV Debate: Is This New Translation Faithful in Its Treatment of Gender? No." *Christianity Today*, October 7, 2002, 37–45.

"Translating λέγω in Acts 1:3." *WTJ* 64, no. 2 (2002): 273–78.

"Gender and Generic Pronouns in English Bible Translation." In *Language and Life: Essays in Memory of Kenneth L. Pike*, edited by

Mary Ruth Wise, Thomas N. Headland, and Ruth M. Brend, 371–80. Dallas: SIL International and the University of Texas at Arlington, 2003.

"How Have Inclusiveness and Tolerance Affected the Bauer-Danker Greek Lexicon of the New Testament (BDAG)?" *JETS* 46, no. 4 (2003): 577–88.

Review of *Narrative, Religion and Science: Fundamentalism versus Irony, 1700–1999*, by Stephen Prickett. *WTJ* 65, no. 2 (2003): 392–96.

"Why Scientists Must Believe in God: Divine Attributes of Scientific Law." *JETS* 46, no. 1 (2003): 111–23.

"Male Meaning in Generic Masculines in Koine Greek." *WTJ* 66, no. 2 (2004): 325–36.

"Prospettive bibliche sugli spiriti territoriali." *Studi di teologia* 16, no. 1 (no. 31) (2004): 20–37. Italian translation of "Territorial Spirits: Some Biblical Perspectives." *Urban Mission* 13, no. 2 (1995): 37–49.

"The Reversal of the Curse." *Tabletalk* 28, no. 3 (2004): 7–12.

Review of *Science and Faith: Friends or Foes?*, by C. John Collins. *WTJ* 66, no. 2 (2004): 468–73.

The TNIV and the Gender-Neutral Bible Controversy. Coauthored with Wayne A. Grudem. Nashville: Broadman and Holman, 2004.

"Small Changes in Meaning Can Matter: The Unacceptability of the TNIV." *JBMW* 10, no. 2 (2005): 28–34.

Redeeming Science: A God-Centered Approach. Wheaton, IL: Crossway, 2006.

"Truth and Fullness of Meaning: Fullness versus Reductionistic Semantics in Biblical Interpretation." In *Translating Truth: The Case for Essentially Literal Bible Translation*, by Wayne Grudem, Leland Ryken, C. John Collins, Vern S. Poythress, and Bruce Winter, 113–34. Wheaton, IL: Crossway, 2006. With minor variations, this article also appeared in *WTJ* 67, no. 2 (2005): 211–27.

"Why Must Our Hermeneutics Be Trinitarian?" *The Southern Baptist Journal of Theology* 10, no. 1 (2006): 96–98.

"Millennio" ("Millennium"). In *Dizionario di teologia evangelica*, edited by Pietro Bolognesi, Leonardo De Chirico, and Andrea Ferrari, 451–52. Marchirolo (Varese): Edizioni Uomini Nuovi, 2007.

"New Testament Worldview." In *Revolutions in Worldview: Understanding the Flow of Western Thought*, edited by W. Andrew Hoffecker, 71–99. Phillipsburg, NJ: P&R, 2007.

"The Presence of God Qualifying Our Notions of Grammatical-Historical Interpretation." *JETS* 50, no. 1 (2007): 87–103.

Review of *Science and Grace: God's Reign in the Natural Sciences*, by Tim Morris and Don Petcher. *WTJ* 69, no. 1 (2007): 213–15.

"Canon and Speech Act: Limitations in Speech-Act Theory, with Implications for a Putative Theory of Canonical Speech Acts." *WTJ* 70, 2 (2008): 337–54.

"A 'Day of Small Things': Get Ready to Serve the Casualties of a Coming Cultural Ugliness." *World*, March 8/15, 2008, 64.

"Feeling Guilty? Then You Probably Are, and Christ Is the Remedy." *World*, October 4/11, 2008, 35.

"He Makes the Wind Blow: Storms and Natural Disasters Proclaim the Regularity of God." *World*, May 31/June 7, 2008, 62.

"History of Salvation in the Old Testament: Preparing the Way for Christ." In *ESV Study Bible*, edited by Wayne Grudem, J. I. Packer, C. John Collins, and Thomas R. Schreiner, 2635–61. Wheaton, IL: Crossway, 2008.

"It's Not Fair: We Need a God Who Is Just." *World*, October 18/25, 2008, 27.

"Kinds of Biblical Theology." *WTJ* 70, no. 1 (2008): 129–42.

"The Marriage of Biblical and Systematic Theology." *Westminster Today* 1, no. 1 (2008): 11–13. Condensed from "Kinds of Biblical Theology." *WTJ* 70, no. 1 (2008): 129–42.

"Me, Myself, and iPhone." *World*, July 26/August 2, 2008, 54.

"Overview of the Bible: A Survey of the History of Salvation." In *ESV Study Bible*, edited by Wayne Grudem, J. I. Packer, C. John Collins, and Thomas R. Schreiner, 23–26. Wheaton, IL: Crossway, 2008.

"The Quest for Wisdom." In *Resurrection and Eschatology: Theology in Service of the Church: Essays in Honor of Richard B. Gaffin Jr.*, edited by Lane G. Tipton and Jeffrey C. Waddington, 86–114. Phillipsburg, NJ: P&R, 2008.

"Second Coming: It's a Reality That Should Not Be Ignored." In *World*, December 13, 2008, 33.

"Small Wonders: Do You Matter to God?" *World*, November 15/22, 2008, 31.

"Appearances Matter." Review of *The Lost World of Genesis 1: Ancient Cosmology and the Origins Debate*, by John Walton. *World*, August 29, 2009, 61.

"Fountain of Youth: There Is a Way, but Only One, to Live Forever."
World, January 17, 2009, 63.

In the Beginning Was the Word: Language—A God-Centered Approach.
Wheaton, IL: Crossway, 2009.

"The Mind of God: Would Discovering a 'God Particle' Bring Us Any
Closer to Him?" *World*, May 23, 2009, 69.

"Multiperspectivalism and the Reformed Faith." In *Speaking the Truth
in Love: The Theology of John M. Frame*, edited by John J. Hughes,
173–200. Phillipsburg, NJ: P&R, 2009.

2010s

"Some Biblical Contributions to Business Ethics." Coauthored with Galen
Radebaugh. In *Business Ethics Today: Adding a Christian Worldview
as Found in the Westminster Confession of Faith: Conference Papers*,
179–210. Philadelphia: Westminster Theological Seminary and Center
for Christian Business Ethics Today, 2010.

"Vern Poythress Responds to John Walton." *Biologos*. February 10, 2010.
http://biologos.org/blogs/archive/vern-poythress-responds-to-john
-walton.

What Are Spiritual Gifts? Basics of the Faith Series. Phillipsburg, NJ:
P&R, 2010.

"Gender Neutral Issues in the New International Version of 2011." *WTJ*
73 no. 1 (2011): 79–96.

Redeeming Sociology: A God-Centered Approach. Wheaton, IL: Crossway, 2011.

"Comments on Mark Strauss's Response." *WTJ* 74, no. 1 (2012): 133–48.

¿Dónde está el sabio? No hay científicos ateos: Los atributos divinos de
las leyes naturales. Translated by Guillermo Green. San José, Costa
Rica: Confraternidad Latinoamericana de Iglesias Reformadas, 2012.
Spanish translation of "Why Scientists Must Believe in God: Divine
Attributes of Scientific Law." *JETS* 46, no. 1 (2003): 111–23.

"Evaluating the Claims of Scientists." *New Horizons*, March 2012, 6–8.

"God and Language." In *Did God Really Say? Affirming the Truthfulness
and Trustworthiness of Scripture*, edited by David B. Garner, 93–106.
Phillipsburg, NJ: P&R, 2012.

*Inerrancy and the Gospels: A God-Centered Approach to the Challenges
of Harmonization*. Wheaton, IL: Crossway, 2012.

Inerrancy and Worldview: Answering Modern Challenges to the Bible. Wheaton, IL: Crossway, 2012.

"An Overview of the Bible's Storyline." In *Understanding the Big Picture of the Bible: A Guide to Reading the Bible Well*, edited by Wayne Grudem, C. John Collins, Thomas R. Schreiner, and Darrell L. Bock, 7–18. Wheaton, IL: Crossway, 2012. Reprint of "Overview of the Bible: A Survey of the History of Salvation." In *ESV Study Bible*, edited by Wayne Grudem, J. I. Packer, C. John Collins, and Thomas R. Schreiner, 23–26. Wheaton, IL: Crossway, 2008.

Review of *Remythologizing Theology: Divine Action, Passion, and Authorship*, by Kevin J. Vanhoozer. *WTJ* 74, no. 2 (2012): 443–55.

Review of *Trinity, Revelation, and Reading: A Theological Introduction to the Bible and Its Interpretation*, by Scott R. Swain. *WTJ* 74, no. 2 (2012): 455–56.

"A Survey of the History of Salvation." In *Understanding Scripture: An Overview of the Bible's Origin, Reliability, and Meaning*, edited by Wayne Grudem, C. John Collins, and Thomas R. Schreiner, 169–80. Wheaton, IL: Crossway, 2012. Reprint of "Overview of the Bible: A Survey of the History of Salvation." In *ESV Study Bible*, edited by Wayne Grudem, J. I. Packer, C. John Collins, and Thomas R. Schreiner, 23–26. Wheaton, IL: Crossway, 2008.

"Adam versus Claims from Genetics." *WTJ* 75, no. 1 (2013): 65–82.

Christian Interpretations of Genesis 1. Phillipsburg, NJ: P&R, 2013.

"Divine Meaning of Scripture." In *Thy Word Is Still Truth: Essential Writings on the Doctrine of Scripture from the Reformation to Today*, edited by Peter A. Lillback and Richard B. Gaffin Jr., 1053–76. Phillipsburg, NJ: P&R, 2013. Reprint of an article in *WTJ* 48, no. 2 (1986): 241–79.

"The Inerrancy of Scripture." *China Evangelical Seminary Bulletin*, September/October 2013.

"The Inerrancy of Scripture." In *Is the Bible Really without Errors? Revisiting the Doctrine of Inerrancy*, edited by Peter K. Chow. New Taipei City: China Evangelical Seminary Press, 2013. Edited version of an article in *China Evangelical Seminary Bulletin*, September/October 2013.

"An Information-Based Semiotic Analysis of Theories concerning Theories." *Semiotica* 2013/193 (February 2013): 83–99.

"Information-Theoretic Confirmation of Semiotic Structures." *Semiotica* 2013/193 (February 2013): 67–82.

Logic: A God-Centered Approach to the Foundation of Western Thought. Wheaton, IL: Crossway, 2013.

"Presuppositions and Harmonization: Luke 23:47 as a Test Case." *JETS* 56, no. 3 (2013): 499–509.

"The Purpose of the Bible." In *Thy Word Is Still Truth: Essential Writings on the Doctrine of Scripture from the Reformation to Today*, edited by Peter A. Lillback and Richard B. Gaffin Jr., 1076–83. Phillipsburg, NJ: P&R, 2013. Reprint of a chapter in *God-Centered Biblical Interpretation*. Phillipsburg, NJ: P&R, 1999, 51–61.

"Why Lying Is Always Wrong: The Uniqueness of Verbal Deceit." *WTJ* 75, no. 1 (2013): 83–95.

Chance and the Sovereignty of God: A God-Centered Approach to Probability and Random Events. Wheaton, IL: Crossway, 2014.

"A Christian Approach to Mathematics." Translated into Korean. 2014. Originally chapter 22 in *Redeeming Science: A God-Centered Approach*. Wheaton, IL: Crossway, 2006.

"A Christian Approach to Physics and Chemistry." Translated into Korean. 2014. Originally chapter 21 in *Redeeming Science: A God-Centered Approach*. Wheaton, IL: Crossway, 2006.

Christian Interpretations of Genesis 1. Korean ed. 2014. Translation of the same title published by P&R, 2013.

Did Adam Exist? Phillipsburg, NJ: P&R, 2014.

"Dispensing with Merely Human Meaning: Gains and Losses from Focusing on the Human Author, Illustrated by Zephaniah 1:2–3." *JETS* 57, no. 3 (2014): 481–99.

"A Misunderstanding of Calvin's Interpretation of Genesis 1:6–8 and 1:5 and Its Implications for Ideas of Accommodation." *WTJ* 76, no. 1 (2014): 157–66.

Redeeming Philosophy: A God-Centered Approach to the Big Questions. Wheaton, IL: Crossway, 2014.

"Rethinking Accommodation in Revelation." *WTJ* 76, no. 1 (2014): 143–56.

"Three Modern Myths in Interpreting Genesis 1." *WTJ* 76, no. 2 (2014): 321–50.

"Why Is Science Possible?" In *Faith and Science Conference: Genesis and Genetics: Proceedings of the 2014 Faith and Science Conference*, edited by David R. Bundrick and Steve Badger, 15–22. Springfield, MO: Logion, 2014.

Christian Interpretations of Genesis 1. Farsi ed. Phillipsburg, NJ: P&R, 2015. Translation of *Christian Interpretations of Genesis 1.* Phillipsburg, NJ: P&R, 2013.

"Christian Interpretations of Genesis 1." In *Science through the Eye of Genesis 1.* Korean ed., by Yung-Eun Sung, Vern S. Poythress, and Cornelis Van Dam, 77–119. Seoul: Sungyak, 2015. The book contains three chapters by the three authors respectively. The middle chapter is a translation of *Christian Interpretations of Genesis 1.* Phillipsburg, NJ: P&R, 2013.

"Correlations with Providence in Genesis 1." *WTJ* 77, no. 1 (2015): 71–99.

"Foreword" to *Apologetics: A Justification of Christian Belief*, by John M. Frame, edited by Joseph E. Torres, xiii–xviii. Phillipsburg, NJ: P&R, 2015.

"Foreword" to *Computer Science: Discovering God's Glory in Ones and Zeros*, by Jonathan R. Stoddard, 3. Phillipsburg, NJ: P&R, 2015.

"Foreword" to *General Epistles in the History of Redemption: Wisdom from James, Peter, John, and Jude*, by Brandon D. Crowe, ix–xi. Phillipsburg, NJ: P&R, 2015.

"Rain Water versus a Heavenly Sea in Genesis 1:6–8." *WTJ* 77, no. 2 (2015): 181–91.

Redeeming Mathematics: A God-Centered Approach. Wheaton, IL: Crossway, 2015.

"Semiotic Analysis of the Observer in Relativity, Quantum Mechanics, and a Possible Theory of Everything." *Semiotica* 2015/205 (June 2015): 149–67.

"Biblical Hermeneutics." In *Seeing Christ in All of Scripture: Hermeneutics at Westminster Theological Seminary*, edited by Peter A. Lillback, 9–16. Philadelphia: Westminster Seminary Press, 2016.

"Correlations with Providence in Genesis 2." *WTJ* 78, no. 1 (2016): 29–48.

The Lordship of Christ: Serving Our Savior All of the Time, in All of Life, with All Our Heart. Wheaton, IL: Crossway, 2016.

The Miracles of Jesus: How the Savior's Mighty Acts Serve as Signs of Redemption. Wheaton, IL: Crossway, 2016.

Racheter la science: Une approche centrée sur Dieu. Translated by Evelyne Pankar and Gérald Pech. Le Séquestre, France: La Lumière, 2016. French translation of *Redeeming Science: A God-Centered Approach.* Wheaton, IL: Crossway, 2006.

Reading the Word of God in the Presence of God: A Handbook for Biblical Interpretation. Wheaton, IL: Crossway, 2016.

Teologia sinfônica: a validade das múltiplas perspectivas em teologia. Tradução de A. G. Mendes. São Paulo: Vida Nova, 2016. Portuguese translation of *Symphonic Theology.* Zondervan, 1987. Reprint, Phillipsburg, NJ: P&R, 2001.

Contributors

G. K. Beale (PhD, University of Cambridge) is J. Gresham Machen Professor of New Testament at Westminster Theological Seminary.

Camden M. Bucey (PhD, Westminster Theological Seminary) is pastor of Hope Orthodox Presbyterian Church in Grayslake, Illinois, and president of the Reformed Forum.

Robert J. Cara (PhD, Westminster Theological Seminary) is Hugh and Sallie Reaves Professor of New Testament and provost and chief academic officer at Reformed Theological Seminary in Charlotte, North Carolina.

Brandon D. Crowe (PhD, University of Edinburgh) is associate professor of New Testament at Westminster Theological Seminary.

Iain M. Duguid (PhD, University of Cambridge) is professor of Old Testament at Westminster Theological Seminary.

John M. Frame (DD, Belhaven College) is professor of systematic theology and philosophy emeritus at Reformed Theological Seminary in Orlando, Florida.

Richard B. Gaffin Jr. (ThD, Westminster Theological Seminary) is emeritus professor of biblical and systematic theology at Westminster Theological Seminary.

Wayne Grudem (PhD, University of Cambridge) is research professor of theology and biblical studies at Phoenix Seminary.

Pierce Taylor Hibbs (MAR, Westminster Theological Seminary) is associate director for theological curriculum and instruction in the Theological English Department at Westminster Theological Seminary.

John J. Hughes (ThM, Westminster Theological Seminary) is director of academic development for P&R Publishing.

In Whan Kim (PhD, University of Wales, Lampeter) is president and vice chancellor of Swaziland Christian University in Mbabane, Swaziland.

Peter A. Lillback (PhD, Westminster Theological Seminary) is president and professor of historical theology and church history at Westminster Theological Seminary.

Luke P. Y. Lu (PhD, Westminster Theological Seminary) is pastor of Bible Reformed Church (OPC) in San Jose, California, and professor of systematic theology and church history at China Reformed Theological Seminary in Taipei, Taiwan.

Diane Poythress (PhD, Westminster Theological Seminary) is visiting professor of church history at China Reformed Theological Seminary, Taipei, Taiwan.

Justin Poythress (ThM, Westminster Theological Seminary) is pastoral intern at Lansdale Presbyterian Church in Hatfield, Pennsylvania.

Ransom Poythress (PhD, Boston University) is assistant professor of biology at Houghton College.

Lane G. Tipton (PhD, Westminster Theological Seminary) is Charles Krahe Chair of Systematic Theology at Westminster Theological Seminary.

Carl R. Trueman (PhD, University of Aberdeen) is Paul Woolley Chair of Church History at Westminster Theological Seminary.

Jeffrey C. Waddington (PhD, Westminster Theological Seminary) is stated supply for Knox Orthodox Presbyterian Church in Lansdowne, Pennsylvania.

Brian Courtney Wood (ThM, Westminster Theological Seminary) is English pastor of Grace Christian Church in Herndon, Virginia.

General Index

Muslims, 168–69
mutual indwelling, 174. *See also*
  perichoresis
mystery, made known to the church,
  50–52

name of God, 85–86
narrative, 80
naturalism, 313, 326
natural laws. *See* laws of nature
natural revelation, 208–9, 313n7,
  315n12
natural theology, 208–9
"Nazianzen circle," 179
Nebuchadnezzar, 124–25
Nestorians in China, 292–96, 309
Nestorian Stone Tablet, 291, 292–95
Nestorius, 292
new birth, 325
new covenant, 137, 141, 273
new heaven and new earth, 152
new science, 199, 204, 207–9, 211
New Testament prophecy, 113,
  121–26
Newton, Isaac, 207, 209
new world, 149, 151–52, 161–64
Nicholas IV, Pope, 297
Nicholi, Armand, 218
Nicodemus, 317
Niebuhr, H. Richard, 230
noetic effects of sin, 223, 224
nominalism, 175
non-conflicting absolutism, 333, 339,
  350
non-conflicting biblical demands,
  333–34
normative perspective, 245, 249,
  375–78, 382
  in metaethics, 382–85
nouthetic counseling, 14

obedience, to all of God's commandments, 353–54, 358
occasionalism, 201, 203, 204–7, 210
old covenant, fading glory of, 273,
  277
Old Testament
  canon of, 135

as Christ-centered, 136
"elusive quality" of, 132
telos and redemptive substance of,
  143
yearning for greater revelation, 143
Old Testament prophecy, 113,
  117–21, 135, 141–42
Oliphint, K. Scott, 190n24
one and many, 169–72
Ong, Walter, 182–83n2
ontology, 180
Opium War, 302
organic Christotelism, 144
Orthodox Presbyterian Church, 115
ousia, 171, 176, 179

panentheism, 203–4, 209
Pantaleon, Heinrich, 327n46
pantheism, 203–4
parents, disobedience toward, 343
Parish, Helen, 327n46
Parmenides, 179n32
Pascal, Blaise, 266
Passover lamb, 101
pastors and teachers, as prophets,
  127–28
Paul
  on the gospel, 133–37, 145
  use of ἐκκλησία, 49–55
peace, 361, 369–70, 374
  and the situational perspective, 375,
  377, 381
Pentecost
  and breaking the curse of Babel,
  193–94
  and prophecy, 121
People's Republic of China, 306, 308
perichoresis, 174–75, 179
Perkins, William, 116
person, as center of self-consciousness,
  172–73
personhood, 191–92
perspectivalism, 229, 234
  and presuppositionalism, 235–50
perspectives
  as inclusive, 379–82
  as interdependent, 379–82

Scripture Index